# ENFORCING RESTRAINT

*Collective Intervention in Internal Conflicts*

Edited by Lori Fisler Damrosch

COUNCIL ON FOREIGN RELATIONS PRESS

NEW YORK

## COUNCIL ON FOREIGN RELATIONS BOOKS

The Council on Foreign Relations, Inc., is a nonprofit and nonpartisan organization devoted to promoting improved understanding of international affairs through the free exchange of ideas. The Council does not take any position on questions of foreign policy and has no affiliation with, and receives no funding from, the United States government.

From time to time, books and monographs written by members of the Council's research staff or visiting fellows, or commissioned by the Council, or written by an independent author with critical review contributed by a Council study or working group are published with the designation "Council on Foreign Relations Book." Any book or monograph bearing that designation is, in the judgment of the Committee on Studies of the Council's Board of Directors, a responsible treatment of a significant international topic worthy of presentation to the public. All statements of fact and expressions of opinion contained in Council books are, however, the sole responsibility of the author.

---

*If you would like more information on Council publications, please write the Council on Foreign Relations, 58 East 68th Street, New York, NY 10021, or call the Publications Office at (212)734-0400.*

Copyright © 1993 by the Council on Foreign Relations®, Inc.
All rights reserved.
Printed in the United States of America.

Library of Congress Cataloging-in-Publication Data

---

Enforcing Restraint: collective intervention in internal conflicts / [edited by] Lori Fisler Damrosch
    p. cm.
   Includes bibliographical references and index.
   ISBN 0-87609-155-9 : $17.95
  1. Intervention (International law)  2. Civil war.  3. Sanctions (International law)  4. United Nations—Armed Forces.  5. United States—Foreign relations—1989–   I. Damrosch, Lori F. (Lori Fisler)

JX4481.E54 1993
342.5'84–dc20
                                        93-11304
                                          CIP

Cover Design: Michael Storrings

# Contents

# Acknowledgments

This study originated under the auspices of the Project on International Organizations and Law of the Council on Foreign Relations. It is one of a number of activities in which the Council has addressed the role of international organizations and law in contemporary world affairs.

In early 1992 the Council convened a study group on the subject "Collective Involvement in Internal Conflicts," which met in eight sessions from May 1992 through February 1993 to discuss the case studies and cross-cutting themes that formed the basis for the essays collected in this volume. A core group of about 30 members, supplemented by speakers and guests with expertise on each of the conflicts addressed at the respective sessions, participated in the discussions and made invaluable contributions to the authors' thinking on these topics. Ambassador Max M. Kampelman chaired the study group, and Lori Fisler Damrosch and Enid C.B. Schoettle codirected it; Anna D. Tapay served as rapporteur.

Many persons at the Council on Foreign Relations contributed to the conceptual development of the project and to its execution. Special thanks are due to Enid C. B. Schoettle, director of the Council's Project on International Organizations and Law and senior fellow at the Council, who was instrumental at all stages. Nicholas X. Rizopoulos, vice president and director of Studies, oversaw the project and gave astute advice. From the Council's Studies Department, Lawrence Hamlet, Jennifer Hobbs, and Arleen O'Brien were responsible for administrative support; and from the Publications Department, David Haproff and Judy Train shepherded the manuscripts through the editorial process. Dore Hollander, copyeditor, Virginia Parrot, word processor, Liz Cunningham, indexer, and Joseph Ascherl, cartographer, deserve thanks for their skillful services.

Finally, we are grateful to the Ford Foundation, which has provided generous financial support for the Project on International Organizations and Law at the Council. We are particularly indebted to Franklin A. Thomas, president of the Foundation, Barry D. Gaberman, deputy vice president and program officer responsible for the grant to the project, and Shepard Forman, director of the Foundation's International Affairs program.

# Foreword

## MAX M. KAMPELMAN

It was evident to me, as a member of the United States Delegation to the Heads of State Summit of the Conference on Security and Cooperation in Europe (CSCE) held in Paris in November 1990, that the prevailing mood of Europe at that time was one of euphoria, optimism, confidence. The Charter of Paris for a New Europe, coupled with the earlier Copenhagen Declaration on the Human Dimension of June 1990, proudly declared a new order for Europe based on democracy as an indispensable ingredient for the realization of peace and security.

The next CSCE Heads of State Summit took place in Helsinki, 19 months later in July 1992. I was again a member of the American delegation. This time, the European mood was one of impotence, deep concern, dismay. Europe understood that with the escalating brutality in the former Yugoslavia seemingly out of rational control, it had failed its first post–Cold War test. The United States had abandoned its leadership role and shifted the burden and primary responsibility for dealing with the irresponsible and devastating violence in Yugoslavia to a rudderless Europe, which was unable to utilize any of its institutions to cope effectively with the accompanying ethnic hatreds and butchery.

It is this reality which was ever-present in the deliberations sponsored by the Council on Foreign Relations that I had the privilege of chairing and that produced this important volume.

Are we entering a new form of Dark Age? Is the defeat of order and decency that is now so evident in Europe only a temporary barrier on the path to a new civilized order? If Europe fails, how can we expect Asia and Africa to succeed? What changes in our political thinking are required if we are constructively to affect the direction of our evolving civilization?

For hundreds of years, international society has been organized on the basis of separate sovereign states whose territorial integrity and political independence are guaranteed by international law. The United Nations Charter, in embodying and reflecting the values of the state system, reaffirmed the principles of non-use of force across international boundaries and non-intervention in internal affairs. These principles were at the core of the collective effort, led by the United States, to defend Kuwait against external attack. But do these principles possibly impede a collective response to equally brutal warfare occurring *within* national boundaries?

As the crises of the 1990s have exploded and persisted, there is a growing awareness of the need to look beyond state boundaries to the sources of instability within states. It is surely not now possible—if indeed it ever was—to take at face value the claims of ruling elites that whatever goes on within state boundaries is solely a matter of domestic jurisdiction. As long ago as the United Nations Charter of 1945, an explicit commitment to human rights and fundamental freedoms has been found in the basic documents of international law, serving as a reminder that state sovereignty is not and has probably never been absolute. The framers of the Charter understood the linkage between the protection of basic human dignity and the preservation of peace and security. The participants in the CSCE also understood this linkage as they built upon the pledges made at Helsinki in 1975, and moved decisively toward an ever stronger acceptance of the legitimacy of international concern about internal repression.

There is a shifting dividing line between "internal affairs" to be protected against intervention and the responsibility of the international community to intervene in order to preserve peace and important human values. When I began negotiating with the Soviet Union within the CSCE context in 1980, there was some world sentiment in support of the Soviet position that our concern with their human rights practices was indeed an improper interference in their internal affairs. Yet, by 1986, the Soviets informed us they were removing their objection, and a rational discourse ensued.

In November 1990, the CSCE countries, including the Soviet Union, signed the Charter of Paris and agreed to "cooperate and support each other with the aim of making democratic gains irreversible."[1] A few months later, at a CSCE meeting of experts on national minority problems held in Geneva, there was a clear statement that "issues concerning national minorities, as well as compliance with international obligations and commitments concerning the rights of persons belonging to them, are matters of legitimate international concern and consequently do not constitute exclusively an internal affair of the respective state."[2]

In late 1991, a CSCE Conference on the Human Dimension was held in Moscow. Again, Europe unanimously declared that "commitments undertaken in the field of the human dimension of the CSCE are matters of direct and legitimate concern to all participating States and do not belong exclusively to the internal affairs of the State concerned."[3]

When the United States in August 1991 denounced the attempted coup against the established Soviet government, the White House specifically referred to "commitments to domestic reforms made by Soviet leaders under the CSCE's Paris Charter and Helsinki Final Act."[4] There was no concern that this statement was an undue interference in the internal affairs of another state. In that same spirit, Russian Foreign Minister Andrei Kozyrev wrote in the Spring 1992 issue of *Foreign Affairs*: "Wherever threats to democracy and human rights occur, let alone violations thereof, the international community can and must contribute to their removal. . . . Such measures are regarded today not as interference in internal affairs but as assistance and cooperation in ensuring everywhere a 'most favored regime' for the life of the peoples—one consistent with each state's human rights commitments under the UN Charter, international covenants and other relevant instruments."[5]

Most recently, the United Nations has sent troops into Somalia where internal instability is causing hunger and death. There are no guidelines or rules and no adequate precedents by which to determine just where the dividing line is or should be. What is clear is that there is a shifting line and it is evident that it is the UN Security Council, which, by its decisions, places the legal imprimatur between what is justifiable and unjustifiable international intervention.

Images, ideas, and problems are not confined by national boundaries. Cameras, satellites, telephones, computers, fax machines—all of these are able to bring distant horrors instantaneously into our homes and offices. Unlike past generations, we do not have the excuse that we do not know the facts. With knowledge comes responsibility.

Human institutions are capable of growth and change, and, indeed, we have seen in our day a rapid evolution of both ideas and institutions. The European Community and the Council of Europe illustrate that change. The UN Security Council has been a focal point for many of the efforts to respond constructively to internal conflicts. It has power under the Charter to respond not only to acts of aggression and breaches of peace, but also to threats to peace. The UN Security Council has been increasingly willing to treat internal conflicts as presenting such threats. In so doing, it is making new law and creating new precedents. These new directions, however, have not come easy or remained unchallenged. They have produced internal stress and strains as UN mechanisms have shown themselves to be creaky and unsteady. Member states have also resisted and even resented the price to be paid for the Security Council to be an effective instrument in helping the world improve the lives of human beings now suffering from violence, ignorance, and hunger.

We should recognize that an already exceedingly overburdened Security Council, even if it were capable of addressing each situation clamoring for attention, may not be the best vehicle for an adequate response. The Charter envisioned a system of regional organizations capable of addressing regional threats, but it is only now that such organizations are beginning to be asked to carry out real responsibilities. It will require tremendous creativity and ingenuity on the part of leaders around the globe to strengthen the available capacities and create new ones of various sorts to meet developing and unpredictable challenges.

One of the most serious challenges to peace and stability is the highly incongruous and self-defeating growth of ethnic and tribal violence at a time when, stimulated by the unifying force of amazing technological, scientific, and communications accomplishments, the nation-states of the world have become ever more interdependent. The drive for self-respect and identification is understandable following the lifting of the lids of repression in areas long dominated by totalitarian rule. But that drive now seriously appears to be getting out of hand. This brings us to the Wilsonian principle of "self-determination of peoples."[6]

It is vital to make it unmistakably clear to all "peoples" that this principle does not legitimize violence and does not include within it the right to secede. A group that wishes to secede from a state which is a member state of the United Nations or of the CSCE cannot find in the Wilsonian principle any justification for doing so unilaterally or by violent means. Its only recourse is to seek its aims peacefully through negotiation or through an appeal to the conscience and judgment of the world community for moral and political assistance. Any other interpretation will produce chaos, instability, and violence and runs contrary to the United Nations Charter and the Helsinki Final Act, both of which emphasize the inviolability of existing boundaries. This does not mean that the boundaries are necessarily just, fair, or historically justified. What it does mean is that the international community has a stake in preventing war, maintaining stability, and resolving problems through negotiations.

The United States is in an agonizing process of redefining its national interest in the post–Cold War era. A new administration in Washington is haltingly and with an uncertain trumpet attempting to formulate its overall strategies and its responses to specific crises. The willingness or unwillingness of the United States to become engaged in addressing a conflict elsewhere that does not appear to affect our immediate national interests power-fully shapes the attitudes of other states. There are, for the moment, no other viable leaders in the world.

There is much at stake during this critical stage of international development, not only in relation to our immediately observable interests in particular conflicts, but also in setting the direction for the evolution of international law and institutions. If the United States fails to provide active diplomatic leadership to harness and contain, if not resolve, the ethnic, national, and religious conflicts that have emerged with the collapse of total-itarianism and repression, those conflicts will continue to turn violent. If the United States does not provide the leadership and power to make certain that aggression does not prove profitable to the aggressor, we will have failed in our duty to build an international community based on law.

The contributors to the present volume have reflected deeply on these issues and have brought to bear their expertise across a wide range of fields. I commend this study to the attention of all those who seek to understand the recent past as a source of ideas for future leadership and direction.

## NOTES

1. *Charter of Paris for a New Europe*, Conference on Security and Cooperation in Europe, Paris, 1990.
2. Report of the CSCE Meeting of the Experts on National Minorities, Geneva, 1991, p. 4.
3. *Document of the Moscow Meeting of the Conference on the Human Dimensions of the CSCE*, October 3, 1991, p. 2.
4. Morton H. Halperin, "Guaranteeing Democracy," *Foreign Policy* (Summer 1993), no. 91, p. 110.
5. Andrei Kozyrev, "Russia: A Chance for Survival," *Foreign Affairs*, vol. 71, no. 1, pp. 1–16.
6. See "Secession and the Right of Self-Determination: An Urgent Need to Harmonize Principle with Pragmatism," by Max M. Kampelman, *The Washington Quarterly* (Summer 1993), pp. 5–12.

# Introduction

## LORI FISLER DAMROSCH

The title of our volume—*Enforcing Restraint: Collective Intervention in Internal Conflicts*—reflects the complexities of our subject. Above all, it suggests the emergent capabilities of the international community to restrain those who are bent on destruction and oppression within their own societies. "Intervention"—a controversial term with multiple connotations—here refers to affirmative international efforts to separate combatants and enforce peace.

Yet the emphasis on restraint is deliberately ironic. In the eyes of many, collective institutions have done little to restrain internal conflicts: rather, it is the institutions themselves that seem under restraint. Those who might have galvanized collective action have innumerable excuses for passivity—lack of legal authority, shortage of financial resources, deference to "sovereignty," the asserted need to obtain consent from the affected state or contending factions, unwillingness to commit oneself unless others will join in, absence of sufficient interest, the fear of creating precedents with unpredictable consequences, other priorities elsewhere, and so on, and so on. While Gulliver mulls over these problems, the Lilliputians wrap him in miles and miles of red tape—or worse, he has tied his own hands.

The present study seeks to contribute to the current debate through an analysis of six case studies of collective responses to internal conflicts and an examination of two strong forms of outside involvement. The case studies consider the situations in the former Yugoslavia, Iraq, Haiti, Liberia, Somalia, and Cambodia in the period from approximately 1991 to the beginning of 1993. Two separate essays take up problems involving economic sanctions (including the impact on civilian populations) and forcible intervention. Cross-cutting themes addressed in all of the essays include the evolution of new standards for collective involvement in restraining internal conflict, the role of the United Nations and regional or other subglobal organizations, and the relevance of international law to the control of internal violence.

## SCOPE OF THE STUDY

We have defined the scope of the study to include cases in which a *collective* decision has been (or could be) made to *intervene* (or otherwise become *involved* in) an *internal conflict*. Each of the italicized terms calls for a brief comment.

*Collective.* Our focus is on collective activities, as opposed to unilateral actions of states. This emphasis takes account of opportunities arising with the end of the Cold War for concerted efforts to promote widely shared values and objectives. The term "collective" suggests a range of possibilities for action by the international community as a whole or by groups of concerned states, whether through the UN, through other international institutions, or on an ad hoc basis. Our case studies endeavor to understand the strengths and weaknesses of current institutional structures, as well as to shed light on why some promising collective initiatives have been taken outside the formal charters of existing organs.

As the international community evolves in the direction of greater capabilities for collective action, it is important to focus on whether standards for evaluating an activity do or should differ depending on whether the activity is undertaken by one state acting unilaterally or by a community of states acting in a collective capacity. Much of the preexisting system of international law has sought to constrain states from unilateral projections of power into other states' "internal affairs" or "domestic jurisdiction." It is not obvious that the same constraints should necessarily apply when an authorized organ acts on behalf of all humanity, or on behalf of a community with common values. What normative conceptions and procedural safeguards may render it acceptable for collective organs to do what no one state should be allowed to do alone?

*Intervention/Involvement.* The term "intervention" evokes different sets of meanings for different speakers and hearers, and thus needs to be used with caution and explanation. Its Latin etymology is straightforward (*inter*, meaning "between," and *venire*, meaning "to come"), and its simplest connotations are morally neutral, as suggested by one dictionary's definition: "to come between as an influencing force, as in order to modify, settle, or hinder some action, argument, etc."[1] Yet contemporary usages include normative implications that are so different as to be practically opposites.

In the field of international law, "intervention" generally indicates an external power's unlawful interference with the territorial integrity or political independence of a state, such as by means of invasion, intimidation, or subversion. Thus the classic international law treatises speak of intervention as "dictatorial interference" resulting in the "subordination of the will" of one sovereign to that of another.[2] Political scientists and others, however, frequently employ the term in a benign sense, to suggest a form of conflict resolution in which the intervenor "comes between" contending parties as a mediator would, but armed with the means to impose a settlement. Compounding these longstanding difficulties in interdisciplinary discussions about intervention is the fact that not only the terms but the very premises of debate in every relevant discipline are undergoing profound change in the post–Cold War period.

In full awareness of the wide range of connotations of the term "intervention," we have tried to proceed as concretely as possible to examine the techniques available to the international community for mitigating the level of violence or repression in an internal conflict, and to explore the legitimacy of those techniques only in light of the context and circumstances relevant to each case. Where the term "intervention" seems more likely to confuse or annoy than to clarify, we have referred instead to "involvement" or "influence."

Techniques of involvement can be either forcible or nonforcible (such as economic sanctions, granting or denying recognition, and concerted diplomatic activity).[3] The various techniques present themselves to some extent as alternative courses of action, but they can also be used sequentially or cumulatively.

In each of the conflicts we have chosen for study, collective *military* involvement either has been under way or has received serious contemplation. UN peacekeeping forces, comparable forces under the auspices of a regional organization, national contingents acting with the support of an international body, and ad hoc multinational coalitions are among the variants for collective military activity. As of the time we began planning the study in late 1991, collective military activity had taken place only with respect to Iraq and Liberia (where a West African force was striving to keep a tenuous peace); but military operations concerning the other crises were in various phases of discussion, debate, or preparation for deployment. By the time we concluded the study in early 1993, international military involvement was in progress in every case except Haiti, and the numbers of troops involved had become quite substantial: in Yugoslavia, more than 22,000 (and the total could conceivably rise to 50,000 or higher during 1993); in Cambodia, nearly 20,000; in Somalia, approximately 28,000.[4]

*Internal Conflict.* Within the scope of this study, internal conflicts are ones in which the conflict is located primarily within the borders of an existing nation-state at the time the issue of collective involvement arises. Internal conflicts include ethnic strife, overthrow of an established government, disintegration of civil order, interference with humanitarian relief efforts, and other violence occurring within a state. Of course, many internal conflicts entail some transboundary elements, either as contributing factors (for example, cross-border arms transfers or ethnic affinities) or as effects of the crisis (for example, refugee flows). A principal theme of this study is the extent to which the international community is now prepared to treat certain internal problems as warranting a collective response, whether or not a specific threat to international peace can be demonstrated. International organizations' practice concerning this issue has undergone a significant evolution even during the time that our study was in progress.

Transborder aggression as such is not the concern of this study, even though it overlaps with our subject. Thus in the chapter concerning Iraq, we are concerned chiefly with repression and violence directed to indigenous population groups, such as the Kurds and Shi'ites, rather than with Iraq's invasion of Kuwait; we do consider the latter as part of the relevant context, however, since the collective measures adopted to protect domestic populations beginning in April 1991 would probably not have been conceivable in isolation from the chain of events beginning with Iraq's invasion of Kuwait the previous summer.

The phenomenon of fragmentation of existing nation-states has transformed some internal conflicts into interstate ones, even short of spillover of the conflict into the territories of third states. The Yugoslav crisis is illustrative: when the crisis began, the Serbian-dominated federal government contended that boundaries between Yugoslav republics had no significance in the eyes of international law, and that its own actions to prevent secession fell within exclusive domestic jurisdiction. With the disintegration of the federation and eventual international recognition of most of the republics as separate states, the conflict became clearly international rather than predominantly internal. The overlapping issues of self-determination, secession, and the contested legal significance of internal borders emerge vividly in other parts of the world as well.

## Selection of Cases

We have chosen a representative sample—far from an exhaustive survey—of crises that engaged the world's attention at the beginning of the 1990s. Each had deep roots in history, going back decades or even centuries. Despite the prevailing impression that such conflicts had been suppressed or held in check during the Cold War (which may have been true of intercommunal strife in Yugoslavia), nothing in the dynamics of superpower confrontation had stopped Saddam Hussein from using chemical weapons and other techniques of extermination against Kurdish village populations in the Anfal campaign of 1988, or Pol Pot from overseeing the massacre of as many as one million Cambodians in the late 1970s. What seemed different as the 1990s began was that the major powers would no longer have to view such situations through the lens of superpower competition.

The Persian Gulf crisis was a watershed event, which made clear both that international and internal peace were closely linked, and that the international community could act collectively with respect to both sets of concerns. Then, in rapid succession, came a series of crises that pressed the international community to decide whether to attempt to respond, and if so, how. Our study includes only cases that have elicited some form of collective response and thus does not cover other situations with equally compelling objective circumstances (such as comparably high levels of deaths and devastation).

A powerful determinant of whether a collective response would occur has been the level of interest on the part of the United States and the willingness of the U.S. government to exercise leadership. In each of our cases, to varying degrees, U.S. responsibilities are implicated because of historical ties, geopolitical interests, or other considerations. That does not necessarily mean that the United States would be the initiator of a constructive collective response: it has stayed aloof in the case of Liberia, has taken a back seat to the Europeans in the case of Yugoslavia, and has seemed ambivalent in the Haitian situation. Nor was there necessarily a palpable self-interest even in the cases where the United States did make a direct commitment to collective action, as with Somalia. But our selection of cases not coincidentally focuses on those where there was some reason to hope or expect that the United States would not remain indifferent.

A variety of roughly comparable situations arose during the course of our study, but just as the international community has been able to react only selectively if at all, we have thought it preferable to focus on a few cases rather than survey a large number.[5] Our six cases span the major regions of the world and thus give an opportunity to consider the capabilities and limitations of several regional organizations, including the Organization of American States (OAS) with respect to Haiti, the Economic Community of West African States (ECOWAS) with respect to Liberia (and to a lesser extent the Organization of African Unity, which had at least a nominal interest in the Liberian and Somalian cases), the Association of Southeast Asian Nations with respect to Cambodia, and a variety of evolving European institutions with respect to Yugoslavia. Under the rubric of "treating like cases alike," the final chapter of concluding reflections gives some attention to the problem of failure of collective response to situations that would arguably warrant comparable treatment with the ones we have studied.

We have not attempted to explore the complex problem of conflicts internal to the former Soviet Union, some of which cross the boundaries of newly independent states, but others of which are confined within a given republic's territorial borders. Nor have we considered China and Tibet, or the multiple ethnic and religious conflicts that have led to enormous loss of life in India. Some might think that these situations are inherently different from the ones in our case studies, since it might seem to stretch the bounds of plausibility for the international community to become involved in a conflict occurring within the territory of one of the major powers. That assumption is not necessarily correct. Indeed, one could profitably examine the several missions to the former Soviet Union undertaken by personal emissaries of the UN secretary-general; efforts of the Conference on Security and Cooperation in Europe (CSCE); and the role of the Commonwealth of Independent States, which may perform functions analogous to peacekeeping within the former Soviet Union.

All of these could constitute collective involvement within the meaning of the study. But since these problems easily deserve a book or books of their own, we leave them for another day.

## STATES AND THE INTERNATIONAL SYSTEM: PREEXISTING FRAMEWORK OF ASSUMPTIONS

The international system is going through a period of revolutionary change. But despite dramatic political transformations, the essential features of a structure of independent states are likely to remain relatively stable. Moreover, the UN Charter does express enduring values worthy of preservation even as the system evolves to meet new challenges. An understanding of the preexisting framework of assumptions will help shed light on the problems of the present and the future.

The UN Charter reflects two clusters of values, which intersect with each other and may sometimes work at cross-purposes.[6] In a cluster which we may call "state system values" are principles inherent in a system of separate states, including nonuse of force, political independence of states, and sovereign equality. In a cluster which we may call "human rights values" are principles relating to the fundamental rights and freedoms of human beings. These two clusters of values interrelate with two types of objectives relevant to international legal rules on intervention: objectives of conflict prevention or containment, and objectives of realization of autonomy.

Because of the overriding importance of containing conflict, the international legal system has sought to restrain states from projecting military power into one another's territory; for similar reasons, traditional international legal doctrine has aimed at restraining states from instigating or exacerbating civil strife in other states. Underlying the traditional rules against intervention (even though they were widely ignored) was the idea that outside involvement in internal strife would risk widening and escalating the conflict.

The autonomy value is sometimes formulated in terms of the political independence of a *state*, but the underlying value is the human rights of the people within state boundaries to organize themselves into political communities and to create their own political institutions. Along with such related principles as self-determination, the norm of nonintervention aims at securing the rights of people within a state to exercise political freedoms without external domination.

These values of conflict containment and autonomy are at the heart of the international legal system's commitment to a norm against external involvement in internal affairs. The norm originated in unwritten custom (systematized by scholars beginning in the eighteenth century) and has been codified in the present century in a series of treaties and other documents. A typical formulation is found in the Charter of the OAS:[7]

> No State or group of States has the right to intervene, directly or indirectly, for any reason whatever, in the internal or external affairs of any other State. The foregoing principle prohibits not only armed force but also any other form of interference or attempted threat against the personality of the State or against its political, economic, and cultural elements.

The UN Charter addressed its intervention provision to the new organization, rather than to member states, in article 2(7):

> Nothing contained in the present Charter shall authorize the United Nations to intervene in matters which are essentially within the domestic jurisdiction of any state or shall require Members to submit such matters to settlement under the present Charter; but this principle shall not prejudice the application of enforcement measures under Chapter VII.

Other provisions of the UN Charter reflecting duties on the part of states and the organization to refrain from intervention in internal affairs are articles 1(2) and 55, which affirm the "principle of equal rights and self-determination of peoples"; article 2(1), which provides that "the Organization is based on the principle of the sovereign equality of all its Members"; and article 2(4), which requires states to "refrain in their international relations from the threat or use of force against the territorial integrity or political independence of any state."

The prohibition in UN Charter article 2(7) is qualified by the reference to "enforcement measures under Chapter VII," which is the chapter dealing with the powers of the Security Council to maintain and restore international peace and security. The title of that chapter refers to "threats to the peace, breaches of the peace, and acts of aggression"; and both because of that title and by virtue of similar terms in various Charter provisions,[8] it has been thought that the Council must at a minimum be able to make a finding of a "threat to the peace" as a prerequisite to the exercise of its enforcement powers.

Yet in two cases arising long before the present wave of internal conflicts—the cases of Rhodesia and South Africa—the Council did take an inclusive view of the concept of "threats to peace" in order to act under chapter VII with respect to situations that were essentially internal. In both cases, of course, the crux of the matter was apartheid; transboundary elements were present, but were distinctly secondary to the grievances that prompted the Council to act. Both cases involved considerable controversy over whether the Council possessed authority under chapter VII to exercise compulsory authority unless a threat to *international* peace could be shown, and in response to this controversy the Council referred in the resolutions to what various members considered significant transboundary factors. Thus, for example, the preamble to the resolution imposing an arms embargo on South Africa identifies not only the South African government's "resort to massive violence against and killings" of its own people, but also "the military build-up by South Africa and its persistent acts of aggression against the neighbouring States," as the predicate for a determination "that the acquisition by South Africa of arms and related *materiel* constitutes a threat to the maintenance of international peace and security."[9]

Another feature of the first four decades of UN experience is also relevant: namely, the actions of both the Security Council and the General Assembly in authorizing deployment of peace-keeping forces. Although a number of UN peacekeeping operations have involved the placement of a force along an international boundary or cease-fire line to separate armies that had been engaged in transboundary conflict, it is significant that several of the largest and most significant UN peacekeeping operations have involved essentially internal conflicts. The

Congo operation is illustrative: the situation was primarily a civil war within the newly decolonized state of the Congo, and secondarily entailed external elements.[10]

UN peacekeeping typically proceeds on the basis of consent given by the affected states or factions. The rationale for insisting upon consent is partly legal and partly prudential. Legally, unless the Security Council is prepared to conclude that a situation meets the requisites for chapter VII (and thus is prepared to make a "threat to peace" finding), it has been thought that consent from appropriate authority within a state is the most satisfactory response to the objection that external involvement constitutes impermissible intervention. In prudential terms, UN peacekeeping usually entails an essentially symbolic, lightly armed force that has neither the mandate nor the means for large-scale conflict. Thus obtaining the effective consent of all combatants has seemed the best way to ensure that they can carry out a feasible mission.

As the following chapters will indicate, however, "consent" in some of the recent cases has been either fictional or even nonexistent. This shift from consent-based peacekeeping toward nonconsensual peace enforcement is another of the main themes of the present study.

## NEW CHALLENGES: NORMATIVE AND INSTITUTIONAL QUESTIONS

Our study explores whether a normative consensus is in the process of emerging, and indeed may have already emerged in part, concerning the conditions under which international involvement in an internal crisis is justified. Through the case studies we are able to observe certain areas of consensus taking shape, although the contours of the consensus are certainly still controversial.

In our cases, the international community typically began by attempting to fit its response into the classical paradigms of UN actions of the 1945–1990 period, even though those paradigms may have been of dubious applicability in the new circumstances. Thus, as we will see, several of the peacemaking and peacekeeping efforts were initially grounded on the rationale of consent, even though the person or body supposedly granting consent might have had little control over the situation on the ground. Moreover, in each instance in which the Security Council has become directly involved (that is, in all of our cases), it has been careful to recite that the situation entailed a "threat to peace," even though to do so in particular cases has entailed quite a stretch from previous conceptions. The threat of expansion of warfare across an international boundary can easily be classified as a threat to peace; the proposition that flows of refugees into neighboring states may also be a sufficient threat is achieving greater (but not universal) acceptance.

On the normative dimension, our case studies establish that large segments of the international community have been willing to endorse strong collective action in a wide range of situations, of which the following are illustrative and not exclusive:

- Genocide, "ethnic cleansing," war crimes, crimes against humanity, and similar atrocities entailing loss of life on a mass scale (Yugoslavia, Iraq, Liberia)

- Interference with the delivery of humanitarian relief to endangered civilian populations (Yugoslavia, Iraq, Somalia)

- Violations of cease-fire agreements (Yugoslavia, Liberia, Cambodia. In each of those cases, collective measures have been targeted selectively at the party perceived as principally responsible for the violations.)

- Collapse of civil order, entailing substantial loss of life and precluding the possibility of identifying any authority capable of granting or withholding consent to international involvement (Liberia, Somalia)

- Irregular interruption of democratic governance (Haiti. As noted, the collective response has not yet crossed the threshold of military action, but strong measures of economic and diplomatic pressure have been taken. The normative consensus would be shared in Latin America and Europe.)

Obviously, the effort to identify and describe potential areas of consensus in such a rapidly changing area is fraught with difficulty, and the preceding formulations should in no way be taken as an attempt to codify normative rules. Whether the present subject would even be amenable to codification is a question addressed in the chapter of concluding reflections.

On the legal-institutional dimension, our study asks questions both about *legitimacy* and about *effectiveness*. The quest for *legitimacy* may begin, but need not end, with the powers and authorities granted to international institutions by their own charters, which by and large were written at a time when the perceptions of threats and needs were quite different from those of today. Existing institutions are being asked to take on functions that they were never intended to perform; they are being pushed to the limits of their own constitutions, or perhaps beyond them. Moreover, some regions of the world suffer from a vacuum of institutional authority to deal with even the most traditional kinds of threats, let alone unprecedented ones. Thus ad hoc groups of states have formed themselves into novel coalitions in response to crisis situations. Assuming that a normative consensus can exist on the desirability of collective involvement, what must done to ensure that the collective organs or groups act legitimately, in compliance with general international law and with their own specific terms of reference, and with the authority of the international community behind them?

Regarding *effectiveness*, the case studies show that even where institutions exist that could potentially become involved, their capabilities are far from optimal. Even the UN, with greater expertise and at least potentially greater resources than regional groups, has found its effectiveness hampered by a variety of circumstances, some of which pertain to the nature of the conflict and some to structural aspects of the organization.

As the case studies will show, the existence of multiple organizations with overlapping mandates can be both a strength

and a weakness. Rarely can there be an ideal allocation of responsibilities: indeed, confusion about who should be doing what
could limit the effectiveness of response and might result in one
institution's undercutting another's efforts.

## OVERVIEW OF THE CASE STUDIES
## AND THEMATIC ESSAYS

We begin with the crisis in the former Yugoslavia, because it has
presented the most acute tests of the international community's
ability to respond to post–Cold War conflicts. We will see in
operation almost every technique of collective involvement mobilized in the other crises, and more besides. Yet we also see the
utter failure of the international community to achieve the objective of quelling the conflict in question.

James B. Steinberg's treatment of the Yugoslav crisis divides
the international community's involvement into five phases, following the collapse of the Yugoslav Communist Party in 1990:
efforts to preserve Yugoslavia as a single entity; efforts following
the Slovenian and Croatian declarations of independence of June
25, 1991, to halt the fighting that broke out between the Slovenian militia and the Yugoslav army; efforts to achieve and maintain a cease-fire in Croatia and broker a political settlement
between the breakaway republics and the remnants of the
Yugoslav federation; efforts addressed to the conflict in Bosnia-
Herzegovina following that republic's referendum on independence in February 1992; efforts to prevent the conflict from
spreading to Kosovo and Macedonia. Steinberg traces the respective roles of European institutions and later the UN in a range of
activities, including sponsorship of a series of negotiations toward an overall political settlement, economic sanctions, humanitarian relief, measures to protect minorities and safeguard
human rights, and the deployment of military observers and
eventually a large-scale peacekeeping force. He also considers
conflicting approaches to the problem of self-determination,
which came to a head when Germany pushed for recognition of
Croatia and Slovenia despite concerns in the UN and elsewhere
about this course of action.

On the normative dimension, Steinberg observes that several justifications have been proffered for international involvement in the Yugoslav crisis, including consent of the parties, transborder aggression, humanitarian needs and human rights, and indirect impact on other states (mainly from refugee flows). As for institutions, Steinberg explains the widespread view at the beginning of the crisis that primary responsibility should lie with European institutions, and he traces the subsequent shift to strategies centered on the UN. Notably, the Yugoslav crisis erupted at a moment when all relevant European institutions (including the European Community, the CSCE, the North Atlantic Treaty Organization, and the West European Union) were undergoing major transformations and redefinition of their respective mandates. The crisis pointed up the urgency of dramatic institutional reform and accelerated and affected the processes of change.

The Yugoslav crisis compels us to ask whether well-intentioned—but weak and ineffectual—efforts from outside parties only made the situation worse. What were the crucial mistakes? What, if anything, could the international community have done to stop the fighting from spreading to Bosnia-Herzegovina? Once the conflict had spread, could an earlier or more forceful intervention have interrupted it? Did the half-hearted international involvement only disable the victims from defending themselves, without in any way hampering the attackers? Did the arrival of international personnel as observers and peacekeepers promote efforts at settlement, or did those outsiders turn out to be little more than hostages, whose presence only complicated the prospects for effective international intervention?

It is hard to do a postmortem on a patient who is still on the operating table; but if the international response to the Yugoslav crisis deserves any credit at all, it may be because it contained the conflict within the boundaries of the former Yugoslavia (and indeed confined it within a few former Yugoslav republics and restrained its spread to other vulnerable Yugoslav regions). Past Balkan crises have been not only virulent but contagious. Perhaps the international measures in Yugoslavia are analogous to early public health achievements in breaking the chain of transmission of infectious diseases, so as to avoid or mitigate an epidemic, even though breakthroughs in treatment or cure still lie in the future.

The international response to Iraq's treatment of its Kurdish and Shi'ite populations beginning in 1991 has been more success- ful than that of the Yugoslav case in achieving both conflict containment and realization of autonomy. When Baghdad turned its guns on its own people in the wake of an international conflict, a prompt international intervention established a secure zone in which Iraqi Kurds could not only live relatively safely but even enjoy a measure of self-government for the first time. Yet this outcome has been controversial; it may not be sustainable over the long term or reproducible elsewhere.

Jane E. Stromseth locates the international response to Iraq's internal conflicts in the context of a long history in which Kurdish aspirations for self-determination have consistently been subor- dinated to the strategic and economic interests of global and regional powers. The international community had done essen- tially nothing for the Kurds, even in the face of extensive evidence of a genocidal extermination campaign in the late 1980s. The turning point came in the immediate aftermath of the successful collective military action to eject Iraq from Kuwait, when the Kurds in northern Iraq and the Shi'ites in the south mounted popular uprisings that elicited a swift and brutal response from Saddam Hussein. Thousands upon thousands fled toward and across the borders with Turkey, Iran, and Kuwait, and a human- itarian crisis of vast proportions ensued.

Stromseth analyzes the debates in the UN Security Council over what became resolution 688, which condemned Iraq's re- pression of its civilian populations and found that the conse- quences of that repression threaten international peace and security. She identifies three rationales put forward by Security Council members to justify international involvement in Iraq's internal crisis: the massive flow of refugees across borders; the severity of Iraq's violations of human rights; and the special responsibility of the UN as a consequence of its previous decision to authorize use of force against Iraq in defense of Kuwait. Stromseth then examines the implementation of resolution 688 through Operation Provide Comfort and the subsequent negotiations with Iraq over the terms of a UN presence on Iraqi territory for humanitarian purposes. She discusses the establishment by allied forces of a secure zone to protect the Kurds in the north, and later a no-fly zone over the southern marshlands. The precariousness of the situation is evident from Saddam Hussein's repeated harassment and probing of the limits of the international commitment. Stromseth considers the advantages and disadvantages of addressing an internal conflict through the lens of humanitarian relief, and she notes that the Iraqi experience has raised expectations that may not be fulfilled in future crises.

The Iraqi case raises questions with profound implications. By creating protected zones in parts of Iraq, has the U.S.–led coalition hastened the disintegration of that state (a development that some would fear because of its effects on regional stability, and others because of the possible precedent elsewhere)? Does the success of the venture depend too heavily on cooperation from states that have only a transient interest in protecting vulnerable Iraqi groups? Can UN resolutions from 1990 and 1991 authorize into the indefinite future any and all actions supporting their purposes that the coalition's leaders deem necessary? This last question relates to the cross-cutting theme of enhancing authority and legitimacy, to which we will return in the concluding chapter.

The case of Haiti offers a different perspective on the mix of principles and interests that can motivate collective intervention. The principle at stake was restoration of a democratically elected government, but few interests of outside parties were involved— except the interest of the United States in dealing with a new wave of boat people. Ironically, the economic sanctions that became the chosen instrument of international involvement turned out only to exacerbate that problem for the United States, while bringing the crisis no closer to resolution.

Domingo E. Acevedo examines the international response to the military coup of September 29, 1991, which overthrew the elected president of Haiti, Jean-Bertrand Aristide. The countries of the American region had established a commitment to political organization on the basis of representative democracy as long ago as the 1948 Charter of the OAS, but that organization's commitment to promote and consolidate democracy has always been qualified by a parallel Charter provision calling for "due respect for the principle of non-intervention." Acevedo traces the history of OAS efforts in support of democracy within member states, culminating in a June 1991 commitment to respond immediately in the event of irregular interruption of democratic governance within a member state.

With respect to the Haitian situation, Acevedo reviews the history of a long succession of dictatorships and the period of instability from the departure for exile of Jean-Claude Duvalier in 1986 through the completion of an internationally supervised election in December 1990, in which Father Aristide won an overwhelming majority of the popular vote. Acevedo then examines the measures of diplomatic and economic isolation the OAS adopted immediately after the coup, and he considers the objections on legal and political grounds within the OAS to forcible action in support of democracy, as well as the reasons why the international response did not entail an exercise of the UN Security Council's enforcement powers until a very late stage (even though the UN did become involved in intensified diplomatic activity by late 1992). Acevedo concludes that the OAS is better at protecting states against external threats than at protecting democratic governments against internal ones.

What accounts for the inability of the OAS to bring about a resolution of the Haitian crisis? Would it have been better for the OAS to do nothing at all than to apply severe measures of economic pressure that have only worsened the already dire conditions of the Haitian people? Or would it have been best to intervene militarily at the outset, with precisely targeted force that might have quickly displaced the usurpers and restored Father Aristide? Could the UN have done a better job than the OAS, or was the actual allocation of responsibility between global and subglobal organizations the best available? These issues growing out of the Haitian case study are also explored in the separate essays on economic sanctions and forcible intervention later in this volume.

The savagery of Liberia's civil war is almost unimaginable. The brutal murder of American nuns brought the story back onto the front pages of American newspapers in late 1992. In the two years before that event, a regional peacekeeping force had assumed responsibility for restoring and maintaining some semblance of order in the country. Does that effort deserve credit for mitigating an internal conflict, or blame for prolonging it? Should the dominant regional power, Nigeria, be commended for taking the lead role in peacekeeping, or condemned for interposing a military force to influence another state's internal struggle?

David Wippman examines the civil war that broke out in Liberia at the end of 1989 and was held in abeyance from approximately August 1990 until August 1992 through the efforts of the West African peacekeeping force. Despite Liberia's long-standing links with the United States, going back to the settlement of what is now Monrovia by emancipated American slaves, the United States saw no post–Cold War interests to be advanced in Liberia. The U.S. preference that Africans address the matter contributed to a disinclination on the part of the UN Security Council to take it up. The locus of regional efforts to resolve the crisis became the Economic Community of West African States, which, as its name suggests, is a subregional organization with the primary mandate of promoting economic integration. ECOWAS attempted a political mediation of the Liberian crisis that produced a plan for cease-fire and eventual elections. But Charles Taylor's faction, which saw military victory almost within its grasp, viewed the ECOWAS initiative as a Nigerian-inspired plot to keep Taylor from power. ECOWAS authorized the dispatch of a "peacekeeping" force to Liberia even before there was any peace to keep.

Wippman analyzes the series of justifications that have been proffered on behalf of the ECOWAS intervention, including its claim to be a peacekeeping force operating with the consent of the principal Liberian factions, the contention that a humanitarian intervention was justified to prevent massive atrocities and restore civil order, and the argument that the ECOWAS action was a regional enforcement action under chapter VIII of the UN Charter. He also considers the compatibility of the operation with the charters both of ECOWAS and of the Organization of African Unity. In addition, Wippman looks at the Security Council's November 1992 measures endorsing the ECOWAS initiatives and adopting a sanctions program complementary to that of ECOWAS.

The ECOWAS intervention in Liberia illustrates several of the cross-cutting themes of this volume. What makes a regional intervention legitimate? Is legitimacy cast in doubt if the intervening body has to stretch for authority that is difficult to find in its own charter? Should the UN become more assertive in approving, supervising, or enforcing regional activities? If effective collective action can only occur when a relatively strong state (such as Nigeria) takes the lead, how can regional or international organizations ensure that the effort advances truly collective or universal interests, rather than the mere self-interest of the initiating state? The Liberian case sheds light on these questions in the African context, and also offers a comparative perspective on similar questions about the role of other dominant powers (such as the United States) in other organizations (such as the OAS).

Somalia—across the African continent from Liberia—is a strikingly different case study. No African organization came to Somalia's rescue as it descended into civil war and famine, nor did African leaders make any real headway on the problem at the UN. The situation continued to deteriorate until President Bush, in the final days of his administration, offered to send in the marines.

Jeffrey Clark's treatment of the Somalian crisis sharply criticizes the failure of the international community to make an effective response to a humanitarian tragedy of virtually unprecedented dimensions. Hundreds of thousands of Somalians died while the world did nothing. Clark demands that organizations and leaders who squandered available opportunities and committed outright errors be held to strict account. He condemns the UN for having withdrawn its staff from Mogadishu (citing security concerns), and for having remained absent even while humanitarian relief organizations bravely continued their work. He identifies a number of blunders in the UN efforts at diplomatic mediation between the warring clans, which undermined UN credibility and doomed the several diplomatic missions to failure. The Security Council busied itself with a series of weak resolutions, including authorization of a pathetically small number of peacekeepers (only 500, as compared to an initial request for 7,000 and the 24,000 American troops who eventually landed in December 1992). Finally, acting at the request of the United States, the Security Council in resolution 794 of December 3, 1992, authorized "all necessary means to establish as soon as possible a secure environment for humanitarian relief operations in Somalia"; the resolution identified the "magnitude of human tragedy in Somalia" as itself constituting a threat to international peace and security.

Clark aptly characterizes the UN authorization of the U.S. military intervention as unprecedented. Yet he trenchantly criticizes the United States as well as the UN for having failed to exercise leadership much earlier in the tragedy. He calls for strict accountability in both UN and U.S. programs to ensure that the Somali debacle is not repeated.

This condemnation of the international failure through the end of 1992 is well justified, but it may be harder to pronounce an eventual verdict on the initiatives that began at year end. Could any measure of success redeem the past two years? Those who died of starvation cannot be restored to life, but perhaps the international community can assist in creating conditions for reconciliation and reconstruction within Somalia. Should it attempt to do so? Or would such an aspiration—or pretension—be nothing other than colonialism in another guise? Can the international community act altruistically to restore Somalia for the sake of Somalians, or will outside powers inevitably pursue their own interests instead?

These questions about the international role in reconstructing a national society are not unique to Somalia. The last of our case studies—that of Cambodia—offers a relevant body of experience that may hold lessons for Somalia and elsewhere.

Steven R. Ratner examines the Cambodian conflict, which differs from the others in that it entails not only an internal struggle (involving four factions, each of which has once governed the country since Cambodia attained independence), but also a long-running regional conflict with direct involvement by Cambodia's neighbors and several global powers. The end of the Cold War made possible a comprehensive settlement agreement that placed the UN at the center of efforts to bring about national reconciliation. Ratner examines the unique responsibilities of the UN Transitional Authority in Cambodia (UNTAC) in relation to the Supreme National Council, which acts as the embodiment of Cambodian sovereignty. He identifies problems that have arisen in the implementation phase, including the refusal of the Khmer Rouge to carry out its obligations under the settlement agreement, and he explains the steps that UNTAC and the Security Council have taken to try to execute and enforce the agreement notwithstanding the Khmer Rouge's noncompliance.

Ratner then considers whether the UNTAC model of direct UN involvement in internal governance during a transitional period might point the way to a new concept of international "conservatorships" for states that have proven to be incapable of governing themselves—what Ratner calls "failed states." Ratner compares the conservatorship model to other precedents, including UN trusteeship of non–self-governing territories.

The UNTAC model will hardly prove attractive in other situations if it fails on its own terms. The central point is that UNTAC is to be "transitional," but to what? Will the process that has unfolded under UN supervision give birth to a genuine Cambodian political structure, or will the country descend once again into chaos after the UN leaves? What instruments are available to the international community to ensure that all Cambodian parties live up to their obligations under the comprehensive settlement agreement, during and after the period of on-site UN involvement? The latter question brings us to the essays on economic sanctions and forcible intervention, which address two different instruments of collective action that are potentially available for enforcement of international obligations, as well as for other purposes.

My own chapter, entitled "The Civilian Impact of Economic Sanctions," focuses on *nonforcible* collective responses to internal conflicts, including the imposition of arms embargoes on the areas of conflict and more drastic programs of comprehensive economic sanctions aimed at severe isolation of a target state. In contrast to most literature on economic sanctions, which concentrates on the effectiveness of sanctions in terms of likelihood of achieving declared objectives, this essay seeks to evaluate sanctions on the basis of deeper values and principles. One of these is the conflict containment value, which may give a principled basis for choosing nonforcible over forcible means of response to most (but not necessarily all) situations of internal crisis. I also argue that sanctions should be differentiated so that wrongdoers are penalized and induced to desist from wrongful behavior, and that a threshold of moral concern is crossed if sanctions cause a significant segment of the civilian population to fall below the level of minimal subsistence. The crossing of that threshold does not necessarily mean that sanctions would have to be terminated; they may have to be kept in place in deference to the conflict containment value, which in my view is hierarchically superior. (Thus, in my opinion, continuation of sanctions against Iraq is proper until such time as Iraq fully carries out the obligations of demilitarization and disarmament that the Security Council imposed at the end of the 1991 Gulf War.) In rare cases when a forcible response might be able to achieve the objectives of a sanctions program at lower cost to innocent civilians, it may be acceptable to invert the usual preference for nonforcible over forcible courses of action.

The chapter by Tom J. Farer, entitled "A Paradigm of Legitimate Intervention," considers conditions bearing on the legitimacy of use of force. After a review of the original understanding embodied in the UN Charter and the interpretive issues that arose in the Cold War period, Farer proposes elements of a possible new normative paradigm. When the putative intervenor would be a state acting unilaterally, restrictive substantive criteria should be applied; moreover, in the interests of ensuring impartial review, the intervening state should be required to report to the Security Council (and to appropriate subglobal arrangements) and to accept the jurisdiction of the International Court of Justice to rule on challenges to its action. With respect to UN intervention, Farer believes that the appropriate analogy is to parliamentary supremacy, so that the Security Council's decisions would be legitimate as long as they command the support of the great majority of the states that matter in international relations. He finds sufficient built-in checks (the requirement of unanimity among the permanent members, the need to muster an additional five votes to pass a resolution, and the need to maintain the support of states that will be called upon to participate in funding) to make it unlikely that the Council will abuse its powers. Indeed, the greater threat is that the Council will be unable to act at all.

Finally, Farer considers authorization of intervention by subglobal—not necessarily regional—institutions. One possibility is a voluntary agreement among like-minded states providing for the reestablishment of constitutional government, by force if necessary, in the event of an unconstitutional seizure of power in a member state. He takes up objections to the exercise of authority to intervene by organizations that are either not geographically defined or are underinclusive or overinclusive of the states in a given region, and also addresses the problem of the relationship of the authority of subglobal organizations to that of the UN.

In the final chapter, entitled "Concluding Reflections," I return to some of the most prominent of the cross-cutting themes. Among these are the following: Can the international community develop patterns of response to internal conflicts so as to deter the eruption of such conflicts in the first place? What can be done to ensure that collective actions not only are normatively sound and accepted on a de facto basis, but also are perceived as having the full weight of international authority behind them? To what extent should collective organs be passing judgment on actors or actions in situations of internal conflict, as opposed to preserving strict impartiality? Is the international community prepared to move toward the objective of treating like cases alike?

We come back, finally, to our title—*Enforcing Restraint.* Only within the last few years has any significant collective enforcement come to seem possible; yet, new constraints have arisen almost as quickly. Budgetary limitations, while very real, are just one factor inhibiting collective action to restrain internal conflicts. Ironically, a more serious obstacle may be the perception that early and tentative collective efforts have failed or even backfired. Such perceptions, unfortunately, may undermine the attempt to forge a new normative consensus on criteria for legitimate collective intervention. A more hopeful interpretation of the cases we have examined is that the process of casting off unnecessary self-restraints is under way and irreversible.

The case studies take account of developments through early 1993, and an epilogue covers events through fall 1993.

## NOTES

1. *Webster's New World Dictionary of the American Language, Second College Edition* (New York: The World Publishing Company, 1972).
2. L. Oppenheim, *International Law*, eighth ed. (London: Longmans, Green, 1955), vol. 1, sec. 134; see also E. Stowell, *Intervention in International Law* (Washington, D.C.: J. Byrne & Co., 1921).
3. Forcible intervention is the subject of sixteen essays and commentaries in L. F. Damrosch and D. J. Scheffer, eds., *Law and Force in the New International Order* (Boulder, Colo.: Westview Press, 1991). This collection covers (among other topics) intervention by invitation, against illegitimate regimes, for humanitarian purposes, and against criminal activity. For a treatment of nonforcible techniques of unilateral influence, see L. F. Damrosch, "Politics across Borders: Nonintervention and Nonforcible Influence over Domestic Affairs," *American Journal of International Law*, vol. 83 (1989), p. 1.
4. See, for example, Paul Lewis, "Peacekeeper to Peacemaker: U.N. Confronting New Roles," *New York Times*, January 25, 1993, pp. A1 and A10; and Paul Lewis, "U.N. Will Increase Troops in Somalia," *New York Times*, March 27, 1993, p. A3.
5. See David Binder and Barbara Crossette, "As Ethnic Wars Multiply, U.S. Strives for a Policy," *New York Times*, February 7, 1993, pp. A1 and A14. The article enumerates 48 current ethnic conflicts; the list would be even longer if it included instances (such as Haiti) of politically motivated violence.

6. For further elaboration, see L. F. Damrosch, "Changing Conceptions of Intervention in International Law," in L. W. Reed and C. Kaysen, eds., *Emerging Norms of Justified Intervention* (Cambridge, Mass.: American Academy of Arts and Sciences, 1993); and Damrosch, "Politics across Borders." See also L. Henkin, *International Law: Politics, Values and Functions* (General Course on Public International Law), 216 Collected Courses of the Hague Academy of International Law (Dordrecht: Martinus Nijhoff, 1989), pp. 24–29, 129–137.

7. Article 18. Texts from other regions are cited in Damrosch, "Politics across Borders," p. 7.

8. For example, articles 24, 34, and 39, and throughout chapter VII.

9. Resolution 418 (November 4, 1977); see discussion of the Security Council's treatment of the Rhodesian and South African situations in Damrosch, "Commentary on Collective Military Intervention to Enforce Human Rights," in Damrosch and Scheffer, *Law and Force in the New International Order*, pp. 215 and 217–219.

10. See United Nations, *The Blue Helmets: A Review of United Nations Peace-Keeping*, 2d ed. (New York: 1990), pp. 213–259.

# International Involvement
# in the Yugoslavia Conflict

## JAMES B. STEINBERG

The grim story of Yugoslavia's breakup and the ensuing ethnic conflict seems all the more disturbing because it has shattered the hope that the Cold War's end might herald a new era of peace. In the smoldering ruins of Dubrovnik, Vukovar, and Sarajevo lie the crumpled dreams of a new cooperative security order in Europe, in which reason and peaceful mediation would replace war as the tools of conflict resolution. The failure first to head off and later to stop the bloodshed has tattered the reputations of regional and international organizations charged in one form or another with protecting human rights, halting aggression, and restoring the peace.

The war in the former Yugoslavia continues, and there remains a risk that it will spread, not only to other parts of Yugoslavia, but to its neighbors, as well. Moreover, Yugoslavia's fate may well serve as an exemplar for ethnic conflict elsewhere in Europe. Thus the lessons—good and bad—learned during the Yugoslavia conflict could have profound consequences for the future of European stability.

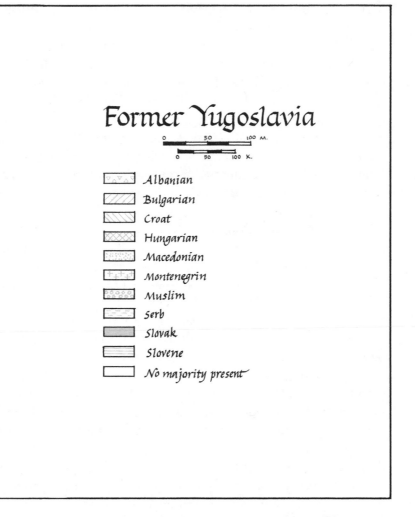

# Former Yugoslavia

0   50   100 M.

0   50   100 K.

- Albanian
- Bulgarian
- Croat
- Hungarian
- Macedonian
- Montenegrin
- Muslim
- Serb
- Slovak
- Slovene
- No majority present

## YUGOSLAVIA'S TROUBLED HISTORY

The history of the territory known for the better part of the 20th century as Yugoslavia is a history of trying to amalgamate what nature seems determined to fragment—to "balkanize." Modern Yugoslavia arose after World War I from the ashes of millennia of conflict and two great empires: the Austro-Hungarian empire (which at its height embraced all of Slovenia, Croatia, Bosnia, and Vojvodina) and the Ottoman empire (which conquered Kosovo in 1389[1] and at one time controlled virtually all of the region, but whose influence diminished until the empire was finally expelled during the First Balkan War in 1912). Neither empire ever exerted full control over the various ethnic and national groups in the Balkans: during the Middle Ages both Bulgaria and Serbia dominated large portions of the Balkan land mass; the Croatians, Albanians, and Bosnians all had relatively short-lived states.[2]

Modern Serbia (along with Montenegro) achieved its independence from Ottoman rule in 1878. By 1914, Serbia also included the area that became known as Macedonia in the Yugoslav federation. Serbian nationalists in Bosnia played a key role in the assassination of the Hapsburg Archduke Ferdinand in Sarajevo, triggering the outbreak of the First World War.

After World War I, the Allies created the Kingdom of the Serbs, Croats, and Slovenes, uniting all of the Serb population of the area in a single state. Yugoslavia was one of the most concrete manifestations of President Woodrow Wilson's vision of bringing democracy and self-determination to Europe. Although Serbs were the dominant group, Slovenes and Croats initially welcomed the new arrangement because it freed them from past domination by Germany, Italy, Austria, and Hungary.[3] But conflict grew between Croats and Serbs, and a violent nationalist movement (Ustashe) began to agitate for Croatian independence. Although moderates on both sides reached an agreement on autonomy for Croatia in 1939, extremist Croatian forces joined with the Nazi invaders in 1941 to create an independent Croatia, massacring hundreds of thousands of Serbs in the process. A Serbian nationalist group, the Chetniks, retaliated, causing significant Croat casualties. While the precise number of those killed is a matter of some dispute (particularly among propagandists for both sides), the legacy of the violence remains vivid to the survivors and their descendants. A third movement, the Communist partisans led by Josip Broz (Marshal Tito), ultimately succeeded in ousting the Axis forces at the end of 1944, with the support of the Soviet Union.

Tito's Communist state was built as a federation with six republics: Bosnia-Herzegovina, Croatia, Macedonia, Montenegro, Serbia, and Slovenia. The internal borders (which remained until the country's breakup in 1991) did not attempt to consolidate populations along ethnic lines; indeed, it appeared that Tito (a Croat) intentionally sought to limit the Serbs' clout by the way he drew the administrative divisions. Thus the borders of Serbia did not embrace all areas with large Serb populations; both Bosnia and Croatia contain large Serb enclaves.

The Constitution of 1974 decentralized Yugoslavia even further, giving the republics greater autonomy and recognizing two key national/ethnic groups that the division of Yugoslavia into six republics did not reflect. It created two new autonomous regions, the Albanian Muslim Kosovo in the southern part of Serbia; and Vojvodina, with a large Hungarian population in the northern part. The Constitution also recognized the Muslims of Bosnia as a "nation." The two principal "Yugoslav" institutions were the League of Communists of Yugoslavia (LCY) and the Yugoslav National Army (JNA).

Tito's death in 1980 led to the creation of a new governmental structure, designed to balance the competing ethnic groups and interests by rotating the Yugoslav presidency among the six republics.

The post-Tito arrangement in effect contained the seeds of its own destruction. The prosperous Catholic republics of Slovenia and Croatia resented sharing their economic good fortune with their poorer Muslim and Orthodox compatriots, while Serbs, embittered by the fetters imposed by Tito, chafed under the new structure, which, in their view, denied them their due. During the 1980s the relatively successful Yugoslav economy came under growing strains in part as a result of mismanagement. Nationalist movements gained strength throughout the country. In Serbia in 1986, a group of intellectuals prepared a memorandum through the Academy of Arts and Sciences calling for a Serbian nationalist awakening. Dobrica Cosic, a writer who later became president of the "rump" Federal Republic of Yugoslavia (Serbia and Montenegro), was a leading force behind the memorandum. Slobodan Milosevic, who became the Serbian leader in 1987, seized on the ideas.

Partially in response to growing Serbian nationalism and fueled by growing anticommunism, independence movements in Croatia and Slovenia gained momentum in the late 1980s. The Yugoslav Communist Party collapsed in January 1990, and leaders in Slovenia and Croatia began to push for constitutional negotiations to reconfigure Yugoslavia into a loose confederation of sovereign republics, a move that Serbia and its allies resisted. Serbian President Milosevic warned in June 1990 that the internal borders of Yugoslavia were predicated on the continuation of a federal state, and that moves to break the country up into constituent parts would open the question of redrawing the borders.[4] At the same time, Croatian leader Franjo Tudjman, whose nationalist Croatian Democratic Union (HDZ) party won Croatia's election in May 1990, promulgated a draft constitution with no mention of protection for the Serb minority. In response, Serbs in the area around Knin launched an uprising in August 1990, demanding autonomy for Serbian-dominated areas.

The deadlock over a negotiated approach accelerated the movement toward unilateral steps leading to referenda in favor of independence for Slovenia in December 1990 and Croatia in May 1991. A constitutional crisis precipitated the final break: under the system of rotating presidency, a Croat, Stipe Mesic, was due to become federal president on May 15, 1991, but Serbia (supported by Montenegro) blocked his appointment.[5] The last thread holding the federation together had been broken, and on June 25, 1991, Slovenia and Croatia declared their independence, triggering a conflict that has resulted in more than 100,000 deaths and the displacement of at least three million persons.

## THE INTERNATIONAL COMMUNITY'S ROLE IN THE YUGOSLAVIA CONFLICT

During the Cold War era, the international community viewed Yugoslavia through the East-West prism: For the West, Yugoslavia was a thorn in the side of the Soviet Union, nominally communist but more market-oriented in its economics and open politically. For the USSR, Yugoslavia was a wayward child, but a member of the family nonetheless, and the Soviet leaders were wary of Western attempts to detach Yugoslavia completely from the socialist camp. Yugoslavia was a field on which the Cold War competition was subtly played out, with the small but present risk that instability in Yugoslavia could build into a direct East-West confrontation.

The history of the international community's involvement in the current Yugoslavia crisis falls into five phases. The initial phase centered on the primarily political effort to preserve Yugoslavia as a single entity following the collapse of the Yugoslav Communist Party in January 1990. The next phase, following the declarations of independence by Slovenia and Croatia on June 25, 1991, focused on halting the fighting between the Slovenian militia and the Yugoslav army. The third phase, triggered by the outbreak of fighting between Serbs (with the support of the Yugoslav army) and Croats in Croatia, featured efforts to achieve and maintain a cease-fire and broker a political settlement between the breakaway republics and the remains of the Yugoslav federation. Bosnia-Herzegovina's referendum in favor of independence at the end of February 1992 initiated the fourth phase, which embraces a range of international actions associated with the conflict in that former Yugoslav republic. The most recent phase has focused on efforts to prevent the conflict from spreading to Kosovo and Macedonia.[6]

### Phase 1: The International Community Supports Yugoslavia's "Integrity"

This phase can be treated briefly, but it is important because it reflected the traditional understanding of the role and limits of international involvement at the outset of the post–Cold War era. Virtually the entire international community strongly hoped that Yugoslavia would remain intact as a result of a political negotiation that might revise the constitutional structures and balance between central government and republics.[7] For some, the main argument in favor of this solution was the fear, tragically realized, that ethnic conflict over borders and minority rights would follow Yugoslavia's breakup. A U.S. National Intelligence Estimate, leaked to the press in the autumn of 1990, presciently warned of these dangers; the fear was widespread.[8]

Others were concerned about the example that Yugoslavia's breakup might set for other multiethnic countries, including Czechoslovakia, Romania, and, most important, the USSR. The Soviet leadership was well aware of the implications of Yugoslavia for its own country. Shortly after the conflict broke out, Soviet President Mikhail Gorbachev stated: "We are looking for ways to resolve the problem by peaceful means, respecting the peoples of Yugoslavia but proceeding from the premise that we favor Yugoslavia's integrity and are committed to the inviolability of borders." If nations fail to respect this principle, he went on, "developments in Europe will be out of hand."[9] However, the international community had few tools at its disposal to halt the movement toward breakup, and so relied primarily on exhortation. The European Community (EC) was the most active: it offered economic assistance and trade concessions to Yugoslavia as an incentive to keep the federation together, while asserting that the Community would refuse to recognize breakaway republics or offer them benefits (including membership in the EC itself).

The United States shared this approach. Just days before Slovenia and Croatia declared independence, U.S. Secretary of State James Baker traveled to Belgrade and announced: "We support democratization, protection of human rights, territorial integrity and preservation of the unity of Yugoslavia."[10]

The operative principle guiding these policies stemmed from the Helsinki Final Act: no changes in international borders except by consent.[11] The international community chose to interpret this rule to apply against unilateral efforts to secede from an established state. This principle in effect gave Serbia a veto over the constitutional negotiations at a stage when Slovenia and Croatia might still have accepted some form of loose confederation with the other republics. Some commentators have even suggested that this principle offered Serbia (acting under the color of the federal government, which it dominated) an implicit green light to crush the unilateral declarations of independence, on the grounds that they represented an effort to alter the country's borders without the federal government's consent.

Whether alternative courses of action might have headed off the bloody conflict is the subject of considerable debate. At least two other options were available. The international community could have accepted the inevitability of Yugoslavia's dissolution and worked to assure that the split was more peaceful, either by taking active measures to assure minority rights within the constituent republics under current borders, or by working with the parties to consider border changes in appropriate circumstances. Alternatively, the international community could have retained its policy preference for a single state, but it could also have made clear to Serbian leaders that the use of force to maintain the federal state would be met with a swift international response (political, economic, or even military).

## Phase 2: Intervention to Halt the Fighting in Slovenia

Slovenia's and Croatia's declarations of independence were immediately followed by the outbreak of fighting between Slovenian and JNA forces. The Conference on Security and Cooperation in Europe (CSCE) became involved by virtue of a newly adopted crisis "emergency" mechanism, which provided for holding a special meeting of the CSCE at the request of one member, if that request received support from twelve other member states.[12] Austria initiated the emergency mechanism on June 28. A day earlier, Austria had triggered a requirement that Yugoslavia clarify its military intentions through the CSCE's Conflict Prevention Center in Vienna, a "confidence-building" measure established by the Stockholm treaty of 1986. But the CSCE was hobbled by the requirement that it act unanimously, and soon receded as a locus of efforts to resolve the crisis.

The EC quickly took on a more active role, sending the three EC foreign ministers who made up the Troika[13] to mediate. Their efforts led to the Brioni Accords, initialed on July 8, which established a cease-fire, a three-month moratorium on implementing the declarations of independence, and a commitment to begin political negotiations on Yugoslavia's future. As part of the agreement, the parties accepted the EC's offer to send thirty to fifty observers to monitor compliance with the agreement.

Following the Brioni Accords, the Yugoslav federal government withdrew its forces from Slovenia and appeared to concede Slovenia's independence, de facto if not de jure. The decision was presumably based on the fact that there is no significant Serb minority in Slovenia. Instead, the central government turned its attention to Croatia.

## Phase 3: International Efforts to Resolve the Conflict in Croatia

The interethnic fighting in Croatia proved much fiercer. The Serb population there was significant—12 percent, according to the 1991 census. Even more important, the Serb population was concentrated geographically, constituting a majority in the Krajina and parts of western Slavonia, and a significant minority in parts of eastern Slavonia. Serbs in Croatia were well armed and organized politically, and they were backed by JNA forces stationed in Croatia.

The EC sought to follow a two-track strategy for Croatia: establish a cease-fire supported by EC monitors (increased from 50 to 300 as a result of decisions in summer 1991); and pursue political negotiations under an EC-sponsored peace conference chaired by Lord Carrington, former British foreign secretary and secretary-general of the North Atlantic Treaty Organization (NATO).[14] A panel of experts drawn from the constitutional courts of France, Italy, Germany, Spain, and Belgium, chaired by Judge Robert Badinter of France, assisted Carrington. The conference formed three working groups: on constitutional arrangements, minority rights, and economic relations.

Throughout much of the fall of 1991, Carrington, backed by most EC leaders, continued to press for some way to keep

Yugoslavia together. In October Carrington and Dutch Foreign Minister Hans van den Broek (representing the presidency of the EC) released a proposed constitutional plan for a loose association among the Yugoslav republics (modeled to some extent on the EC itself), retaining the existing interrepublic borders. All of the republics except Serbia (but including Montenegro, which had been closely associated with Serbia) accepted the proposal. The EC voted on November 8 to impose economic sanctions against Yugoslavia, but to exempt any republic that agreed to the constitutional plan. On December 2 the EC restored aid and trade privileges to Bosnia, Croatia, Macedonia, and Slovenia, leaving only Serbia and Montenegro subject to the sanctions. The EC action thus meant treating the republics differently, even though the Community continued to recognize only the federal government of Yugoslavia.

As the negotiations dragged on, some European states, especially Germany and Austria, began to push for formally recognizing Slovenia and Croatia. Some advocates for recognition based their arguments on the right of self-determination,[15] while others saw recognition as a means to halt the fighting, by putting new pressure on Serbia and mobilizing support for international involvement on behalf of Croatia. Although Carrington, United Nations representatives, and U.S. officials all opposed recognition and warned that it would impede peace efforts,[16] Germany pressed ahead and threatened to recognize unilaterally if the EC as a whole did not agree. Eager to preserve EC unity during the difficult Maastricht negotiations, Germany's partners agreed to establish a process for deciding on whether and which states to recognize.

The compromise EC agreement charged the Badinter panel with reviewing all requests for recognition from Yugoslav republics, on the basis of a number of criteria, including respect for individual and minority rights, a commitment not to alter borders by force, democratic government, and accepting the EC peace process. Although most EC countries agreed to abide by the panel's findings, German leaders threatened to recognize Croatia and Slovenia regardless of the outcome of the review.

The Badinter panel found that Slovenia and Macedonia met the criteria for recognition. It raised questions about Croatia's commitment to human rights, and sought further assurances from Bosnia, including a guarantee that the republic would hold a referendum to establish public support for independence. Faced with German pressure, however, and a cosmetic change in Croatia's constitution in response to the Badinter report, the Community voted to recognize Slovenia and Croatia on January 15, 1992, while deferring action on Bosnia and Macedonia. Greek objections blocked EC action on recognizing Macedonia; Greece feared that by using the name Macedonia, the Yugoslav republic was fueling irredentist designs on northern Greece.[17]

While the EC pursued political negotiation, it simultaneously sought to broker a durable cease-fire to aid in the peace process. But the Community was largely unsuccessful in its efforts, and throughout the summer and early fall it debated the idea of sending peacekeeping or peacemaking troops to Croatia, under the aegis of the Western European Union (WEU).[18] But there was little consensus in support of this step. Instead, several European states, led by France and Austria, turned to the UN for assistance in the effort to establish a cease-fire in Croatia.[19]

Initially the UN Secretariat was reluctant to support UN involvement in the conflict. After the outbreak of fighting in Slovenia, Secretary-General Pérez de Cuéllar rejected UN intervention in an "internal" matter and noted that Slovenia was not a member of the UN. But with the continued failure of EC-led efforts, attention increasingly focused on the UN as an alternative forum. France (a permanent member of the Security Council, and the Council's chair in September) and Austria (serving a term membership on the Council) continued to lead the effort. France's interest in UN action was stimulated by the continued political disagreements within the EC on how to proceed and by a general unwillingness to use the WEU, while Austria was a neighbor concerned about possible widening of the conflict and responding to its close historical and cultural ties to Croatia and Slovenia.

Finally, on September 25, the Security Council concluded that continuation of the fighting constituted a threat to international peace and security; invoking chapter VII of the UN Charter, the Council voted an arms embargo (resolution 713). The vote on the resolution was unanimous after the Yugoslav government assured China and the nonaligned members of the Council that it did not oppose the embargo. The Security Council also endorsed the peace efforts the EC had undertaken "with the support of" the CSCE. On October 8 Pérez de Cuéllar appointed former U.S. Secretary of State Cyrus Vance as his personal envoy to Yugoslavia.

At a meeting with Vance in Geneva on November 23, the presidents of Serbia and Croatia and the Yugoslav state secretary for national defense agreed to request UN peacekeepers. On the basis of that understanding, on November 27 the Security Council adopted resolution 721, urging the secretary-general to present "an early recommendation" for a peacekeeping force if a cease-fire between the parties could be arranged. In response, the secretary-general prepared a report outlining a plan, contingent on a cease-fire, for a peacekeeping force in Croatia;[20] the Security Council endorsed the plan on December 15 (resolution 724).

The Vance plan called for the complete withdrawal of the JNA and other Serbian military units from Croatia. In addition, it provided for establishing three UN Protected Areas in areas with large Serb populations that had come under the effective control of the JNA or Serb militias: eastern and western Slavonia, and the Krajina.[21] Within the protected areas, the plan required the complete withdrawal or demobilization of all military units, including the Croatian national guard and army, as well as all territorial paramilitary forces (Serb and Croat). Only lightly armed police forces (whose composition must reflect the ethnic mix in the area) could remain in the protected areas to maintain order, and these were subject to supervision by UN forces (UN Protection Force, or UNPROFOR I)[22] to assure nondiscrimination and protection of human rights. UNPROFOR I would have the authority to control access to the protected areas to assure that no new military forces or equipment were introduced. In addition, UNPROFOR I was to have responsibility for facilitating the voluntary return of residents displaced from the protected areas.

Vance's effort to achieve a cease-fire began to bear fruit in early January 1992, and a small deployment of UN monitors arrived in Zagreb and Belgrade on January 14.[23] Despite some continued fighting, on February 12 Vance recommended to the secretary-general that the UN begin to deploy a peacekeeping force of around 12,000–13,000 troops. This recommendation followed fresh assurances from Croatia's Franjo Tudjman that his government would comply with the plan. The Security Council endorsed the recommendation on February 21 (resolution 743); authorized an initial deployment of troops; and, in a departure from normal procedure, provided an initial mandate for one year (instead of the usual six months), to give both Serbs and Croats in Croatia greater assurance that their interests would be protected.

Resolution 743, while noting that "the Government of Yugoslavia" had requested a peacekeeping force, left the legal basis of the UNPROFOR I deployment vague. It made no explicit reference to chapter VII of the Charter, but did state that "the situation in Yugoslavia continues to constitute a threat to international peace and security," referencing resolution 713, the arms embargo, which was based on chapter VII.

The secretary-general initially estimated the cost of the deployment in excess of $600 million, but the Security Council provided only $250 million to begin the operation.

UNPROFOR I began to deploy on March 8, under the command of Indian General Satish Nambiar; the Security Council authorized full deployment on April 7 (resolution 749). Deployment was scheduled to be completed by the end of April, but was delayed because of continued disagreements over UNPROFOR's role and failures to comply with the agreed provisions on disarming militias in the protected areas. Although UNPROFOR I succeeded to some degree in calming the conflict in those areas, tensions remained high in the east and south sectors, and problems of noncompliance were wide-ranging.[24]

Problems were also growing in the surrounding areas (the "pink zones"). Under the Vance plan, the JNA was obliged to withdraw from all of Croatia, while the Croatian forces had to withdraw from (or disband in) the protected areas only. It soon became apparent that areas adjacent to the protected areas had significant Serb populations subject to the authority of the Croatian military, and that Serbia and the JNA were unwilling to comply with the Vance plan without some assurances that the Serbs in these adjacent areas would be protected. While the Security Council rejected Belgrade's request to expand the protected areas, on June 30, 1992, it agreed (in resolution 762) to establish a joint commission of representatives of the Croatian government and local Serbs to monitor the police authorities and to assure the withdrawal of the Croatian army and the JNA from those areas. But the joint commission was largely frustrated in its work, and Secretary-General Boutros Boutros-Ghali concluded that implementation of resolution 762 was "largely incomplete."[25]

By the end of 1992, Tudjman was threatening to oppose extending UNPROFOR's mandate, on the grounds that Serb militias were blocking the agreed resettlement of Croatians displaced from the protected areas. Whether Croatia's withdrawal of consent would end the current mandate is a matter of debate, and is discussed below.

## Phase 4: The Conflict in Bosnia

In January 1992 the Badinter panel had concluded that Bosnia met most of the conditions for EC recognition, but recommended that the republic hold a referendum to confirm popular support for independence. The referendum was held at the end of February, and the vote was overwhelmingly in favor, partly because of the Bosnian Serbs' decision to boycott the referendum. Serbs made up 31 percent of Bosnia's population of 4.4 million in 1991; Muslims, 44 percent; Croats, 17 percent; and others (including self-described Yugoslavs), 8 percent.

Even before the referendum, tensions between Bosnia's three ethnic/religious groups ran high, and in early February the EC peace conference turned its attention to seeking a political solution to meet all sides' concerns. Despite an agreement by leaders of the three factions to respect the republic's borders, Bosnian Serbs began to consolidate control over Serb-dominated areas, with the avowed aim of joining the republic of Serbia.[26] The EC initially delayed acting in response to the Bosnian referendum, but as the security situation deteriorated on April 7, 1992, both the EC and the United States recognized Bosnia in the hopes that this would help to stabilize the political situation. At the same time, the Security Council called on the parties in Bosnia to cooperate with the EC peace efforts (resolution 749, April 7). These efforts had little impact: instead, the Bosnian Serbs, aided by the JNA, accelerated the violence, focusing on forcible removal, intimidation, and even killing of Bosnian Muslims and Croats to create ethnically pure Serb enclaves—a process that became known as "ethnic cleansing."

As the situation continued to deteriorate in Bosnia, the international community followed a multidimensional, multi-institutional strategy to address the conflict there: economic sanctions to end Serbia's support for the conflict; UN-supported humanitarian relief operations; refugee assistance; investigations of human rights abuses and war crimes; and negotiations for a political settlement. At various stages there were discussions of more direct military involvement, but this idea was rejected. The UN's actions were facilitated to some extent by the General Assembly's decision on May 22, 1992, to admit Slovenia, Croatia, and Bosnia to the UN, while declining to accept Serbia's and Montenegro's claim to act as the successor to Yugoslavia.[27]

*Economic Pressure to Halt Outside Support for the Warring Parties.* In April and May the international community initially focused its efforts on halting Serbia's support for Bosnian Serbs, especially the use of the JNA against the Bosnian government, and threatened new diplomatic and economic sanctions.[28] The effort briefly appeared to bear fruit when, on April 27, the leaders of Serbia and Montenegro announced a new constitution for the "Federal Republic of Yugoslavia," raising hopes that Milosevic might finally agree to accept the other republics' independence. But the violence continued, and on May 6 the EC was forced to withdraw its monitoring mission after an EC observer was killed.

Although a number of European countries began to press for sending UN peacekeepers to Bosnia,[29] the secretary-general demurred in the absence of a cease-fire.[30] Instead, on May 15, the Security Council adopted resolution 752, calling for the end of outside interference in Bosnia by both Serbs and Croats, an end to ethnic cleansing, and noninterference with humanitarian relief. Under U.S. prodding, the Security Council escalated the pressure on May 30, with mandatory economic sanctions against Serbia and Montenegro to enforce resolution 752 pursuant to chapter VII of the Charter (resolution 757). The vote was 13–0, with China and Zimbabwe abstaining. The sanctions represented a broad-ranging cutoff of trade and financial transactions, exempting only foodstuffs and medicine; on June 18 the exemptions were extended to other essential humanitarian supplies (resolution 760).

The initial sanctions contained no explicit enforcement mechanism, although both the WEU and NATO sent naval forces to the Adriatic to monitor compliance.[31] In the face of widespread evidence of large-scale violations, both on overland shipments and on the Danube, the Security Council voted on November 16 to tighten enforcement. It authorized states "acting nationally or through regional agencies or arrangements to use such measures commensurate with the specific circumstances as may be necessary" to halt shipments on the Adriatic and the Danube that would violate either the arms embargo or the economic sanctions,[32] and prohibited transshipment of key commodities through Serbia, which had been a major loophole for sanctions avoidance. Monitors (including inspectors from the U.S Customs Service) were to be placed along the borders and international waterways.[33]

*Humanitarian Relief.* As the fighting continued, concern over the plight of Bosnian Muslims in besieged cities grew. Heavy shelling closed the Sarajevo airport to relief operations; in early June the UN stepped in to broker an agreement to place the airport under UNPROFOR control. The Security Council agreed in principle to extend UNPROFOR's mandate to include securing the airport with an additional 1,100 troops, as well as supervising the withdrawal of heavy weaponry from the area (resolution 758, June 8, 1992). But for the most part the airport remained closed until French President François Mitterrand's surprise visit to Sarajevo following the EC summit in Lisbon at the end of June; even the Mitterrand-inspired cease-fire did not hold for long.

Public pressure to take a more activist approach to humanitarian relief increased throughout the summer, spurred on by grisly revelations of prison camps, torture, and killings of Muslim civilians. After considerable debate, and at U.S. prodding, on August 13 the Security Council adopted resolution 770, which "called upon all states to take nationally or through regional agencies or arrangements all measures necessary to facilitate in coordination with the United Nations" the delivery of humanitarian aid.[34] After a period of uncertainty over how to implement this provision, France, Britain, Spain, and Canada ultimately agreed to contribute to a new UN deployment, UNPROFOR II, to help assure the delivery of humanitarian aid.[35]

Logistical problems associated with moving troops into Bosnia as Serb forces continued to harass relief convoys hindered deployment of UNPROFOR II. Although the UN forces were authorized to use force in conjunction with their mission, the UN commanders were reluctant to confront Serb militias. UN and U.S. analysts concluded that only about one-quarter of the needed humanitarian supplies were reaching the target population. With the approach of winter, experts began to forecast 100,000–400,000 possible deaths in Bosnia from war, hunger, exposure, and disease.

Although (as discussed below) the Bosnian Serbs agreed at the August 1992 London Conference to end military flights, mounting evidence indicated that they were violating that commitment. As a result, on October 9, acting pursuant to resolution 770 to ensure "the safety of the delivery of humanitarian assistance," the Security Council banned all military flights other than those in aid of the various UN activities (resolution 781). While the Security Council agreed to station monitors to observe compliance with the ban, the European countries with peacekeeping forces in Bosnia resisted the U.S. effort to include stronger provisions for enforcement. This resistance continued when the United States promoted a new effort at enforcement in December, in view of continuing Bosnian Serb violations of the UN flight ban.

*Human Rights.* As reports of human rights violations grew during the spring and summer, pressure to take action intensified. In August Tadeusz Mazowiecki was appointed special rapporteur of the UN Commission on Human Rights and was sent to the former Yugoslavia to investigate. He issued two reports, concluding that "massive and grave violations of human rights are occurring throughout the territory of Bosnia" and "human rights violations are being perpetrated by all parties to the conflicts. There are also victims on all sides. However, the situation of the Muslim population is particularly tragic: they feel that they are threatened with extermination."[36] The Security Council also adopted resolution 771, condemning the violation of the Geneva Conventions of 1949 and other international humanitarian law, and called on governments and others to compile data on human rights violations. Thereafter, the Security Council requested the secretary-general to establish a commission of experts to review the available information (resolution 780, October 6, 1992). On October 23 the secretary-general appointed a five-member commission of experts from the Netherlands, Egypt, Canada, Senegal, and Norway. Pressures to act mounted throughout the fall of 1992, as the United States stepped up calls for convening a war crimes tribunal and the EC appointed a special commission to investigate reports of mass rape by Serb forces in Bosnia.

The UN, acting through the UN High Commissioner for Refugees (UNHCR), also became involved in providing refugee assistance, both in and outside Bosnia. Refugee efforts included the convening of an interagency conference on July 29, 1992, involving UNHCR, UNICEF, the World Food Programme, and the World Health Organization; and the establishment of the Consolidated Inter-Agency Programme of Action and Appeal for Former Yugoslavia for the period September 1992 through March 1993.[37]

*Political Negotiations.* In Bosnia the international community initially pursued the "division of labor" approach followed in Croatia: the UN took responsibility for negotiating and monitoring cease-fires, while the EC led the effort to find a political

solution to the crisis. But this bifurcated strategy proved difficult
to sustain. Matters came to a head in July 1992, when the EC's
chief negotiator, Lord Carrington, brokered a cease-fire agreement that called, among other things, for Serb forces to place
their heavy weaponry under UN supervision. This provoked an
immediate outcry from Secretary-General Boutros Boutros-
Ghali, who criticized the EC for committing the UN without
prior consultation. As a result, the EC and the UN decided to
merge their efforts and involve the UN directly in the peace
negotiations, beginning with a joint conference in London
on August 26–28, bringing together all of the parties to the
conflict.[38]

At the London Conference the parties adopted the Statement
of Principles, including nonrecognition of territorial gains achieved
by force, unconditional release of civilian detainees, and protection of minority rights. They agreed to a ban on military flights
over Bosnia, international monitoring of the Serbia-Bosnia border, tougher sanctions enforcement, and full cooperation in permitting the delivery of humanitarian relief. The Bosnian Serbs
agreed to place their heavy weaponry under UN supervision. The
parties also agreed to set up the open-ended International Conference on the Former Yugoslavia, with a permanent steering
committee, cochaired by Vance (on behalf of the UN) and Lord
Owen, a former British foreign secretary, who took over from
Lord Carrington (on behalf of the EC).[39]

On October 27 Vance and Owen unveiled their proposal for
dividing Bosnia into seven to ten largely autonomous (but not
ethnically pure) regions, with a limited central government.[40]
Under the Vance-Owen plan, the international community would
have an ongoing involvement in assuring the peace settlement: it
would, for example, appoint senior government officials, establish an independent judiciary, and continue stationing UN forces
to assure observance of the terms of the agreement.

The continued difficulties in the peace negotiations, coupled
with the limited efficacy of the humanitarian relief effort, led the
Bosnian government to call for selectively lifting the arms embargo to permit it to acquire arms. This position gained the
backing of the Organization of the Islamic Conference, as well as

influential Western public figures and eventually President Clinton,[41] but Vance and Owen stoutly resisted, arguing that lifting the embargo would only prolong the fighting.

As of early 1993, the fate of the plan remained unclear, in part because of doubts whether the Bosnian Serbs were really prepared to give up much of the roughly 70 percent of Bosnian territory under their de facto control, or to relinquish their claims to sovereignty over the Serb-controlled areas. Similarly, it was not clear that the Bosnian Muslims would relinquish their hopes for a truly unitary state.

## Phase 5: Kosovo, Macedonia, and the Wider Balkans

As the conflict persisted in Bosnia, international concern that it might spread to other parts of the former Yugoslavia and beyond deepened. The situation in Kosovo was particularly volatile. Since 1990, when Milosevic suspended the Constitution of 1974 and ended Kosovo's status as an autonomous province, Serbian authorities had intensified their crackdown on the rights of Kosovo Albanians, who make up some 90 percent of the province's population, closing Albanian schools, firing Albanian professionals and managers, and harassing the populace. Many feared that Milosevic would unleash ethnic cleansing in Kosovo, creating huge refugee flows into Albania and Macedonia, and potentially triggering Albanian military involvement.[42]

The situation in Macedonia also threatened to trigger a wider Balkan conflict. Although the Badinter panel had concluded in early 1992 that Macedonia largely met the EC's criteria for recognition as a state, Greek objections continued to block EC action. Despite misgivings by most EC leaders, at the Community's Lisbon summit in June 1992, the EC agreed not to recognize Macedonia unless it agreed to change its name to meet Greece's objections.[43]

The international community's refusal to recognize Macedonia aggravated what was already a highly unstable situation. Macedonia, one of the poorest regions of the former Yugoslavia, suffered heavily from the economic sanctions against Serbia, which accounted for some 60 percent of Macedonia's trade. In addition, Greece blocked vital oil shipments to Macedonia, further damaging the latter's economy. This in turn exacerbated the ethnic tensions between Slavs and Albanians, which a fragile coalition government including Albanians and a Turk, as well as Slavs, had kept in check.[44]

Macedonia's weak condition posed a number of dangers for widening the conflict. First, there was a risk that Serbia might seek to reassert its authority over the republic, although the small Serb population and the republic's poverty suggested that this was unlikely to be a high priority for Milosevic. More likely was the risk of deeper internal conflict or collapse, fueled by an influx of refugees from Kosovo. A breakdown of the central authority in Skopje could tempt Albania, Greece, and Bulgaria to intervene to defend their interests, and potentially lead to a confrontation between Greece and Turkey.

To forestall this spillover of the conflict, the CSCE, with the agreement of the Serbian government, sent civilian monitors to Kosovo, the Sandzak, and Vojvodina, and agreed to double the number of observers at the December Stockholm CSCE meeting. On December 11 the Security Council voted to deploy some 700 peacekeepers to Macedonia (resolution 795), in accordance with the recommendation of the secretary-general, who proposed establishing the force "with an essentially preventive mandate of monitoring and reporting any developments in the border area which could undermine confidence and stability in Macedonia or threaten its territory."[45] The force constitutes "an extension of the UNPROFOR mandate" under the UN Force Commander's control and is paid for out of the UN budget. The deployment appears to be based on consent, since the Security Council resolution references the original UNPROFOR resolution, notes the "request by the Government in the former Yugoslav Republic of Macedonia for a United Nations' presence," and makes no explicit reference to chapter VII or a threat to peace and security.

As concerns about the spread of the conflict grew, the United States specifically warned that it was prepared to use force against Serbia in response to military actions in Kosovo, a position that had widespread support in Western Europe. Finally, in April 1993 Greece agreed to a compromise that would allow Macedonia to become a UN member under the temporary name "Former Yugoslav Republic of Macedonia," thus partially defusing the crisis.

## INTERNATIONAL INVOLVEMENT

The unraveling of Yugoslavia offered the international community a daunting challenge in devising substantive principles and institutional arrangements to resolve or at least contain the conflict. The issues raised have profound implications for the future, and go to the heart of the nature of the international order and international law in the post–Cold War era.

Broadly speaking, the international community repeatedly faced the question: Should the international community intervene, and if so, who should do it, for what purpose, and with what means? The elements of the question are interrelated, since different institutions, for historical and political reasons, seemed oriented toward different objectives—the UN toward peacekeeping and humanitarian objectives, the CSCE toward human rights, the EC toward political mediation and economic "carrots and sticks," and NATO and the WEU toward military operations.

The effort to answer this question unleashed a fundamental reexamination of a series of difficult questions relating to the underlying issues of self-determination, individual and group rights, and the exercise and limits of sovereignty: When should the international community support the breakup of a recognized state? Under what circumstances does the international community have the right to intervene to limit a government's right to exercise authority over its residents free from outside interference? With what means may it do so, and who decides?

### The Justifications for Intervention

During the course of the crisis, the international community offered a variety of rationales for intervening in the conflict; each rationale in effect derogated from the general prohibition in article 2(7) of the UN Charter barring interference "in matters which are essentially within the domestic jurisdiction of any state." Generally, the rationales fell into four categories: involvement by consent of the parties, transborder aggression, respond-

ing to humanitarian needs and violations of human rights, and
indirect impact on other states (primarily as a result of refugee
flows).

*Consent and Good Offices.* In the initial stages of the crisis the
international involvement was primarily limited to actions with
the consent of the parties, or offers of mediation and good offices.
The EC began its mediation efforts in response to the outbreak of
fighting without expressly articulating a basis for becoming involved: ministers, who were in the middle of a complex debate on
improving the foreign policy capability of the EC, seemed to take
it for granted that the Community should prove its fitness for a
more assertive foreign policy role by attempting to mediate. Most
of the EC's initial steps had the consent of the parties;[46] for
example, the decision to deploy monitors was endorsed in the
Brioni Accords.

By the fall of 1991, the EC adopted a somewhat more
activist approach to intervention in Yugoslavia's "internal" affairs, including imposing differential sanctions on those republics
that did not agree to the EC's peace plan, even before the Community had recognized the independence of Croatia and Slovenia. The EC did not directly explain the rationale or legal basis
for its actions; it was seeking to provide leverage for Lord Carrington's peacemaking efforts. Several EC states were prepared to
go even further—including sending military forces for peacekeeping or peacemaking—although some, especially Germany, argued that only the UN had the authority to intervene (under
chapter VII of the Charter) without the parties' consent. Despite
considerable debate over whether the EC (or WEU) had the
authority to act under these circumstances, and under what
rationale, the issue remained moot, because the lack of political
consensus on what objectives to pursue, as well as what means to
use, blocked more assertive EC actions.

The CSCE's early involvement was limited to action supported by consensus of all members, including the Yugoslav
government, although the CSCE's decision to take up the issue
was triggered by the newly adopted emergency mechanism, which
required the support of only 12 of the 35 members. The con-

sensus requirement was a major barrier to an activist CSCE role, especially in the early stages of the crisis.

From the beginning of the crisis through the winter of 1992, the UN also was largely limited to actions with the consent of the parties (thus implicitly acting under chapter VI), although the arms embargo, which the Security Council adopted in September 1991, was predicated on chapter VII of the Charter.[47] The deployment of UNPROFOR to Croatia was based on the parties' agreement to the Vance-Owen plan, although it remains unclear whether the withdrawal of consent (or the refusal by one or more parties to renew UNPROFOR's mandate, which was temporarily extended in March 1993) would require withdrawing the UN forces. Certainly the Security Council could revise the mandate and base the deployment on chapter VII, without Croatia's or Serbia's consent.

The decision to deploy UNPROFOR to Macedonia also appears predicated on consent, since the Security Council resolution specifically notes the Macedonian government's request. But this action raises a potentially difficult question about whether and under what circumstances a government of a state that is not a member of the UN or widely recognized by the international community is entitled to consent to UN involvement. In this case, the General Assembly had declined to allow the Federal Republic of Yugoslavia (Serbia and Montenegro) to succeed to Yugoslavia's seat at the UN, so there was no recognized government to withhold consent either.

*Beyond Consent: Threats to Peace, Security, and Human Rights.* Over the course of the Yugoslavia crisis it became increasingly clear that consent of the parties to traditional mediation and peacekeeping would not by itself halt the fighting, relieve the increasingly desperate plight of civilians caught up in the conflict, or bring about a durable peace settlement; new rationales were necessary to justify international actions.

The best-established justification for international involvement (either by nations individually or by institutions) is in response to transborder aggression. Article 39 of the Charter authorizes the Security Council to act in cases of aggression, and article 51 specifically reserves the right of individual or collective self-defense in response to an armed attack against a UN member state. This principle formed the basis for the UN-authorized coalition that forced Iraq out of Kuwait. But this rationale has played only a limited role in the Yugoslavia conflict.

During the early stages of the crisis, it seemed unlikely that the conflict would be transformed from an internal to an international one extending beyond the borders of Yugoslavia. However, the Security Council's first enforcement action with respect to Yugoslavia, the arms embargo, specifically made reference to the Council's concern about "the consequences [of the fighting] for the countries of the region, in particular in the border areas of neighboring countries" (resolution 713). During the initial fighting in Slovenia, minor incidents occurred at the Austrian border. Later, problems arose in connection with Serbian/JNA overflights of Hungary and the bombing of a border village, and potential problems emerged involving withdrawing JNA forces transiting Italian territory. But few non-Yugoslav nationals were caught up in the conflict (limiting the need for a rescue operation), and most of the initial impetus for international involvement came from concerns about long-term political consequences or the more immediate humanitarian plight, rather than the risk of an international war.

Once the international community recognized Croatia, Slovenia, and Bosnia, the situation was converted, at least in part, to an international conflict. This helped pave the way for the Security Council to adopt economic sanctions against Serbia and Montenegro: the preamble to resolution 757 imposing the embargo specifically reiterated the principle that "the borders of Bosnia and Herzegovina are inviolable," and noted that Serbia and Montenegro had failed to heed the Security Council's earlier demand for an end to outside interference.[48]

But this rationale was insufficient to justify UN involvement in the "civil war" aspects of the Bosnian conflict. Arguably, the UN involvement could have been based on the "consent" of the government of Bosnia, at least after Bosnia was admitted to the UN. The use of UN forces to put down civil insurrection could thus be analogized to the 1960 Congo deployment. But the

Bosnian government has been ambivalent about the relief mission, indicating that it would prefer that the UN lift the arms embargo, even at the cost of ending UN-supported humanitarian relief if necessary. As a result, the Bosnian government did not formally request the UN humanitarian role.

As a result, the UN and other international organizations have increasingly turned to three alternative theories to justify their involvement. These theories find, respectively, that the massive movement of refugees, the grave humanitarian crisis brought on by the war, and the Bosnian Serbs' human rights violations (including the notorious ethnic cleansing) threaten peace and security.

There is little doubt that the dimensions of the refugee problem and the humanitarian crisis, especially as the conflict spread to Bosnia, were major factors in increasing international willingness to intervene. The refugee problem clearly had a transboundary impact: more than 500,000 Yugoslav refugees fled to other European countries, and Croatian and Bosnian Serbs were resettled in Serbia, while hundreds of thousands of Bosnian Croats and Muslims filled camps and other temporary facilities in Croatia.

Equally grave was the humanitarian crisis. As the result of Bosnian Serb military strategy, which focused on besieging Muslim-controlled cities, large parts of the population were cut off from food and medicine; power and water facilities were destroyed; other basic public services were disrupted; and the risk of death from starvation, exposure, and disease was growing. As for human rights, the reports of atrocities against civilian detainees and of widespread rapes of Bosnian women conjured up chilling memories from Yugoslavia's (and Europe's) not-too-distant past.

The human rights dimension also propelled the CSCE to take a more assertive stance, a concern rooted in the Helsinki Final Act and the Paris Charter.[49] In the Moscow Declaration of October 1991, the CSCE leaders suggested that they were prepared to intervene to enforce a member nation's obligation to respect human rights, at least to the extent of sending rapporteurs without the target government's consent.[50] However, the CSCE moved cautiously in this direction, following the EC's (and later the UN's) lead. Only in mid-1992 did the CSCE move to send human rights observers into Serbia (to Kosovo, Sandzak, and Vojvodina).[51]

On the question of whether human rights and humanitarian concerns were sufficient in themselves to justify action under chapter VII, or whether intervention was justified only because the human rights and humanitarian situation was a threat to international peace and security, the Security Council record is somewhat ambiguous. The ambiguity could be seen in two Security Council resolutions passed on a single day (August 13, 1992): Resolution 770, authorizing, pursuant to chapter VII, nations and organizations to take "all measures necessary" to assure delivery of humanitarian relief, specifically noted that "the situation in Bosnia and Herzegovina constitutes a threat to international peace and security and that the provision of humanitarian assistance . . . is an important element in the Council's effort to restore international peace and security." By contrast, in resolution 771 the Security Council, also acting under chapter VII, demanded that all parties facilitate ICRC access to prison camps. The resolution referred to the parties' obligation to comply with the Geneva Conventions, but failed to make specific reference to any threat to international peace and security.

By the summer of 1992, growing concern that the conflict might spill over to involve neighboring countries refocused attention on the more traditional, security-related threats to peace. The increasingly desperate situation of the Bosnian Muslims and the perceived inefficacy of international organizations' efforts generated deep public outrage in Islamic countries, which threatened to intervene unilaterally unless the international community took stronger action. The international community grew increasingly worried that the conflict would spread to Kosovo or Macedonia, heightening the danger that outside parties would either intervene or be drawn in as a result of the spillover of fighting or mass refugee movements. This was an important impetus to the Security Council's decision to authorize the deployment of a "preventive peacekeeping force" in Macedonia (although, as noted above, the deployment is not pursuant to chapter VII, and the formal basis for the deployment appears to be the Macedonian government's consent), as well as to the U.S. threat to take military action against Serbia in the event that Serbia provoked a conflict in Kosovo.

It is difficult to know whether the need to articulate an international law justification for intervention in Yugoslavia's (or Croatia's, or Bosnia's) internal affairs constrained international institutions' willingness to act or the nature of their actions. Certainly they have all been reluctant to act, and especially reluctant to use force, but it seems equally plausible that for most relevant actors, the reticence stemmed more from underlying disagreements about the political aims to be achieved, or the efficacy of intervention, than from precedent-setting effects.

It is clear, however, that the Security Council is prepared (at least in principle) to authorize the use of force for humanitarian purposes. Although the Council's decision to use UNPROFOR II in Bosnia to help deliver humanitarian relief recited the talismanic "threat to peace and security," the authorization of "all measures necessary" was not directed to removing or reducing those threats, but to the humanitarian goal, a decision that foreshadowed the UN-authorized, U.S.–led deployment in Somalia.

## The Choice of Institutions

A broadly shared consensus at the beginning of the Yugoslav conflict held that primary responsibility for helping to resolve the conflict lay with regional institutions. This contention is attributable to a number of factors. First, as previously noted, the UN viewed the problem (especially in its early stages) through the self-denying optic of noninterference in internal affairs. That instinctive reluctance to avoid involvement was reinforced by the Cold War tradition that the UN did not become involved in European conflicts, if for no other reason than that the Cold War East-West division virtually guaranteed that one side or the other would use its Security Council veto. A third reason for preferring a regional approach was the growing interest in the recently institutionalized CSCE as the post–Cold War locus for European conflict resolution. In addition, as noted above, EC leaders were especially eager in the run-up to the Maastricht summit on European economic and political union to demonstrate that the Community had come of age in the field of foreign policy, especially on a question that was so close to home for EC members. Finally, the limited interest of the superpowers—and especially the limited interest of United States—tended to push the European organizations to the forefront.

For a number of reasons, however, the regional organizations, both European and transatlantic (CSCE, EC, WEU, and NATO), proved of limited use. In part, the problem stemmed from institutional weaknesses in each of the organizations, which all were in the early stages of adapting to the post–Cold War era.[52]

Although the EC moved rapidly on the diplomatic front after the conflict broke out in June 1991, it has had only a limited impact on the conflict, and has attracted much harsh criticism for its failures. EC defenders point to several successes of the Community's efforts. These include brokering the Brioni Accords, establishing criteria for recognizing the new states, and, perhaps most important, preserving a degree of harmony among EC members in their approach to the crisis that prevented the kind of Europe-wide conflict that followed on the heels of the Balkans crises at the beginning of the century. EC defenders argue that its limited success stemmed from a lack of the tools needed for a more effective response. In particular, they have cited the absence of an integrated "common foreign and security policy" mechanism among the Twelve, and of on-call military capability for joint action—two areas that were under discussion in the intergovernmental conference on political union (which led to the December 1991 Maastricht treaty) when the Yugoslav conflict broke out.

In the Maastricht treaty, the EC members agreed to establish the Common Foreign and Security Policy (CFSP), with limited majority voting and a new concept of "joint" and "common" actions.[53] They also took steps to increase their cooperation in defense matters, agreeing that the CFSP "shall include all questions related to the security of the Union, including the eventual framing of a common defence policy, which might in time lead to a common defence," and tighten the link between the EC and WEU by requesting that the WEU elaborate and implement EC decisions that have defense implications. Commentators and EC leaders themselves frequently cited the Community's limitations in responding to Yugoslavia as an impetus to the Maastricht provisions on foreign and security policy.

Similarly, the CSCE was at the beginning of a dramatic transformation, a process that the Yugoslavia crisis itself helped accelerate. In November 1990, only seven months before the fighting broke out, the CSCE members agreed, in the Charter of Paris, to establish permanent institutions for the organization: the Conflict Prevention Center, the Office for Democracy and Human Rights, and a small secretariat. Just days before the fighting began in Slovenia, the CSCE finally agreed to a crisis response procedure that would allow for an emergency meeting of its members.

The Yugoslavia crisis contributed considerably to improving the CSCE's ability to act in response to an "internal" conflict. At the time the crisis began, the CSCE acted strictly by consensus, allowing the offending state to block action. As a result of the Yugoslavia experience, the CSCE elaborated the concept of "consensus minus one," and in the face of Yugoslavia/Serbia's continued intransigence, it acted for the first time to suspend a member's participation. As noted earlier, in the Moscow Declaration the CSCE strengthened the tools available for human rights enforcement. At the Helsinki Follow-Up Conference in July 1992, the CSCE took a number of steps, many motivated by the Yugoslavia crisis. At Helsinki the CSCE members created the post of high commissioner for national minorities, charged with providing early warning of potential conflicts and early action to prevent the outbreak of conflict; established a more extensive menu of actions for conflict prevention and crisis management, including fact-finding and rapporteur missions and CSCE peacekeeping (which may draw on the EC, NATO, and the WEU, as well as the peacekeeping mechanism of the Commonwealth of Independent States); and agreed to explore other ideas for conciliation and arbitration mechanisms.

In addition, the crisis in Yugoslavia helped accelerate the evolution of the two regional defense organizations, NATO and the WEU. Two factors—the self-denying limitation against out-of-area actions and the military orientation of NATO forces toward defense of members' territory, rather than peacekeeping and peacemaking missions—had hampered NATO's initial ability to respond. Under the 1949 Washington treaty, the only formal constraint on NATO action is members' commitment to refrain from using force "in any manner inconsistent with the purposes of the United Nations" (article 1).[54] Nonetheless, the principal affirmative obligation of NATO members is to come to each other's assistance in the event of "an armed attack against one or more of them in Europe or North America" (article 5), and as a matter of practice, this has been interpreted to bar NATO action out-of-area—that is, in matters that do not directly affect the territorial security of member states.[55] As a result, NATO kept a very low profile during the first year of the conflict: the Allies consulted (as provided for under article 4 of the Washington treaty), but took no action, since the crisis did not appear to affect NATO members' security directly.

The WEU faced even greater institutional limitations. Until the mid-1980s, it was almost entirely a paper organization; even with its subsequent revitalization, it had no forces under its direct command. The WEU's previous military operations had been limited to naval activities: coordinating mine-sweeping operations in the Persian Gulf in 1987, and the embargo against Iraq in response to its invasion of Kuwait in August 1990.

Yugoslavia led to innovations for both NATO and the WEU that not only permitted them to play a greater role as the crisis unfolded, but also may improve both the likelihood and the efficacy of future involvement in similar crises. At their June 1992 summit in Bonn, WEU leaders adopted a package of reforms to "operationalize" the WEU, including establishing a permanent planning staff and compiling a list of forces available to the organization. They also agreed on a list of possible WEU missions: humanitarian and rescue missions, peacekeeping (on behalf of the UN or CSCE), and "tasks of combat forces in crisis management, including peacemaking."[56]

NATO followed a similar evolution, finding a new role and rationale for out-of-area activities: acting as the operational arm of the CSCE and the Security Council. In the June 1992 Oslo Declaration, NATO leaders began to enlarge the scope of potential NATO action by noting that the "Alliance has the capacity to contribute to effective actions by the CSCE in line with its new and increased responsibilities for crisis management," and stating that "we are prepared to support, on a case-by-case basis in accordance with our own procedures, peacekeeping activities under the responsibility of the CSCE, including by making available Alliance resources and expertise."[57]

The NATO and WEU decisions led almost immediately to greater involvement in the Yugoslavia crisis. In July 1992 both organizations agreed to send naval forces to the Adriatic to monitor compliance with trade sanctions against Serbia and Montenegro; that mission was expanded to include enforcing the embargo after the adoption of Security Council resolution 787 on November 16. NATO also contributed AWACS aircraft to monitor the no-fly zone established by resolution 781 and, at the secretary-general's request, prepared a study of options for creating safe havens and enforcing the no-fly resolution. NATO also considered acting on its own initiative to implement the Security Council resolution authorizing "all measures necessary" for assuring the delivery of humanitarian relief.

Still, the NATO and WEU reaction has remained cautious. Although UNPROFOR II is composed almost entirely of NATO nations' forces, it has remained a UN, rather than NATO, mission, under UN command, though supported with NATO assets. Similarly, NATO has remained divided about whether enforcement of the no-fly resolution should be conducted by NATO qua NATO, or under UN command.

There seems little doubt that all of the European security-related institutions have implemented significant changes in response to the Yugoslavia crisis. Had these been in place in June 1991, or even earlier, the regional organizations might have acted more quickly, or more decisively, or more effectively.

But simple institutional reform cannot cure much of the regional organizations' failure. The EC was largely paralyzed by fundamental disagreements over which course to pursue, and what price members were prepared to pay to bring about an end to the fighting and a political settlement. Old ties—historical cultural, religious, and ethnic—as well as contemporary disagreements about western Europe's interests in eastern and southeastern Europe played a role in producing these divergent perspectives. The problem was exacerbated because serious domestic political problems with ethnic, national, and religious minorities colored some, but not all, EC states' approach to the Yugoslav crisis.[58] Even if the EC had already established a "defense arm" through the WEU or otherwise, it is unlikely that Community members would have decided to deploy an intervention force. Even if some form of majority voting had been in place to carry out EC foreign and security policy, it is unlikely that the EC leaders would have risked the serious divisions that would follow from trying to impose a controversial policy toward Yugoslavia on the deeply divided Community members.

Since the WEU membership is a subset of the EC, most of the political constraints on the latter's action largely applied to the former, although the absence of Denmark and Ireland (perhaps the least enthusiastic among EC members about an independent, activist role for the WEU), as well as Greece (until November 1992), arguably made WEU consensus somewhat easier to achieve. But the WEU faced another difficult internal division: many of its members, especially the Atlanticist countries, such as the United Kingdom and Portugal, were reluctant to use force acting through a European-only institution, fearing that it would contribute over the long run to decoupling the United States from western European security.

NATO too is caught in this web. Despite NATO's growing interest in a more active role in regional conflict beyond direct collective defense, its involvement as an institution remains halting. Some of this hesitancy stems from France's reluctance to give NATO a broader mission, preferring arrangements conducted by Europeans under the WEU. Many of France's WEU partners, however, are reluctant to act without the United States. This has led to jury-rigged arrangements, such as the parallel (and overlapping) NATO/WEU naval forces in the Adriatic, or complex and confusing command relationships, such as UNPROFOR I and II. The result of this internal NATO conflict has been to force many activities back to the UN level.

This political disagreement among members was, of course, replicated in the CSCE, with the further complication that several multiethnic CSCE members faced similar dangers of internal conflict. For Romania, Bulgaria, the Baltic countries, and Russia, the precedent-setting effects of international involvement in ethnically based civil conflict might have profound implications in the future. Thus, even with the innovation of "consensus minus one," agreement in the CSCE proved daunting.

Ironically, what many considered the regional organizations' comparative advantage—proximity to and interest in resolving the conflict—also proved a serious limitation. Because many states in the region had historical alliances or adversary relations with the parties to the Yugoslav conflict, their impartiality as mediators was questioned. Russia, France, and, to a lesser extent, the United Kingdom were viewed as sympathetic to Serbia, while Germany's support for recognizing the independence of Croatia and Slovenia was attributed to past political, cultural, and religious ties. Some (not only in Serbia, but also in western Europe) even hinted darkly about German designs to establish a "Fourth Reich." These concerns about partiality were blamed for the limited success of the EC-sponsored peace conference.

Yet it is surprising that the UN—or, more accurately, the Security Council—should seem a "fairer" venue (at least in contrast to the CSCE), since four of the Council's five permanent members are also members of the CSCE. It is somewhat more understandable that Serbian leaders initially preferred that action proceed through the Security Council, since it offered Serbia the protection of both the Russian and Chinese vetoes and the constraints of article 2(7). Nevertheless, in the end, the Security Council was at least as successful in generating support for interventionary steps as was the EC or the CSCE. This success is attributable to a number of factors, including the recognized legal and moral legitimacy of the Security Council acting under chapter VII; the U.S. preference (once the United States took a more active interest in the spring of 1992) to exert its leadership through the Security Council rather than the CSCE, where it is only one among equals; and the growing impetus to expand the UN's role in the post–Cold War environment.

The division of labor the regional organizations and the UN initially attempted was hard to maintain. UN action was needed for mandatory sanctions, not only because many states insisted that only the UN had the authority to act, but also because many measures, such as the arms and oil embargo and more general trade sanctions, required more than regional compliance to be effective. By the summer of 1992, the tension between the regional and UN approach broke into the open.

UN Secretary-General Boutros-Ghali has strongly urged an expanded role for regional organizations, and has made clear that he believes that the regional organizations in Europe have a special responsibility to relieve the already overburdened UN machinery. Yet, despite the decision at the Helsinki Follow-Up Conference to establish the CSCE as a chapter VIII organization under the UN Charter, and CSCE institutional reforms that should facilitate the use of CSCE (rather than UN) peacekeepers and CSCE mediation, it seems likely that in future crises, the parties will have a natural tendency to look to the UN as the ultimate arbiter. It will require a strong self-denying restraint by the permanent members of the Security Council to convince the parties that the European regional organizations should lead in conflict resolution; such a role for these organizations will be particularly hard to achieve because the Security Council retains the exclusive right to authorize enforcement actions under article 53, even where a regional organization becomes a chapter VIII organization. More promising is the use of regional organizations as the implementing arm of the Security Council: the actions of NATO- and WEU-organized flotillas in support of the trade sanctions is a promising model, particularly in view of the barriers to establishing well-trained and well-supported on-call UN forces for missions other than traditional peacekeeping.

### The Means of Involvement: Sanctions, Peacekeeping, Peacemaking, and Beyond

The international community's involvement in Yugoslavia has proven a dramatic illustration of the expanding tools of international efforts to influence conflict. Some of the means the EC, CSCE, and UN used fall into traditional patterns. These include mediation and good offices (peacemaking, in the sense used by Secretary-General Boutros-Ghali in *An Agenda for Peace*),[59] which all three institutions pursued in one form or another in the summer and fall of 1991, and the imposition of economic sanctions to influence parties' behavior. But from the beginning there was considerable innovation. In some cases, the innovation had more to do with the institution than with the activity: the EC's unarmed observers in Slovenia, and later Croatia and Bosnia (known as the "ice-cream men" for their all-white uniforms), followed in a tradition of peacekeeping with the consent of the parties, but represented a new step for the EC.

These innovations pushed the boundaries of "peacekeeping" and the tradition of peacekeepers' neutrality. While the UNPROFOR I force deployment had the consent of the parties, its mission is much greater than observing a cease-fire or marking a line of separation between belligerents: the forces' task is to disarm militias, facilitate the withdrawal of the JNA, and oversee the resettlement of displaced persons.[60] Despite the parties' agreement in principle, resistance to complying has been widespread on all sides, raising the difficult question of whether the UN is entitled to become a "peace enforcer," enforcing the agreed-on mandate.[61] The failure thus far to do so has fueled criticism (led by the Croats, including Croatian President Tudjman) that UNPROFOR is in reality simply preserving the fruits of the Serbs' illegal use of force.

In Bosnia the situation is even more complicated. Although the UN has criticized the actions of all parties, it has singled out Serbia and the Serb forces in Bosnia as the main culprits, and taken measures directly against Serbia. But the Security Council has been unwilling to intervene on behalf of the Bosnian government, and the humanitarian aid effort is, at least nominally, designed to be neutral, assisting Serbs, as well as Muslims and Croats. The effort to maintain the UN's "neutrality" in Bosnia faces an inherent contradiction: any effort to bring in humanitarian aid helps the Bosnian forces in the struggle with the Serbs, since the Serbs are attempting to use starvation and exposure to force the Bosnian government to capitulate. On the other hand, if UNPROFOR declines to use force to overcome Serb barriers to the delivery of humanitarian aid, the UN is capitulating to the Serbs' strategy. What is worse, from the Muslims' perspective, is that some members of the Security Council have cited their concern over their forces' safety as a reason not to take more assertive action against the Serbs or allow the Bosnians to arm themselves. Thus, from the Bosnian government's perspective, it has the worst of two worlds: in the guise of neutrality, the UN will neither guarantee the delivery of humanitarian aid nor allow the Bosnians to take their own effective measures.

The Yugoslavia crisis has also seen the realization of another of Boutros-Ghali's concepts for UN action: the "preventive deployment" of UN forces in Macedonia at the request of the Macedonian government to help prevent the spread of the conflict.[62] If the parties to the Bosnia conflict had accepted the Vance-Owen plan, the UN would play an even greater ongoing role in trying to reconstruct political order in the war-torn republic: the plan draws on some of the concepts used in the UN role in Cambodia, and incorporates elements of what some have called a "trusteeship" approach to peace-building.[63]

The choice of legal theories or rationales has shaped the means that the international community has been prepared to use. Thus the humanitarian rationale provided a justification for extending UNPROFOR's mandate to aid in the delivery of food and medicine, while the establishment of the no-fly zone was predicated on protecting the humanitarian aid. Similarly, the human rights rationale led to moves to open the prison camps and to begin collecting data on prisoners of war. The fact that UNPROFOR I's deployment depended on the agreement of the parties meant that the UN forces acted with extreme caution in carrying out their mandate, leading to Croatian charges that the UN forces were siding with the Serbs. More generally, the UN forces' effort to maintain their impartiality in both Croatia and Bosnia subjected them to criticism from all parties that the UN was siding with the adversary. Although the UNPROFOR II deployment was based on chapter VII, not chapter VI, the UN forces in Bosnia were reluctant to use force to achieve their mission (other than in self-defense).

### Preserving International Borders and the Right of Self-Determination

Throughout the Yugoslavia conflict, the international community has struggled to reconcile apparently conflicting principles enshrined in the Helsinki Final Act: nonintervention in internal affairs and no altering international borders except by consent; and the right of self-determination. The international community on the whole has believed that the best way to achieve European stability was to maintain the existing international borders, which largely reflected the post–World War I territorial settlements (augmented by the consolidation of the Soviet internal empire in the years following the Russian Revolution). These states were to be the constitutive units within which individuals would exercise the rights guaranteed by the UN Charter and the Helsinki Final Act (including the right to self-determination).[64]

The Helsinki Final Act dealt only with international borders and was silent on internal political arrangements such as regional government and local autonomy, which was a feature of a number of European governments, East and West. These internal arrangements took on particular significance in multiethnic states such as Yugoslavia, because they reflected to varying degrees a measure of ethnic self-government.

But the long-term success of these federal arrangements depends largely on the consent of all the groups involved. In Yugoslavia, as in the Soviet Union, the glue that held the state together was coercion, exercised through both state organs and the Communist Party. With the collapse of communism in Yugoslavia, the international community hoped to promote consent as an alternative basis for maintaining the federation. But long-standing ethnic, cultural, and religious rivalries, fueled by economic disparities among the republics, made consensus difficult.

From Serbia's point of view, breaking up the country into its constituent parts would leave large numbers of Serbs at the mercy of ethnic groups perceived as hostile to them. Milosevic made clear that the government of Serbia would not accept Tito's internal borders as the basis for external borders of a dissolved Yugoslavia. Meanwhile, for the dominant ethnic groups of the other republics, continuing the federation meant acquiescence in increasingly nationalistic Serb domination.

Initially, the international community approached the problem through the Helsinki prism: self-determination and human rights, but within existing borders. But the ongoing crisis, and the unwillingness of the parties to respond to the rather limited incentives the international community offered, forced the international community to adapt its principles to the political reality. Although the international community was reluctant to accept the right of secession, it was faced with a federal government that was prepared to use force to maintain the internal status quo. Thus it had three choices: in the name of noninterference in internal affairs, allow Serbia to assert control; intervene to protect the rights of non-Serbs in Yugoslavia; or de facto recognize the right of secession, at least under limited circumstances. Most countries preferred a combination of the first and second options: limited diplomatic and economic pressure on Serbia, but no direct military involvement and no recognition for Slovenia and Croatia. Germany, however, strongly advocated recognition, motivated by the inapt analogy of German unification. Faced with the political necessity of accommodating Germany's fixed determination to recognize the breakaway republics, the EC cobbled together a decisional rule to justify its actions: no changing of "internal borders" by force, thus arguably accepting de facto that internal borders are the appropriate unit for applying the right to self-determination.[65]

The EC's decision, followed by the UN vote to admit Bosnia, Croatia, and Slovenia, establishes a precedent with unclear implications. Although the Community referred to the principle of not altering internal borders by force, the goal of the Serbian-dominated federal government was not to change internal borders, but to preserve the federal structure in the face of other republics' attempts to create a looser federation and, failing that, to gain independence. The EC's decision could be read to permit the citizens of a well-defined political subdivision to decide for themselves what state they wish to live in—following the example of the U.S. Declaration of Independence (but pointedly not the U.S. Civil War). This interpretation finds support in the Badinter panel's insistence that all of the republics hold referenda on independence as a condition for EC recognition.

It seems unlikely that the international community would be prepared to accept such a broad view of the meaning of self-determination. It would open up a never-ending question of which internal subdivision could claim that right—for example, does it apply to each *rayon* (region) or *oblast* in Russia? More pointedly, in the case of the former Yugoslavia, does it apply to the citizens of Kosovo, which not only has recognizable borders, but which, before Milosevic came to power, had considerable autonomy in the federal structure? Broad application of the principle of self-determination to mean a right of secession for any administrative unit could contribute powerfully to growing fragmentation in Europe and produce conflict in other areas, as well. For example, it is inconsistent with well-established practice in Africa, where newly independent states have agreed to maintain colonial boundaries in an attempt to limit intertribal conflict. Moreover, elevating administrative boundaries to the status of international law impedes sovereign nations' rights to arrange their own political structures.

It is possible to identify a number of features unique to the situation in Yugoslavia that justify the international community's accepting secession: the constitutional coup by Serbia in blocking the normal rotation of the Yugoslav presidency, the gross violations of human rights, and the absence of good faith in seeking a confederal solution that protects the interests of all parties. Moreover, the republics that made up the former Yugoslavia had considerable autonomy under the old structure, and the actions of Serbia and its allies seemed aimed at strengthening the central government at their expense. There is a clear need to define the limits of the international community's decision to recognize the Yugoslav republics, to understand potential applicability of this decision to future ethnic conflicts. In particular, if the international community is prepared to pursue a more activist approach to guaranteeing individual and minority rights in the future, such an approach could prove an alternative to recognizing the right of secession as a corollary to the right of self-determination. The CSCE's decision to establish a high commissioner for national minorities is a step in this direction, although how forceful the international community might be in the event that diplomatic efforts (the focus of the high commissioner) are unsuccessful remains to be seen.

## CONCLUSION

This history of the international community's role in the Yugoslavia crisis can point to two quite contradictory conclusions, depending on one's overall approach to the nature of the international order in the post–Cold War world.

One approach argues that with the end of the East-West struggle, the international community can and must play a more active role in civil and ethnic conflict. Adherents of this approach base their arguments on two, not mutually exclusive, theories: either they believe in the principle that fundamental civil rights are superordinate to claims of sovereignty, or they see that growing interdependence means that all conflicts pose a threat to international peace and security. For advocates of this approach, the international community's record in the former Yugoslavia seems abysmal: brave rhetoric backed up at best by half measures and an unwillingness to risk significant national blood or treasure.

Opposing this view is the contention that without the threat of escalation to superpower confrontation, conflicts such as those in the former Yugoslavia, while tragic in their human toll, pose little danger to stability and are too intractable to be resolved by outside intervention. From this viewpoint, the international community was right to limit its role primarily to good offices and exhortation (perhaps with a little humanitarian aid thrown in); the fatal mistake was not doing too little, but succumbing to the temptation to do too much and risking an open-ended involvement of more than 20,000 international troops for an unattainable goal.

In practice, the international community was torn between the two conceptions, and this ambivalence affected not only national leaders, but also the public, who were simultaneously outraged by the brutal atrocities in the heart of Europe and leery of committing their sons and daughters. It should come as no surprise that the solutions developed in the course of the crisis seem ambiguous and sometimes self-contradictory. But these ambiguities are unlikely to remain in their current form for long, since new ethnic and national crises in Europe and beyond are virtually certain to test these emerging precepts concerning international involvement in internal conflict.

## NOTES

1. On June 28, 1389, Serbian forces lost the battle of Kosovo field to the Ottomans, inaugurating five centuries of Ottoman rule. Kosovo holds a special place in Serbian memory, not only because of the battle, but because important historical and religious sites are located there.
2. See Barbara Jelavich, *History of the Balkans*, vol. 1 (Cambridge: Cambridge University Press, 1983), pp. 4–36.
3. See John Zametica, *The Yugoslav Conflict*, Adelphi Paper, no. 270 (London: International Institute for Strategic Studies/Brassey's, 1992); and James Gow, "Deconstructing Yugoslavia," *Survival*, vol. 33, no. 4 (July/August 1991), pp. 291–311.
4. Zametica, *The Yugoslav Conflict*, p. 22.
5. See Gow, "Deconstructing Yugoslavia," p. 291.
6. This sequencing of the phases reflects when each phase "began," but it is important to note that phase 3, concerning the conflict in Croatia, has continued in parallel with ongoing events in Bosnia (phase 4) and the more recent steps to prevent the conflict from spilling over into Kosovo and Macedonia (phase 5).

   For a more detailed account of the international community's role in the Yugoslavia crisis, see James B. Steinberg, *The Role of European Institutions in Security after the Cold War: Some Lessons from Yugoslavia* (Santa Monica, Calif.: Rand, 1992); and a revised and updated version, "The Response of International Institutions to the Yugoslavia Conflict: Implications and Lessons," in F. Stephen Larrabee, ed., *Europe's Volatile Powderkeg: Balkan Security after the Cold War* (Washington, D.C.: American University Press, forthcoming).
7. For the views of the international community prior to Slovenia's and Croatia's declaration of independence, see Gow, "Deconstructing Yugoslavia," pp. 303–307.

8. See David Binder, "Evolution in Europe: Yugoslavia Seen Breaking Up Soon," *New York Times*, November 28, 1990, p. 7.

9. Michael Parks, "Gorbachev Sees Major Peril in Yugoslav Crisis," *Los Angeles Times*, July 10, 1991, p. A6.

10. Tanjug, June 21, 1991 (FBIS-EEU-91-121, June 24, 1991, p. 37).

11. This injunction derives from three of the Helsinki Principles: Principle 1 (sovereign equality) declares that the participating states "consider that their frontiers can be changed, in accordance with international law, by peaceful means and by agreement." According to Principle 3 (inviolability of frontiers), the participating states "regard as inviolable all one another's frontiers as well as frontiers of all States in Europe and therefore they will refrain now and in the future from assaulting those frontiers." Principle 4 (territorial integrity of states) declares that the participating states "will refrain from any action inconsistent with the purposes and principles of the Charter of the United Nations against the territorial integrity, political independence or the unity of any participating State, and in particular refrain from any such action constituting a threat or use of force." See Helsinki Final Act, 14 *International Legal Materials* 1292 (1975).

12. The CSCE foreign ministers had adopted the emergency mechanism the preceding week. The United States and the Soviet Union had blocked an effort to develop emergency response procedures in connection with the November 1990 Paris CSCE summit, but as the potential for instability in Eastern Europe became clearer through the first half of 1991 (including in Yugoslavia itself), the two nations relented, although the Soviet Union made clear that accepting the emergency mechanism did not alter the requirement of unanimity in CSCE actions or amend the principle of noninterference in internal affairs. See "Conference on Security and Co-Operation in Europe: Document of the Moscow Meeting on the Human Dimension," October 3, 1991, 30 *International Legal Materials* 1670 (1991).

13. The Troika consists of the current EC presidency nation and the immediate preceding and successor presidency holders (the presidency of the EC rotates alphabetically every six months).

14. The initial effort to establish a peace conference centered on the CSCE, but Yugoslavia vetoed the proposal.

15. As early as July, the chairman of the German Christian Democratic Party (CDU) stated: "We won our unity through the right to self-determination. If we Germans think everything else in Europe can stay just as it was, if we follow a status quo policy and do not recognize the right to self-determination in Slovenia and Croatia, then we have no moral or political credibility. We should start a movement in the EC to lead to such recognition." See *Guardian*, July 2, 1992, p. 8.

16. UN Secretary-General Javier Pérez de Cuéllar wrote to Carrington that he was "deeply worried that any early selective recognition could widen the present conflict and fuel an explosive situation." See David Binder, "Bonn's Yugoslav Plan Faces More Flak," *New York Times*, December 14, 1991, p. 3. U.S. Deputy Secretary of State Lawrence Eagleburger echoed this sentiment in a message to EC leaders and reflected a view shared by many EC leaders. Ibid. See also U.K. Foreign Secretary Douglas Hurd, "Averting a Balkan Tragedy," *Times* (London), December 3, 1991, p. 14.

17. The debate over the existence and origin of a Macedonian nationality is convoluted and passionate. The most fervent Macedonian partisans claim that the nation descends from Philip of Macedon, while the Greek government insists that the population is merely "Slavophone Greek," and some Bulgarians view Macedonians as Bulgarian in nationality. The modern republic of Macedonia was created in 1946, putting the imprimatur on a nationalist identity separate from Serbs and Bulgarians. The 1991 census put the population at 69 percent "Macedonian"; 20 percent Albanian (although many Albanian leaders claim the proportion is as high as 40 percent); and smaller proportions of Turks, Muslims, and Gypsies. Only 2 percent are Serb. See Duncan Perry, "The Republic of Macedonia and the Odds for Survival," *RFE/RL Research Reports*, vol. 1, no. 46, November 20, 1992, pp. 12–19.

18. Willem van Eekelen, the WEU secretary-general, first proposed sending lightly armed WEU peacekeeping forces in mid-July, and France picked up the idea at a July 29 EC foreign ministers meeting; Denmark, Germany, Portugal, and the United Kingdom opposed the notion. The idea of some kind of WEU intervention surfaced again in mid-September, when the WEU developed four options, ranging from providing logistical assistance to the unarmed EC observers to a full peacekeeping force of 25,000–35,000 troops. See Steinberg, *The Role of European Institutions*, pp. 16–17. However, continued British and German opposition led proponents of a peacekeeping force to turn their attention to the UN.

19. France, chairing the Security Council in September 1991, proposed that the UN establish an emergency force under chapter VII of the Charter and impose an arms embargo. Most other states preferred a more limited, peacekeeping role.

20. See UN Report S/23280, December 11, 1991.

21. For UN administrative purposes the protected areas were divided into four sectors: East (eastern Slavonia), West (western Slavonia), and North and South (the northern and southern parts of the Krajina protected area).

22. The designation UNPROFOR I is used to distinguish this deployment from the subsequent force involved in protecting humanitarian relief operations in Bosnia. The division between the two forces is somewhat artificial, however, since the original UNPROFOR forces, charged with carrying out the Croatia peacekeeping agreement, were headquartered in Sarajevo, the capital of Bosnia, and as fighting spread to that republic, the forces there assumed a role in protecting the Sarajevo airport and facilitating the peace talks in Bosnia. Nonetheless, there are important distinctions between UNPROFOR I and UNPROFOR II. UNPROFOR I is paid for out of the UN peacekeeping account, while UNPROFOR II was until 1993 financially the responsibility of the contributing nations. But both forces come under the overall command of a single UN Force Commander. See "Further Report of the Secretary General Pursuant to Security Council Resolution 743 (1992)," S/24848, November 24, 1992 (hereinafter Secretary General's November 24th Report).

    In addition, UNPROFOR II acts specifically under chapter VII, and with the authorization to take "all measures necessary" to carry out the humanitarian relief effort, while UNPROFOR I is arguably acting pursuant to the parties' consent.

23. On January 2, 1992, the parties signed an "implementing accord" establishing the details of the cease-fire agreed to in principle in Sarajevo on November 23, 1991. On January 8 the Security Council endorsed the sending of an advance party of military liaison officers. See resolution 727.

24. The secretary-general identified a number of areas of noncompliance with the Vance plan, including cease-fire violations in all sectors and the surrounding areas; failure of the Serbian militia forces to demobilize; terrorism against members of minority groups; failure of Serb authorities to allow stationing of UN personnel at border crossings; and, in three of the sectors (all except West), failure to permit the return of refugees and displaced persons. He noted that all sides bore some responsibility for the violations, but that "the root cause of UNPROFOR's inability to make further progress" was the self-constituted "Government of the Republic of Serbian Krajina." See Secretary General's November 24th Report, para. 44.

25. Ibid., para 25.

26. On March 27, 1992, the Bosnian Serbs proclaimed their own constitution.

27. On September 22 the General Assembly rejected Serbia's and Montenegro's claim to be the successor state to the Socialist Federal Republic of Yugoslavia and insisted that the new Federal Republic of Yugoslavia apply for membership in its own right.

28. On April 24 the presidency of the Security Council issued a statement on behalf of the Council calling for the end of outside interference in Bosnia.

29. On April 29 the secretary-general sent Marrack Goulding, the undersecretary for peacekeeping operations, to Bosnia to consider the feasibility of a peacekeeping operation.

30. Report S/23900, May 12, 1992.

31. The WEU and NATO decisions were taken in conjunction with the CSCE Helsinki Follow-Up Conference, held on July 10, 1992. Both the WEU and NATO had recently taken steps to broaden their role beyond territorial defense of their member states. The WEU had decided to undertake not only peacekeeping on behalf of the CSCE or UN, but also other crisis management military activities and humanitarian operations. See Council of Ministers, Western European Union, Petersberg Declaration, Bonn, June 19, 1992, para. 2.4. NATO had agreed to make its forces available ("on a case by case basis") to the CSCE for peacekeeping activities. See Final Communiqué, Ministerial Meeting of the North Atlantic Council in Oslo, Norway, June 4, 1992, para. 11.

32. Resolution 787. These measures were authorized under chapters VII and VIII.

33. See "Further Report of the Secretary General Pursuant to Security Council Resolution 787 (1992)," S/25000, December 21, 1992, setting forth options for deploying UN forces to monitor or enforce various UN resolutions.

34. The Security Council also adopted resolution 771, demanding that the parties to the conflict open the camps to inspection by humanitarian organizations.

35. "The financial arrangements agreed for the expansion of UNPROFOR under Resolution 776 (1992) are also innovative. The addition to UNPROFOR of contingents financed and supported entirely by their national governments has given rise to some teething troubles, especially as regards command and control. I have had to seek the help of the contributing governments in ensuring that all concerned recognize that the new units are an integral part of UNPROFOR, under the overall command of the force commander, and that newly arrived troops wearing United Nations insignia pass under United Nations command as soon as they reach the mission area." See Secretary General's November 24th Report, para. 50.

   As deployed, the UNPROFOR II force consisted of 7,500 troops, drawn primarily from France, the United Kingdom, Spain, and Canada. UNPROFOR II brought the total UN deployment in the former Yugoslavia to 23,000, and made it the largest UN operation in history, surpassing both the Congo operation of 1960 and the UN Transitional Authority in Cambodia, which was operating at the same time as UNPROFOR.

36. See reports A/47/418, September 3, 1992; A/47/635, November 6, 1992. See also "The Situation in Bosnia and Herzegovina," Report of the Secretary General, A/47/747, December 3, 1992, para. 22.

37. "The Situation in Bosnia and Herzegovina," paras. 34–36. The UN estimated that more than three million refugees, displaced persons, and other victims of the conflict in the former Yugoslavia required assistance.

38. In addition to representatives of the EC countries, the participants were the heads of the six former Yugoslav republics; the president and prime minister of the self-proclaimed Federal Republic of Yugoslavia; the foreign ministers of the United States, Russia, Japan, China, Turkey, Canada, Switzerland, and former Yugoslavia's neighbors (Albania, Austria, Bulgaria, Hungary, and Romania); and representatives from the CSCE, the EC Commission, the International Committee of the Red Cross (ICRC), and the Organization of the Islamic Conference. Representatives of Bosnian Serbs and Croats, Kosovar Albanians, and Vojvodina's Hungarians attended as observers.

39. The other members of the steering committee were representatives of the EC and CSCE troikas, the permanent five members of the UN Security Council, the Organization of the Islamic Conference, and two neighboring states. The steering committee created six working groups, on Bosnia, ethnic and national communities and minorities, seccession issues, humanitarian issues, economic issues, and confidence- and security-building and verification measures.

40. See "Report of the Secretary General on the International Conference on the Former Yugoslavia," S/24795, November 11, 1992, annex 7.

41. The Islamic Conference threatened to act unilaterally to aid the Bosnian Muslims unless the international community took action by January 15, 1993, to come to their assistance.

42. According to some reports, Serbian nationalist forces, perhaps with the tacit support of right-wing elements in Serbia's government, have begun ethnic cleansing of Hungarians, Croats, Ukrainians, and Ruthenians in Vojvodina. See Hugh Poulten, "Rising Ethnic Tension in Vojvodina," *RFE/RL Research Report*, vol. 1, no. 50, December 18, 1992, pp. 21–27.

43. Russia, Bulgaria, Turkey, Slovenia, Croatia, and the self-declared Turkish Republic of Cyprus have recognized Macedonia.

44. See Duncan Perry, "Macedonia: A Balkan Problem and a European Dilemma," *RFE/RL Research Report*, vol. 1, no. 25, June 19, 1992, pp. 35–45.

45. "Report of the Secretary General on the Former Yugoslav Republic of Macedonia," S/24923, December 9, 1992. This report became the basis for the Security Council's action.

46. Early EC steps also included limited nonconsensual actions, such as suspending economic aid and reducing or eliminating trade preferences.

47. The resolution stated that the Security Council was "concerned that the continuation of this situation constitutes a threat to international peace and security." However, the government of Yugoslavia indicated that it did not object to the embargo.

48. Resolution 757 grew out of resolution 752, which demanded "that all forms of interference from outside Bosnia-Herzegovina . . . cease immediately and that Bosnia-Herzegovina's neighbors take swift action to end such interference and respect the territorial integrity of Bosnia-Herzegovina." Resolution 752 was adopted on May 15, 1992, after most of the international community had recognized Bosnia, but a week before Bosnia was admitted to the UN. Resolution 757 was adopted one week after Bosnia was admitted.

49. See Helsinki Principle 7, "Respect for human rights and fundamental freedoms"; and "Charter of Paris for a New Europe," 30 *International Legal Materials* 190 (1991).

50. Conference on Security and Cooperation in Europe, "Document of the Moscow Meeting on the Human Dimension," October 3, 1991, 30 *International Legal Materials* 1670 (1991).

51. See "Exploratory Missions to Be Sent," *Financial Times*, July 9, 1992, p. 3.

52. See Steinberg, *The Role of European Institutions*, for a more detailed assessment of the performance of the European institutions and some suggestions for reform.

53. Maastricht treaty, title 5, "Provisions on a Common Foreign and Security Policy."

54. The treaty also states that it does not affect "the primary responsibility of the Security Council for the maintenance of peace" (article 7).

55. The out-of-area constraint has a long history in NATO. During NATO's early years, the United States invoked this limitation to avoid NATO involvement in members' colonial affairs; the most dramatic early application was the U.S. refusal to become involved (or allow NATO to become involved) in the 1956 Suez crisis. In later years, the out-of-area limitation allowed Europeans to remain at arm's length from U.S. involvement in Vietnam and other U.S. military activities outside of Europe.

56. Council of Ministers, Western European Union, Petersburg Declaration, para. II. 4.

57. Ministerial Meeting of the North Atlantic Council in Oslo, Final Communiqué, para. 11.

58. France, Italy, Spain, and the United Kingdom all had, to varying degrees, problems with ethnic groups seeking greater autonomy or independence. In approaching the problem of what to do in Yugoslavia, the United Kingdom

was especially mindful of the situation in Northern Ireland, which made it wary of other countries' intervening in internal ethnic or religious conflicts, and also sensitized the government to the difficulty of imposing a solution through the use of military forces.

59. Boutros Boutros-Ghali, *An Agenda for Peace* (New York: United Nations, 1992). The secretary-general writes: "Peacemaking is action to bring hostile parties to agreement, essentially through such peaceful means as those foreseen in Chapter VI of the Charter of the United Nations" (para. 20).

60. Thus the UNPROFOR operation clearly fits Boutros-Ghali's description of "peace-building": "Through agreements ending civil strife, these may include disarming the previously warring parties and the restoration of order, the custody and possible destruction of weapons, repatriating refugees" (ibid., para. 55).

61. This appears to be the sense in which Boutros-Ghali uses the term "peace-enforcement": "the United Nations has sometimes been called upon to send forces to restore and maintain the cease-fire" (ibid., para. 44).

62. Ibid., para. 28: "preventive deployment could take place when a country feels threatened and requests the deployment of an appropriate United Nations presence along its side of the border alone."

63. Thus the International Conference on the Former Yugoslavia would be responsible for establishing a constitutional court, ensuring ethnic balance for the Bosnian military and police and protecting human rights.

64. The text of the provision (principle 8) is somewhat ambiguous. It refers to the right of self-determination of "peoples," but qualifies this by the clause "acting at all time in conformity with the purposes and principles of the Charter of the United Nations and with the relevant norms of international law, including those related to territorial integrity of States." This qualification would appear to exclude secession.

65. The EC, the United States, and the UN enunciated the principle. Dutch Foreign Minister van den Broek observed in August 1991, "It is not acceptable that *internal* or external borders be changed unilaterally by force" (emphasis added). See Celestine Bohlen, "Fragile Truce in Yugoslavia: The Fighting Wanes, but Hatreds Smolder," *New York Times*, August 8, 1991, p. A3. U.S. Secretary of State James Baker later reiterated this sentiment, declaring that: "the United States, the European Community and the entire CSCE community have sent a clear message to the peoples of Yugoslavia: the use of force to solve political differences or to change external or internal borders in Yugoslavia is simply not acceptable." See U.S. Department of State Dispatch, September 30, 1991, pp. 723–724. Security Council resolution 713 enshrined the principle: "noting the Declaration of 3 September 1991 of the states participating in the Conference on Security and Cooperation in Europe that no territorial gains or changes within Yugoslavia are acceptable." See Philip Zelikow, "The New Concert of Europe," *Survival*, vol. 34, no. 2 (Summer 1992), p. 19. Even before the conflict began, the European Parliament enunciated the idea: "the constituent republics and autonomous provinces of Yugoslavia must have the right freely to determine their own future in a peaceful and democratic manner and on the basis of recognized international and internal borders." See European Parliament Resolution on Yugoslavia, March 13, 1991, quoted in Gow, "Deconstructing Yugoslavia," p. 28.

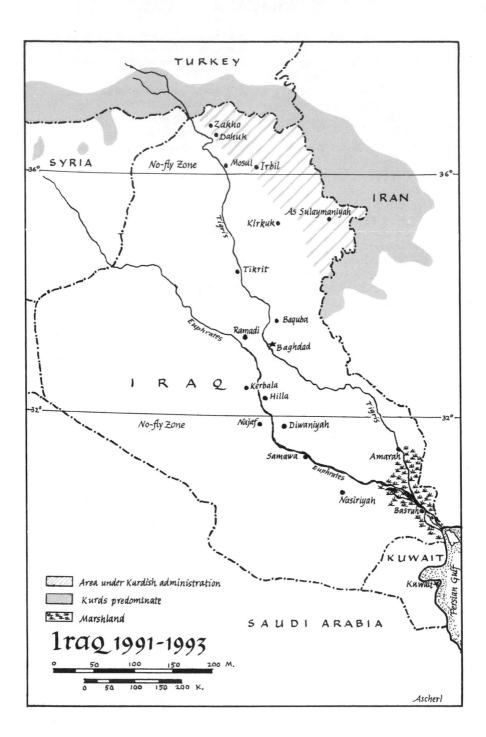

TURKEY

SYRIA

•Zakho
•Dahuk

No-fly Zone

36° ———— 36°

•Mosul •Irbil

IRAN

•As Sulaymaniyah

Kirkuk•

Tigris

•Tikrit

•Baquba

Euphrates

Ramadi•
✕ Baghdad

I R A Q

•Kerbala
•Hilla

32° 32°

No-fly Zone

Najaf• •Diwaniyah

Samawa• Amarah

Euphrates
Tigris

•Nasiriyah

Basrah•

KUWAIT

Kuwait•

Persian Gulf

▨▨▨ Area under Kurdish administration

▨ Kurds predominate

❉❉❉ Marshland

# IRAQ 1991-1993

0    50    100    150    200 M.

0    50    100    150 200 K.

SAUDI ARABIA

Ascherl

# CHAPTER TWO: IRAQ

# Iraq's Repression of Its Civilian Population: Collective Responses and Continuing Challenges

## JANE E. STROMSETH

Two years after the end of the Persian Gulf War, the situation in northern Iraq is both hopeful and precarious. On the hopeful side, Iraq's Kurdish minority is administering its own affairs and held elections in May 1992 for a Kurdish National Assembly and for the leader of the Kurdish political movement. The election took place over the opposition of Saddam Hussein and with the assistance of international observers, while allied air forces hovered overhead to provide reassurance to the Kurds voting below. The election initiated a new chapter in the Kurdish struggle for autonomy and self-determination, a struggle with a long and tragic history. Fully aware of the sharp tension between the territorial integrity of existing states and the principle of self-determination *if* it takes the form of secession, Iraqi Kurdish leaders have for now chosen to seek greater autonomy and political rights within Iraq rather than a separate Kurdish state.

The situation in northern Iraq remains unstable, however. Saddam Hussein continues an economic embargo against the Kurds, denying the Kurds vital food, medicine, and fuel. Turkey's agreement allowing allied air forces to use Incirlik air base to monitor developments in northern Iraq is contingent upon renewal by the Turkish Parliament every six months. Moreover, Iraq's agreement with the United Nations accepting the deployment of UN armed guards on its territory likewise depends on periodic extensions. Given Saddam Hussein's opposition to the Kurdish elections and his proven willingness to use force against the Kurds, continuation of the allied air umbrella over northern Iraq and the UN presence on the ground is crucial to the well-being and even survival of Iraq's Kurdish population.

The plight of Shi'ite Muslims in the marshlands of southern Iraq is also precarious. Saddam Hussein's documented repression of and military attacks against the Shi'ites prompted the United States, Britain, and France to declare a "no-fly" zone in southern Iraq below the 32nd parallel, similar to the one in effect in northern Iraq above the 36th parallel. In contrast to the situation in the north, however, Iraq has not allowed UN guards in the south, and few international relief organizations conduct operations there.

As unsettled as the situation in Iraq is today, the collective monitoring of Iraq's treatment of its Kurdish and Shi'ite citizens stands in stark contrast to the tragic chain of events in the immediate aftermath of the Persian Gulf War. Shortly after Operation Desert Storm ended in late February 1991, after allied forces liberated Kuwait from the forces of Saddam Hussein, President George Bush declared that a "new world order" had begun—in which the UN would fulfill the vision of its founders, and "respect for human rights [would] find a home among all nations."[1] At first glance, the vindication of both the territorial integrity of Kuwait and the political independence of the Kuwaiti people through collective action by the international community seemed to set a promising precedent for such a "new world order." Yet by late March 1991, Saddam Hussein's forces were brutally crushing rebellions in northern and southern Iraq, sending thousands of Kurdish and Shi'ite refugees fleeing toward neighboring Turkey and Iran. Although President Bush had earlier encouraged Iraqis to rise up and challenge Saddam Hussein, he initially took the position that the predicament of the Kurdish and Shi'ite rebels was an "internal affair" for Iraq, a matter that did not justify intervention by the United States or its allies.[2]

As the refugee flows escalated and the human suffering mounted, however, many people found it increasingly difficult to view the situation of the Kurds and Shi'ites as a strictly "internal" matter, particularly when the allied coalition had just engaged in major military action against Iraq and when the terms of the Security Council's cease-fire resolution[3] gave the UN continuing and pervasive oversight of Iraq's weaponry and economy. If the "new world order" meant order for the Kuwaitis but not for the Kurds—order between states but not *within* them—it did not appear to be a particularly attractive or new or just form of order. As the media brought the suffering of Iraqi civilians into homes around the world, and as Turkey and Iran pleaded for international help in responding to the refugee crisis, the Security Council took action, adopting resolution 688.[4] That path-breaking resolution demanded that Iraq stop repressing its civilian population and insisted that Baghdad allow international humanitarian organizations immediate access to all those in need of assistance.

Although the international community felt a special sense of responsibility toward Iraqi Kurds and Shi'ites in the aftermath of the Gulf War, the collective response to their predicament is "precedential" in at least four respects. First, it indicated that the Security Council is willing to condemn internal repression as a threat to international peace and security, at least when it results in substantial cross-border refugee flows. Second, it illustrated the international community's preference for viewing a crisis in humanitarian terms, sidestepping more difficult political issues of self-determination. Third, it revealed the Security Council's clear reluctance to explicitly authorize the use of force to stop a state from repressing its own citizens, although some Security Council members undertook military measures that other states implicitly tolerated. Fourth, it spurred institutional reforms to make UN humanitarian responses more prompt and effective, such as through the use of corridors of peace or zones of tranquillity, even in cases where a state may be reluctant to consent formally. Larger questions remain, however, including whether the international community will be willing to assist other repressed groups in situations similar to that in Iraq.

## HISTORICAL BACKGROUND

Although many world leaders focused on the plight of the Kurds for the first time in March 1991, the Kurds' struggle for self-determination and for basic human rights has been ongoing for decades, even centuries. But Kurdish self-determination consistently has been subordinated to the strategic and economic interests of regional and global powers.

The Kurds are a non-Arab people, numbering about 20 million. They reside primarily in the mountainous areas spanning northeastern Iraq, southeastern Turkey, northwestern Iran, and northeastern Syria. Smaller Kurdish populations reside in Armenia, Azerbaijan, and Lebanon. Largely Sunni Muslims, the Kurds represent an estimated 23–27 percent of the population in Iraq, 19–24 percent in Turkey, 10–16 percent in Iran, and 8–9 percent in Syria.[5] The Kurds have their own language, although markedly different dialects exist, as well as a distinctive culture with strong tribal and family ties.[6] At the same time, divisions among Kurdish groups have often been fierce and sometimes violent.

Kurds have aspired to establish an independent state at least since 1880, when a Kurdish religious leader led a revolt against the Ottoman empire and called for an autonomous Kurdistan.[7] As part of the breakup of the Ottoman empire at the end of World War I, the 1920 Treaty of Sèvres, signed by the allies and the Turkish government, promised the Kurds "local autonomy." Indeed, that treaty contemplated creation of a Kurdish state if the Kurds demonstrated to the League of Nations that a majority of the population wished to become independent of Turkey and if the League Council so agreed.[8] The Treaty of Sèvres was never ratified or implemented, however, and the 1923 Treaty of Lausanne divided Kurdistan among Turkey, Iraq, and Iran. Although Britain recognized the ethnic distinctiveness of the Kurdish people and sought to protect their rights within Iraq, Britain abandoned the notion of a separate Kurdish state in favor of including the oil-rich region around Mosul as part of Iraq, which became a British mandate territory.[9]

Since attaining statehood in 1932, Iraq has had an uneasy relationship with its Kurdish minority, which today numbers 3.5–4 million people and is Iraq's largest non-Arab minority group. On the one hand, the Iraqi government has, at least nominally, recognized a degree of Kurdish autonomy in the northeastern provinces of Dahuk, Irbil, and As Sulaymaniyah. A 1974 decree established Kurdish, along with Arabic, as an official language in these areas, and established a separate Legislative Assembly and Executive Council, with certain delegated powers.[10] However, Baghdad largely dominated these institutions. A 1970 autonomy agreement between the Kurds and the Baath regime had spelled out additional rights,[11] but the Iraqi regime has never adequately implemented this agreement.

On the other hand, Iraqi paper promises aside, the Kurds have been subject to ruthless attacks when it has suited the political purposes of Iraq's ruling Baath party. During the final two years of the Iran-Iraq war, Iraqi repression of both Kurdish rebels and civilians was particularly brutal. Beginning in 1986, Iraqi forces systematically destroyed Kurdish villages.[12] Throughout 1988, Iraqi forces engaged in a comprehensive campaign—the Anfal—to exterminate the Kurds; they rounded up and murdered as many as 100,000 Kurdish men, women, and children, placing many in mass graves to be shot by soldiers and buried by bulldozers.[13] In March 1988 Iraqi air forces attacked the city of Halabja with chemical weapons.[14] In August 1988, after accepting a cease-fire in the Iran-Iraq war, Iraq attacked scores of Kurdish villages with chemical weapons, killing non-combatant men, women, and children.[15] The purported rationale for these attacks was retaliation for Kurdish sympathy for Iran during the war.

Iraq's genocidal violence against its Kurdish population in the 1980s went essentially unsanctioned. French President François Mitterrand and the Reagan administration denounced Iraq's use of chemical weapons, but the international community failed to impose sanctions on Iraq for its attacks against the Kurds[16] as political and strategic considerations once again overrode humanitarian concerns. The Soviet Union had been an ally and chief arms supplier of the Baath regime since its ascendancy to power in 1968, although the Soviet invasion of Afghanistan strained the relationship.[17] The United States, together with Iran, supported Kurdish rebels in their struggle against the Baath regime in the early 1970s, but that assistance halted abruptly in 1975, when Iran and Iraq signed the Algiers Agreement resolving certain outstanding territorial disputes.[18] In 1984, five years after the fall of the shah of Iran, the United States resumed diplomatic relations with Iraq, considering Saddam Hussein a useful counterweight to the Islamic fundamentalism of Khomeini's Iran.[19] France became an increasingly important arms supplier of Iraq in the late 1970s and 1980s, second only to the Soviet Union.[20]

Turkey was not likely to condemn Iraq's treatment of the Kurds, given the two countries' common interest in suppressing Kurdish guerrilla activities, as well as Turkey's own refusal to protect the basic human rights of its substantial Kurdish minority.[21] Iran under Khomeini was willing to provide sanctuary to Iraqi Kurds fleeing the violence of Saddam Hussein, viewing Iraq's Kurdish resistance as a useful thorn in the side of the Iraqi regime. Yet Iran refused to provide any degree of autonomy to its own Kurdish minority.[22]

In short, for years regional and global powers have shaped and manipulated the Kurdish struggle for self-determination and for protection of basic human rights to serve their own political purposes. As Professor Hurst Hannum of Tufts University aptly stated: "In the Middle Eastern world of oil and geopolitics, the interests of the Kurds have been at the bottom of everyone's list, except insofar as they promoted the strategic goals of weakening one or another of the states in the region."[23] The initial nonresponse of the international community in the immediate aftermath of the Persian Gulf War seemed to follow the pattern of neglecting Kurdish interests unless strategic considerations dictated otherwise.

## THE POST–GULF WAR CRISIS

Operation Desert Storm was suspended at midnight on February 27, 1991, following the allied forces' success in reclaiming Kuwait from the forces of Iraqi President Saddam Hussein. On March 2 the UN Security Council adopted resolution 686, indicating that allied military operations would remain suspended so long as Iraq complied with certain conditions, including acceptance of the Security Council's twelve prior resolutions and cessation of all hostile military actions, such as "missile attacks and flights of combat aircraft."[24] For the remainder of March the Security Council focused its energies on reaching a comprehensive cease-fire agreement with Iraq.[25]

The coalition forces' defeat of Saddam Hussein created temporary chaos in Iraq, a development that both rebel Kurdish groups in northern Iraq and Shi'ite opposition forces in southern Iraq viewed as a fortuitous opening. Although Shi'ite Muslims constitute more than 50 percent of Iraq's population, historically they have been disadvantaged both politically and economically within Iraqi society.[26] Galvanized by the 1979 Islamic revolution in Iran, a religiously based Shi'ite opposition took shape, challenging the Baath regime, which is ideologically committed to secularism, and whose leaders and military commanders, including Saddam Hussein, are disproportionately Sunni Muslims.[27] Before and during the Gulf War, President Bush urged the people of Iraq on several occasions to rise up and challenge Saddam Hussein.[28] Some Iraqis, particularly Kurdish leaders, interpreted these statements as an offer of support for such efforts, despite the historical unreliability of Western assistance for their cause.[29]

In early March Kurds in northern Iraq and Shi'ites in the south engaged in popular uprisings against the regime of Saddam Hussein.[30] The rebels initially had considerable success in taking control of cities and territory.[31] Republican guard troops loyal to Saddam Hussein quickly responded with military force against the rebels, however, using helicopter gunships, tanks, and artillery against unarmed civilians. Although the U.S. air force shot down several Iraqi military aircraft for violating the terms of resolution 686, Iraqi helicopter gunships attacking Iraqi civilians operated with impunity.[32] Despite his earlier remarks encouraging revolt against Saddam Hussein, President Bush initially characterized the Kurdish and Shi'ite uprisings and the Iraqi response as an "internal matter" that did not warrant a U.S. military response. He and his advisors expressed unwillingness to entangle American forces in what could be a protracted civil war, and they indicated that U.S. military troops would not be deployed to protect civilian or armed rebel groups.[33] At this point, Britain also favored a policy of nonintervention.[34] Instead, allied leaders expressed their determination to bring their troops home from the region as soon as possible.

By the end of March, Iraqi forces had effectively crushed the rebellion and retaken rebel-held areas first in southern Iraq and then in the Kurdish north, brutally slaughtering captured rebels and unarmed civilians.[35] Thousands of Shi'ites in the south fled to the allied-occupied areas along the Iraq-Kuwait border or to Iran. The Kurds in the north fled into the mountains by the thousands, toward neighboring Turkey and Iran, where they were stranded without food or medicine and were vulnerable to attacks by Iraqi helicopter gunships. As television reports brought their suffering into homes around the world, Western governments could no longer characterize the situation in Iraq as a strictly "internal" matter.[36]

Just as the United Nations served as the umbrella legitimizing collective action to expel Iraq from Kuwait, so too the Security Council became the central forum for articulating a collective response to the situation unfolding in Iraq. The regional organizations in the area— the Arab League and the Gulf Cooperation Council—did not play any significant role in this task. The Arab League had been divided over its response to Iraq's invasion of Kuwait.[37] After the League initially condemned Iraq's action by a vote of 14–4,[38] twelve of its members agreed on a plan to send military forces to Saudi Arabia;[39] three states opposed the plan, and five abstained or expressed reservations.[40] At a meeting in late March 1991, the League issued no condemnation of Iraq's treatment of the Kurds or Shi'ites.[41] The Gulf Cooperation Council[42] condemned Iraq's invasion of Kuwait in August 1990, but did not play a significant role either in coordinating its members' involvement in the allied military action[43] or in responding to the crisis involving the Kurds and Shi'ites.

## THE INTERNATIONAL RESPONSE

As the predicament of the Iraqi refugees grew more desperate in early April 1991, France and Turkey took the lead in placing the matter squarely on the Security Council's agenda.[44] Turkey, with a Kurdish population larger than Iraq's, feared the prospect of an accelerating stream of Kurdish refugees within its borders. Turkish officials estimated that up to a million Iraqi Kurds might flee into Turkey.[45] Iran faced a similar refugee problem as Kurds in the north and Shi'ite Muslims in the south fled Iraqi repression, and Iran estimated that 500,000 Iraqi refugees would cross into Iran in early April alone.[46] Both Turkey and Iran argued that this flow of refugees across borders, as well as Iraqi transborder military incursions on their territory,[47] posed a threat to the security and stability of the region that was properly the subject of Security Council action.[48]

### Security Council Resolution 688

On April 5, 1991, the UN Security Council adopted resolution 688 by a vote of 10–3, with two abstentions.[49] That resolution did several things: First, it condemned Iraq's repression of its civilian population, including most recently the Kurdish population. Second, it characterized the consequences of that repression—"a massive flow of refugees towards and across international frontiers" and "cross border incursions"—as a threat to international peace and security. Third, it demanded that Iraq stop the repression. Fourth, it expressed hope for an open dialogue to "ensure that the human and political rights of all Iraqi citizens are respected." Fifth, it insisted that Iraq allow international humanitarian organizations immediate access to those needing assistance. Sixth, it requested the secretary-general to pursue humanitarian efforts in Iraq, using all the resources at his disposal to respond to the needs of displaced Iraqis, and it demanded that Iraq cooperate with the secretary-general. Finally, it appealed to member states and to humanitarian organizations "to contribute to these humanitarian relief efforts."

The Security Council debate preceding passage of resolution 688 was both a response to urgent human needs and a wide-ranging philosophical discussion of the purpose and limits of the Security Council. The participants understood that the resolution would establish a precedent that would shape perceptions of the proper role of the Security Council in future crises growing out of internal conflict. Under article 39 of the UN Charter, the Security Council has broad authority to take action in response to threats to the peace.[50] But at the heart of the debate over resolution 688 was the meaning and contemporary significance of article 2(7), which provides that nothing in the Charter authorizes the UN "to intervene in matters which are essentially within the domestic jurisdiction of any state." Although article 2(7) contains an exception for enforcement measures adopted under chapter VII of the Charter,[51] resolution 688 did not invoke chapter VII.[52]

Articulating a traditional, state-centric position, three of the Third World states on the Security Council—Zimbabwe, Yemen, and Cuba—opposed the resolution, contending that the UN response it outlined was beyond the authority of the Security Council. These states argued that the UN Charter limits the Security Council's role to protecting inter-national peace and security—that is, protecting order *between* states. They characterized the conflict between Iraq and its civilian population as a "domestic conflict," or "internal struggle."[53] Zimbabwe acknowledged that the "humanitarian situation and the question of refugees" affected Iraq's neighbors.[54] In its view (and the view of Cuba and Yemen), however, such humanitarian problems were matters for other UN organs to address,[55] most notably the General Assembly, which in contrast to the Security Council can only make recommendations to member states.[56] Yemen's representative argued that the resolution "sets a dangerous precedent that could open the way to diverting the Council away from its basic functions and responsibilities for safeguarding international peace and security and towards addressing the internal affairs of countries."[57] Yemen insisted further that practically every state, large or small, will encounter "internal difficulties and transborder problems" at some point, and that resolution

688 was a step toward an "ominous" new world order that could change "the rules that have contributed to stability over the past four decades."[58]

China and India abstained, expressing their concern for the humanitarian needs of the refugees, but also their desire to protect the principle of nonintervention in internal affairs. China's representative, for example, indicated that the situation in Iraq involved both "internal affairs" and "international aspects." While supporting the secretary-general in "rendering humanitarian assistance to the refugees through the relevant organizations," China also reiterated its position that the Security Council "should not consider or take action on questions concerning the internal affairs of any State."[59] India likewise contended that the international community should offer aid to the displaced Iraqi civilian population, but that it "should not prescribe what should be done, for that would impinge on the internal affairs of States."[60]

The ten states that supported resolution 688 relied on three types of arguments. The predominant argument was fully consistent with a traditional state-centric view: namely, that the massive flow of refugees *across international borders* that Iraq's actions caused was a threat to international peace and security in the region. In U.S. Ambassador Thomas Pickering's words:

> . . . it is the Council's legitimate responsibility to respond to the concerns of Turkey and the Islamic Republic of Iran, concerns increasingly shared by other neighbours of Iraq, about the massive numbers of people fleeing, or disposed to flee, from Iraq across international frontiers because of the repression and brutality of Saddam Hussein. The *transboundary impact* of Iraq's treatment of its civilian population threatens regional stability.[61]

Britain,[62] France,[63] and the Soviet Union[64] shared this view, as did six of the ten nonpermanent members of the Security Council then serving (Austria,[65] Belgium,[66] Côte d'Ivoire,[67] Ecuador,[68] Romania,[69] and Zaire[70]).

A second, more human rights–oriented argument was advanced by several members of the Security Council, most notably France and Britain. These states contended that Iraq's violation of its citizens' human rights was itself a matter of international concern and thus not within Iraq's "domestic" jurisdiction.

Britain cited the case of South Africa as a precedent.[71] France argued that human rights violations "become a matter of international interest when they take on such proportions that they assume the dimension of a crime against humanity," as was the case in Iraq.[72]

Ecuador and Romania also stressed human rights, but with certain qualifications that indicated their sensitivity about the prospective implications of resolution 688. For example, Romania's representative declared that "humanitarian cooperation" could help prevent "mass and flagrant violations of human rights," but cautioned that the UN's response to the plight of the Iraqi population "should not create a precedent that could be used—or, rather, misused—in the future for political purposes."[73] In Ecuador's view, the Security Council might not have authority to act "if we were dealing solely with a case of violation of human rights by a country within its own frontiers."[74] In this case, however, Iraq's repression of its civilian population created substantial human displacement across borders and thus affected international peace and security.

The third type of argument made in support of Security Council action to protect the Kurds and Shi'ites was that the UN had a special responsibility to respond to developments growing out of its own decision to authorize the use of force to expel Iraq from Kuwait.[75] As France argued, after adopting 14 resolutions designed to restore peace and security in the region, the Security Council "would have been remiss in its task had it stood idly by" while Iraq massacred innocent men, women, and children.[76]

## Implementing Resolution 688

Resolution 688 was an attempt to respond collectively to the urgent humanitarian needs of displaced Iraqis in the aftermath of the Gulf War and to halt Iraq's repression of its civilian population through diplomatic pressure and the involvement of humanitarian relief agencies under UN coordination. Thus, the resolution demanded that Iraq stop repressing its civilian population and—contrary to standard UN practice requiring host country consent—obliged Iraq to allow international humanitarian organizations immediate access to its territory. Yet the resolution did not address two issues. It did not expressly authorize the use of military force to protect Iraqi Kurds and Shi'ites from Saddam Hussein: the debate preceding the resolution's passage gave no indication that military force was contemplated by its "appeal to all Member States . . . to contribute to these humanitarian relief efforts."[77] Nor did the resolution take a position on the merits of the Kurdish struggle for self-determination,[78] although it did express hope that "an open dialogue will take place to ensure that the human and political rights of all Iraqi citizens are respected."[79]

More than a Security Council resolution was needed, however, to convince the Kurdish and Shi'ite refugees that they would be protected from continued Iraqi repression and thus could safely return to their homes. In southern Iraq, refugee camps were established in early April in the UN-supervised demilitarized zone along the border with Kuwait.[80] In northern Iraq, the difficulties of implementing a UN role in aiding and protecting the Kurds became apparent almost immediately. On April 6, the day after the Security Council adopted resolution 688, the U.S. air force began dropping food, blankets, and clothing to Kurdish refugees. The United States also warned Iraq against undertaking military operations, including any air operations, north of the 36th parallel.[81] Convinced that even more decisive action was needed to ensure the safety of the Kurds, British Prime Minister John Major urged the establishment of a "safe haven" zone in northern Iraq under UN supervision and possibly protected by UN peacekeeping forces.[82] The European Community promptly endorsed the idea, and Turkey's president advanced a similar proposal.[83] The United States initially was cautious about such a plan, voicing concern that it might lead to a long-term allied presence in Iraq and that Kurdish rebel forces would use the safe haven zones as sanctuaries.

## Operation Provide Comfort

Concerted pressure from Britain, France, and Turkey soon persuaded the United States to contribute military forces to a joint operation to create and protect refugee camps within Iraq's northern border.[84] In mid-April troops from the United States, Britain, and France entered northern Iraq and began to establish refugee camps in the Zakho region, creating a de facto safe haven zone for Iraqi Kurds guarded by allied forces.[85]

American and allied officials argued that the purpose of Operation Provide Comfort was humanitarian, not political, and that resolution 688 provided authority for the operation.[86] UN Secretary-General Pérez de Cuéllar cautioned, however, that a foreign military presence on Iraqi territory required Iraqi consent or the express authorization of the Security Council.[87] Iraq denounced the allied operation as an intervention in its internal affairs and insisted that the UN operate any relief centers on Iraqi territory.[88] In light of Saddam Hussein's violence against the Kurds, the allies persisted in their efforts to create a protected safe haven, despite the legal reservations of the secretary-general and the opposition of Iraq.

## A UN Presence in Iraq

Shortly after allied forces entered northern Iraq, Saddam Hussein agreed to accept a UN presence on Iraqi territory for humanitarian purposes. Although Baghdad continued to reject resolution 688, on April 18, 1991, it signed a memorandum of understanding (MOU) with Prince Sadruddin Aga Khan, the executive delegate of the UN secretary-general for the UN Humanitarian Programme for Iraq, Kuwait and the Iraq/Iran and Iraq/Turkey Border Areas.[89] Under this MOU, Iraq consented to a UN humanitarian presence within Iraq wherever it was needed. Baghdad agreed to the establishment of UN humanitarian centers, which would provide assistance to displaced Iraqis with the aim of aiding their voluntary return to their place of origin. The regime also agreed to allow safe passage of emergency relief supplies throughout the country. The MOU extended until December 31, 1991, and was subject to renewal by mutual agreement. It has been extended several times.

In contrast to the allied safe haven zone, the April 18 agreement applied to all of Iraq's territory, both north and south. It also was premised on Iraqi cooperation and provided no military protection for the Kurds. On the heels of this agreement, Iraq asked the UN to assume responsibility for the relief centers that the allied forces had begun to establish in the north.[90] The allies, particularly the United States, were not interested in a long-term military presence in Iraq and hoped to be able to turn the Kurdish relief camps over to the UN as soon as possible. At the same time, the allies wanted a UN police force deployed to protect the Kurds from further attacks by the forces of Saddam Hussein.

In early May Iraq emphatically rejected any deployment of armed UN police forces to protect the Kurds, calling such proposals an intervention in Iraq's internal affairs.[91] The United States and its allies initially argued that resolution 688 provided sufficient authority to deploy UN police forces in Iraq.[92] Secretary-General Pérez de Cuéllar again took issue with them, indicating that under established UN practice, deployment of UN peacekeeping forces or police on Iraqi territory would require Iraq's consent, unless the Security Council explicitly authorized the forces.[93] France, Britain, and the United States considered returning to the Security Council for such authorization, but Soviet and Chinese officials were opposed to deploying UN forces to protect Iraqi civilians without Iraq's consent.[94] Given these political realities and the desperate situation of the Kurds, the allies chose not to force the issue. Instead, allied troops continued to provide a de facto safe haven zone by virtue of their presence, even as allied leaders hoped a compromise might emerge in negotiations between Iraq and the UN that would permit the UN to take over operation of the refugee camps and adequately protect the Kurdish population.

## Agreement on UN Guards

In late May 1991 the UN reached an agreement with Iraq allowing deployment of a UN guards contingent in Iraq, within the framework established by the April 18 MOU.[95] Iraq consented to deployment of up to 500 UN guards to be assigned to various UN humanitarian centers in Iraq, wherever they were needed. The guards would be allowed to move freely between humanitarian centers, reception points, and suboffices, and they would be authorized to carry sidearms such as pistols or revolvers. On Iraq's insistence, the agreement made no mention of UN police protection for the Kurds. As Sadruddin Aga Khan described it, the UN guards' basic mandate was to protect UN humanitarian workers and assets deployed in Iraq: "They are neither peace-keepers nor policemen where UN resources are not involved."[96] Nevertheless, the guards could observe and report on the human-itarian situation in Iraq, and they provided a symbolic international presence. UN officials clearly hoped that their very presence would deter Iraq from taking further action against the Kurds.

In June, once the UN guards were in place and the situation appeared to be stabilizing, allied troops gradually began leaving the northern security zone, over the protest of Kurds who were skeptical that the UN presence was sufficient to protect them. Allied forces turned over responsibility for humanitarian relief operations to the UN High Commissioner for Refugees. By mid-July 1991, allied forces were fully withdrawn,[97] except for a small military monitoring team in Zakho called the Military Coordina-tion Center. The eight to ten allied officers who constitute this team oversee security issues in the northern security zone and help resolve conflicts between Kurds and Iraqi forces.[98] With the permission of the Turkish government, a joint allied force is stationed at Incirlik air base in southeastern Turkey,[99] from which it conducts daily overflights of the Kurdish safe haven zone and remains poised to intervene to protect the Kurds if necessary.[100]

## SUBSEQUENT DEVELOPMENTS AND CHALLENGES

Once the safe haven zone was relatively secure, Kurdish leaders Massoud Barzani of the Kurdistan Democratic Party (KDP) and Jalal Talabani of the Patriotic Union of Kurdistan (PUK) began to negotiate with Saddam Hussein over an autonomy agreement for Iraqi Kurdistan based on the 1970 accord.[101] Disagreements soon surfaced, however, over international guarantees for any such agreement, which Saddam Hussein emphatically rejected. Other disputed points were the territory to be included in the autono-mous region, a Kurdish share in the oil revenues from Kirkuk, and Kurdish demands for democratic elections throughout Iraq.[102] In late October 1991 Saddam Hussein imposed an internal eco-nomic embargo against the Kurdish areas of northern Iraq, bar-ring supplies of food, medicine, and fuel, and rendering the Kurds totally dependent on outside assistance.[103] The Iraqi ruler also withdrew his remaining forces from Kurdish-controlled territory.[104] In December Kurdish leaders halted autonomy negotiations with Baghdad in protest over the economic embargo and announced that they would hold elections for leader of the Kurdish political movement and for the new Kurdish National Assembly.

## The Kurdish Elections

During the election campaign, Massoud Barzani expressed greater optimism than Jalal Talabani about ultimately achieving an acceptable autonomy agreement with Saddam Hussein. Talabani instead urged that the Kurds wait to negotiate a federal arrangement with a subsequent Iraqi government.[105] The elections, held on May 19, 1992, produced a draw between the two major Kurdish parties; the KDP and the PUK each won 50 seats in the Kurdish National Assembly.[106] Neither Barzani nor Talabani received an absolute majority for the Kurdish leadership position, and they agreed to share power, pending a runoff election.[107] As both Barzani and Talabani are well aware, the issue of a separate Kurdish state remains an explosive one, not only to Baghdad but also to the neighboring governments of Turkey, Iran, and Syria.[108] Thus, for now, Iraq's Kurdish leadership has chosen a middle way, seeking political autonomy within the Iraqi state rather than independence. In October 1992 the Kurdish Assembly endorsed the idea of Kurdish self-rule within a federal, democratic Iraq.[109] But the long-term direction of the Kurdish leadership and the newly elected legislature remains to be seen.

A coalition of Iraqi opposition parties shares the Kurds' desire for a federal Iraqi state. That coalition, the Iraqi National Congress (INC), met in northern Iraq in October 1992 and elected as its three leaders Massoud Barzani, a Shi'ite Muslim cleric, and a Sunni Muslim who is a retired general.[110] The INC called for a federal, democratic system in Iraq, and its members expressed hope that the Iraqi people eventually will overthrow Saddam Hussein. Despite this determined opposition, Saddam Hussein's hold on power continues to appear as strong as ever.

## Operation Southern Watch

Since allied troops left Iraq, Saddam Hussein's forces have engaged in periodic military attacks against Kurds in the north and Shi'ites in the south.[111] Iraqi warplanes and helicopter gunships bombed Shi'ite villages in the marshes of southern Iraq, evoking strong criticism during a special Security Council meeting in August 1992.[112] The marshes are home to a combination of displaced civilians, Shi'ite rebels, Iraqi army deserters, and indigenous residents. Numerous Security Council members denounced Iraqi repression against the Shi'ites as a violation of resolution 688, citing repeated Iraqi artillery bombardment and air attacks, forced resettlement of villages, manipulation of food supplies, and restrictions on relief operations.[113]

The United States, Britain, and France announced two weeks later, on August 26, that they were imposing a "no-fly" zone in southern Iraq below the 32nd parallel banning all Iraqi planes and helicopters.[114] As in Operation Provide Comfort in the north, the allies invoked resolution 688 as authority for Operation Southern Watch. That resolution did not expressly authorize the use of force to monitor Iraq's treatment of its civilian population; but few objected to the no-fly zone on that basis, given the clear vulnerability of Iraqi Shi'ites to the brutality of Saddam Hussein.[115] The minimal international presence on the ground in southern Iraq made aerial surveillance all the more vital.[116] Allied forces based in the region conduct daily overflights of southern Iraq, just as allied air forces monitor the no-fly zone in effect above the 36th parallel.

Iraqi forces regularly probe and test allied determination to protect both the Kurds in the north and the Shi'ites in the south. Baghdad escalated its pattern of defiance in the final weeks of the Bush presidency by sending Iraqi warplanes into both no-fly zones and threatening coalition aircraft with antiaircraft weapons.[117] When Iraq ignored allied warnings and refused to guarantee the safety of UN flights carrying UN weapons inspectors, allied forces launched a series of tailored responses in January 1993, bombing Iraqi air defense radars and antiaircraft weapons in the two no-fly zones.[118] In addition, American cruise missiles attacked an Iraqi military-industrial facility near Baghdad,[119] prompting several Gulf War allies to express their concern about the lack of explicit Security Council authorization for this action.[120] As President Bill Clinton took office, Saddam Hussein declared a "cease-fire" with respect to Iraqi attacks against allied aircraft,[121] but Iraq has continued to threaten allied forces policing the no-fly zones.[122]

In light of Iraq's pattern of intransigence, continued enforcement of the no-fly zones may be required indefinitely in order to guard against a repeat of the massacres of March 1991. The future of the southern no-fly zone depends on the willingness of the Gulf War allies to continue the operation and on the political support of Arab states in the region.[123] The northern no-fly zone is contingent on Turkey's continuing willingness to renew the agreement allowing the allies to operate from Incirlik air base.

Whether the Turkish Parliament will continue to renew that agreement remains an open political question. Turkey's treatment of its own Kurdish minority is a turbulent domestic issue, as is its struggle against the outlawed Kurdish Workers' Party (PKK), which seeks Kurdish statehood.[124] So far, Iraqi Kurdish leaders have had a tacit understanding with the Turkish government: Turkey will allow use of its territory to monitor the situation in northern Iraq, so long as Iraqi Kurds oppose the separatist efforts of PKK guerrilla forces.[125] Turkey's anxiety about the future political direction of Iraqi Kurdistan, including its potential galvanizing effect on Turkey's sizable Kurdish population, makes long-term Turkish support for allied protection of Iraqi Kurds an exceedingly delicate political issue.[126]

## A New MOU

Like allied air monitoring, international humanitarian relief operations in Iraq face an uncertain future. In the summer of 1992, Saddam Hussein dragged his feet on renewing the MOU with the UN governing humanitarian operations.[127] As negotiations stalled and the agreement expired,[128] Iraq refused to issue or renew visas and travel permits for UN guards and relief workers. Moreover, UN personnel became regular targets for violence and harassment.[129] Finally, after months of delay, in October 1992 Iraq and the UN concluded a new MOU,[130] which represented an Iraqi retrenchment from the original accord.[131]

Iraq has continued to impede humanitarian relief operations since concluding the MOU. Saddam Hussein has not permitted UN guards or humanitarian centers in the south, although UN officials do monitor some specific programs, and very few humanitarian relief organizations operate there.[132] In the north, the UN was forced to halt relief convoys temporarily when bombs exploded on relief trucks after they passed through government-controlled territory or checkpoints.[133] Only after Iraq agreed to permit UN guards on the trucks did the convoys resume.[134]

In March 1993, the UN and Iraq conducted negotiations on a one-year humanitarian plan for Iraq extending from April 1, 1993, to March 31, 1994.[135] UN officials expect to implement this plan, although certain funding issues still must be resolved. If Iraq refuses to cooperate, the UN will have to confront the question of whether to continue relief operations and deploy armed guards on Iraq's territory without its consent. To be sure, Iraq's "consent" was compelled in the first place (and was influenced, no doubt, by the allied forces' entry into Iraqi territory to establish a safe haven zone). Diplomatic pressure and continued allied air monitoring may be sufficient to assure Iraq's consent again. If not, the UN may have to decide whether the Iraqi people's support for continuing the humanitarian operation, of which the UN guards are a critical part, supplies sufficient consent.[136] Alternatively, the Security Council will need to consider whether to expressly authorize UN forces on Iraqi territory under chapter VII.

In Iraqi Kurdistan, the combination of a UN presence on the ground and an allied air umbrella appears sufficient, as of the summer of 1993, to deter the kind of repression and refugee flows that occurred in March and early April of 1991. Withdrawal of either the UN ground presence or the allied air monitoring, however, would invite a recurrence of that desperate crisis. The situation in southern Iraq will remain especially precarious so long as no substantial UN presence exists there. In light of Saddam Hussein's proven willingness to use military force against

Iraqi civilians, international monitoring of developments in both northern and southern Iraq—including a capability and willingness to provide military protection, if necessary—is essential to the safety of Iraq's civilian population.

## NORMATIVE AND INSTITUTIONAL ISSUES

Does the international response to Iraq's repression of its Kurdish and Shi'ite citizens suggest that a consensus is beginning to emerge regarding the legitimacy of collective involvement in "internal conflicts," or is the Iraqi situation so unique as to be a nonprecedent? The extent of the collective commitment to aid and protect the Kurds (backed up by allied military force) was unusual because of the shared sense of postwar responsibility and the influential role of the media in galvanizing public opinion.[137] Nevertheless, that experience has broader significance: it reveals the current boundaries on the willingness of UN members to take action in response to a state's repression of its own citizens.

First, the Iraqi case showed that the Security Council was willing to act in response to internal repression when it resulted in substantial transborder refugee flows. Because violation of human rights within a state is a frequent cause of mass exoduses,[138] this is a potentially far-reaching precedent. Yet the limits of the precedent are also apparent: only ten of the fifteen Security Council members supported the resolution,[139] and all of them emphasized the spillover effect of Iraq's repression *across borders*. Only France and Britain suggested that a state's violation of its citizens' human rights might by itself justify Security Council action if it reached a certain level of egregiousness. In sharp contrast, five members expressed great apprehension about a larger Security Council role in conflicts they viewed as essentially "domestic."

The Iraqi case thus reflects the tensions that exist within the UN on the question of collective involvement in internal conflicts. On the one hand, UN member states are increasingly aware that the distinction between internal and inter-national conflicts is breaking down, and that conflicts that begin within a state's borders, such as human rights violations or struggles for self-determination, may ultimately pose a threat to international peace and security subject to Security Council action.[140] Most UN members no longer view the principle of domestic jurisdiction as a barrier to action in such cases.[141] On the other hand, substantial *political* barriers to action remain. Not only China, but also nonaligned countries, such as India and Zimbabwe, are reluctant to accept international oversight of matters they view as primarily domestic. These states fear that "internal conflicts" or human rights issues will be "used as a pretext for the intervention of big Powers in the legitimate domestic affairs of small States."[142] Such concerns, coupled with the threat of China's veto, will hamper efforts to obtain Security Council authorization in the future, just as they have impeded strong Security Council action with respect to Haiti,[143] despite the desperate refugee flows caused by that internal conflict.

Second, the Iraqi case illustrated the international community's clear preference for approaching a crisis as a humanitarian problem, sidestepping more contentious political questions of self-determination.[144] Allied leaders repeatedly stated that they were creating a humanitarian safe haven zone in northern Iraq, not a political zone, and they took no position on the issue of Kurdish autonomy or self-determination. Similarly, resolution 688 focused on the urgent humanitarian needs of the refugees, expressing "hope" that "an open dialogue" would be possible "to ensure that the human and political rights of all Iraqi citizens are respected."[145] The goal, in short, was to stop the suffering of the Iraqi Kurds and Shi'ites, and to establish enough peace to permit a "dialogue" among the parties, rather than to advocate a particular political solution.

Viewing a crisis in humanitarian terms has certain advantages. For one, it allows a greater possibility of normative agreement in favor of collective involvement. In other words, if the international community widely perceives a response to be humanitarian in nature, and if the risk of long-term military involvement is minimized, the possibility of collective action increases.[146] Thus, former Secretary-General Pérez de Cuéllar argued in his final annual report in favor of a "collective *obliga-*

*tion* of States to bring *relief* and redress in human rights emergencies," instead of a more open-ended right of intervention.[147]

Another benefit of establishing a humanitarian enclave for delivery of relief supplies is its potential to provide the first step on the way to resolving deeper conflicts. If violence can be halted even in a limited area, combatants may be willing at least to begin seeking a negotiated solution to their differences. Without the safe haven zone in northern Iraq, Saddam Hussein probably would never have begun to negotiate with the Kurds over an autonomy agreement, and the Kurds would not have been able to hold an election. But a humanitarian approach will not work in all cases—for instance, when armed factions completely refuse to cooperate, especially if UN member states are unwilling to commit peacekeeping or other forces to back up the humanitarian relief.

Moreover, viewing a crisis through a strictly humanitarian lens has certain drawbacks. Humanitarian relief alone will not resolve deep-seated political problems, and the international community, as well as the parties to a conflict, may stop at the provision of humanitarian aid and not work hard enough at resolving the underlying conflict. If deeper political differences are not resolved, the international community may find itself providing assistance indefinitely. Furthermore, even purportedly humanitarian efforts have significant political consequences for the division of power among the contending parties, especially if the international presence is long-term. In short, humanitarian and political issues cannot be neatly compartmentalized.

Third, the UN response to Iraq's treatment of the Kurds and Shi'ites revealed the Security Council's clear reluctance to explicitly authorize the use of military force to stop a state from repressing its own citizens. Resolution 688 did not invoke chapter VII of the UN Charter, nor did it expressly authorize forcible measures to protect Iraqi citizens. Reaching agreement simply on ordering Iraq to open up its territory to humanitarian relief organizations and cooperate fully with them was hard enough. Britain, France, and the United States decided quite sensibly, however, that allied military protection was critical to assisting the Kurds and protecting them from Saddam Hussein's military attacks.

Although the former secretary-general argued that the allied military action needed more explicit authorization,[148] allied officials saw the matter differently. In their view, resolution 688 was sufficiently open-ended to provide a legal basis for the allied action.[149] The resolution did not expressly mandate Operation Provide Comfort, they acknowledge, but it did call the situation in Iraq a threat to peace and security, and it appealed to member states to assist the humanitarian relief effort. It also demanded that Iraq allow immediate access to those in need. Allied officials argued that this demand, together with the fact that Iraq was already subject to enforcement action under chapter VII, provided adequate legal authority for allied military assistance to the relief effort. Security Council members opposed to a more direct legal approach did not challenge this view. In other words, resolution 688's open-endedness was both a necessity and a virtue—a necessity because of the unwillingness of the Security Council to provide a more definitive authorization, and a virtue because it permitted the allies to take action during this period of evolving norms while not forcing the hand of the Chinese and others who were willing to tolerate actions de facto that they would not authorize de jure. Likewise, few states raised legal objections when the United States, Britain, and France invoked resolution 688 in imposing the southern no-fly zone.

Such an approach has worked acceptably with respect to Operation Provide Comfort and Operation Southern Watch. Indeed, had the allies not committed troops to northern Iraq in April 1991 or monitored Iraqi airspace, Saddam Hussein's brutal military attacks against innocent civilians undoubtedly would have continued unabated. Nevertheless, taking military action under a UN "umbrella" without clear authorization by the Security Council poses certain risks.[150] In circumstances not linked so directly to prior UN enforcement action, the use of military force without clear Security Council authorization could damage the legitimacy of the operation. Moreover, as the secretary-general concluded in the Iraq case, the UN cannot deploy peacekeeping or police forces on a state's territory unless the Security Council mandates them under chapter VII of the Charter or unless the parties and the Security Council give their consent.[151] In short, the unusual manner in which resolution 688 was implemented—safe havens guarded by allied forces replaced by a UN presence on the ground in northern Iraq, and allied air umbrellas in both the north and the south—worked effectively in this case, without much opposition from anyone except Saddam Hussein. In the future, however, allied forces are not likely to have the same latitude in the absence of clearer authorization from the Security Council.

Fourth, and finally, the UN experience in Iraq gave impetus to institutional reforms designed to facilitate UN humanitarian responses, such as through creation of corridors of peace or zones of tranquillity. In December 1991 the General Assembly adopted by consensus resolution 46/182 to strengthen UN coordination of humanitarian emergency assistance.[152] Introduced by Sweden, the resolution contains a lengthy annex that, among other things, establishes guiding principles for humanitarian assistance that address both state sovereignty and the needs of "victims of natural disasters and other emergencies."[153] The guiding principles reflect a shift away from the traditional focus on the primacy of state sovereignty and on state-initiated requests for assistance.[154] To be sure, resolution 46/182 underscores that the "sovereignty, territorial integrity and national unity of states must be fully respected."[155] But rather than requiring the express consent of the affected *state*, the resolution takes a more flexible approach: "humanitarian assistance should be provided with the consent of the affected *country* and *in principle* on the basis of an appeal by the affected country."[156]

Resolution 46/182 requested the secretary-general to appoint a high-level UN official to coordinate emergency humanitarian assistance.[157] The General Assembly also urged the secretary-general to establish a $50 million emergency revolving fund and additional standby capabilities to ensure prompt responses in a crisis. In early 1992 Secretary-General Boutros Boutros-Ghali appointed Sweden's ambassador to the UN, Jan Eliasson, to the position of under-secretary-general and emergency relief coordinator in the newly established Department of

Humanitarian Affairs. Although ad hoc arrangements may still be useful in particular cases, building on these institutional reforms should enable the UN and the humanitarian agencies working with it to respond more quickly and effectively to humanitarian emergencies.

## CONCLUSION

In the years ahead, the member states of the UN will need to rethink the proper balance between the sovereignty of states and legitimate international involvement in internal conflicts. As pressures in favor of greater international involvement increase, so too will interest grow in the articulation of normative standards governing collective assistance to victims of repression and human rights abuses.[158] The Group of 7 industrialized countries, for instance, have urged the UN to prepare to take "exceptional action" as in Iraq if human suffering from "war, oppression, refugee flows" or from natural disasters such as famine, disease, or floods reaches "urgent and overwhelming proportions."[159] Professor Stanley Hoffmann of Harvard University has argued for a standard that "would justify collective intervention by international or regional organizations, or by states with these agencies' consent, whenever domestic disorders or policies threaten a region's peace or security, and when fundamental human rights are violated on a large scale."[160] Former Secretary-General Pérez de Cuéllar argued in his last annual report that any action to protect human rights must fulfill three criteria: consistency, meaning that protection of human rights should not be invoked in one situation and disregarded in a similar one; collectivity, meaning that any action to protect human rights should be taken in accordance with the UN Charter and should not be unilateral; and proportionality, meaning that the response must be commensurate with the wrong that has been committed.[161]

Even more difficult than articulating normative standards, however, is obtaining political agreement to act in concrete cases. The Security Council has broad authority under chapter VII of the Charter to take action when it determines that an internal conflict threatens international peace and security. In our interdependent world, most cases of systematic repression and large-scale violation of human rights will create such a threat.[162] The barriers to collective action in such cases will be political, not legal.

Consistency may be, in the end, the hardest criterion of all to satisfy. Many minority groups experiencing severe repression are likely to seek support from the international community as they struggle for protection of their basic human rights. Whether the collective response to Iraq's repression of its Kurdish and Shi'ite citizens will someday be seen as the beginning of a new trend or as a completely special case is yet to be determined. One thing is certain, however. That experience has raised expectations that similar responses will be forthcoming in other conflicts. For years to come, the UN will receive pleas like that of Bosnian Foreign Minister Haris Silajdzic, who has asked: Why can't we have a safe haven zone like the Kurds?[163] The fate of many suffering men, women, and children depends on the answer.

## NOTES

1. Address Before a Joint Session of the Congress on the Cessation of the Persian Gulf Conflict, March 6, 1991, *Weekly Compilation of Presidential Documents*, March 11, 1991, vol. 27, no. 10, p. 259.
2. Ann Devroy and R. Jeffrey Smith, "Neutrality in Iraq Reaffirmed by U.S.," *Washington Post*, March 27, 1991, p. A1.
3. Resolution 687 (April 3, 1991).
4. Resolution 688 (April 5, 1991).
5. Hurst Hannum, *Autonomy, Sovereignty, and Self-Determination* (Philadelphia: Univ. of Pennsylvania Press, 1990), p. 179.
6. H.C. Metz, ed., *Iraq: A Country Study* (Washington, D.C.: Library of Congress, 1990), pp. 83–84. There is, however, considerable linguistic, religious, and social diversity among Kurds. See Martin van Bruinessen, "Kurdish Society, Ethnicity, Nationalism and Refugee Problems," in P. G. Kreyenbroek and S. Sperl, eds., *The Kurds: A Contemporary Overview* (London: Routledge, 1992), pp. 34–45.
7. Hannum, *Autonomy, Sovereignty, and Self-Determination*, p. 182.
8. Ibid., p. 183.
9. Ibid., p. 184, n. 588; and p. 185. See also Metz, ed., *Iraq: A Country Study*, pp. 32, 37–40.
10. Hannum, *Autonomy, Sovereignty, and Self-Determination*, pp. 192–193; and Metz, ed., *Iraq: A Country Study*, pp. 186–187.
11. Metz, ed., *Iraq: A Country Study*, pp. 60–61 and 186–187. Among the provisions of the 1970 agreement are that in areas populated by a Kurdish

majority, Kurdish shall be the language of instruction and, along with Arabic, the language for official business; that administrative officials shall be Kurdish or persons fluent in Kurdish; that Kurdish organizations may be freely established; and that the Iraqi Constitution will be amended to guarantee that Kurds enjoy "self-rule" within Kurdish majority areas in Iraq, as well as share in legislative power within Iraq in a manner proportionate to their numbers. See Hannum, *Autonomy, Sovereignty, and Self-Determination*, pp. 190–192.

12. Kanan Makiya, "The Anfal: Uncovering an Iraqi Campaign to Exterminate the Kurds," *Harper's Magazine*, May 1992, p. 57.

13. Ibid., pp. 58–61. See also Judith Miller, "Iraq Accused: A Case of Genocide," *New York Times Magazine*, January 3, 1993, p. 15; U.S. Senate Committee on Foreign Relations, *Kurdistan in the Time of Saddam Hussein*, staff report, November 1991, pp. 20-21; U.S. Senate Committee on Foreign Relations, *Saddam's Documents*, staff report, May 1992; and Middle East Watch and Physicians for Human Rights, *Unquiet Graves: The Search for the Disappeared in Iraqi Kurdistan* (New York, 1992).

14. U.S. Senate Committee on Foreign Relations, *Chemical Weapons Use in Kurdistan: Iraq's Final Offensive*, staff report, October 1988, pp. 30–31.

15. Ibid., pp. 11–31.

16. See Elisa D. Harris, "Towards a Comprehensive Strategy for Halting Chemical and Biological Weapons Proliferation," *Arms Control*, vol. 12, no. 2 (September 1991), pp. 134–137; U.S. Senate Committee on Foreign Relations, *Chemical Weapons Use in Kurdistan*, pp. 38–40; Deanne E. Maynard, "Iraq: United States Response to the Alleged Use of Chemical Weapons Against the Kurds," *Harvard Human Rights Yearbook*, vol. 2 (1989), pp. 179–186; and Jonathan C. Randal, "Chemical War Conference Forgets Kurd Gas Victims," *Washington Post*, January 7, 1989, p. A16.

    On August 26, 1988, in response to the secretary-general's investigation of chemical weapons use during the Iran-Iraq war, the Security Council adopted a resolution of condemnation (resolution 620), and decided to consider "appropriate and effective measures . . . should there be any *future* use of chemical weapons" (para. 4 [emphasis added]).

17. Metz, ed., *Iraq: A Country Study*, pp. 203–204.

18. Ibid., p. 61; and U.S. Senate Committee on Foreign Relations, *Civil War in Iraq*, staff report, May 1991, p. 2.

19. Metz, ed., *Iraq: A Country Study*, p. 206.

20. Ibid., pp. 204–205.

21. Over ten million Kurds live in Turkey. For many years Turkey followed a policy of forced assimilation and suppression of Kurdish ethnic identity and culture. See Hannum, *Autonomy, Sovereignty, and Self-Determination*, p. 188. Turkey has made some modest improvements in its laws governing the Kurds. For example, it decriminalized use of the Kurdish language in the home in 1990—but it continues to ban publications in Kurdish. "Turkey's Kurds," *Washington Post*, October 12, 1992, p. A22. Moreover, torture inflicted by Turkish security forces and unexplained executions of villagers, journalists, and local politicians are common in

Kurdish areas of Turkey. See Amnesty International, *Turkey: Walls of Glass* (New York: 1992). As the Lawyers Committee for Human Rights concluded in 1992: "Turkey has failed to protect the rights of its Kurdish population. Although violations against the Kurds in Turkey have not reached the same level as they have in Iraq, the human rights situation of the Kurds remains dire and calls for concerted attention on the part of the U.S. and others in the international community." Lawyers Committee for Human Rights, *Human Rights and U.S. Foreign Policy* (New York, 1992), p. 63.

22. Hannum, *Autonomy, Sovereignty, and Self-Determination*, p. 196.

23. Ibid., p. 200.

24. Resolution 686, paras. 2 and 3.

25. The Security Council adopted resolution 687, the formal cease-fire resolution, on April 3, 1991; Iraq accepted it on April 6, 1991. See Minister of Foreign Affairs of Iraq, letter to the president of the Security Council, S/22456, April 6, 1991, and president of the Security Council, letter to the Permanent Representative of Iraq to the United Nations, S/22485, April 11, 1991.

26. Metz, ed., *Iraq: A Country Study*, pp. 63 and 96-97; and Yasmine Bahrani, "Iraq's Silenced Majority," *Washington Post*, October 4, 1992, p. C4.

27. Metz, ed., *Iraq: A Country Study*, pp. 64, 86, and 96. Iraq's Shi'ite Muslim population is diverse, however, and most Shi'ites do not seek separation from Iraq. Rather, they desire greater political and economic opportunity within the country. Caryle Murphy, "Iraqi Shi'ites Say Goal is Power Sharing, Not Independence," Washington Post, August 23, 1992, p. A19.

28. Middle East Watch, *Endless Torment: The 1991 Uprising in Iraq and Its Aftermath* (New York, 1992), p. 38 and n. 20. See also Barton Gellman, "Kurds Contend U.S. Encouraged Rebellion via 'Voice of Free Iraq,'" *Washington Post*, April 9, 1991, p. A17; and Michael Wines, "Kurd Gives Account of Broadcasts to Iraq Linked to the C.I.A.," *New York Times*, April 6, 1991, p. A1.

29. Jonathan C. Randal, "Kurds' Spring of Hope Collapses amid Feelings of Betrayal," *Washington Post*, April 3, 1991, p. A1.

30. Middle East Watch, *Endless Torment*, pp. 29–66.

31. U.S. Senate Committee on Foreign Relations, *Civil War in Iraq*, pp. 1–3.

32. Caryle Murphy, "U.S. Jet Downs 2nd Iraqi Plane," *Washington Post*, March 23, 1991, p. A1. Indeed, on March 26 White House spokesperson Marlin Fitzwater indicated that the United States would not shoot down helicopters used against rebel groups unless they posed a threat to U.S. forces in the region. See Ann Devroy and R. Jeffrey Smith, "Neutrality in Iraq Reaffirmed by U.S.," *Washington Post*, March 27, 1991, p. A1. On the equivocation in U.S. policy concerning helicopters, see Middle East Watch, *Endless Torment*, pp. 40–42.

33. See Devroy and Smith, "Neutrality in Iraq Reaffirmed by U.S." As President Bush subsequently put it: "I do not want one single soldier or airman shoved into a civil war in Iraq that's been going on for ages." Remarks at Maxwell Air Force Base War College in Montgomery, Alabama, April 13,

1991, *Weekly Compilation of Presidential Documents*, April 22, 1991, vol. 27, no. 16, p. 433.

34. Matt Bigg, "Kurds Ask Thatcher to Intervene," Press Association Limited Newsfile, April 2, 1991.

35. Middle East Watch, *Endless Torment*, pp. 29–32 and 45–66; and U.S. Senate Committee on Foreign Relations, *Civil War in Iraq*, pp. 3–4. Major Kurdish cities fell under Iraqi control on March 31 and April 1. See *Civil War in Iraq*, p. 4. Thousands of Iraqis, particularly in southern Iraq, are still being detained by Iraqi security forces. Many others have been executed or have simply "disappeared." See *Endless Torment*, pp. 7–9.

36. In the view of one observer, allied policy finally changed "not because of a reassessment of international obligations towards those who have had their rights systematically abused, but because the attention devoted by the Western media to the plight of the Kurds along the Turkish border threatened the political dividends that Western governments had secured from the conduct of the war itself." James Mayall, "Non-Intervention, Self-Determination and the 'New World Order,'" *International Affairs*, vol. 67, no. 3 (July 1991), p. 426.

37. The 21 members of the Arab League are Algeria, Bahrain, Djibouti, Egypt, Iraq, Jordan, Kuwait, Lebanon, Libya, Mauritania, Morocco, Oman, Qatar, Saudi Arabia, Somalia, Sudan, Syria, Tunisia, the United Arab Emirates, Yemen, and the Palestine Liberation Organization.

38. Arab League resolution 195 (August 10, 1990); and "The Arab League," *Los Angeles Times*, August 10, 1990, p. 4.

39. "Arab Leaders Agree to Send Troops to Help Defend Saudi Arabia," *Los Angeles Times*, August 12, 1990, p. 1.

40. The twelve members voting in favor of the resolution were Bahrain, Djibouti, Egypt, Kuwait, Lebanon, Morocco, Oman, Qatar, Saudi Arabia, Somalia, Syria, and the United Arab Emirates. The three voting against were Iraq, Libya, and the Palestine Liberation Organization. Algeria and Yemen abstained. Jordan, Sudan, and Mauritania expressed reservations, and Tunisia was absent. See Carol Berger, "Crisis in the Gulf: Arab Leaders Agree on 12-Nation Gulf Force," *Independent*, August 11, 1990, p. 8.

41. See Youssef M. Ibrahim, "After the War: Gulf Allies Lay Down Rules for Postwar Arab Relations," *New York Times*, March 31, 1991, p. 8; and Patrick Werr, "Egypt Emerges as Power Broker in Arab Politics," *Reuter Library Report*, March 31, 1991.

42. The six members of the Council are Bahrain, Kuwait, Oman, Qatar, Saudi Arabia, and the United Arab Emirates.

43. John Chipman, "Third World Politics and Security in the 1990s: 'The World Forgetting by the World Forgot?'" in Aspen Strategy Group, *Facing the Future: American Strategy in the 1990s* (Lanham, Maryland: University Press of America, 1991), p. 220. Syria, Egypt, and the Gulf Cooperation Council states signed an agreement on security cooperation in March 1991. See "Rafsanjani, Assad Hold Talks on Postwar Security," Reuters, April 27, 1991.

44. See Permanent Representative of Turkey to the United Nations, letter to the president of the Security Council, S/22435, April 2, 1991; and Chargé

d'Affaires of the Permanent Mission of France to the United Nations, letter to the president of the Security Council, S/22442, April 4, 1991.
45. Provisional Verbatim Record of the Two Thousand Nine Hundred and Eighty-second Meeting of the Security Council, S/PV.2982, April 5, 1991, p. 7 (remarks of Mr. Askin). The United Nations High Commissioner for Refugees estimates that approximately 400,000 Iraqis actually fled to Turkey. Lawyers Committee for Human Rights, *Asylum under Attack: A Report on the Protection of Iraqi Refugees and Displaced Persons One Year after the Humanitarian Emergency in Iraq* (New York, 1992), p. 30. For an assessment of Turkey's treatment of those refugees, see pp. 30–43 of that report.
46. Permanent Representative of the Islamic Republic of Iran to the United Nations, letter to the secretary-general, S/22447, April 4,1991. The Lawyers Committee for Human Rights estimates that 1.2–1.4 million Iraqi refugees entered Iran between March 1 and April 10, 1991. See the committee's *Asylum under Attack*, p. 48; for a discussion of Iran's treatment of those refugees, see pp. 43–59.
47. Permanent Representative of the Islamic Republic of Iran to the United Nations, letter to the secretary-general, April 3, 1991; and S/PV. 2982, p. 6 (remarks of Mr. Askin, Turkey).
48. S/PV. 2982, p. 8 (remarks of Mr. Askin, Turkey); and pp. 13–15 (remarks of Mr. Kharrazi, Islamic Republic of Iran).
49. Austria, Belgium, Côte d'Ivoire, Ecuador, France, Romania, the Soviet Union, the United Kingdom, the United States, and Zaire voted in favor of the resolution. Cuba, Yemen, and Zimbabwe voted against it; China and India abstained.
50. Article 39 provides: "The Security Council shall determine the existence of any threat to the peace, breach of the peace, or act of aggression and shall make recommendations, or decide what measures shall be taken in accordance with Articles 41 and 42, to maintain or restore international peace and security."
51. Article 2(7) provides: "this principle shall not prejudice the application of enforcement measures under Chapter VII."
52. The resolution made no reference to chapter VII, although it did characterize the cross-border consequences of Iraq's repression as a threat to "international peace and security." Several commentators, including the UN legal counsel, have concluded that the resolution was not adopted under chapter VII. See statement of Carl-August Fleischhauer, under-secretary-general and legal counsel of the United Nations, in *Proceedings of the 86th Annual Meeting of the American Society of International Law*, April 1–4, 1992 (Washington, D.C.: American Society of International Law, 1992), p. 588; and David J. Scheffer, "Use of Force after the Cold War: Panama, Iraq, and the New World Order," in L. Henkin et al., *Right v. Might: International Law and the Use of Force*, 2d ed. (New York: Council on Foreign Relations, 1991), p. 146.
53. S/PV. 2982, p. 31 (remarks of Mr. Zenenga, Zimbabwe); pp. 27–31 (remarks of Mr. Al-Ashtal, Yemen); and pp. 44–50 (remarks of Mr. Alarcon de Quesada, Cuba).

54. Ibid., pp. 31–32 (remarks of Mr. Zenenga, Zimbabwe).
55. Ibid., pp. 31–32 (remarks of Mr. Zenenga, Zimbabwe); p. 46 (remarks of Mr. Alarcon de Quesada, Cuba); and p. 27 (remarks of Mr. Al-Ashtal, Yemen).
56. See UN Charter, article 10.
57. S/PV. 2982, pp. 28–30 (remarks of Mr. Al-Ashtal, Yemen).
58. Ibid., pp. 28–30, 31.
59. Ibid., p. 56 (remarks of Mr. Li Daoyu, China).
60. Ibid., p. 62 (remarks of Mr. Gharekhan, India).
61. Ibid., p. 58 (remarks of Mr. Pickering, United States [emphasis added]).
62. Ibid., pp. 64–65 (remarks of Sir David Hannay, United Kingdom).
63. Ibid., p. 53 (remarks of Mr. Rochereau de la Sabliere, France).
64. Ibid., p. 61 (remarks of Mr. Vorontsov, USSR).
65. Ibid., p. 56 (remarks of Mr. Hohenfellner, Austria).
66. Ibid., p. 67 (remarks of Mr. Noterdaeme, Belgium, president of the Security Council).
67. Ibid., p. 41 (remarks of Mr. Bechio, Côte d'Ivoire).
68. Ibid., p. 36 (remarks of Mr. Ayala Lasso, Ecuador).
69. Ibid., p. 22 (remarks of Mr. Munteanu, Romania).
70. Ibid., p. 38 (remarks of Mr. Kibidi Ngovuka, Zaire).
71. Ibid., pp. 64–65 (remarks of Sir David Hannay, United Kingdom). Britain also stressed Iraq's obligations under the Geneva Conventions of 1949 to protect innocent civilians in the event of internal armed conflict. Ibid., p. 66. See also p. 67 (remarks of Mr. Noterdaeme, Belgium, president of the Security Council). In addition, several states not serving on the Security Council but present at the meeting placed a particularly strong emphasis on the duty of the UN to protect human rights, and condemned Iraq for violating internationally accepted human rights standards. See, e.g., ibid., pp. 72–73 (remarks of Mr. Rantzau, Germany); p. 88 (remarks of Mr. Huslid, Norway); p. 81 (remarks of Mr. Viqueira, Spain); and pp. 79–80 (remarks of Mr. Hayes, Ireland).
72. Ibid., p. 53 (remarks of Mr. Rochereau de la Sabliere, France).
73. Ibid., pp. 24–25 (remarks of Mr. Munteanu, Romania). Romania also qualified its emphasis on human rights by stating: "Questions pertaining to the situation of various segments or components of populations from the ethnic, linguistic or religious points of view are matters of the national jurisdiction of States." (p. 23).
74. Ibid., p. 36 (remarks of Mr. Ayala Lasso, Ecuador).
75. Ibid., p. 53 (remarks of Mr. Rochereau de la Sabliere, France); and p. 82 (remarks of Mr. Eliasson, Sweden). Sweden was present at the Security Council meeting but was not a member of the Council at the time. See also ibid., pp. 24–25 (remarks of Mr. Munteanu, Romania) (Security Council was "addressing a special case in the aftermath of the Gulf War").
76. Ibid., p. 53 (remarks of Mr. Rochereau de la Sabliere, France).
77. Resolution 688, para. 6. See Scheffer, "Use of Force after the Cold War," pp. 145–146.
78. The debate underlying resolution 688 focused on the urgent humanitarian needs of the refugees. Little discussion of the Kurds' struggle for greater political participation occurred.

79. Resolution 688, para. 2.

80. The Lawyers Committee for Human Rights estimates that 30,000–50,000 Iraqi civilians sought refuge in the allied-occupied areas. See the committee's *Asylum under Attack*, pp. 60–63. Allied forces withdrew from southern Iraq by early May. See "Allied Forces Exit Gulf Demilitarized Zone," *Washington Post*, May 11, 1991, p. A22; and Michael R. Gordon, "Southern Iraq Flights Halted and Troops Will Pull Back," *New York Times*, May 8, 1991, p. A16.

81. John E. Yang and Ann Devroy, "U.S. Seeks to Protect Kurd Refugee Areas," *Washington Post*, April 11, 1991, p. A1.

82. William Drozdiak and David B. Ottaway, "U.S., Allies Want Refugee Havens Established in Iraq," *Washington Post*, April 19, 1991, p. A1.

83. Ibid.

84. David Hoffman and Ann Devroy, "Allies Urged Bush to Use Land Forces," *Washington Post*, April 18, 1991, p. A1. The article cites a U.S. diplomat who said that "our main concern" was that "refugee concentrations in Turkey were threatening to become semi-permanent locations for the Kurds that could spell political and economic headache for Ankara for years to come."

85. Barton Gellman and William Drozdiak, "U.S. Troops Enter Northern Iraq to Set Up Camps," *Washington Post*, April 18, 1991, p. A1; and Patrick E. Tyler, "U.S. Scouting Refugee Sites Well Inside Iraq's Borders, Aiming to Lure Kurds Home: Misgivings at U.N.," *New York Times*, April 18, 1991, p. A1.

86. Barton Gellman and William Drozdiak, "U.S. Troops Enter Northern Iraq to Set Up Camps," p. A38.

87. Ibid.; Andrew Rosenthal, "A Risky Undertaking," *New York Times*, April 18, 1991, pp. A1 and A16; Tyler, "U.S. Scouting Refugee Sites Well Inside Iraq's Borders," *New York Times*, pp. A1 and A16; and Fleischhauer, statement, *Proceedings*, p. 588.

88. Alan Cowell, "Iraq, Assailing Bush's Plan, Says U.N. Will Run Havens," *New York Times*, April 18, 1991, p. A16.

89. Memorandum of understanding, April 18, 1991, annex to secretary-general, letter to the president of the Security Council, S/22663, May 31, 1991.

90. Minister for Foreign Affairs of Iraq, letter to the secretary-general, S/22513, April 21, 1991.

91. R. W. Apple, Jr., "Baghdad Rejects U.N. Police Force to Protect Kurds," *New York Times*, May 10, 1991, p. A1; and David Hoffman and Glenn Frankel, "Iraq Rejects U.N. Force to Police Refugee Havens," *Washington Post*, May 10, 1991, p. A1.

92. R. W. Apple, Jr., "Baghdad Rejects U.N. Police Force to Protect Kurds."

93. Ibid.; and Fleischhauer, statement, *Proceedings*, p. 588.

94. Patrick E. Tyler, "Bush May Seek U.N. Ruling for Force in Kurdish Zone," *New York Times*, May 16, 1991, p. A16; and David Hoffman, "Soviets Reluctant to Back Wider U.N. Role in Iraq," *Washington Post*, May 14, 1991, p. A8.

95. May 25, 1991, annex on deployment of a UN guards contingent, S/22663. Like the April 18 MOU, this agreement extended until December 31, 1991, and was subject to renewal by mutual agreement.

96. Sadruddin Aga Khan, "U.N. Protection Born of Necessity," *Washington Post*, June 12, 1991, p. A23.

97. Eric Schmitt, "Last U.S. and Allied Troops Begin Withdrawal from Northern Iraq," *New York Times*, July 13, 1991, p. 3; and Barton Gellman, "Last Coalition Units Are Leaving Iraq," *Washington Post*, July 13, 1991, p. A1.

98. Lawyers Committee for Human Rights, *Asylum under Attack*, p. 18 and n. 23.

99. R. Jeffrey Smith and Barton Gellman, "U.S., Allies Agree to Form Force for Protection of Kurds," *Washington Post*, June 26, 1991, p. A9. The original base agreement, signed in June 1991, was for a six-month period. It was renewed in December 1991, June 1992, and December 1992.

100. Both French President Mitterrand and President Bush indicated that the allied strike force would respond if Saddam Hussein resumed massacring the Kurds. See The President's News Conference with French President François Mitterrand in Rambouillet, France, July 14, 1991, *Weekly Compilation of Presidential Documents*, July 22, 1991, vol. 27, no. 29, p. 954; and William Drozdiak, "U.S., France Back Force if Needed," *Washington Post*, July 15, 1991, p. A1. President Clinton also affirmed his determination to bring Iraq "to full compliance" with UN resolutions. See Rick Atkinson, "Clinton Will Face Decisions on U.S. Force on Day One," *Washington Post*, January 19, 1993, pp. A1 and A16.

101. Jonathan C. Randal, "Kurds Seek Guarantees for Pact," *Washington Post*, May 2, 1991, p. A29.

102. Ibid.; and "Under Allied Umbrella, Iraq's Kurds Turn to Ballot Box," Agence France Presse, May 10, 1992.

103. See UN Commission on Human Rights, Report on the situation of human rights in Iraq, prepared by Mr. Max van der Stoel, Special Rapporteur of the Commission on Human Rights, in accordance with Commission resolution 1991/74, E/CN.4/1992/31, February 18, 1992.

104. Lawyers Committee for Human Rights, *Asylum under Attack*, p. 9.

105. International Human Rights Law Group, *Statement on the May 1992 Elections in Northern Iraq* (Washington, D.C., 1992), p. 4.

106. Ibid., pp. 6–7; and Jonathan Randal, "Kurds Declare Election a Draw; Result Imperils Talks with Iraq," *Washington Post*, May 23, 1992, p. A20.

107. Jonathan Randal, "Kurdish Rivals Face Delicate Tasks: Build Alliance, Credibility," *Washington Post*, May 24, 1992, p. A47. The two main Kurdish parties agreed in September 1992 to combine their guerrilla forces into a single force under a unified Kurdish command. See "2 Kurdish Parties Agree to Merger," *New York Times*, September 16, 1992, p. A15.

108. See Chris Hedges, "Kurds in Iraq Warned by Turkey, Iran, and Syria," *New York Times*, November 15, 1992, p. 9; and Caryle Murphy, "Key States Warn U.S. over Kurds," *Washington Post*, November 15, 1992,

p. A33. Kurdish leaders contend that Iran, Syria, and Iraq are aiding Turkey's separatist Kurdish Workers' Party (PKK) in order to undermine the Iraqi Kurds' efforts at self-rule and autonomy. See Caryle Murphy, "Iraqi Kurds Say Iran Is Backing a Rival Faction," *Washington Post*, November 2, 1992, p. A18; and "Iran Is Reported to Aid Turkish Kurds in Iraq," *New York Times*, October 25, 1992, p. 15.

109. See Caryle Murphy, "With West's Protection, Kurds Realize a Precarious Dream," *Washington Post*, November 9, 1992, p. A1; and Caryle Murphy, "Key States Warn U.S. over Kurds." For a perceptive analysis of the Kurds' struggle for self-determination and its implications for regional stability, see Graham E. Fuller, "The Fate of the Kurds," *Foreign Affairs*, vol. 72, no. 3 (Spring 1993), pp. 108–121.

110. "Hussein Foes Create Joint Front for a Federal Iraq," *New York Times*, November 2, 1992, p. A7; and Caryle Murphy, "Iraqi Opposition Meets in Kurdistan to Prepare for Post-Saddam State," *Washington Post*, October 28, 1992, p. A21. See also Jonathan C. Randal, "Iraqis Form Anti-Saddam Front," *Washington Post*, June 30, 1992, p. A20.

111. Reports that Iraq was attacking Shi'ites in the southern marshlands prompted Sadruddin Aga Khan to visit that area in July 1991 in the hope of establishing a UN humanitarian center to provide food and other relief, and to deter further Iraqi aggression. Unfortunately, Baghdad thwarted UN efforts to establish a UN presence in southern Iraq until March 1992, when it finally agreed to a UN office in Nasariya for the distribution of humanitarian assistance. See Middle East Watch, *Endless Torment*, p. 15. By September 1992, that office was closed.

   In late March 1992 Iraqi forces engaged in shelling and shooting at Kurdish civilians along the safe haven zone. See Chris Hedges, "Iraqi Forces Shell Kurdish Rebels in Apparent Cease-fire Violation," *New York Times*, March 31, 1992, p. A1.

112. See Provisional Verbatim Record of the Three Thousand One Hundred and Fifth Meeting of the Security Council, S/PV.3105, August 11, 1992. At this meeting, Max van der Stoel, special rapporteur of the UN Commission on Human Rights, reported on Iraq's continued repression of its civilian population (pp. 16-23). His interim report on the situation of human rights in Iraq appears as an annex to Charge d'Affaires of the Permanent Mission of Belgium to the United Nations, letter to the President of the Security Council, S/24386, August 5, 1992.

113. See, e.g., S/PV.3105, pp. 35–39 (remarks of Mr. Perkins, United States); pp. 42–45 (remarks of Mr. Vorontsov, Russian Federation); pp. 51–53 (remarks of Mr. Rochereau de la Sabliere, France); pp. 54–57 (remarks of Mr. Hannay, United Kingdom); and pp. 59–62 (remarks of Mr. Arria, Venezuela). See also pp. 41–42 (remarks of Mr. Van Daele, Belgium); p. 46 (remarks of Mr. Hatano, Japan); p. 48 (remarks of Mr. Hajnoczi, Austria); and pp. 57–59 (remarks of Mr. Budai, Hungary).

   Both India and China, however, expressed their reservations about the Security Council's jurisdiction to consider human rights matters. See pp. 6–7 (remarks of Mr. Gharekhan, India); and p. 12 (remarks of Mr. Li, China). See also pp. 7–10 (remarks of Mr. Ayala Lasso, Ecuador); and pp. 11–12 (remarks of Mr. Mumbengegwi, Zimbabwe).

114. John Lancaster, "Allies Declare 'No-Fly Zone' in Iraq," *Washington Post*, August 27, 1992, p. A1; Michael Wines, "U.S. and Allies Say Flight Ban in Iraq Will Start Today," *New York Times*, August 27, 1992, p. A1; and "Excerpts from Bush's Talk: Off-Limits Zone to Iraqi Jets," *New York Times*, August 27, 1992, p. A14.

115. But see "No-Fly in Iraq. Why?" *New York Times*, August 28, 1992, p. 24 ("Unlike other resolutions on Iraq, 688 did not invoke Chapter 7 of the U.N. Charter, the legal basis for armed enforcement"). The no-fly zone came under sharp criticism on other grounds. A number of Arab states, for example, expressed fears that the plan might lead to a de facto partition of Iraq and create an opening for Iranian influence. See Caryle Murphy, "Many Arabs Critical of 'No-Fly Plan,'" *Washington Post*, August 26, 1992, p. A7. Iraq denounced the ban as a violation of international law. See Trevor Rowe, "Iraq Says Ban on Flight Breaks International Law," *Washington Post*, August 27, 1992, p. A27.

116. By September 1992, there was no UN international presence in southern Iraq. See Provisional Verbatim Record of the Three Thousand One Hundred and Thirty-Ninth Meeting of the Security Council, S/PV.3139, November 23, 1992, p. 118 (remarks of Mr. Eliasson, under-secretary-general for humanitarian affairs and emergency relief coordinator). Some Iraqi Shi'ites question the effectiveness of the flight ban when Saddam Hussein continues artillery fire and economic and political repression against residents in the southern marshlands. See Nora Boustany, "Iraqi Opposition Figure Urges Internal Resistance," *Washington Post*, October 13, 1992, p. A17; and Caryle Murphy, "Iraqi Exiles Allege New Brutality in South," *Washington Post*, November 21, 1992, p. A21.

117. See "Bush's Last Message to Hill Is about Iraq," *Washington Post*, January 21, 1993, p. A18. On December 27, 1992, U.S. forces shot down an Iraqi plane in southern Iraq for violating the no-fly zone and refusing to turn back when challenged. See Helen Dewar, "U.S. Fighter Downs Iraqi Military Jet in Flight-Ban Zone," *Washington Post*, December 28, 1992, p. A1; and Michael R. Gordon, "U.S. Shoots Down an Iraqi War Plane in No-Flight Zone," *New York Times*, December 28, 1992, p. A1.

118. Barton Gellman and Ann Devroy, "U.S., Allied Jets Batter Iraq's Air Defenses," *Washington Post*, January 19, 1993, p. A1; Michael R. Gordon, "U.S. Leads Further Attacks on Iraq Antiaircraft Sites; Admits Its Missile Hit Hotel: Targets in South," *New York Times*, January 19, 1993, pp. A1 and A8; Thomas L. Friedman, "Limiting the Response," *New York Times*, January 19, 1993, pp. A1 and A8; Barton Gellman and Ann Devroy, "U.S. Delivers Limited Air Strike on Iraq," *Washington Post*, January 14, 1993, p. A1; and R.W. Apple, Jr., "U.S. and Allied Planes Hit Iraq, Bombing Missile Sites in South in Reply to Hussein's Defiance," *New York Times*, January 14, 1993, p. A1.

119. Ann Devroy and Barton Gellman, "U.S. Attacks Industrial Site Near Baghdad; MiG Downed as Gulf Allies Display Might," *Washington Post*, January 18, 1993, p. A1; and Michael R. Gordon, "Bush Launches Missile Attack on Weapons Site Near Baghdad as Washington Greets Clinton," *New York Times*, January 18, 1993, p. A1.

120. See Sharon Waxman, "France Criticizes Attack on Iraq," *Washington Post*, January 21, 1993, p. A18; Michael Dobbs, "Moscow Seeks Talks in Security Council about Gulf Crisis," *Washington Post*, January 19, 1993, p. A17; John Murray Brown, "Kurdish Pressures, U.S. Use of Base Worrying Ankara," *Washington Post*, January 19, 1993, p. A17; Paul Lewis, "Iraqi Crisis Appears to Ease but Raids Put Allies at Odds," *New York Times*, January 20, 1993, p. A1; and Eugene Robinson, "Criticism from Gulf War Allies Strains U.S.–Led Coalition," *Washington Post*, January 20, 1993, p. A25.

121. Saddam Hussein also said that he would allow UN flights carrying UN weapons inspectors to resume. See Michael R. Gordon, "Iraq Says It Won't Attack Planes and Agrees to U.N. Flight Terms," *New York Times*, January 20, 1993, p. A1; and R. Jeffrey Smith and Julia Preston, "Baghdad Declares Goodwill Cease-Fire," *Washington Post*, January 20, 1993, p. A1. Whether Iraq actually observes this "cease-fire" remains to be seen.

122. See Eric Schmitt, "Iraqi Gunners Fire on American Jets in North, U.S. Says," *New York Times*, April 10, 1993, p. 1; John Lancaster and R. Jeffrey Smith, "U.S. Jets Bomb Iraqis After Being Fired On," *Washington Post*, April 10, 1993, p. A12; Robert D. Hershey, Jr., "U.S. Says 2 of Its Planes Attacked Iraqi Radar That Imperiled Them," *New York Times*, April 19, 1993, p. A2; Guy Gugliotta, "U.S. Jets Attack Iraqi Radar Site," *Washington Post*, April 19, 1993, p. A19.

123. Kuwait publicly supports the no-fly zone, and Saudi Arabia quietly provides assistance, including air bases; most other Arab states are ambivalent or negative about the operation and fear a de facto partition of Iraq, as well as greater Iranian influence. See John H. Cushman Jr., "Saudis in Supporting Role to Allied Flights over Iraq," *New York Times*, August 30, 1992, p. 10; William E. Schmidt, "Rebellion a Factor Keeping Egypt Out of U.S. Air Campaign in Iraq," *New York Times*, September 1, 1992, p. A6; and William Drozdiak, "Moroccan Warns U.S. about Iraq," *Washington Post*, September 6, 1992, p. A1.

124. Turkey's treatment of its Kurdish population has prompted strong criticism. See, e.g., Marc Fisher, "Bonn Condemns Turkey for Attacks on Kurds," *New York Times*, March 27, 1992, p. A23; and Lawyers Committee for Human Rights, *Asylum under Attack*, pp. 19–21. See also note 21, above.

125. See Chris Hedges, "An Odd Alliance Subdues Turkey's Kurdish Rebels," *New York Times*, November 24, 1992, p. A1; Caryle Murphy, "Turkish Army Presses Offensive in Iraq," *Washington Post*, October 25, 1992, p. A29; and John Murray Brown, "Rival Kurds Embroiled in Battle," *Washington Post*, October 18, 1992, p. A29.

126. See Laurie Mylroie, "Kurdistan after Saddam Hussein," *Atlantic*, December 1992, pp. 49–50. Yet discontinuation of the basing agreement could lead to another refugee crisis similar to that in March 1991, which would hardly be in Turkey's interest.

127. Trevor Rowe, "Iraq Lags on Renewal of U.N. Accord," *Washington Post*, June 25, 1992, p. A35; and Trevor Rowe, "Iraq Refuses to Renew Accord

That Permits U.N. Role There," *Washington Post*, August 22, 1992, p. A14. The Security Council, in a statement by its president on September 2, 1992, criticized Iraq's refusal to renew its agreement with the UN. See Paul Lewis, "U.N. Agencies Ordered to Continue Efforts in Iraq," *New York Times*, September 3, 1992, p. A10.

128. The original MOU between Iraq and the UN, concluded in April 1991, was due to expire on December 31, 1991, but Iraq and the UN agreed in late November to extend it until June 30, 1992. Negotiations over extension of that agreement were not concluded until October 22, 1992, four months after it expired.

129. In July 1992 a UN guard was murdered while he slept. See "Peace Keeper Killed in Iraq," *Washington Post*, July 17, 1992, p. A16. See also "U.N. Unit in Iraq Attacked," *New York Times*, July 29, 1992, p. A6; Chris Hedges, "Baghdad Said to Sponsor Attacks on Aid Missions," *New York Times*, July 30, 1992, p. A8; Trevor Rowe, "U.N. Personnel's Safety Stirs Concern," *Washington Post*, August 28, 1992, p. A28; William E. Schmidt, "U.N. Reports an Attempt to Bomb Guards' Car in Iraq," *New York Times*, August 31, 1992, p. A3; and S/PV.3139, November 23, 1992, p. 126 (remarks of Mr. van der Stoel).

By early October, the number of UN guards in Iraq had dwindled to just over 100, and relief workers stayed on at their own peril. See Trevor Rowe, "Iraq Shows Flexibility on Aid to Kurds," *Washington Post*, October 2, 1992, p. A39; and S/PV. 3139, November 23, 1992, p. 118 (remarks of Mr. Eliasson.)

130. Memorandum of understanding, October 19, 1992; Frank J. Prial, "U.N. Chief in Accord with Iraqis on Food and Medicine for Kurds," *New York Times*, October 23, 1992, p. A11. This MOU was extended until March 31, 1993. By then, Iraq and the UN essentially had agreed to a one-year plan for continued humanitarian aid. See note 135, below.

131. Iraq agreed in October to accept only 300 UN armed guards, down from the earlier 500. See MOU, October 19, 1992, para. 9. The October MOU provides that the guards will be posted as needed in northern Iraq, with a small administrative component in Baghdad. The MOU does not preclude posting of guards in southern Iraq, but neither does it expressly authorize it. Moreover, the MOU gives the Iraqi government greater logistical control over UN operations outside of northern Iraq. See John M. Goshko and Ruth Marcus, "U.S. Assails U.N.-Iraq Relief Pact," *Washington Post*, October 20, 1992, p. A9.

132. See S/PV.3139, November 23, 1992, p. 126 (remarks of Mr. van der Stoel). Undersecretary Eliasson reported that UNICEF was operating a vaccination campaign throughout Iraq, the World Health Organization would distribute medicine, and the World Food Programme planned to distribute food in both northern and southern Iraq. Ibid, pp. 119–120.

133. Iraqi security agents reportedly planted the bombs. See "U.N. Suspends Aid to Kurds in Iraq," *New York Times*, October 23, 1992, p. A11; and John Lancaster, "Iraq Accused of Sabotaging Kurdish Relief," *Washington Post*, December 19, 1992, p. A8.

134. John M. Goshko, "Iraqis Again Violate 'No-Fly' Zone Ban," *Washington Post*, December 30, 1992, p. A12.

135. See UN Department of Humanitarian Affairs, *United Nations Inter-Agency Humanitarian Programme in Iraq: Cooperation Programme, 1 April 1993–31 March 1994* (New York, 1993).

136. See General Assembly resolution 46/182, Strengthening of the Coordination of Humanitarian Emergency Assistance of the United Nations (adopted without a vote on December 19, 1991), annex, para. 3 (referring not to the consent of the state or government, but to "the consent of the affected *country*" [emphasis added]). This resolution is discussed below in the text accompanying notes 152–157.

137. Southern Iraq has received considerably less media attention, as well as far less international assistance. Baghdad's restrictions on press access in the south, where journalists generally are allowed only on "official" trips, exacerbate this situation. See Caryle Murphy, "Iraqi Exiles Allege New Brutality in South," *Washington Post*, November 21, 1992, p. A21. Reports of detentions and executions thus go unmonitored by international observers.

138. See General Assembly resolution 45/153, Human Rights and Mass Exoduses (adopted without a vote on December 18, 1990). Among other things, that resolution notes the clear connection between violations of human rights and substantial refugee flows. See also UN Commission on Human Rights, *Study on Human Rights and Mass Exoduses*, E/CN.4/1503, December 31, 1981. Sadruddin Aga Khan was the special rapporteur for this study.

139. This gave the resolution only one more than the nine votes it required to pass. See UN Charter, art. 27, para. 3.

140. Under article 39 of the UN Charter, the Security Council determines "the existence of any threat to the peace, breach of the peace, or act of aggression." At the UN summit in January 1992, the Security Council members indicated a more expansive understanding of the threats to security today when they declared that "non-military sources of instability in the economic, social, humanitarian and ecological fields have become threats to peace and security." See Provisional Verbatim Record of the Three Thousand and Forty-sixth Meeting of the Security Council, S/PV.3046, January 31, 1992, p. 143.

141. As former UN Secretary-General Pérez de Cuéllar put it: "It is now increasingly felt that the principle of non-interference with the essential domestic jurisdiction of States cannot be regarded as a protective barrier behind which human rights could be massively or systematically violated with impunity." See Javier Pérez de Cuéllar, *Report of the Secretary-General on the Work of the Organization* (New York: United Nations, 1991), p. 12.

142. S/PV.3046, p. 131 (remarks of Mr. Shamuyarira, Zimbabwe). See also p. 93 (remarks of Mr. Li Peng, China); S/PV.2982, pp. 62–63 (remarks of Mr. Gharekhan, India).

143. See Thomas R. Pickering, "The U.N. Contribution to Future International Security," *Naval War College Review* (Winter 1993), p. 97.

144. For a discussion of collective responses to secessionist disputes, see Jane E. Stromseth, "Self-Determination, Secession and Humanitarian Interven-

tion by the United Nations," in *Proceedings of the 86th Annual Meeting of the American Society of International Law*, April 1–4, 1992 (Washington, D.C.: American Society of International Law, 1992), pp. 370–374.

145. Resolution 688, para. 2.

146. In the case of Somalia, the Security Council acted under chapter VII and authorized the secretary-general and member states "to use all necessary means to establish as soon as possible a secure environment for humanitarian relief operations in Somalia." See resolution 794, para. 10 (December 3, 1992). As that experience and the Iraqi case both show, however, humanitarian operations inevitably confront deeper political problems, which may lead to a longer-term commitment than originally contemplated.

147. Pérez de Cuéllar, *Report of the Secretary-General*, p. 13 (emphasis added).

148. See note 87 and page 90, above.

149. See, e.g., Patrick E. Tyler, "10,000 American Troops to Build Camps over a 2-Week Period," *New York Times*, April 18, 1991, pp. A1 and A16.

150. For example, several Gulf War allies, including France, Russia, and Turkey, expressed unease about some allied military actions taken in January 1993 in response to Iraqi defiance of the no-fly zones. See note 120, above.

151. See Fleischhauer, statement, *Proceedings*, note 52, p. 588.

152. For an analysis of the resolution, see Lawyers Committee for Human Rights, *Asylum under Attack*, pp. 76–84.

153. Resolution 46/182, annex, para. 1.

154. Lawyers Committee for Human Rights, *Asylum under Attack*, p. 77.

155. Resolution 46/182, annex, para. 3.

156. Ibid. (emphasis added).

157. Ibid., para. 34. The emergency relief coordinator's responsibilities, listed in paragraph 35(d), include "actively facilitating, including through negotiation if needed, the access by the operational organizations to emergency areas for the rapid provision of emergency assistance by obtaining the consent of all parties concerned, through modalities such as the establishment of temporary relief corridors where needed, days and zones of tranquility and other forms."

158. India and Zimbabwe, though skeptical about greater international involvement in internal conflicts, have stated that they favor an effort to articulate standards governing such action. See S/PV.3046, p. 98 (remarks of Mr. Rao, India); and p. 131 (remarks of Mr. Shamuyarira, Zimbabwe).

Yet as Ambassador Thomas Pickering cautioned: "We are unlikely to see the rapid elaboration of sweeping tenets of international law to provide automatic external guarantees for minority rights, democratically elected governments, or hungry people caught up in a civil war. A significant number of U.N. members do not see such principles as leading to order but as subversive of it, or at least subversive of an order based on firm doctrines of state sovereignty and nonintervention." See Pickering, "The U.N. Contribution to Future International Security," p. 98.

159. Political Declaration Strengthening the International Order, London Economic Summit 1991, para. 4.

160. Stanley Hoffmann, "Delusions of World Order," *New York Review of Books*, April 9, 1992, p. 41. Hoffmann suggests negotiating a treaty that

defines the circumstances under which collective action for humanitarian purposes would be permitted, and setting up a treaty secretariat that would coordinate action by the parties.

A complete set of normative criteria would need to identify the kinds of responses—humanitarian aid, diplomatic and economic sanctions, peacekeeping forces, and ultimately the use of force—that would be warranted and when. See, e.g., David J. Scheffer, "Toward a Modern Doctrine of Humanitarian Intervention," *University of Toledo Law Review*, vol. 23, no. 2 (Winter 1992), pp. 286–293.

161. Pérez de Cuéllar, *Report of the Secretary-General*, p. 13.

162. Large-scale repression is likely to cause refugee flows and regional instability, among other consequences. In two prior cases, Southern Rhodesia and South Africa, the Security Council essentially concluded that systematic violation of human rights created a threat to international peace and security subject to Security Council action under chapter VII. Thus, in 1965 the Security Council called upon states to apply sanctions against Southern Rhodesia (resolution 217), and in 1966 it authorized Britain to take limited forcible steps to enforce those sanctions (resolution 221). The Council imposed comprehensive mandatory economic sanctions on Southern Rhodesia in 1968 (resolution 253), and imposed an arms embargo against South Africa in 1977 (resolution 418).

163. Laura Silber, "Leaders of Bosnia, Croatia Reportedly Discuss Two-Republic Confederation," *Washington Post*, May 20, 1992, p. A24.

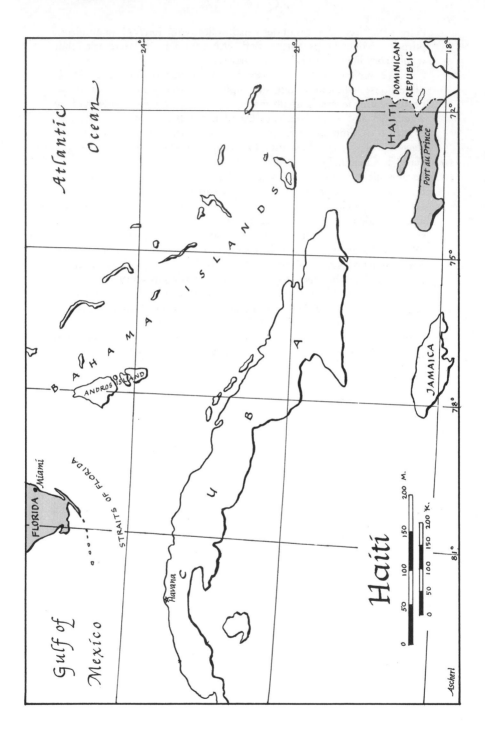

Haíti

Ascherl

# The Haitian Crisis and the OAS Response: A Test of Effectiveness in Protecting Democracy

## DOMINGO E. ACEVEDO*

In February 1991, Father Jean-Bertrand Aristide took office as the first president in the history of Haiti who had won a free and fair election. He carried with him the hopes of his supporters—an overwhelming majority of Haiti's desperately poor people—for an end to decades of abusive authoritarian rule and the beginning of a new era founded on principles of democracy and social justice.

Less than eight months later, on September 30, those hopes were dashed when President Aristide was overthrown in a military coup whose perpetrators defied not only the will of the Haitian majority but also a commitment to representative democracy undertaken on a hemisphere-wide basis through the Organization of American States (OAS). In fact, observers from the OAS, the United Nations, and nongovernmental organizations had monitored the election that resulted in Aristide's victory. Thus the international community had established a baseline

---

*The views expressed in this chapter are entirely those of the author and should in no way be attributed to the Organization of American States.

of expectations both legitimizing Aristide's government and supporting its continuation.

The OAS immediately reacted to the coup with a package of diplomatic and economic sanctions, and the UN lent support to these efforts. Yet a solution to the crisis has proved elusive.

The Haitian crisis, though unique in many respects and certainly different from the other cases in this volume, shares with them the element of human suffering in an environment of gross violation of human and political rights. Moreover, it demonstrates that regardless of how clearly and categorically popular sovereignty may be expressed, general international law leaves little margin for effective multilateral assistance on behalf of the majority of people seeking vindication of their rights to political participation[1] and to a democratic, representative government.

This study analyzes the role of the OAS and, secondarily, the UN in response to the coup d'état in Haiti. In so doing, it will address some of the questions that arise from the conflict between sovereignty and collective action for the purpose of protecting democracy. It will also examine the extent to which regional organizations and the UN are legally empowered to undertake or authorize actions of a unilateral or collective nature against a government that comes to power by means other than the free expression of the will of the people.

## OAS LEGAL FRAMEWORK RELEVANT
## TO THE HAITIAN CRISIS: A SUMMARY

This section will briefly examine those legal standards of the inter-American system that are relevant in the case of the Haitian crisis. It will also look at how the OAS member states have interpreted and applied those standards.

### The OAS Charter and Past OAS Actions

For decades, even before the OAS was formally established in 1948, the countries of the Western Hemisphere repeatedly expressed their allegiance to democracy and to the "democratic ideal."[2] While the U.N. Charter does not require any one form of government, the preamble to the OAS Charter expresses the member states' conviction "that representative democracy is an indispensable condition for the stability, peace and development of the region." The OAS Charter includes a more explicit articulation of that principle in article 3(d), which reads as follows: "The solidarity of the American States and the high aims which are sought through it require the political organization of those States on the basis of the effective exercise of representative democracy."

In article 2(b), the Charter proclaims the following as one of the essential purposes of the OAS: "To promote and consolidate representative democracy, with due respect for the principle of non-intervention." But article 1 provides that the Organization "has no powers other than those expressly conferred upon it by the Charter, none of whose provisions authorizes it to intervene in matters that are within the internal jurisdiction of the Member States."

While the OAS has for many years espoused the ideal of representative democracy, several important policy objectives related to that ideal and favored by the majority of the member states are sometimes unattainable through coordinated collective action because of excessive reliance on the primacy of the principle of nonintervention.[3]

Gonzalo Facio, a former minister of foreign affairs of Costa Rica, has noted that "the OAS' traditional failure to act in defense of democracy, which became characteristic of the decades of the seventies and the eighties, was not the result of an absence of legal authority to act."[4]

As far back as 1959, the Organization's Fifth Meeting of Consultation of Ministers of Foreign Affairs adopted the Declaration of Santiago, which specifically states that the governments of the American republics should be the product of free elections and that "perpetuation in power, or the exercise of power without a fixed term and with the manifest intent of perpetuation, is incompatible with the effective exercise of democracy."[5]

Some 20 years later, the Seventeenth Meeting of Consultation adopted a resolution declaring that the solution to the problem confronting Nicaragua during the civil strife in 1979 was

"exclusively within the jurisdiction of the people of Nicaragua." In an obvious inconsistency, however, the same resolution also stated that the solution should be based on:

> i. Immediate and definitive replacement of the Somoza regime.
> ii. Installation in Nicaraguan territory of a democratic government, the composition of which should include the principal representative groups which oppose the Somoza regime and which reflects the free will of the people of Nicaragua.
> iii. The guarantee of the respect for human rights of all Nicaraguans without exception.
> iv. The holding of free elections as soon as possible, that will lead to the establishment of a truly democratic government that guarantees peace, freedom and justice.[6]

It is interesting to compare the decisive action the OAS took against the Somoza government in 1979 with the Organization's handling of subsequent crises of a similar nature. For example, in the Panamanian crisis in 1989, the OAS Meeting of Consultation considered that "the abuses by General Manuel Antonio Noriega in the crisis and the electoral process of Panama . . . have abridged the right of the Panamanian people to freely elect their legitimate authorities; that the outrageous abuses perpetrated against the opposition candidate and citizenry violate human, civil, and political rights." The meeting then went on to note that an essential purpose of the OAS is "to promote and consolidate representative democracy with due respect for the principle of nonintervention . . . a purpose that is being seriously jeopardized," and concluded that "a transfer of power in the shortest possible time and with full respect for the sovereign will of the Panamanian people" should be implemented.[7]

The 1989 Panamanian crisis demonstrated that when it comes to the supersensitive issues of nonintervention, sovereignty and collective action against an illegitimate regime, a powerful restraint operates on many governments of the region. The result is all too frequently a peculiar form of windfall profit to undemocratic and de facto governments that, despite their illegitimacy, manage to preserve their position, survive, and even thrive, against the wishes of the great majority of the population.

One could cite several other declarations and cases of purported defense of democratic principles by the OAS member countries—for example, responses to the overthrow of the constitutional government of Guatemala in 1954, the case of Cuba in 1962, and the Dominican Republic case in 1965. Even though from a mechanistic standpoint the reasons invoked in some of those cases were the defense of democratic principles, the underlying reasons were to be found more in the imperative of the East-West competition than in a desire to promote and protect democracy.[8]

## The Santiago Commitment to Democracy and OAS Resolution on Representative Democracy (1991)

The Organization's concern for the effective exercise of representative democracy took a quantum leap with approval in 1991 of the Santiago Commitment to Democracy and the Renewal of the Inter-American System and a resolution on representative democracy. The latter calls for an automatic meeting of the OAS Permanent Council

> . . . in the event of any occurrences giving rise to the sudden or irregular interruption of the democratic political institutional process or of the legitimate exercise of power by the democratically elected government in any of the Organization's member states, in order, within the framework of the Charter, to examine the situation, decide on and convene an ad hoc meeting of the Ministers of Foreign Affairs, or a special session of the General Assembly, all of which must take place within a ten-day period.

It further states that the purpose of any such meeting should be "to look into the events collectively and adopt any decisions deemed appropriate, in accordance with the Charter and international law."

Less than four months after their approval, the new procedures would be put to their first test, when the constitutional president of Haiti was forced from office and expelled from the country.

## HAITI BEFORE THE CRISIS

For decades, the Haitian people had endured a long succession of de facto authoritarian rulers.

Haiti won its independence after a series of long and bloody slave revolts that freed the black majority from colonial domination. At the time independence was declared in 1804, Haiti was one of the most profitable territories for the colonial power. In fact, it played an important part in the economic life of eighteenth-century France.[9]

The Haitian struggle for independence was particularly significant in that it posed a radical challenge not just to colonialism but to slavery, as well: the war for independence, therefore, was also a civil war between the white residents, backed by Napoleon's army, and the rest of the population; it was, in some measure, a social revolution fundamentally different from other independence movements in the Western Hemisphere. After becoming an independent state, Haiti spent several decades in isolation, largely because other states feared that recognition would trigger similar slave revolts and perhaps even secession in their territories.[10]

In 1915 the United States invaded the island of Hispaniola and occupied both Haiti and the Dominican Republic. Its occupation of the Dominican Republic lasted until 1924, but its occupation of Haiti continued until 1934. Professor Anthony Maingot remarks that the U.S. occupation "did little more than leave a bad memory which all Haitian groups use to their own advantage." In addition, he observes:

> Those who have studied the occupation from the Haitian perspective agree that racial antagonism was probably the single most important reason why the Americans failed to achieve anything of enduring value despite some significant contributions to improved health, roads and the infrastructure in general.[11]

The U.S. occupation's most obvious legacy was the Haitian army, which was then called the Haitian Guard and was run by American officers.[12]

Although Haiti was the second country in the Western Hemisphere to win its independence, it never managed to establish anything even remotely resembling a democratic tradition. Violence has always been the means of settling conflicts and choosing leaders in Haiti.[13] That method became institutionalized when François Duvalier, commonly known as Papa Doc, came to power after "winning" an election in 1957 that was widely viewed as rigged. The terror, coercion, and intimidation Duvalier routinely used to maintain control were nothing new for Haiti. But unlike previous rulers, Duvalier was prepared to use these reprehensible tactics against not just the peasantry, but a substantial sector of the elite, as well.[14]

During the first seven years of his regime, Duvalier's efforts were directed at securing his position by eliminating potential opposition. The primary targets were, not surprisingly, his political opponents, particularly those who had refused to accept the outcome of the 1957 elections and were determined to overthrow him by whatever means.[15]

Many of his opponents were powerful members of the business community in Port-au-Prince, a group that had played a significant role in the politics of Haiti since the early days of independence.[16] While waging a violent campaign against them, Duvalier cleverly engineered, at least for the first two years of his rule, the support of the Roman Catholic church and, for a much longer period, that of the U.S. embassy in Port-au-Prince.[17]

In 1964 François Duvalier devised a means of dispensing with elections once and for all. Claiming that he was responding to popular demand, he encouraged the Haitian legislature to adopt a new constitution, which it did on May 25, 1964, declaring him "president-for-life." The 1964 constitution also declared Duvalier to be "the unquestioned leader of the Revolution," "the Apostle of National Unity," "the Worthy Heir of the Founders of the Haitian Nation," and "the Restorer of the Fatherland."[18]

Upon the death of François Duvalier in April 1971, his title of president-for-life passed to his nineteen-year-old son, Jean-Claude. The succession was "legalized" with enactment of the 1970 and 1971 amendments to the 1964 constitution, which lowered the minimum age requirement for the presidency from 40 to 18 years of age and authorized François Duvalier to appoint his own successor. Under article 104 of the 1971 constitution, Jean-Claude's term of office was also for life.[19]

Like his father's, the regime of Jean-Claude Duvalier was marked by gross violations of fundamental human rights and the denial of political rights. In fact, most of the individual rights the so-called Duvalier constitutions guaranteed were never respected. Government forces, particularly the Volunteers for

National Security (more commonly known as the Tontons Macoutes), were routinely identified as being responsible for the harassment, persecution, kidnapping, and killing of aspiring political leaders, journalists, labor organizers, youth organizers, lawyers, and human rights activists.[20]

On February 7, 1986, Jean-Claude Duvalier was overthrown. He and his closest supporters fled into exile on a United States Air Force plane, marking the end of a family dynasty that had ruled for almost 30 years. The National Council of Government (CNG), a civilian-military junta headed by Lt. Gen. Henry Namphy, replaced Duvalier.

Duvalier's departure raised hopes that Haiti might emerge from decades of political and economic hopelessness and despair.[21] Those hopes began to fade, however, as the country drifted through a seemingly unending "transitional" period that at times trod perilously close to a return to dictatorship. Since the fall of Duvalier, Haiti has had a succession of short-term governments, each of them the product of either a coup d'état or an election whose validity was questionable at best. Between 1988 and January 1991 the following persons, in addition to Namphy, occupied the presidency: Leslie Manigat, Prosper Avril, Herard Abraham, and Ertha Pascal-Trouillot. Neither the government of Namphy nor any that succeeded him introduced major changes in either the structure of political power or the basis of economic power or public administration.[22] Furthermore, the overall human rights situation improved only marginally in the years after the fall of the Duvalier dynasty.

As the Inter-American Commission on Human Rights (IACHR) pointed out in 1988, "whether the military 'seized' power on February 7, 1986, as it claimed, or was placed in power by other forces, the CNG during its period in power demonstrated no vocation for democracy." The IACHR concluded that the military-led democratization process served, in fact, to consolidate its hold on power. Namphy, who proclaimed himself commander-in-chief of the armed forces in 1987, in open defiance of the provisions of the Constitution, "proclaimed himself President *sine die*, expelled the civilian President, suppressed the legislature, abrogated the 1987 Constitution, and, in effect, established a military dictatorship."[23]

The IACHR included in its 1988 report on Haiti an important—and at that time revolutionary—recommendation to the OAS General Assembly: that a timetable be established in order that free and fair elections could be held in Haiti, and that "the electoral process be made subject to international supervision in light of the traumatic experience of the November 29, 1987 elections."[24] The November 29, 1987 "experience" refers to the massacre of voters that took place on election day, and the CNG's decision to disband the Provisional Electoral Council, which put an end to the democratization process that ostensibly began immediately after the departure of Jean-Claude Duvalier.

## INTERNATIONAL SUPERVISION OF THE 1990 ELECTORAL PROCESS IN HAITI

The period leading up to the 1990 elections was marked by heightened political and social instability in Haiti. When the elections of November 1987 failed because of widespread violence, vandalism, and terror,[25] the OAS Permanent Council took note of the "deplorable acts of violence and disorder" and stated that all necessary measures must be adopted for the Haitian people to express their will through free elections, without any form of pressure or interference.[26]

Another election took place on January 17, 1988, but "numerous irregularities prevailed," according to the IACHR: the four major candidates for the presidency refused to participate, and three other candidates later joined them in the election boycott. Leslie Manigat won the election and took office on February 7, 1988, but on June 20 of that year was overthrown by a military coup and forced to leave the country. General Namphy immediately announced that he would govern by decree, and nullified the 1987 constitution. He also declared that no elections would take place until appropriate conditions had been established.[27]

Namphy was deposed by a military coup in September 1988 and Gen. Prosper Avril was installed as president. In March 1989 the constitution was partially put into effect by a decree that also ordered suspension of 36 articles regarded as "incompatible with the government of General Avril."[28]

After effectively resisting several coup attempts, Avril was forced to resign on March 10, 1990, and Gen. Herard Abraham temporarily took over the presidency. Three days later, Ertha Pascal-Trouillot, a judge of the Court of Cassation (Haiti's highest court), was sworn in as president.[29]

## The Elections of December 16, 1990

In February 1990 the OAS Permanent Council recommended that the Organization support the provisional government of Haiti in its efforts to hold elections and asked the secretary-general to establish an observer mission, should the government request OAS cooperation.[30] Shortly thereafter, the Haitian government expressed interest in having OAS assistance prior to the election and having the Organization's presence during the election; between March and May 1990, several OAS preparatory missions visited Haiti. In July the government approved an electoral law drafted by the Provisional Electoral Board (PEB) of Haiti.[31]

As provided in the agreement between the OAS and the Government of Haiti,[32] two OAS groups participated in the electoral process: observers and advisors. The function of the observers was to "follow the progress of each of the operations connected with the electoral process, to receive and forward to the competent authorities complaints concerning any irregularity brought to their attention, to ascertain the facts following receipt of complaints and to report their findings to the appropriate quarters." The role of the advisors was to "provide the PEB and each of its subordinate bodies with all the expertise and legal, professional, logistic and technical assistance required in the context of the preparation and implementation of the electoral process."[33]

Between October and December 16, 1990, the OAS group increased steadily, and by election day, it consisted of approximately 200 persons from 26 member states. Four days before the elections, the OAS secretary-general traveled to Haiti to head the OAS group that observed and verified the elections.[34]

The OAS teams of observers and advisors, as stated, performed functions that went beyond the mere ballot count. The same must also be said, of course, of the United Nations Observer Group for the Verification of the Elections in Haiti (ONUVEH), which the UN General Assembly established to monitor the elections. The ONUVEH mission included three groups: a group for electoral observation, composed of 39 international staff, with the addition of 154 observers at the time of the elections; a group for security observation, consisting of 64 security experts; and a group for administration. Teams of ONUVEH electoral observers and security observers were deployed throughout Haiti's nine departments. In addition, ONUVEH established a countrywide communications network.[35] Several countries and a significant number of nongovernmental organizations also helped oversee the election and verify that the electoral process was open, free, and fair. For example, the National Democratic Institute and the Council of Freely Elected Heads of Government sent a delegation, led by former U.S. President Jimmy Carter, who chairs that council.[36]

The question of whether the OAS monitoring of the electoral process could be considered impermissible in the absence of exceptional peacemaking requirements (as several governments argued in the UN General Assembly at the time the ONUVEH was established)[37] was never raised in the OAS. The probable reason is that the OAS monitoring took place at the request of the provisional government. Thus, the question of the Organization's interference in Haiti's domestic affairs was not at issue. With reference to the authority of a state to bind itself by agreement in relation to a question of domestic policy, the International Court of Justice had stated in 1986 that it could not find "within the range of subjects open to international agreement, any obstacle or provision to hinder a State from making a commitment of this kind."[38]

## THE ELECTION OF ARISTIDE

After nearly five years of political uncertainty, the internationally supervised elections held on December 16, 1990, produced the first democratically elected president in the history of Haiti. In a landslide victory, the Reverend Jean-Bertrand Aristide, backed by the Haitian masses, won 67 percent of the popular vote, overwhelming Marc Bazin, a moderate candidate alleged to have ties with the old Duvalier regime.[39] (Bazin became prime minister of the de facto government in 1992, some months after Aristide's overthrow.)

Despite Aristide's unequivocal mandate from the Haitian people, many doubted his ability to improve relations with the United States, the Haitian military, the upper classes, and the business community. Fears of a military coup were realized even before he could take office: on January 6, 1991, only three weeks after the election and one month before Aristide was to be inaugurated, a former interior minister under the Duvalier government and prominent leader of the Tontons Macoutes, Roger Lafontant, successfully engineered a bloodless military coup.[40] The next day, however, troops loyal to Aristide stormed the presidential palace and arrested Lafontant.

On February 7, 1991, Aristide was sworn in as Haiti's first democratically elected president. He advocated radical reforms in the socioeconomic structure of Haitian society and championed liberation theology.[41] But shortly after his election, an important faction in the coalition that had supported Aristide's presidential candidacy criticized him for having selected a close friend, Rene Preval, as prime minister.

In the first few months of his administration, President Aristide undertook several measures to assert civilian control over the military. The most important—and, in hindsight, perhaps ill-advised—was Aristide's retirement of Lt. Gen. Herard Abraham, commander-in-chief of the army. Abraham had earned domestic and international praise for his role in suppressing Lafontant's attempted coup. In his place, President Aristide appointed Brig. Gen. Raoul Cédras on July 3, 1991.

The following were among other measures President Aristide undertook: he had a list drawn up with the names of 162 persons who could not leave Haiti until their bank accounts had been checked, among them Ertha Pascal-Trouillot, the previous "provisional" president; he initiated efforts to recover some of

Duvalier's ill-gotten gains by filing lawsuits in France; to end the period of "popular justice" (*dechoukaj*) in Haiti, he convened a special government committee to investigate notorious human rights violations to bring to trial and punish those responsible; and he instituted trials against several well-known Macoute figures who had not managed to flee abroad.[42] Although the frequency of certain types of abuses diminished considerably under the Aristide government, international human rights groups continued to express concern over a number of issues related to detainees, political opponents of Aristide, and certain methods of interrogation and incarceration.[43]

Not surprisingly, traditionally entrenched groups that had always represented the power of wealth, privilege, and violence in Haiti—particularly the upper classes and the army—viewed Aristide's populist approach as a threat.

## THE COUP D'ETAT OF SEPTEMBER 30, 1991

On September 30, 1991, the Haitian military, led by General Cédras, seized power and displaced the government constitutionally elected by the people of Haiti just eight months earlier.[44] One of the reasons the leaders of the coup advanced to justify the overthrow of the elected government was that Aristide used his position to wage a virulent campaign against the National Assembly[45] and the armed forces. They provided, as evidence, copies of Aristide's speeches calling for the demise of politicians and military officers who opposed his programs.[46]

As Gonzalo Facio points out, "Against these arguments it can be asserted that a military coup is not the appropriate response to Aristide's alleged constitutional and human rights violations."[47] The Haitian constitution provides, indeed, the mechanisms and means to deal with any illegal action by a president, which is denunciation before the National Assembly and a request for impeachment.

On October 7 a "provisional" government was installed, purportedly in conformity with article 149 of the Haitian constitution, a peculiar legalism for a patently unconstitutional situation.[48]

## THE OAS AND UN RESPONSE TO THE COUP

Immediately after the coup, the OAS Permanent Council held an emergency meeting on September 30 and condemned the events that occurred in Haiti. The Council demanded adherence to the constitution and respect for the government legitimately established through the free expression of the popular will.[49]

The ad hoc Meeting of Consultation of Ministers of Foreign Affairs, which the Permanent Council convoked in response to the situation created by the coup, condemned the disruption of the democratic process in Haiti, calling it a violation of the Haitian people's right to self-determination. The ministers demanded "full restoration of the rule of law and of the constitutional regime, and the immediate reinstatement of President Jean-Bertrand Aristide in the exercise of his legitimate authority."[50]

The resolution the ministers of foreign affairs adopted also provided that the Organization would recognize as legitimate only representatives designated by the constitutional government of President Aristide, and that the OAS Inter-American Commission on Human Rights would immediately take all measures within its competence to protect and defend human rights in Haiti and to report thereon to the Permanent Council. Furthermore, the resolution recommended action to bring about the diplomatic isolation of those who held de facto power in Haiti, and the suspension, by all states, of their economic, financial, and commercial ties with Haiti, except aid for strictly humanitarian purposes. Although not without precedent,[51] this was undoubtedly the strongest resolution the OAS had adopted against any government.

When the de facto government of Haiti refused to comply with the OAS request that President Aristide be immediately reinstated, the Meeting of Consultation passed another resolution[52] on October 8, 1991, which strongly condemned the use of violence and military coercion, as well as the decision to illegally replace the constitutional president of Haiti.[53] The ministers also declared that "no government that may result from this illegal situation" would be accepted and that no representative of such a government would be recognized. In addition, the ministers agreed to President Aristide's request that "a civilian mission be constituted to reestablish and strengthen constitutional democracy in Haiti to facilitate the reestablishment and strengthening of democratic institutions, the full force and effect of the Constitution, respect for human rights of all Haitians, and to support the administration of justice and the adequate functioning of all the institutions that will make it possible to achieve these objectives . . ."[54] The civilian mission was entrusted with the very difficult task of negotiating with the military and political forces that either participated in or supported President Aristide's deposal, to work out a compromise to facilitate his return to power.

On October 10, 1991, the UN General Assembly "strongly condemn[ed] both the illegal replacement of the constitutional President of Haiti and the use of violence, military coercion and the violation of human rights" in Haiti, and urged UN member states "to consider the adoption of measures in keeping with those agreed on by the Organization of American States."[55]

On February 25, 1992, President Aristide, under the auspices of the OAS, signed an agreement with leaders of the Senate and of the Chamber of Deputies to install Rene Theodore as the new prime minister. The agreement, known as the Protocol of Washington, also provided for the eventual restoration of the Aristide government, the lifting of the economic sanctions the OAS had recommended in October 1991, and a general amnesty for the coup plotters. On March 27, 1992, the Court of Cassation ruled that the agreement was unconstitutional and could not be ratified by the parliament. Almost immediately, the OAS Permanent Council issued a declaration condemning the de facto government's failure to ratify the agreement and the invocation of "constitutionality by those who have violated the Constitution which they claim to defend."[56]

On May 17, 1992, the OAS ad hoc Meeting of Consultation of Foreign Ministers passed a resolution[57] that urged OAS member states "to adopt whatever actions may be necessary for the greater effectiveness of the measures referred to" in the ministers' earlier resolutions in response to the coup. This new resolution requested OAS member states to "deny access to port facilities to any vessel" that violates the embargo and to monitor compliance with the embargo. The resolution also urged states to deny visas to "perpetrators and supporters of the coup" and to freeze their assets. The foreign ministers stopped short, however, of considering a naval blockade to enforce the embargo, or a ban on commercial passenger flights to and from Haiti, as some had urged.[58]

In May 1992, the OAS General Assembly adopted an Argentine proposal to convene a special session before the end of 1992 to consider amendments to the OAS Charter to permit the Organization to exclude governments that violate political rights.[59]

Also in May 1992, the de facto government made public a "tripartite agreement for the formation of a government of consensus and public salvation for the consolidation of democracy." Neither President Aristide nor his political supporters, however, were invited to participate in it. Purportedly in compliance with the terms of the "agreement," on June 19, 1992, Marc Bazin was installed as Haiti's prime minister, over President Aristide's objections. The de facto president, Joseph Nerette, resigned from office with the swearing in of Bazin, as provided for in the "agreement."

In a resolution passed on December 13, 1992, the OAS ad hoc Meeting of Consultation of Ministers of Foreign Affairs urged any members of the OAS and of the UN that had not done so to take the necessary steps to implement fully the measures agreed upon within the framework of the OAS.[60] By the end of 1992, it seemed that OAS efforts were exhausted and a new approach would be necessary. The locus of activity shifted to the UN, which had previously maintained a low profile and had done little beyond lending moral support to the endeavors of the OAS.

On December 11, 1992, the UN secretary-general appointed Dante Caputo, a former minister of foreign affairs of Argentina and once president of the UN General Assembly, as his special representative for Haiti.[61] Thereafter, the UN, working through the secretary-general's special representative and in coordination with the OAS and the U.S. government, took the lead in an initiative to work with the interested Haitian parties to restore democracy in that country. This shift to the UN forum was prompted, at least in part, by the prospect of a massive influx of refugees, which drew high-level attention to Haiti's crisis in early January 1993, both from the outgoing Bush administration and from President-elect Bill Clinton.[62]

On January 13, 1993, in remarks before the OAS Permanent Council, U.S. Ambassador Luigi Einaudi described the new shape of the initiative, which he said was "built on three pillars that [had] emerged clearly over the past month":

- Internationally, a new pattern of coordination between the OAS and the UN, in which are combined the special strengths of regional sensitivity and global power

- In Haiti, a desire among the most varied of sectors to put an end to this tragic crisis

- In the United States, close cooperation in the national interest between incoming and outgoing administrations of different political parties.[63]

## COLLECTIVE INVOLVEMENT THROUGH COERCIVE MEANS: ECONOMIC SANCTIONS AND FORCIBLE INTERVENTION

This section will analyze the extent to which the OAS as a regional organization is empowered to impose sanctions of a forcible and nonforcible nature. It also touches upon the authority of the OAS vis-à-vis that of the UN Security Council in respect to matters not covered under chapter VII of the UN Charter.

### Economic Sanctions

The economic measures the OAS imposed against Haiti were intended to compel the illegitimate government to restore power to the lawfully elected authorities. Thus they were an application of compulsory or coercive means vis-à-vis Haiti. Yet in relation to the members of the OAS, the action was recommendatory.

Whether the OAS is entitled to determine that the economic sanctions against Haiti will be *compulsory* on OAS members other than Haiti (rather than recommendatory) is, from a legalistic-mechanistic standpoint, doubtful. The OAS Charter contains no provision whatsoever with reference to enforcement measures by the Organization. It is, on the other hand, rather specific regarding the prohibition of any action of an enforcement nature, whether against a single state or a group of states.[64] Moreover, under article 53 of the UN Charter, regional arrangements are not empowered to apply measures of an enforcement nature without the authorization of the Security Council.

Nevertheless, the OAS did apply *compulsory* diplomatic and economic measures against the Dominican Republic in 1960.[65] In January 1962 it excluded the government of Cuba from participation in the OAS[66] and resolved that its members were to suspend all trade in arms with that government. In 1964 the Organization again authorized its members to apply additional measures against Cuba.[67] In each of these cases several members of the OAS argued that the concept of enforcement measures applied only to the use of force as contemplated in article 42 of the UN Charter and did not, therefore, apply to the measures provided for in article 41, which fall short of the use of armed force.[68]

In practice, whether the OAS labels the sanctions compulsory or recommendatory in nature is irrelevant. The plain fact is that the OAS has no institutional means to "enforce" compulsory measures; in other words, there are no sanctions against states that do not comply, particularly when the noncompliant state is either the most powerful or among the most powerful members of the Organization. For example, Mexico's refusal to comply with the compulsory sanctions against Cuba did not elicit any reaction.

The lack of authority on the part of the OAS to compel its members to participate in a trade embargo was one factor in a situation of significant noncompliance with the embargo against Haiti. Equally important is the absence of any authority to require states outside the OAS to join in the embargo. Thus, it was not as effective a measure as it might have been had the OAS had the means to enforce compliance on the part of its members, and the means to seek compliance and cooperation of states outside the hemisphere.

Documents assembled by the General Accounting Office (GAO) indicate that at least a dozen countries in Europe, Latin

America, and Africa "routinely ignored the embargo" and detail "the shipment of nearly a million barrels of petroleum to Haiti from France, Colombia, Portugal, Senegal, and the Netherlands Antilles." [69]

While the United States sponsored the economic embargo,[70] on February 4, 1992, Washington modified its policy after it became clear that U.S. businesses with interests or operations in Haiti would sustain severe losses were the embargo to continue. As a result, the administration announced a number of exemptions (on a case-by-case basis) for the Haitian assembly sector. Under these exemptions the Treasury Department was authorized to grant licenses to individuals and companies operating in the assembly sector in Haiti, and to permit export of materials manufactured in the United States, assembly of the finished product in Haiti, and its importation back into the United States.[71] The decision to modify the policy was also justified as necessary to reduce the exodus of Haitian refugees to the United States.[72]

These loopholes in the OAS embargo give rise to the question whether the embargo could have been rendered more effective through an exercise of the UN Security Council's compulsory powers under chapter VII of the UN Charter. The Security Council could hardly be expected to require all members of the UN to comply with an embargo or other compulsory measures approved by the OAS. The same is not true, however, of sanctions approved by the Security Council. As Professor Thomas Franck points out, "The international community long has asserted, in the case of South Africa, a right of all states to take hortatory, economic and—in extreme cases—even military action to enforce aspects of the democratic entitlement, but only when duly authorized by the United Nations" [73]

The obstacles to an invocation by the Security Council of its chapter VII powers are partly political. It should also be noted, however, that several important Council members (especially China, which can veto any Council resolution) object to the application of enforcement measures in what they view as an essentially domestic situation. This objection reflects the continuing view of many governments that the UN Charter does not authorize the Security Council to act as enforcer of democracy or human rights in the absence of a more direct threat to international peace and security than they perceive in the Haitian case (though the Council overcame these qualms by summer 1993).

Of course, from the beginning the OAS and the UN could have considered other nonforcible measures. The OAS has amended its Charter to authorize suspension of any member state whose democratically constituted government has been overthrown by force. This measure could have been matched by others, such as the suspension of bilateral diplomatic relations; the freezing of all state assets; suspension of access to financial institutions such as the Inter-American Development Bank, the World Bank, and the International Monetary Fund; and the suspension of sea and air links and, in general, more effective economic sanctions calculated to take as heavy a toll as possible on the illegitimate government, while minimizing the adverse effect on the population.

In view of the legal issues discussed above, approval of such measures by either OAS or UN decision would have increased the pressure on the Haitian de facto authorities, but it is doubtful that either the regional or the global organization could do much to compel unwilling states to abide by such measures.

## Forcible Intervention

Perhaps the most important issue is the specification of the conditions under which forcible action in support of a democratically elected government should be considered justified. Franck's view is "that all states [should] unambiguously remove the use of unilateral, or even regional, military force to compel compliance with the democratic entitlement" in the absence of prior authorization by the UN Security Council.

Franck has summarized the view that the implementation of measures must be the prerogative not of individual states but of organizations such as the UN as follows:

> The international community may only invoke collective enforcement measures such as sanctions, blockade or military intervention in limited circumstances—as when the Security Council finds that it is not engaging in the enforcement *against* a member but is acting at the request of a legitimate government against a usurper. These prerequisite determinations, however, must be made by the ap-

propriate collective machinery of the [international] community and not by individual members.[74]

Using Franck's reasoning, collective forcible action in the case of Haiti would have been permissible had it been requested by President Aristide—whom the OAS considers the only "legitimate authority" in that country—provided that the UN Security Council authorized it. It is unclear, however, whether a de jure government that has only formal but not *actual* power may invite foreign "military intervention" for the purpose of removing the de facto regime.

This writer shares Franck's distaste for unilateralism. Some governments in the Western Hemisphere, particularly those most sensitive to the issue of sovereignty, would likely resist collective armed intervention to vindicate gross violations of human and political rights and the right to representative democracy. Nevertheless, if all nonforcible measures fail, recourse to collective armed intervention will be the only effective alternative.

As to the plausibility of collective military intervention by a regional organization to restore democracy when other measures have failed, no consensus exists among the members of the OAS to undertake an action of that nature. In the opinion of this writer, any effort to build support in that direction would, unfortunately, appear premature. The prime minister of Canada has proposed a naval blockade around Haiti by Canada, the United States, France, Venezuela, and others to bring down Haiti's military dictatorship.[75] This proposal elicited little or no support elsewhere in the hemisphere.

Regarding institutional enforcement, Professor W. Michael Reisman notes that "the given of contemporary international decision making is the absence of such institutions and the need to focus on regulating unilateral decision making." He then eloquently argues that "because rights without remedies are not rights at all, prohibiting the unilateral vindication of clear violations of rights when multilateral possibilities do not obtain is virtually to terminate those rights."[76] While this approach may, in the abstract, appear plausible, as a generic standard it is seriously flawed.

The arguments against unilateral military intervention are indeed compelling. The right to invade a sovereign state with military forces is extremely limited. At the present time there simply is no generally accepted international practice or norm of international law that affords one state the right to intervene merely on the basis of the perceived political or legal illegitimacy of another government.[77] Even if, as in the case of Haiti, the international community has unequivocally established the illegitimacy of the de facto government, international law lacks any explicit set of principles or rules authorizing that government's removal by a unilateral act of force. Moreover, unilateral military action "to protect democratic governments" might, in some cases, be used as a pretext to accomplish objectives that might not necessarily represent a true commitment to either democracy or the right of self-determination. In fact, recent cases demonstrate that unilateral action is often undertaken when some other parallel interest provides the necessary political will for a state to act.[78] On the other hand, many governments could be understandably reluctant to intervene unilaterally in another country for the sole purpose of vindicating human and political rights or the right to representative democracy.

## COLLECTIVE INVOLVEMENT IN THE HAITIAN CRISIS: AN ANALYSIS

At the center of the entire debate with regard to collective—and, of course, unilateral—action by states is the question of state sovereignty, which should be interfered with only in the most extreme circumstances, if even then. The traditional state-centric notion of sovereignty is evolving into a concept based on the will of the people.[79] This view was eloquently summarized as "*de facto* power [that] has been transformed into legal power founded on the idea of juris consensus."[80]

Human rights and, at least in the Western Hemisphere, the international protection of democracy, have been the primary beneficiaries of that transformation.[81] It is, in effect, becoming gradually permissible to consider the denial of a "population's right to participate democratically in the process of governance" in a similar light as governments responsible for gross domestic human rights abuses. Nowhere is this gradual recognition more evident than in the inter-American system, particularly if—as in the cases of Panama and Haiti—international monitoring and supervision of a free electoral process produces a clear indication of the sovereign choice of the people.[82]

In the past, authoritarian regimes that would otherwise have enjoyed no legitimacy among the people they purported to govern, and that retained power only through a pervasive infrastructure of internal coercion and intimidation, were often shielded against collective action by an extremely narrow interpretation of the principle of nonintervention, as happened in the case of the Panamanian government under Manuel Noriega.

For the members of the OAS, the notion that the illegal replacement of a democratically elected government is still a matter essentially within the domestic jurisdiction of its member states, and thus immune from international scrutiny, is no longer the axiomatic precept it once was, as recent practice unequivocally shows: the OAS dealt with the coup in Suriname in December 1990, the attempted coup in Venezuela in February 1992, and the so-called autogolpe by the constitutional president of Peru in April 1992 and of Guatemala in May 1993.[83]

The approval, in June 1991, of the Santiago Commitment to Democracy and the Renewal of the Inter-American System and the accompanying resolution on representative democracy reaffirmed the OAS membership's concern with effective exercise of representative democracy.

Self-interest on the part of the elected governments undoubtedly played an important part in the shift of the majority of OAS members from staunch anti-interventionism to an appreciation of the advantages that collective action in defense of democracy could afford. For the first time, an international organization has explicitly ruled that governments shall be held internationally accountable to the regional community for the means by which they have taken and secured power.

Obviously these pronouncements, resting as they do on resolutions of the OAS General Assembly, lack the normative quality of a treaty. They are, nevertheless, clear evidence of a consensus within the inter-American community that the protection of democracy should be gradually regulated.

Both the Santiago Commitment and the accompanying resolution could be regarded as part of the subsets of what Franck characterizes as the emerging "international democratic order."[84] In his view, the fundamental notions of "democratic entitlement"[85] and what he described as "a prescient glimpse of the legitimating power of the community of nations" are rapidly becoming "a normative rule of the international system."

Basically, Franck envisions an international community in which representative democracy is an essential condition for legitimacy and is inextricably linked to human and political rights. As he puts it, "The symbiotic linkage among democracy, human rights and peace is now widely recognized."[86]

From that perspective, democracy is the fundamental, irreducible common denominator from which all other basic individual rights flow. The logical extension of this argument is that the promotion and protection of human rights can be effective only within the confines of the democratic and representative system of government. Conversely, it could also be argued that human rights are the fundamental common denominator from which democracy flows, as the form of government that best ensures the protection of those rights. Professor Fernando Tesón asserts that "the rights of states derive from human rights," and therefore "a government that engages in substantial violations of human rights betrays the very purpose for which it exists and so forfeits not only its domestic legitimacy but its international legitimacy as well."[87]

The question of "the emergence of democracy as a global normative entitlement" involves several collateral issues that deserve far more consideration than can be given by this chapter.[88] Among them is the need to determine first what constitutes a legitimate government. There is a simplistic tendency to equate elected governments with democratic ones. While fair and free elections are a necessary condition and a key part of democracy, as Thomas Carothers observes, they "are undeterminative of democracy."[89]

Next is the suggestion that a neutral multilateral normative regime should be established to authorize and supervise collective action if and when such action is deemed necessary. Reisman advanced this view; for him, "the most satisfactory solution to this question is the creation of centralized institutions, equipped with decision-making authority and the capacity to make it effective."[90]

It is noteworthy, nevertheless, that many of Franck's observations and ideas are particularly relevant to the Haitian crisis. For example, by placing the right of self-determination at the core of democracy and then linking that right with the other two components of democratic entitlement (freedom of expression and electoral rights), Franck portrays the ongoing stalemate in Haiti as a denial of the normative entitlement to democracy. Under this norm, the de facto government of Haiti would be both domestically and internationally illegitimate and subject, therefore, to international action.

Equally important is the suggestion that monitoring of internal elections should be established as a "systemwide" obligation "owed by each government to its own people and to the other States of the global community."[91]

## CONCLUSION

The OAS—although usually depicted as an organization with no enforcement mechanisms and with a long record of avoiding direct confrontation[92]—has been resolute in its efforts to restore the deposed president of Haiti by imposing nonforcible measures against the military junta that illegally seized power there. More than two years later, however, that strategy has not yet succeeded. Worse still, the economic sanctions have had a crushing impact on the poorest Haitians (paradoxically, those who most enthusiastically support President Aristide), rather than on the perpetrators and supporters of the coup. As a result, the political and human rights situations that the OAS measures were intended to vindicate have deteriorated even further.[93]

Haiti's case seems to suggest, therefore, that across-the-board nonforcible measures could be useful against an illegitimate regime in a limited range of situations; in addition, it demonstrates the shortcomings of the regional institutional mechanisms of enforcement available in this particular case. As the permanent representative of Chile to the OAS pointed out: "One important lesson from Haiti will be that we need to improve the efficiency of our instruments and actions on behalf of democracy, while still respecting international law." [94]

The failure of the political organ of the OAS to resolve the Panamanian crisis (before the U.S. invasion) and the Haitian crisis (for at least two years) lends support to the view that as a regional organization, the OAS is devoted first and foremost to the protection of sovereignty against external threats; it is, however, far less effective in protecting democracy.

It would appear, therefore, that if regional action to protect political rights and democracy is to be more effective, both the enforcement mechanisms and the selectivity of the measures, as the Haitian case shows, need to improve procedurally and substantively.

The UN's active involvement, strongly supported by the United States, provides an unusual opportunity to find a solution to the Haitian crisis. As the Reverend Jesse Jackson pointed out during a visit to Haiti: "If real pressure is applied, and the United States and the United Nations express their resolve fully and totally, the issue will become the exodus of the coup leaders and not the exodus of the people who fear them." [95]

After intensive international pressure and shuttle diplomacy between Washington and Port-au-Prince by UN mediators, in mid-April 1993 a settlement was reportedly reached calling for Father Aristide's return to power, the removal of those army officers involved in the coup, and a program to rebuild the country. At the last minute, however, the army's commander, Lt. Gen. Raoul Cédras, apparently backed away from the settlement. [96]

With negotiations at an impasse, President Clinton announced application of additional U.S. sanctions against Haiti's military leaders, other members of government, and prominent members of the business community. The president explained that, "In light of their own failure to act constructively, I have determined that the time has come to increase the pressure on the Haitian military, the de facto regime in Haiti, and their supporters."[97]

Then, on June 16, the UN Security Council imposed a worldwide ban on shipments of oil and arms to Haiti and the "freezing of Haitain assets."[98]

The heightened U.S. and UN pressure on the de facto government brought the parties back to the negotiating table. On July 3, 1993, Lt. Gen. Raoul Cédras and President Aristide signed an agreement to restore the latter to power by October 30, 1993. The resounding support that the nonforcible measures won in the UN Security Council undoubtedly sent a very clear message to the de facto Haitain authorities. Perhaps even more persuasive in getting them to negotiate in earnest was the specter of the forcible measures that the international community could have authorized against them had the nonforcible measure been ineffective.

## NOTES

1. See Gregory H. Fox, "The Right to Political Participation in International Law," *Yale Journal of International Law*, vol. 17, no. 2 (1992), p. 609.
2. At the same time, however, democratic governments in Latin America in the past were often toppled by coups d'état, and many countries in the region lived for years under a variety of oppressive, authoritarian regimes. Margaret Ball has noted that "to preach democracy without otherwise supporting it was to engage in empty oratory. Self-determination, in an absolute sense, could justify dictatorship—so long as it was popularly based—just as readily as democracy. And nonintervention—again in an absolute sense—could prevent the organization [the OAS] from ever enforcing any decision in the face of member opposition, up to and including decisions which the members had previously agreed should be enforced." See *The OAS in Transition* (Durham, N.C.: Duke University Press, 1969), p. 485. On this subject see also Dinah Shelton, "Representative Democracy and Human Rights in the Western Hemisphere," *Human Rights Law Journal*, vol. 12, no. 10 (1991), pp. 353–359.
3. See Shelton, "Representative Democracy," p. 359.
4. See Gonzalo Facio, *The Haitian Crisis Is Testing the Democratic Will of the OAS*, Special Report (Council for Inter-American Security Foundation, 1992), p. 2.
5. See resolution I, Declaration of Santiago de Chile, on Representative Democracy, OEA/Ser.F/III.5, August 18, 1959, p. 301 (Spanish version).
6. Resolution II, OEA/Ser.F/II.17, doc. 49/79, rev. 2, June 23, 1979.

7. See resolution I, The Serious Crisis of Panama in Its International Context, OEA/Ser.F/II.21, doc. 8/89, rev. 2, May 17, 1989.

8. For example, on June 26, 1954, ten members of the OAS requested that a Meeting of Consultation be convened to consider the danger to the peace and security of the hemisphere and to agree upon measures in view of the "demonstrated intervention of the international communist movement in the Republic of Guatemala." See OAS General Secretariat, *The Inter-American Treaty of Reciprocal Assistance: Applications, 1948–1956* (Washington, D.C.: 1973), p. 165.

9. David Nicholls, *From Dessalines to Duvalier: Race, Color and National Independence in Haiti* (Cambridge: Cambridge University Press, 1979), p. 3.

10. Ibid., p. 5. According to Nicholls, racial prejudice and the fear of similar revolts were essentially responsible for the refusal of the United States to recognize Haitian independence until 1862.

11. See Anthony P. Maingot "Sovereign Consent vs. Statecentric Sovereignty: The Haitian Case." Paper for the Inter-American Dialogue meeting on Reconstructing Sovereignty in a Democratic Age (April 1993), p.6.

12. One commentator has written: "In a society with few functioning civil institutions, the army rapidly became the pivotal power broker, installing and toppling presidents regularly after the Marines departed." See Lee Hockstader, "Haitians Look for U.S. Hand in Whatever Befalls Their Nation," *Washington Post*, June 17, 1992, p. A23.

13. See "Electoral Assistance to Haiti," UN doc. A/45/870, p. 9. Since independence, Haiti has had over 20 constitutions and has always been governed by authoritarian rulers, including two emperors and a king.

14. As John Canham-Clyne noted, "under the U.S.-backed family dictatorship of François 'Papa Doc' Duvalier and Jean-Claude 'Baby Doc' Duvalier, Haiti was plagued by military intimidation, political corruption, and elite control of national resources." See "Haiti after the Coup," *World Policy Journal*, vol. IX, no. 2 (Spring 1992), p. 349.

15. See Nicholls, *From Dessalines to Duvalier*, p. 215.

16. Ibid., pp. 215–216 and 237.

17. For example, he invited the U.S. Marine Corps mission to train the Haitian forces and made frequent remonstrations against communism, thus portraying himself as being on the side of the free world. Ibid., p. 216.

18. See Inter-American Commission on Human Rights (IACHR), "Report on the Situation of Human Rights in Haiti," doc. OEA/Ser. L/V/II.74, doc. 9 rev. 1, September 7, 1988, p. 29. The title "president for life" did not originate with François Duvalier. It was introduced in the 1807 constitution, which made Henry Christophe Haiti's first president-for-life. Prior to 1964, the institution of a presidency for life had last appeared in the constitution of 1846.

19. Ibid.

20. Ibid., p. 37. Thomas Carothers observes that "the Reagan Administration saw Jean-Claude Duvalier as a net positive—although he was a corrupt, repressive, and inept leader, he was firmly anticommunist and pro-United States." See *In the Name of Democracy: U.S. Policy toward Latin America in the Reagan Years* (Berkeley: University of California Press, 1991), p. 183.

21. Haiti has long been desperately poor; approximately 80 percent of Haitians earn less than U.S. $100 annually and live, therefore, "far below the critical poverty level of US$150 per year." Some 78 percent of the people are illiterate. See "First Report of the United Nations Observer Group for the Verification of Elections in Haiti," in "Electoral Assistance to Haiti," UN doc. A/45/870, December, 14, 1990, p. 9.

22. Ibid., p. 10.

23. See IACHR, "Report on the Situation of Human Rights in Haiti," p. 105.

24. Ibid., p. 193.

25. On December 4, 1987, seven Catholic bishops condemned as "atrocities" the violent crimes that had led to the cancellation of the November 29 elections. Ibid., p. 86.

26. See resolution CP/RES. 489 (720/87), December 7, 1987.

27. See IACHR, "Report on the Situation of Human Rights in Haiti," p. 14.

28. Ibid., p. 15.

29. Ibid., p. 21.

30. See resolution CP/RES. 537 (805/90), February 23, 1990. The OAS General Assembly confirmed this resolution through resolution AG/RES. 1048 (XX-0/90), adopted in June 1990.

31. See "Report of the Secretary General on the Organization's Support for the Electoral Process in Haiti," OAS document AG/doc. 2671/91, April 29, 1991, p. 3.

32. See, "Accord Entre le Gouvernement de la Republique d'Haiti et le Secretaire General de l'Organisation des Etats Americains sur les Privileges et Immunites Accordes au Groupe de Conseillers et d'Observateurs du Processus Electoral en Haiti," in OEA/Ser.G CP/doc.2108/90, September 25, 1990, p. 5.

33. Ibid., p. 6.

34. On January 20, 1991, a second round of elections took place, this one to decide the political majority in the Haitian parliament, from which the prime minister would be elected, in accordance with the constitution. Several OAS observers remained in Haiti after the December 16 elections, and the number was increased to 48 for the second round. These observers came from eleven countries, and most of them spent one week in Haiti. See "Report of the Secretary General," p. 17.

35. See "United Nations Electoral Assistance to Haiti," UN Department of Public Information, DPI/1120-91-40244, March 1991.

36. See 1991: A Year in Review (Washington, D.C.: National Democratic Institute for International Affairs, 1991), p. 18.

37. See Thomas Franck, "The Emerging Right to Democratic Governance," American Journal of International Law, vol. 86, no. 1 (1992), p. 81.

38. See "Military and Paramilitary Activities in and against Nicaragua (Nicaragua v. United States of America), Merits, Judgment," ICJ Reports 1986, p. 131 (para. 259).

39. See Howard W. French, "Haitians Overwhelmingly Elect Populist Priest to the Presidency," New York Times, December 18, 1990, p. A1.

40. See H.W. French, "Former Chief of Duvalier's Militia Claims Power after Coup in Haiti," New York Times, January 7, 1992, p. A1. The coup,

needless to say, was engineered to prevent Aristide from taking office. Lafontant was subsequently sentenced to life in prison and was murdered in his cell in circumstances that are still unclear. See "Restoring Haiti's Democracy," *Washington Post*, October 6, 1992, p. C6.

41. See H.W. French, "Haiti Leader Faces Task of Controlling Military," *New York Times*, December 20, 1990, p. 18. See also "Mobilizing Resources for Development: A Retrospect on President Aristide's Economic Strategy for Haiti and His Administration's Record with Aid Donors," *International Policy Update*, vol. 1 (April 1992), p. 3.

42. See Cristina Cerna, "The Case of Haiti before the Organization of American States," in the *Proceedings of the 86th Annual Meeting of American Society of International Law* (1992).

43. See Amnesty International, "Haiti: Human Rights Violations in the Aftermath of the Coup d'Etat" (London, October 3, 1991). In a June 1992 meeting between American human rights experts and Aristide in Miami, a participant cited a speech the deposed president made to Haitian students in which he "praised the presence of a mob armed with gasoline and tires—which are often used in the vigilante justice Father Aristide's critics have suggested he condoned—outside a courthouse where a notorious former Interior Minister [Lafontant] was on trial." See Howard W. French, "Meetings with Aristide Emphasize Human Rights," *New York Times*, June 7, 1992, p. A3.

In January 1993 the *New York Times* reported that "in recent weeks, senior American officials have said that in addition to the troubling remarks of the populist President during his seven-month tenure, they are now convinced, bolstered by an F.B.I. investigation *[sic]* of the matter, that Father Aristide personally ordered the killing in prison of one of his most bitter opponents, Roger Lafontant, while the coup was under way. Father Aristide's supporters deny this." See Howard W. French, "Visiting U.S. General Warns Haiti's Military Chiefs," *New York Times*, January 9, 1993, p. 5.

The unconfirmed FBI "investigation" and a subsequent column in the *Washington Post* accusing Father Aristide of abuses have been described as "part of a campaign of disinformation by his opponents to forestall American action to restore him to power." See Steven A. Holmes, "U.S. Seeks to Bar Retaliation if Haitian Is Restored," *New York Times*, January 28, 1993, p. A11. See also Lally Weymouth, "Haiti's Suspect Savior: Why President Aristide's Return from Exile May Not Be Good News," *Washington Post*, January 24, 1993, p. C2.

44. It is debatable whether Cédras actually led the coup or simply emerged later as its leader. Some observers have suggested that the coup was instigated from within the army rank and file, and not from the top of the military hierarchy. See, for example, John M. Goshko, "Proposal for Aristide's Return Stalls; OAS Efforts Continue after Haiti's Communist Leader Skips Meeting," *Washington Post*, January 21, 1992, p. A15.

45. Aristide indeed sought to bypass the National Assembly by refusing to submit to it appointments of Court of Cassation judges, cabinet members, and ambassadorial nominations, as provided for in the 1987 constitution.

When the National Assembly began to consider a vote of no confidence in Prime Minister Preval, a mob of "at least two thousand Aristide supporters surrounded the National Assembly on August 13, roughing up two deputies and threatening to burn others alive" if they moved ahead with the motion against Preval. A crowd of Aristide's supporters also attacked a senator's home, and a group armed with used tires and gasoline threatened a deputy of the National Assembly with the *surplice de Père Lebrun*, or "necklacing" (burning alive). See Howard W. French, "Ex-Backers of Ousted Haitian Say He Alienated His Allies," *New York Times International*, October 22, 1991, p. A10.

46. See Facio, *The Haitian Crisis*, p. 6.
47. Ibid.
48. A former member of the Court of Cassation, Joseph Nerette, was appointed president and Jean Jacques Honorat, head of the Centre Haitien des Droits et Libertés Publiques (CHADEL)—a nongovernmental human rights organization—was appointed provisional prime minister.
49. See "Support of the Democratic Government of Haiti," CP/RES. 567 (870/91), September 30, 1991.
50. See "Support of the Democratic Government of Haiti," resolution MRE/RES. 1/91, doc. OEA/Ser.F/V.1, October 3, 1991 (operative para. 1).
51. As stated above, in June 1979, the Seventeenth Meeting of Consultation adopted a resolution calling for the "immediate and definitive replacement of the Somoza regime" and declared that government to be "the fundamental cause" of the turmoil in Nicaragua. For a good analysis of this issue, see Cristina Cerna, "Human Rights in Conflict with the Principle of Non-intervention: The Case of Nicaragua before the Seventeenth Meeting of Consultation of Ministers of Foreign Affairs," in *Human Rights in the Americas* (1984), p. 93.
52. See "Support for Democracy in Haiti," resolution MRE/RES.2/91, October 8, 1991.
53. That is, as mentioned, the appointment of Joseph Nerette as president and Jean Jacques Honorat as provisional prime minister.
54. See Request from the President of the Republic of Haiti to the Secretary General of the OAS, doc. MRE/doc.3/91, October 7, 1991.
55. See Crisis of Democracy and Human Rights in Haiti, resolution 46/7, October 11, 1991. On December 17, 1991, and December 2, 1992, the General Assembly passed resolutions concerning the condition of human rights in Haiti. See resolution 46/138 and doc. A/C.3/47/L.73.
56. See OAS doc. CP/SA/896/92 and CP/doc. 2248/92, April 1, 1992.
57. See Restoration of Democracy in Haiti, resolution MRE/RES. 3/92, May 17, 1992.
58. See, for example, David W. Dent, "Haiti Could Become a Pawn in U.S. Politics," *Christian Science Monitor*, March 3, 1992, p. 19; "A Military Force for the Americas," *New York Times*, March 24, 1992, p. A30; and Barbara Crossette, "U.S. Is Discussing an Outside Force to Stabilize Haiti," *New York Times*, June 6, 1992, p. A1.

One commentator suggested that "if the OAS succeeds, the next step should be a permanent collective-security mechanism to defend all Western

Hemisphere democracies. The OAS needs to make it clear that comparable economic and diplomatic sanctions, and collective military action as a last resort, could be repeated automatically if democracy is toppled, whether in large or small countries, such as Argentina and Guatemala, which have suffered military coups in the past." See Robert Pastor, "Haiti Is Not Alone," *New York Times*, October 4, 1991, p. A31. Perhaps a more precise term for this mechanism would be "collective defense," as suggested by, among others, the Inter-American Dialogue in its report *Convergence and Community: The Americas in 1993* (Washington, D.C., 1993).

59. On December 14, 1992, a special session of the OAS General Assembly adopted a new Charter provision, stating that a member of the OAS whose "democratically constituted government has been overthrown by force may be suspended from the exercise of its right to participate in the meetings of the General Assembly" and in the meetings of several other OAS bodies. See Texts Approved by the General Assembly at Its Sixteenth Special Session in Connection with the Amendments to the Charter of the Organization, doc. OEA/Ser.P/AG/doc.11 (XVI-E/92), December 14, 1992. The amendments will enter into force when two-thirds of OAS members have deposited their instruments of ratification.

60. See Reinstatement of Democracy in Haiti, resolution MRE/RES. 4/92, December 13, 1992.

61. On December 21, Agence France Presse reported that the secretary general of the OAS had objected to "the involvement of 'other organizations' in the settlement of the Haitian crisis." Reproduced in OAS Department of Public Information, *Boletín de Noticias*, December 22, 1992, p. 2. However, in early January 1993 he announced that he had asked Caputo to serve as his representative, as well.

    The UN initiative includes mediation efforts intended to get both sides (Aristide and the de facto government) to agree, in principle, "to end human rights abuses and to start negotiations on issues like de-politicizing the armed forces and rebuilding Haiti's shattered economy." See Steven A. Holmes, "Bush and Clinton Aides Link Policies in Haiti," *New York Times*, January 7, 1993, p. A10.

62. In this connection, the *New York Times* reported: "This attention, coming on top of the recent decision by the United Nations to supplement an ineffective Organization of American States as a broker here, appears to have brought a level of urgency to the situation that for the first time in months has raised hopes for an early solution. See Howard W. French, "Visiting U.S. General Warns Haiti's Military Chiefs," *New York Times*, January 9, 1993, p. 5.

    In mid-January 1993 the U.S. Coast Guard began to deploy large cutters, patrol boats, and at least a dozen aircraft to the international waters north of Haiti to block an expected wave of refugees seeking to reach the United States. The deployment, according to U.S. officials, was ordered by the outgoing administration in consultation with President-elect Bill Clinton. It was intended, in part at least, to lend credence to Clinton's announcement on January 14, 1993, that he would continue the Bush policy of returning Haitian boat people, thereby temporarily abandoning a campaign pledge to discontinue the policy of intercepting Haitian boat people on the high seas. See Howard W. French, "Haitians Express Sense of Betrayal," *New York Times*, January 17, 1993, p. 3. See also Steven A. Holmes, "U.S. Sends Flotilla to Prevent Exodus from Haiti by Sea," *New York Times*, January 16, 1993, p. 1. For a criticism of Clinton's reversal, see "For Haitians, Cruelty and Hope," *New York Times*, January 17, 1993, p. 16.

63. Luigi R. Einaudi, "New Hope for Haiti," remarks before OAS Permanent Council, January 13, 1993.

64. For example, article 18 provides: "No State or group of States has the right to intervene, directly or indirectly, for any reason whatever, in the internal or external affairs of any other State. The foregoing principle prohibits not only armed force but also any other form of interference or attempted threat against the personality of the State or against its political, economic, and cultural elements."

   With regard to coercive measures, article 19 stipulates: "No State may use or encourage the use of coercive measures of an economic or political character in order to force the sovereign will of another State and obtain from it advantages of any kind."

65. See Sixth Meeting of Consultation of Ministers of Foreign Affairs, resolution I, in Final Act, doc. OEA/Ser. C/II.6, (1960), pp. 4–6.

66. See Eighth Meeting of Consultation of Ministers of Foreign Affairs, resolution 6, in Final Act, doc. OEA/Ser.C/II.8 (1962), pp. 12–14.

67. See Ninth Meeting of Consultation of Ministers of Foreign Affairs, resolution 1, in Final Act, doc. OEA/Ser.C/II.9 (1964), pp. 5–6.

68. Members of the OAS defended this questionable argument first in September 1960, when the Security Council considered the Dominican case, and on several occasions thereafter. See UN Security Council Records, Fifteenth Year, 893rd, 894th, and 895th Meetings, September 8–9, 1960. See also doc. S/4484, September 8, 1960.

69. See "Countries Ignore Haiti Embargo," *New York Times*, May 31, 1992, p. 3. The documents, assembled in May 1992 by the GAO, were made available to the author by the office of Senator Edward Kennedy.

70. At the ad hoc Meeting of Consultation of Ministers of Foreign Affairs of the OAS on October 2, 1991, Secretary of State James Baker stated that the Haitian junta was "illegitimate" and that "it is imperative that we agree—for the sake of Haitian democracy and the cause of democracy throughout the hemisphere—to act collectively to defend the legitimate government of President Aristide. Words alone are not going to suffice. This is a time for collective action." See OEA/Ser.F/V.1, MRE/ACTA 1/91, October 2, 1991, p. 17.

71. See OAS document CP/INF, 3231/92. See also Al Kamen and John M. Goshko, "U.S. Plans to Ease Embargo on Haiti; OAS Chief Expresses Caution," *Washington Post*, February 5, 1992, p. A1; and Kamen and Goshko, "U.S. Eased Haiti Embargo under Business Pressure; Abrams Pressed Jobs Issue with State Department," *Washington Post*, February 7, 1991, p. A1. On December 22, 1992, the Mexican news agency Noticias Mexicanas reported that trade between the United States and Haiti was in

excess of $140 million during the first seven months of 1992. Reproduced in OAS Department of Public Information, *Boletín de Noticias*, December 23, 1992, p. 2.

72. Between October 1991 and July 1992, more than 37,000 Haitians fled their country to seek refuge in the United States. Their status has been the focus of litigation in the U.S. courts. On May 24, 1992, President Bush issued an executive order denying Haitians intercepted at sea the right to immigration interviews to determine their eligibility for political asylum in the United States. On August 1, 1992, the U.S. Supreme Court agreed to rule on the legality of the executive order, but allowed its implementation, pending a full review. Approximately one-third of the 37,000 Haitians who fled after the coup made a credible case for possible political asylum, before President Bush issued the executive order, and were transferred to the United States so they could apply for asylum. See Barbara Crossette, "Haiti Arrests 150 Intercepted by U.S.," *New York Times*, August 15, 1992, A2.

73. See "The Emerging Right to Democratic Governance," p. 85.

74. Ibid.

75. See "Mulroney Calls for Naval Blockade of Haiti," *New York Times*, December 25, 1992, p. A31.

76. W. Michael Reisman, "Sovereignty and Human Rights in Contemporary International Law," *American Journal of International Law*, vol. 84, no. 4, p. 875. See also Reisman, "Coercion and Self-Determination," *American Journal of International Law*, vol. 78, no. 3 (1984), p. 642. There he asserts that a state could, without violating article 2(4) of the UN Charter, resort to unilateral forcible action in order to remove an authoritarian government in another state.

77. See Oscar Schachter, "The Legality of Pro-Democratic Invasion," *American Journal of International Law*, vol. 78 (1984), p. 645. See also Lori F. Damrosch, "Commentary on Collective Military Intervention to Enforce Human Rights," in L.F. Damrosch and D.J. Scheffer, eds., *Law and Force in the New International Order* (1991), p. 215, and "Politics Across Borders: Nonintervention and Nonforcible Influence over Domestic Affairs," *American Journal of International Law*, vol. 83 (1989), p. 1; and Heraldo Muñoz, "Haiti and Beyond," *Miami Herald*, March 1, 1992, p. 6C.

78. Ted G. Carpenter mentions several examples in "The New World Order," *Foreign Policy*, vol. 84 (1991).

79. Reisman has argued that contemporary international law protects "the people's sovereignty rather than the sovereign's sovereignty." See "Sovereignty and Human Rights in Contemporary International Law," *American Journal of International Law*, vol. 84 (1990), p. 869. Reisman observes that the "contemporary change in content of the term 'sovereignty' also changes the cast of characters who can violate that sovereignty," and states that "in modern international law, sovereignty can be violated as effectively and ruthlessly by an indigenous as by an outside force, in much the same way that the wealth and natural resources of a country can be spoliated as thoroughly and efficiently by a national as by a foreigner" (p. 872).

80. See Heraldo Muñoz and Tom Farer, "Reinforcing the Collective Defense of Democracy." (Prepared for the Inter-American Dialogue, 1992.) With

regard to the evolving notion of sovereignty, one author has argued that "if . . . the State exists only for the purpose of enabling the individuals which comprise it to live their lives relatively peacefully, and for no other purpose, then one cannot say that sovereignty ultimately rests with the State. Rather, it rests with individuals." See Kurt Mills, "Humanitarian Intervention: A Legal, Political, and Moral Analysis." (Presented to the panel Sovereignty and Human Rights in an Interdependent World, Midwest Political Science Association, Chicago, Ill., April 9–11, 1992), p. 22.

81. Franck notes that "there has long been a trend toward global conscience capable of interfering where injustice reigns. Interference against gross domestic human rights abuses has already become relatively normative in the system." See "United Nations-Based Prospects for a New Global Order," *New York University Journal of International Law and Policy* (1990), p. 605

82. The activities of the UN, the OAS, and the nongovernmental organizations in establishing, defining, and monitoring, in independent member states, free and open elections, have contributed to the ongoing reevaluation of norms and principles related to sovereignty. See Fox, "The Right to Political Participation," p. 539.

   Franck observes that "the capacity of the international community to extend legitimacy to national governments, however, depends not only on its capacity to monitor an election . . . but also on the extent to which such international activity has evolved from the ad hoc to the normative: that is, the degree to which the process of legitimation itself has become legitimate." See Franck, "The Emerging Right to Democratic Governance," p. 51.

83. See resolutions CP/RES. 554/90; CP/RES. 576(887/92); MRE/RES. 1/92, Support for the Restoration of Democracy in Peru, April 13, 1992; and MRE/RES. 2/92 Restoration of Democracy in Peru, May 18, 1992.

84. Franck identifies three subsets, or "building blocks," in the creation of a democratic entitlement: self-determination, which is the historic root from which the democratic entitlement grew; freedom of expression, which "developed as part of the exponential growth of human rights since the mid-1950's"; and defining and "monitoring a right to free and open elections." See "The Emerging Right to Democratic Governance," p. 52.

85. The notion of democratic entitlement was the subject of Franck's article "The United Nations-Based Prospects for a New Global Order."

86. See Franck, "The Emerging Right to Democratic Governance," p. 89.

87. See Fernando Tesón, *Humanitarian Intervention: An Inquiry into Law and Morality* (Transnational Publishers, Inc. 1988), pp. 15 and 245. See also Mills, "Humanitarian Intervention."

88. For example, the consolidation of democracy in Europe and the Americas should not obscure the differences between political culture in those regions and elsewhere. Carpenter observes that "merely because movements around the world employ the rhetoric of democracy does not mean that they adopt its fundamental premises." See "The New World Order," p. 36. Against those who, after the Gulf conflict, urged the U.S. government to help establish a democratic regime in Iraq, Carpenter argues that "viable democracies are virtually unknown in the Middle East" (p. 35).

89. See Thomas Carothers, "Empirical Perspectives on the Emerging Norm of Democracy in International Law," in *Proceedings of the 86th Annual Meeting of the A.S.I.L.* (1992). Michael J. Sandel summarized this issue as follows: "Democracy is more than just a procedure for electing officials—it is a way of life and a set of traditions and institutions. Most importantly, it requires an independent judiciary that can enforce rights, protect the opposition and ensure that not only are elections democratic but that daily life is democratic as well." Quoted in Thomas L. Friedman, "A New U.S. Problem: Freely Elected Tyrants," *New York Times*, January 12, 1992, p. E3. Tom Farer notes that during the Reagan administration, "the key criterion of human rights performance [was] a government's ability to trace its authority to victory in competitive elections." See "Elections, Democracy and Human Rights: Toward Union," *Human Rights Quarterly*, vol. 11 (1989), p. 510.

90. See Reisman, "Sovereignty and Human Rights," p. 875.

91. Franck, "The Emerging Right to Democratic Governance," p. 81. The monitoring and supervision of elections by international organizations basically ensures that they are free and fair and that the results, as Reisman points out, "serve as evidence of popular sovereignty and become the basis for international endorsement of the elected government." See Reisman, "Sovereignty and Human Rights," pp. 868–869. See also Fox, "The Right to Political Participation, pp. 570–595. It is important to note, however, that using elections to determine legitimacy raises several questions, as discussed earlier in this paper.

92. See Barbara Crossette, "Hamstrung over Haiti," *New York Times*, May 19, 1992, p. A7.

93. According to a report in 1992, "life has been severely disrupted for all but the richest" in Haiti, and the government "continues to tolerate widespread human rights abuses and defy local and international calls for a return to democracy." See Howard W. French, "Plight of Haiti's Poor Brings Calls to Loosen the Embargo," *New York Times*, August 5, 1992, p. A3. See also Colman McCarthy, "Indifference to Haitian Suffering," *Washington Post*, June 20, 1992, p. A23.

  As to human rights, see Marco Tulio Bruni Celli, "Report on the Human Rights Situation in Haiti," prepared in accordance with Commission on Human Rights resolution 1991/77, docs. E/CN.4/1992/50 and E/CN/1992/50 Add.1, January 31, 1992, and February 17, 1992, respectively. In a report issued on August 18, 1992, Amnesty International states that almost a year after the coup that ousted President Aristide, "human rights abuses reminiscent of the Duvalier era are once again part of most Haitians' daily life." See OAS Department of Public Information, *Boletín de Noticias*, August 19, 1992, p. 6.

94. See Muñoz, "Haiti and Beyond."

95. See Douglas Farah, "Prospects for Prompt Resolution of Haitian Crisis Begin to Dim," *Washington Post*, January 24, 1993, p. A24. See also Howard W. French, "Jackson, in Haiti, Cautions Military," *New York Times*, January 24, 1993, p. A7.

96. See Howard W. French, "Mediators Reach Settlement on Aristide Return," *New York Times International*, April 11, 1993, p. 10. See also H.W.

French, "Haiti Army Spurns Offer of Amnesty," *New York Times*, April 17, 1993, p. 1.

97. See Douglas Farah, "U.S. Tightens Sanctions on Regime in Haiti," *Washington Post*, June 5, 1993, p. A18.

98. See Howard French, "U.N. Approves Ban on Shipments of Oil to Haiti Military," *New York Times*, June 17, 1993, p. A1.

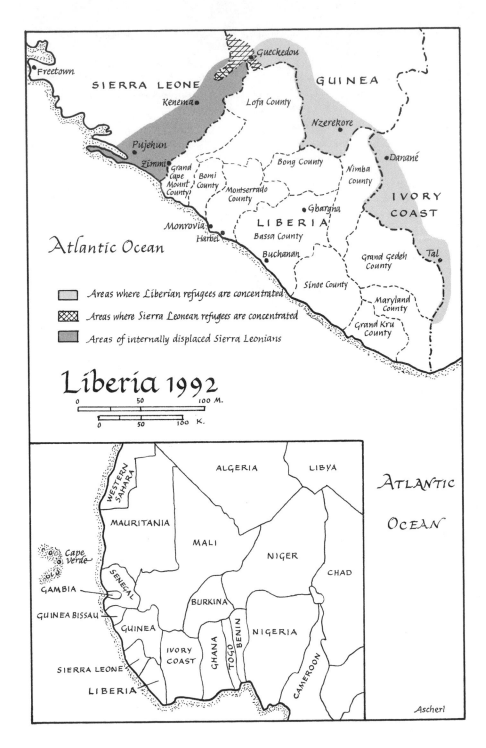

Freetown

SIERRA LEONE    Gueckedou    GUINEA

Kenema    Lofa County

Nzerekore

Pujehun    Danané

Zimmi    Grand    Bong County    Nimba
Cape    Bomi    county
Mount    County
County    Montserrado    IVORY
County    COAST

Gbargha

Monrovia    LIBERIA
Harbel    Bassa County

Atlantic Ocean    Buchanan    Tal
Grand Gedeh
County

Sinoe County

Maryland
County

Grand Kru
County

Areas where Liberian refugees are concentrated

Areas where Sierra Leonean refugees are concentrated

Areas of internally displaced Sierra Leonians

## Liberia 1992

0    50    100 M.

0    50    100 K.

WESTERN SAHARA    ALGERIA    LIBYA    ATLANTIC

OCEAN

MAURITANIA

Cape    MALI    NIGER
Verde

SENEGAL    CHAD

GAMBIA    BURKINA

GUINEA BISSAU    NIGERIA

GUINEA    GHANA    BENIN    CAMEROON
TOGO
IVORY
SIERRA LEONE    COAST

LIBERIA

Ascherl

# CHAPTER FOUR

# Enforcing the Peace: ECOWAS and the Liberian Civil War

## DAVID WIPPMAN*

> So the question then is, where does a country whose government has collapsed, and with warring factions that are unable to reach an agreement, and unable to establish any form of authority, where does this country go, what do the people do, what then becomes the most crucial issue in their survival? Is it the question of their preservation of their own humanity, or is it the question of holding on to some legal notion of sovereignty?
>
> Amos Sawyer, President, Interim Government of
> National Unity, August 1991

On Christmas Eve in 1989, a small band of rebels entered northeastern Liberia from Côte d'Ivoire. The rebels, followers of exiled Liberian official Charles Taylor, hoped to overthrow the government of President Samuel Doe. President Doe sent troops to meet the rebel forces. The ensuing civil war, which was marked by unimaginable brutality, tribalism, and senseless killing, led with astonishing swiftness to the collapse of the Doe government.

---

*The author served as counsel to the Interim Government of Liberia from November 1990 to May 1992; however, the views expressed herein are solely those of the author.

By July 1990, all semblance of civil authority within Liberia had ceased to exist. Rebel forces (which by then had fractured into two opposing factions) held all of Liberia except for the capital city, Monrovia. Fighting street by street, they struggled with the remnants of Doe's army, and with each other, for control of the city. The already extraordinary human toll of the conflict escalated rapidly. All sides regularly tortured and murdered non-combatants; thousands of civilians faced starvation; and tens of thousands were forced into exile, joining some 500,000 of their fellow citizens already seeking refuge in neighboring countries.

On August 23, 1990, armed forces from five member states of the Economic Community of West African States (ECOWAS) intervened in Liberia to stop the fighting. They came under immediate attack by the forces of Charles Taylor, who had promised to resist what he termed an invasion of foreign troops that violated Liberia's sovereignty and territorial integrity. Fighting and negotiations alternated over the next several months. By November 1990, ECOWAS forces controlled Monrovia and a cease-fire was established. At the same time, an interim government was installed in Monrovia under the protection of the ECOWAS troops. In response, Taylor established his own "government" in his own "capital city," Gbargna, effectively partitioning Liberia and prompting ECOWAS to begin a long search for the elusive formula that would unify the country under a freely elected government.

In late August 1992, just when ECOWAS seemed on the verge of exerting sufficient pressure on Taylor to restart a stalled peace process, renewed fighting shattered the nearly two-year-old ECOWAS-brokered cease-fire. Remnants of former President Doe's army launched a fierce assault on Taylor's forces and eventually captured much of northwestern Liberia. Taylor accused ECOWAS troops of supporting his adversaries and launched his own full-scale assault on Monrovia, thus drawing ECOWAS troops into the fighting. After several weeks of intense combat, ECOWAS forces succeeded in reestablishing a protective buffer zone around the capital. But fighting has continued on a sporadic basis, and perhaps more important, the neutrality of ECOWAS, and its ability to fashion a peaceful settlement to Liberia's festering conflict, have been seriously called into question.

Nonetheless, ECOWAS has not given up. Although it has turned to the United Nations for assistance in imposing an arms embargo on Liberia, the Community has reaffirmed its intention to maintain the lead role in seeking a lasting resolution to the Liberian conflict.

In large part, ECOWAS assumed that role by default. At the height of the civil war, the United States refused requests for military intervention, insisting that "an African problem" required "an African solution." The UN Security Council similarly declined even to discuss the Liberian conflict until well after ECOWAS decided to intervene. For many, this reaction confirmed the pessimistic view that the "new world order" spells only neglect for African states, or at least for those not fortunate enough to possess any vital natural resources. The positive side of such neglect is that it enabled the ECOWAS states to fashion their own response to an internal conflict, a response that was more complete and, at least until the collective intervention in Somalia, more effective than the response of the larger international community to most other contemporary internal conflicts. But whether the ECOWAS intervention can, or should, serve as a model for other internal conflicts is not yet clear.

The ECOWAS decision to intervene in a largely internal conflict raises difficult issues of international law and politics. Community members offered a variety of justifications for their actions, ranging from the need to stop the slaughter of Liberian civilians to the need to restore some measure of regional peace and stability. As demonstrated below, these justifications are legally problematic. Nonetheless, the international community on balance seems to have welcomed the ECOWAS decision to attempt to restore peace by force.

Overall, the role of ECOWAS in Liberia and the response of the international community suggest the following "lessons": First, regional organizations at times will have both the capacity and the incentive to intervene in local conflicts that do not engage the interests or attention of the great powers sufficiently to result in an effective response by the UN. Second, the international community now appears willing not only to tolerate but to support a considerable degree of intervention in internal conflicts when necessary to restore order and save lives. Third, many African countries are willing to reconsider, at least to some extent, their traditional hostility to intervention in any form, and to recognize internal human rights violations as a threat to international peace and security warranting the attention of outside states. Fourth, for those who support intervention in Bosnia, Somalia, and elsewhere, the ECOWAS intervention illustrates one obvious point: it is easier to get in than to get out.

## HISTORICAL BACKGROUND

To some degree, the present conflict dates back to 1822,[1] when a small group of emancipated slaves from the United States settled in what is now Monrovia. They were sponsored by the American Colonization Society (ACS), and financed in part by the administration of President James Monroe. The settlers, who came to be known as Americo-Liberians, were initially under the rule of white governors appointed by ACS. In 1847, however, the settlers severed their links with ACS and proclaimed Liberia an independent state.

In many respects, the Americo-Liberians sought to duplicate in Liberia the society they had known in the United States. They established a republican form of government, with executive, legislative, and judicial branches very similar to the U.S. model, and adopted a flag and other national symbols fashioned after those of the United States. The Americo-Liberians also recreated the social hierarchy they had experienced in the ante-bellum South, but with themselves as the socially dominant, landowning class. They considered the indigenous population primitive and uncivilized, and treated it as little more than an abundant source of forced labor.

For more than 130 years, the Americo-Liberians dominated the country's political, economic, and social life, even though they constituted only about 5 percent of the population. By 1931, the subjugation of the indigenous population was so complete that a League of Nations report described Liberia as a "Republic of 12,000 citizens with 1,000,000 subjects."[2] As a result, the Americo-Liberians have been compared with the Europeans who colonized other African countries.

In 1944 President William V. S. Tubman took office, promising to integrate the indigenous population more fully into Liberia's economic and political life. This policy was part of Tubman's overall plan to transform Liberia into a modern state, and to preempt through evolutionary change an emerging African nationalism that he and others saw as a potential threat to the privileged position of the Americo-Liberian elite.[3] Reelected seven times, Tubman served as Liberia's president for 27 years. Although his tenure saw a modest improvement in the lot of indigenous Liberians, political and economic power remained in the hands of a relatively small group of Americo-Liberian families.

When Tubman died in 1971, Vice President William Tolbert replaced him. Although Tolbert retained many of Tubman's policies, Liberia started to experience growing social and economic unrest. Organized opposition movements started to develop and mature. Government corruption, nepotism, and patronage practices, already a serious problem under Tubman, continued to escalate. Economic recession, coupled with the gradual migration of African workers into urban areas, created a tense environment.

On April 12, 1980, a unit of the Liberian National Guard, under the leadership of Master Sergeant Samuel Doe, forced its way into the executive mansion, killed President Tolbert and his security guards, and established a "revolutionary" government. Doe suspended the Constitution, abolished the legislature, banned political parties, and placed the country under martial law. Resistance to the coup was minimal; indeed, the country's indigenous majority initially welcomed it.

The new government promptly tried and shot thirteen of the country's most prominent politicians, including the former ministers of justice and foreign affairs. The televised executions inaugurated a decade of brutal and arbitrary exercise of power. They also marked the end, at least temporarily, of Americo-Liberian rule.

Doe promised to combat corruption and to redistribute the nation's wealth equitably among the country's sixteen recognized ethnic groups. But Doe, a member of the Krahn tribe, did not live up to his promises. Instead, he elevated fellow Krahns to most positions of importance, even though the Krahn constituted less than 4 percent of the Liberian population. He also fostered a climate of rampant corruption and grave human rights abuses, which were directed against indigenous ethnic groups other than the Krahn, as well as against Americo-Liberians. As a result, ethnic tensions and political unrest increased so sharply that in 1986, the Lawyers Committee for Human Rights predicted precisely the "escalating cycle of ethnic violence" and "massive reprisals against the Krahn" that began with Taylor's invasion in 1989.[4]

Notwithstanding the dismal character of the Doe regime, and the manner in which it came to power, U.S. aid to Liberia increased dramatically from 1980 to 1985. U.S. policy was motivated by strategic interests, such as the availability of refueling facilities and telecommunications relay stations, and by a desire to preempt Soviet influence.[5] But while willing to assist Doe, and thereby to confer some measure of legitimacy on his regime, Washington also sought to moderate the character of that regime. Under U.S. pressure, Doe held elections in 1985 to return the country to civilian rule. He claimed a victory margin of 51 percent, but the results were almost universally regarded as fraudulent.[6]

Following the elections, Thomas Quiwonkpa, an exiled former army officer, led an unsuccessful coup attempt against Doe. Krahn soldiers took immediate reprisals against Quiwonkpa's ethnic group, the Gios, and against a closely related group, the Manos. Hundreds were executed after being subjected to "bloodcurdling brutality."[7] Several hundred Gios and Manos then fled to Côte d'Ivoire, where many were later recruited into Charles Taylor's Christmas 1989 invasion force.[8] Thus, although Liberia soon returned to relative calm, the seeds of the coming ethnic conflict had already been planted.

## THE 1989–1990 CIVIL WAR

When Taylor invaded Nimba County with a few hundred men in late December 1989, under the banner of the National Patriotic Front of Liberia (NPFL), the Doe government and most outside observers dismissed the incursion as insignificant. Indeed, on January 2, 1990, Doe's minister of justice, Jenkins Scott, confidently announced that the government had deployed sufficient troops to deal with the rebels, and that the problem was "over."[9] In fact, the government troops dispatched to deal with the rebels found the NPFL's hit-and-run tactics frustrating and elusive, and responded by massacring hundreds of Gio and Mano civilians, whom the government accused of supporting Taylor's largely Gio and Mano forces.[10] This senseless slaughter of civilians "set the tone for the war," and prompted many Gio and Mano residents of Nimba County to join Taylor's forces.[11] In turn, the insurgents savagely attacked both Krahn and Mandingo civilians, the former because Doe and many members of the army belonged to the Krahn, the latter because they were perceived to be in alliance with the Krahn.[12] In no time, Taylor's small-scale incursion mushroomed into a large-scale inter-ethnic war.

Within a month, Taylor's ill-trained recruits, many of them in their early teens, had taken control of Nimba County. Hundreds, perhaps thousands, of noncombatants were killed, and tens of thousands were forced to flee. As Taylor gained additional recruits, the fighting spread rapidly to other counties. By April 1990, hundreds of thousands of Liberians had sought refuge in the bush, or in neighboring Côte d'Ivoire and Guinea.

As the insurgency spread throughout Liberia, over half of the country's population of 2.6 million was displaced; some 600,000–700,000 Liberians fled the country altogether. Those unable to escape were subjected to what has aptly been called "a reign of terror." Thousands were killed, often after suffering horrific physical abuse.

By early June 1990, rebel forces reached Monrovia. An internal dispute led to the formation of a splinter rebel faction known as the Independent National Patriotic Front of Liberia

(INPFL), whose leader was a former Taylor commander named Prince Johnson. NPFL and INPFL forces alternately battled each other and the remnants of Doe's military, the Armed Forces of Liberia (AFL). What remained of the civilian population of Monrovia was caught in the cross-fire.

Although most observers assumed the rebel forces would quickly vanquish the AFL and drive Doe from his fortified mansion, the rebels proved unable to do so. The conflict settled into a military stalemate. The result was anarchy. Each warring faction exercised a slight measure of "de facto executive and judicial power" in its particular area of control, but for the most part, all semblance of civilian authority was gone.[13]

International calls for a cease-fire went unheeded, and mediation efforts ultimately proved fruitless. In the early stages of the conflict, U.S. government officials and various African leaders unsuccessfully encouraged the parties to reach a negotiated settlement. Negotiations held in Sierra Leone under church auspices foundered, principally because Doe refused even to discuss the rebels' demand for his immediate resignation.[14]

As informal mediation efforts fizzled, the ECOWAS heads of state met at their annual summit in late May 1990, where they agreed to establish the five-member Standing Mediation Committee[15] entrusted with the mission of achieving a settlement of the Liberian crisis. Three fundamental principles were to guide the Committee: that the parties should agree to a cease-fire; that all sides should put an end to the "routine destruction of human lives and property"; and that the parties should accept free and fair elections as the only way to restore peace and harmony to the country.

At the insistence of the Standing Mediation Committee, representatives of the NPFL and the government agreed to a series of talks, which took place in Freetown, Sierra Leone. Once again, the talks foundered over Doe's reluctance to resign, even as rebel forces approached to within a mile of the executive mansion.[16]

The collapse of peace talks led to multiple calls for military intervention. Senior Liberian politicians and interest groups, relying on the "special relationship" between Liberia and the

United States, openly called for U.S. marines to stop the fighting or at least to create a safe haven for civilians.[17] But intervention in Liberia would advance no post–Cold War strategic interests for the United States. Moreover, Washington viewed all three warring factions as undesirable, and did not wish to incur blame for assisting any of them into power. Thus, the United States initially took the position that the disintegration of Liberia was an "internal affair," and counseled against an armed intervention undertaken without the consent of the parties.[18]

When the United States refused to intervene, efforts were made to place the Liberian crisis on the Security Council's agenda. Those efforts also proved fruitless, in part because of opposition by Côte d'Ivoire, which was sympathetic to Taylor, and in part because the Council's members shared the U.S. view that the problem should be solved by Africans. In particular, the two African members of the Council, Ethiopia and Zaire, "were not prepared to have the Security Council deal with Liberia."[19] Both evidently wished to avoid creating a precedent that might someday apply to them, and in deference to their views, other Council members chose not to press the issue.[20]

In the end, the international response was limited to the rescue of foreign nationals by U.S. marines, who conducted a helicopter evacuation operation in early August.[21] The international community's refusal to act set the stage for the subsequent ECOWAS intervention.


## THE ECOWAS INTERVENTION

As the conflict persisted into August 1990, the situation in Monrovia became increasingly desperate. Tens of thousands of Liberians, and hundreds of nationals from other ECOWAS states, were trapped without food, water, medicine, or shelter. Pressure on ECOWAS leaders to take action mounted.

On the face of it, however, ECOWAS seemed an unlikely candidate for conducting a large-scale effort to enforce the peace. As its name suggests, the Community is a subregional organization designed primarily to promote West African economic integration. Founded in 1975 under the Treaty of Lagos, ECOWAS has sixteen member states, which were at one time variously under British, French, Portuguese, and (counting Liberia) American colonial domination.[22] This diversity in the colonial heritage of the ECOWAS states, coupled with their radically different levels of economic and political development, has historically posed substantial obstacles to full cooperation on a range of issues.[23] The principal fault line lies between the francophone and anglophone states, traditionally led by Côte d'Ivoire and Nigeria, respectively. Given Nigeria's size (Nigeria has a gross national product and a population "roughly equal to those of the other fifteen members of ECOWAS combined")[24] the francophone states have always been suspicious of any Community initiative that might unduly extend Nigerian influence.

In light of these divisions, the extent to which ECOWAS should involve itself in intra-Community political (as opposed to economic) issues has always been a subject of debate among member states. In recent years, however, many West African leaders have concluded that economic integration cannot be divorced from larger political and security concerns. Acting on this theory, the ECOWAS heads of state agreed at their 1978 summit to modify the organization's treaty, which contained no provisions for collective security, by adopting a protocol on nonaggression. The protocol commits member states that cannot resolve an intra-Community dispute peacefully to submit such disputes to the ECOWAS heads of state for resolution.[25]

While valuable, the protocol dealt only with aggression between or among signatory states. It did not purport to address aggression coming from states outside the region, nor did it address the problem of civil conflicts taking place wholly within signatory states. A defense pact adopted in 1981 dealt with these omissions.[26] Under the pact, the member states agreed to provide mutual assistance for defense in case of any external (i.e., extra-regional) aggression; any conflict between member states that cannot be settled under the terms of the protocol on nonaggression; and any "internal armed conflict within any Member State engineered and supported actively from outside likely to endanger the security and peace in the entire Community."[27] Although several local conflicts in the late 1980s offered opportunities to invoke the defense pact, it was never formally called into play.[28] Nonetheless, the pact's existence reflects the determination on the part of at least some of West Africa's presidents to resolve regional conflicts by regional means.

## The Decision to Intervene

That determination was put to the test in Liberia. In early August 1990, the members of the Standing Mediation Committee, joined by the presidents of Guinea and Sierra Leone, met in the Gambia to review the Liberian crisis. At the conclusion of the meeting, the attending heads of state called on all the warring parties to observe an immediate cease-fire, and announced that "acting on behalf of the ECOWAS Authority [of heads of state and government] . . . an ECOWAS Cease-fire Monitoring Group (ECOMOG) shall be established in Liberia for the purpose of keeping the peace, restoring law and order and ensuring that the cease-fire is respected."[29] The Committee also called for the establishment of a broad-based interim government to rule Liberia until an internationally supervised election could take place.

Although ECOMOG was formally denominated a "cease-fire monitoring," or peacekeeping, body, it was clear from the start that it would have to establish a cease-fire by force before it could begin to monitor it. Unlike Prince Johnson and President Doe, who welcomed the Committee's initiative, Charles Taylor saw it from the outset as an effort to prevent him from taking power.[30] Even in advance of the August summit, he denounced the possibility of armed intervention as "illegal," and warned that his forces would fight to the last man to defend Liberia's sovereignty against any "foreign intervention."[31] The Committee, or at least most of its members, were determined to proceed nonetheless. As President Conté of Guinea put it, "we have . . . decided that whether they [the NPFL] like it or not, the ECOWAS should accomplish its mission."[32]

Charles Taylor was not the only critic of the Committee's decision to intervene. Two of the Committee's own members, Togo and Mali, refused initially to contribute troops to the force, and joined by Côte d'Ivoire and Senegal, they expressed concern that the Committee had overstepped its bounds.[33] President Blaise Compaore of Burkina Faso, long Taylor's most open supporter, was more blunt. He denounced the Committee's decision, declaring that the Committee had "no competence to interfere in member states' internal conflicts," and argued that ECOWAS should not intervene without the consent of all parties to the conflict.[34] Thus, with the exception of Guinea, which was suffering the most from an influx of refugees, all of the francophone states questioned the Committee's peace plan. Their motivation stemmed in part from sympathy for Taylor, and in part from concern over the possible expansion of Nigerian influence.

Nonetheless, the Committee's majority moved ahead with its plan. On August 24, 1990, ECOMOG began to deploy approximately 3,500 troops (later increased to 9,000) to Monrovia. The largest contingents came from Nigeria and Ghana; Guinea, Sierra Leone, and the Gambia also contributed troops. On August 27, the Committee convened the "All Liberia Conference" of seventeen Liberian political parties and interest groups. The participants, noting that "today there is no government in Liberia," and "relying and acting on the inherent sovereign right of the Liberian people to make laws for their governance," declared the suspension of certain portions of the Liberian Constitution, and elected an interim president and legislature.[35] They entrusted the new interim government, headed by Amos Sawyer,[36] with the task of national reconciliation and the conduct of elections. They also endorsed unanimously the Standing Mediation Committee's peace plan.

## Turning Point: The Death of Samuel Doe

As the conference proceeded, ECOMOG troops were already engaged in combat. The moment ECOMOG soldiers landed in Monrovia, they came under attack by Taylor's forces. By early September, however, the monitoring group succeeded in negotiating a temporary cease-fire. The cease-fire lasted until September 10, 1990, when President Doe made the fatal mistake of visiting ECOMOG headquarters. While awaiting the return of the group's commander, Doe was seized by Prince Johnson's men, then tortured and killed.

Doe's demise demonstrated that his removal alone would not end the conflict. But his death did have a significant impact on the course of the conflict. Embarrassed by Doe's capture, ECOMOG abandoned its posture of a peacekeeping body willing to use force only in self-defense, and began a full-scale offensive to drive the NPFL from Monrovia.[37] In doing so, ECOMOG found itself in the uncomfortable position of fighting with two of the warring factions (the INPFL and the AFL) against the third. After several weeks of intensive combat, ECOMOG succeeded in forcing the NPFL out of Monrovia, thus paving the way for the arrival of international relief supplies and the installation of the interim government.[38]

At the insistence of several of the francophone states, ECOWAS scheduled an emergency summit for November, and invited representatives of the warring factions to attend. The summit marked a turning point in the conflict. After heated discussions, the ECOWAS heads of state unanimously agreed to endorse the Standing Mediation Committee's peace plan, including the decision to create ECOMOG and to establish a broad-based interim government.[39] Simultaneously, ECOWAS successfully pressed the NPFL to agree to a cease-fire with the other warring factions.[40]

Despite sporadic violations, the cease-fire largely ended the fighting, and enabled international relief organizations to resume work not only in Monrovia, but throughout much of Liberia. Progress on a political solution came more slowly. Taylor refused to acknowledge the legitimacy of the interim government, insisting that his control over 90 percent of Liberia entitled him to be president. Under pressure from ECOWAS, Taylor agreed with the other warring factions in late December 1990 to the holding of a new All Liberia Conference to select a "future interim government." That government was to disarm the warring factions and govern the country until new elections could take place.[41] But when the conference was finally held, in March 1991, Taylor refused to participate. And when Amos Sawyer was again chosen to be the interim president, Taylor denounced the conference and refused to accept its results.

A detailed cease-fire agreement that ECOWAS brokered in February 1991 met a similar fate. Although the warring parties accepted the agreement's provisions for the encampment and disarmament of all combatants under ECOMOG supervision,[42] Taylor soon found reasons why the NPFL could not comply. His refusal to accept the results of the All Liberia Conference, and his disregard for the ECOWAS disarmament plan, left Liberia effectively partitioned, with the NPFL controlling most of the country.

## The Conflict Widens

From the beginning, prointervention forces had characterized the war in Liberia as a threat to the subregion's peace and security. That characterization proved accurate when NPFL soldiers joined forces with Sierra Leonean dissidents and invaded Sierra Leone in March 1991. Various observers characterized Taylor's involvement as retaliation for Sierra Leone's support for ECOMOG, as a quid pro quo for help he had previously received from Sierra Leonean dissidents, and as an effort to divert attention from his refusal to participate in the All Liberia Conference.[43] Notwithstanding assistance rendered to Sierra Leone from other ECOWAS states, the fighting continues in various parts of the country.

Impatient with the political impasse in Liberia, and goaded by the spread of fighting into Sierra Leone, a new warring faction, the United Liberation Movement of Liberia for Democracy (ULIMO), was formed in late May 1991; its members were primarily Krahn refugees and former AFL soldiers who had sought refuge in Sierra Leone. Shortly thereafter, ULIMO forces began to engage the NPFL in a series of inconclusive skirmishes that ultimately culminated in a major ULIMO offensive.

In late June 1991 heads of state from the major ECOWAS protagonists met in Yamoussoukro at the urging of Côte d'Ivoire President Houphet-Boigny. Responding to concerns of anglophone dominance of the peace process, they formed a five-member committee (consisting of Côte d'Ivoire, the Gambia, Guinea-Bissau, Senegal, and Togo) to serve as an adjunct to the Standing Mediation Committee, and to take the lead in monitoring implementation of the cease-fire and the electoral process in Liberia.

The establishment of the Committee of Five put Taylor's principal ECOWAS supporter, Côte d'Ivoire, in the position of having to assist in brokering an acceptable political solution or admit defeat.

The new committee held a series of meetings that, on October 29, 1991, resulted in an agreement known as Yamoussoukro IV. In that agreement, the NPFL, the INPFL, and the AFL promised to encamp and disarm by January 15, 1992. They also agreed that ECOMOG forces would establish a buffer zone along Liberia's borders with Sierra Leone and Guinea, thus insulating those countries from further incursions by NPFL forces, and simultaneously precluding ULIMO from launching further assaults against the NPFL. In addition, the parties agreed to a series of steps to facilitate elections, including the reopening of roads throughout Liberia and the establishment of an elections commission named jointly by the interim government and the NPFL.[44] But despite relatively promising initial progress, the key terms of Yamoussoukro IV were not fulfilled, in large part because Taylor's forces again refused to disarm.

In an effort to carry out Yamoussoukro IV, ECOMOG began to deploy additional troops in Liberia, especially along its borders with Guinea and Sierra Leone. Progress was slow, as ECOMOG encountered obstructionist tactics from both the NPFL and ULIMO.[45] On several occasions ECOMOG and NPFL forces exchanged fire, resulting in the death of at least six ECOMOG soldiers.[46] Frustrated by Taylor's intransigence, the ECOWAS heads of state issued a communiqué at their July 1992 summit condemning Taylor's obstructionist tactics, and warning him to cooperate with ECOMOG in the implementation of the terms of Yamoussoukro IV by August 31, or face "comprehensive sanctions."[47]

## Imposing the Peace: Round Two

While ECOWAS and virtually everyone else focused on the need to induce Charles Taylor and the NPFL to comply with the Community's peace plan, the growing threat to that plan posed by ULIMO had largely been ignored. For months the NPFL and ULIMO had been engaged in sporadic fighting. Although some clashes were substantial, most analysts considered ULIMO only a minor threat to Taylor, and therefore only a minor factor in the peace process.

But in late July and early August, the fighting escalated sharply, as ULIMO began to force the NPFL to cede ground inside Liberia. As a result of the renewed fighting, the August 31 deadline for Taylor to encamp and disarm or face sanctions passed in silence. Locked in combat, both the NPFL and ULIMO paid lip service to the ECOWAS peace plan, but both refused to disengage, much less to disarm. As a result, Liberian civilians were once again caught in the cross-fire.

As ULIMO continued to advance, Taylor began to accuse ECOMOG of clandestinely supporting ULIMO. Several ECOMOG soldiers died in clashes with Taylor's forces, and in early September Taylor effectively held some 500 ECOMOG troops hostage for several days before allowing them to return to Monrovia.[48]

As relations between ECOMOG and the NPFL deteriorated, calls for UN intervention became more frequent and pronounced. Former President Jimmy Carter, who had periodically sought a role as mediator in Liberia, publicly questioned the capacity of ECOWAS to continue to serve as a neutral broker and urged the dispatch of a UN observer group.[49] Even several of the ECOWAS states, led by Côte d'Ivoire, began to describe ECOWAS as "stymied" in its peacekeeping efforts, and to call for "logistical support" for ECOWAS in the form of UN observers, who would be considered neutral.[50] By contrast, other ECOWAS members, particularly Nigeria and Sierra Leone, wished to increase the pressure on Taylor by imposing economic and military sanctions designed to deny him the means with which to continue fighting.

As ECOWAS debated the most suitable course of action, Taylor launched a full-scale assault on Monrovia. Once again, ECOMOG found itself fighting alongside two warring factions, this time ULIMO and the AFL,[51] against the third. As it had two years before, a rapidly reinforced ECOMOG expelled Taylor's forces from the capital after weeks of heavy combat that created thousands of new civilian casualties and tens of thousands of new refugees. But this time, an ECOWAS call for a cease-fire was largely ignored.

Not surprisingly, the renewed fighting prompted fresh debate over the proper role for ECOWAS. Nigeria and Sierra Leone favored a major military offensive against the NPFL; francophone states resisted, and again pushed for UN involvement. Two further ECOWAS meetings, in late October and early November, produced a compromise. Effective November 5, 1992, ECOWAS finally imposed the sanctions it had threatened since July: it barred the shipment of weapons from member states into NPFL-held territory, and perhaps more important, it barred the export to member states of Liberian products originating in NPFL-held territory.[52] The ECOWAS heads of state also agreed to seek Security Council assistance in rendering these sanctions mandatory on all members of the international community, and to request the appointment of a UN special representative to "cooperate with ECOWAS in the implementation of the ECOWAS peace plan."[53] At the same time, however, they "strongly reaffirmed their trust in ECOMOG and reiterated their confidence in its absolute neutrality."[54]

The ECOWAS heads of state also authorized ECOMOG to enforce the sanctions decision and, more broadly, to ensure respect for the ECOWAS-declared cease-fire, and to implement "the encampment and disarmament of all combatants of the warring parties."[55] ECOMOG pursued this mission in various ways, including the bombing of suspected NPFL strongholds and supply lines. But despite the broad license given ECOMOG to use force against the NPFL, the all-out ground offensive Nigeria favored was put off, at least for the time being.

In late October 1992 ECOWAS requested a meeting of the Security Council to consider imposition of a blockade against all of the warring parties that refused to respect the Yamoussoukro IV accords (i.e., the NPFL), as a means of making the sanctions it adopted binding on the international community as a whole. The Council met on November 19, and for the first time, it conducted a substantive on-the-record discussion of the situation in Liberia.[56] The discussion is notable mostly for its effusive praise of the ECOWAS initiatives in Liberia, and for vague promises of continued Security Council support. At the conclusion of the discussion, the Council unanimously adopted resolution 788, which immediately imposed the requested embargo on "all deliveries of weapons and military equipment to Liberia." The Council also voted to dispatch a special representative to evaluate the situation in Liberia and report to the Council.

However, the Council did not impose an embargo on the export of Liberian products, as the ECOWAS states had requested. Instead, it simply "requested" all states to cooperate with the measures ECOWAS had already undertaken, thus making compliance voluntary. Several statements by Council members suggest that the Council wished to have a report by the secretary-general before proceeding beyond an arms embargo. More likely, however, the decision not to impose economic sanctions reflects a continued lack of enthusiasm for such sanctions on the part of the francophone ECOWAS states, and of France—which is both the primary purchaser of exports from NPFL-held territory and a competitor with Nigeria for influence in West Africa.

But even in the absence of mandated economic sanctions, resolution 788 and the debate leading up to it constitute a clear endorsement of ECOWAS initiatives in Liberia. The resolution and debate also reflect the Council's strong sense of relief that ECOWAS was willing to continue pursuing settlement of a protracted conflict that would otherwise fall to an already overstretched UN to resolve.

The success of the ECOWAS effort, however, remains very much in doubt. Fighting has continued in Liberia, as ECOMOG, ULIMO, and a revived AFL, at times acting in concert and at times acting independently, have challenged NPFL control over the countryside. Interethnic animosities remain strong, and arms are abundant.

Under these circumstances, it is not yet clear whether ECOWAS can muster the political will—and the political unity—to force a political settlement among Liberia's bitterly opposed warring factions. Many of ECOMOG's member countries have already encountered demonstrations and political protests over the commitment of troops and desperately scarce funds to the resolution of an internal conflict in another country. But having gone so far, ECOWAS is unlikely to abandon lightly its self-imposed mandate to reunify Liberia under a democratically elected government, even if ECOMOG must continue using force to do so.

## GROUNDS FOR INTERVENTION

From the outset, the international community's response to the ECOWAS intervention in Liberia has been, for the most part, one of guarded approval. Well before passage of resolution 788, the Security Council, the Organization of African Unity (OAU), the European Community, and a host of individual countries (including the United States) periodically encouraged ECOWAS in its efforts to find a solution to Liberia's course of self-destruction. But apart from Burkina Faso's early denunciation of ECOMOG as an illegal intervention in a sovereign country's internal affairs, most states have said little or nothing about the means ECOWAS chose to establish peace. In short, the international community has responded to the initial ECOWAS intervention in much the same way that it responded to Tanzania's intervention in Uganda in 1979: it has validated the result without formally validating the means.

The people of Liberia, of course, have been far more concerned with the ends than with any questions concerning the legality of the means. For the most part, ECOMOG was (and continues to be) welcomed throughout Liberia. By contrast, many Liberians are bitter toward the larger international community, and toward the United States in particular, for failing to intervene, especially in light of the international community's response to the invasion of Kuwait. But as the United States found out in Grenada, the receptiveness of the local population to an armed intervention does not preclude questions concerning the legality of the intervention under international law, or its desirability as a precedent. Answering those questions requires a close look at the justification for military intervention, and at the possibility of viable alternatives.

The legal objection to the initial ECOMOG intervention is clear. Force was used to determine the outcome of an internal conflict. As Burkina Faso pointed out, the use of force in that manner is ordinarily considered inconsistent with the rules against intervention in a country's internal affairs as established by the UN Charter, the Charter of the OAU, and customary international law. The question for international lawyers, then, is whether the ECOWAS intervention falls, or should fall, within an exception to the principle of nonintervention.

The ECOWAS states themselves have offered a number of justifications for intervening in Liberia, including the need to stop the large-scale killing of civilians; the need to protect foreign nationals; the need for the Community, as a regional organization, to protect international peace and security in West Africa; and the need to restore some measure of order to a state in anarchy.

Although various ECOWAS leaders emphasized different grounds at different times, the Standing Mediation Committee cited all of these bases for intervention collectively as the "background" to the decision to establish ECOMOG:

> The failure of the warring parties to cease hostilities has led to the massive destruction of property and the massacre by all the parties of thousands of innocent civilians, including foreign nationals, women and children . . . contrary to all recognized standards of civilized behaviors. . . . The civil war has also trapped thousands of foreign nationals, including ECOWAS citizens, without any means of escape or protection.
>
> The result of all this is a state of anarchy and the total breakdown of law and order in Liberia. Presently, there is a government in Liberia which cannot govern and contending factions which are holding the entire population as hostage, depriving them of food, health facilities and other basic necessities of life.
>
> The developments . . . have also led to hundreds of thousands of Liberians being displaced and made refugees in neighboring countries, and the spilling of hostilities into neighboring countries.[57]

Against this background, the Committee decided to assume its "responsibility of ensuring that peace and stability is maintained in the subregion." All of these justifications merit careful consideration.

## ECOMOG as a Peacekeeping Force

As its name suggests, ECOMOG was initially conceived as a peacekeeping force. All of the West African states recognized that intervention would be more acceptable—and more likely successful—if it had the consent of the warring parties. Thus, for many months, ECOWAS sought through diplomatic pressure to induce the warring parties to accept a cease-fire, which ECOMOG would monitor, pending a larger political settlement. When the ECOWAS Standing Mediation Committee was formed, its mandate was to achieve a cease-fire through mediation. Similarly, when ECOMOG was created, its mission was described as "keeping the peace, restoring law and order and ensuring that the cease-fire is respected."[58] Abass Bundu, the ECOWAS executive secretary, initially stated that ECOMOG would enter Liberia only after a cease-fire had been achieved.[59] Discussion shifted to the possibility of forcible intervention only when the impossibility of achieving a negotiated cease-fire agreement became apparent. Even when it became clear that the NPFL would forcibly resist ECOMOG's initial deployment, many ECOWAS leaders continued to describe the monitoring group's mission as peacekeeping only.[60]

In an effort to limit ECOMOG to a peacekeeping role, ECOWAS leaders ordered it to avoid any military engagements upon arrival in Monrovia, in the hope that the mere deployment of community forces would induce Taylor to agree to a cease-fire.[61] That strategy proved unworkable when NPFL forces attacked ECOMOG troops. Consequently, ECOMOG began to pursue a "strategy of limited offensive." As described by ECOWAS chairman Dawda Jawara, under that strategy, ECOMOG was still acting principally as a peacekeeping force, but one "obliged to fire back and attack," given the NPFL refusal to accept a cease-fire.[62] Within a month, ECOMOG's strategy had evolved into a conventional offensive, with the aim of driving Taylor's forces out of the capital and creating a protected buffer zone around it.

If Taylor's forces had agreed to the initial deployment of ECOMOG troops, then the subsequent fighting, even the offensive that drove the NPFL out of Monrovia, might have qualified as a lawful exercise of a peacekeeping force's right of self-defense.[63] But Taylor's declaration in advance that he would treat ECOMOG as an invasion force makes it difficult to characterize ECOMOG as a peacekeeping operation: the distinguishing feature of a peacekeeping operation is that it operates, at least at the outset, with the full consent of the primary warring factions. Any dilution of this fundamental principle risks undermining the acceptability of international peacekeeping operations generally. Accordingly, simply designating ECOMOG as a peacekeeping force seems an inadequate legal justification for its initial role in ending the Liberian civil war.

ECOMOG's claim to be a peacekeeping force achieved greater credibility in November 1990, when the warring factions agreed to a cease-fire and accepted ECOMOG as the force to monitor it. For almost two years, ECOMOG successfully fulfilled the neutral interposition function of most peacekeeping forces, until fighting resumed in late 1992. With the NPFL attack on Monrovia in November, however, ECOMOG of necessity again became an active combatant, fighting alongside the AFL and ULIMO to drive NPFL forces out of Monrovia.

As noted earlier, however, a peacekeeping operation has a right to use force in self-defense, and perhaps a limited right to repel by force attacks designed to frustrate its mission.[64] Thus, this time, ECOWAS could credibly defend its drive to oust Taylor's forces from Monrovia as "the right of ECOMOG, as a peace-keeping force, to defend itself against armed attacks from any quarter."[65]

Most states, including the United States, publicly accepted this view and saw no reason to replace ECOMOG with a UN force.[66] Similarly, when the Security Council discussed the situation, it condemned only Taylor's attack on ECOMOG, which it explicitly characterized as a "peacekeeping force"; the Council did not condemn, or even mention, ECOMOG's vigorous armed response.

But even if ECOMOG's use of force in 1992 qualifies as self-defense by a peacekeeping force, its fall 1990 offensive cannot fit comfortably under that rubric. For that offensive, the other justifications the ECOWAS states proffered must be considered.

## ECOMOG and Humanitarian Intervention

The primary reason ECOWAS advanced for its initial deployment of troops to Liberia, and the most compelling one, was to end the carnage. The Standing Mediation Committee cited the "massacre of innocent civilians" as a basis for its decision to create ECOMOG. Similarly, ECOWAS chairman Jawara rejected the charge that the monitoring group was an "invasion force," on the ground that its mission was primarily humanitarian. Moreover, when Nigeria's foreign minister first wrote to advise the Security Council of ECOMOG's deployment, he, too, described the Community's motivation primarily in humanitarian terms.[67]

The legitimacy of humanitarian intervention under international law is, of course, much debated. But for those who believe it is or should be considered lawful, the ECOWAS intervention in Liberia satisfies virtually every proposed test, and in many respects constitutes an excellent model.[68]

By all accounts, the loss of life in Liberia had reached near genocidal proportions; mass starvation and widespread disease were imminent. The continued fighting posed a clear danger to the peace and security of the region, both through the creation of an enormous refugee population in countries ill-equipped to handle such an influx and through the potential (soon realized) for a direct spillover of fighting from Liberia into neighboring states. ECOWAS made all reasonable efforts to obtain the warring parties' consent to a cease-fire, and to a Community interposition force. The decision to intervene was a multilateral one, undertaken by a subregional organization with a direct interest in the preservation of peace in the region. Moreover, although the decision did not initially command the full support of all ECOWAS members, unanimous support for ECOMOG was eventually forthcoming. Further, the intervention was proportional to the humanitarian crisis that precipitated it; a minimum of force was used to end the fighting and to create a modicum of order and security in which relief supplies could be delivered to the Liberian population. A large majority of Liberians, both in Monrovia and in NPFL-held territory, enthusiastically welcomed the intervention. In addition, ECOWAS took great care to minimize the impact of the intervention on Liberian sovereignty interests. The Community did not impose a government on Liberia. Instead, it encouraged the selection of an interim government through two conferences attended by a broad spectrum of Liberian political parties and interest groups, with the understanding that general, internationally supervised elections would take place as soon as feasible. Finally, long after the initial intervention, ECOWAS has continued to shoulder the financial, political, and military burden of efforts to preserve the peace, and has continued to seek a negotiated political solution to the conflict. Notwithstanding warnings of a Vietnam- or Lebanon-style quagmire, ECOWAS has persisted, through a graduated combination of diplomatic, economic, and military pressures, in pursuing a viable political settlement.

In light of the above, it is not surprising that the international community has acquiesced in the initial decision to impose peace. As noted earlier, the Security Council, the OAU, and the European Community have applauded ECOWAS for bringing a measure of peace and humanitarian relief to a shattered country, but in terms that have glossed over the initial use of force. The Security Council's statements, for example, all follow the imposition of peace, and focus on the need for all parties to cooperate with ECOWAS in its plan for a peaceful resolution of the conflict; the statements largely ignore ECOMOG's use of force. In fact, even the ECOWAS heads of state, when they first endorsed the Standing Mediation Committee's peace plan, referred only obliquely to the initial need for force, and concentrated instead on the parties' subsequent agreement to the Committee's plan. Thus, for the most part, the international community, and ECOWAS itself, implicitly approved of the Committee's decision to use force, without overtly endorsing the principle of humanitarian intervention.

Nonetheless, the ECOWAS intervention is not without precedential value for advocates of humanitarian intervention. Perhaps most important, it reflects a nascent willingness on the part of many African states, long among the most vociferous defenders of absolute state sovereignty, to recognize that massive human rights abuses can transform an internal, domestic problem into a problem for the larger international community. As in the case of Iraqi repression of the Kurds, substantial cross-border migration of refugees played an important role in the determination that outside intervention was warranted. The threat to foreign nationals was also a significant factor.[69] Perhaps even more important was the fear among many ECOWAS states that the popular overthrow of a military dictatorship in a neighboring state might prove contagious. But if public statements are to be credited, the threat to Liberians themselves was the most important factor motivating the decision to intervene.

Comments by several prominent African leaders endorsing ECOMOG's role in Liberia would have been unthinkable just a few years ago. For example, Salim A. Salim, the secretary-general of the OAU, rejected the claim that ECOMOG's use of force constituted a violation of the OAU Charter prohibition on intervention in the internal affairs of other countries. While applauding the principle of nonintervention, Salim took the position that "non-interference should not be taken to mean indifference." He argued that it was a "misinterpretation" of the OAU Charter to suppose that it required member states to ignore massive human rights violations in other member countries:

> . . . for an African government to have the right to kill its citizens or let its citizens be killed, I believe there is no clause in the charter that allows this.
>
> To tell the truth, the charter was created to preserve the humanity, dignity, and the rights of the African. You cannot use a clause of the charter to oppress the African and say that you are implementing the OAU charter. What has happened is that people have interpreted the charter as if to mean that what happens in the next house is not one's concern. This does not accord with the reality of the world.[70]

Other African leaders—including the chairman of the OAU and president of Uganda, Yoweri Museveni; and the president of Zimbabwe, Robert Mugabe—expressed similar views.[71] While most African states would not endorse the interpretation of the OAU Charter Secretary-General Salim suggested, the mere fact that such proposals receive serious attention in Africa is itself a significant change.

## Intervention to Restore Order

In a justification closely related to the humanitarian rationale, several ECOWAS leaders also asserted that the principle of domestic jurisdiction does not bar intervention in the context of a total breakdown of law and order. The chairman of the OAU, President Museveni, agreed with that view, and argued that the intervention in Liberia did not violate the OAU's rule of noninterference "because the state of Liberia ha[d] effectively collapsed."[72] Similarly, President Mugabe of Zimbabwe took the position that the "'domestic affairs' of a country must mean affairs within a peaceful environment, but . . . when there is no government in being and there is just chaos in the country, surely the time would have come for an intervention to occur."[73]

As with all proposed exceptions to the rule of nonintervention, the obvious danger of this approach lies in the possibility of abuse by powerful states.[74] Moreover, as President Mugabe was quick to point out, a principle permitting intervention in cases of anarchy might impede legitimate efforts by oppressed peoples to overthrow tyrannical governments,[75] since a time lag typically ensues between the disorder that accompanies the overthrow of an existing government and the establishment of renewed order under a new government.

Nonetheless, an absolute rule of nonintervention does little to protect values of sovereignty, political independence, and territorial integrity in a civil conflict that results in a protracted military stalemate and continuing anarchy, such as existed in Liberia in 1990. In such cases, intervention that helps to restore the capacity of the affected people to reestablish order in a democratic fashion seems to promote, rather than to undermine, the affected country's sovereignty.

An alternative approach is to reconsider the requirement of consent for outside intervention in an internal conflict. When no government exists to provide such consent, then arguably a rule should apply that would legitimate intervention for humanitarian purposes when any of the primary warring factions requests it. Such an approach, which has not yet gained acceptance as an exception to the usual rules governing intervention, would legitimate the intervention in Liberia, since the forces of two of the three warring factions then operating in Liberia welcomed the arrival of ECOMOG. However, like the somewhat broader approach presidents Mugabe and Museveni proposed, reconsideration of the consent requirement also runs the risk of serious abuse by powerful states. Even in fundamentally internal conflicts, one or more of the various warring factions frequently receives some help from interested outside states. A rule that permitted intervention whenever one of the warring factions requested or consented to it might open the door too widely to intervention by states acting to further self-interest rather than to further the interests of the affected state or the international community.

## Intervention Under Chapter VIII

Under chapter VII of the UN Charter, the Security Council may determine that a particular situation constitutes a threat to international peace and security, and order or authorize the use of enforcement measures, including armed force, as necessary to restore and maintain international peace. But chapter VIII of the Charter empowers regional organizations to undertake enforcement action to address threats to international peace and security, provided that the Security Council authorizes such action.[76]

The exact meaning of the provisions authorizing regional enforcement action has always been the subject of dispute. In the discussions leading to the adoption of the UN Charter, the proper allocation of authority between regional organizations and the UN was second only to voting procedure in the Security Council as a subject of debate.[77] During the Cold War, regional organizations were sometimes viewed as a means to circumvent the veto-blocked Security Council. Thus, until recently, the political views of the various Cold War protagonists have colored discussion of the legal authority of regional organizations to act in particular cases.

Because the Charter contains no definition of a chapter VIII regional organization, no consensus exists even on what constitutes such an organization, or whether a subregional organization such as ECOWAS might qualify. In general, though, it appears that the requirements are few, and that most geographically concentrated groups of states that habitually act in concert under a governing charter or similar set of rules can qualify as a regional organization. But even if a particular subregional organization can legitimately claim to be a chapter VIII organization, its authority to use force against a member state depends on compliance with its own charter and rules; compliance with the rules of any larger regional organization to which its members belong; and authorization of the Security Council.

These issues have all been subject to intense debate in the context of prior interventions. The most recent and one of the most heated of these debates centered on the 1983 U.S. intervention in Grenada. The United States argued that its use of force in Grenada was justified in part because it undertook the intervention under the auspices of the Organization of Eastern Caribbean States (OECS).[78] But most states rejected this and other justifications the United States advanced; blocked only by the U.S. veto, the UN Security Council voted 11–1 to condemn the intervention.[79]

Although similar objections could be made to the ECOMOG intervention in Liberia, a stronger case exists for treating it as valid under chapter VIII. The principal difficulty in doing so lies in the fact that the Security Council never formally authorized the use of force. In July 1990 Liberia's representative to the UN attempted without success to place the Liberian crisis on the Council's agenda.[80] Not until January 1991, after ECOMOG had forced a cease-fire, did the Council issue its first public pronouncement. In a general statement, the Council lauded ECOWAS for working to bring peace to Liberia and encouraged all parties to cooperate with ECOWAS in the further implementation of its peace plan.[81] The Council made no specific mention of the use of force.

Seventeen months later, the Council issued another general statement, again praising ECOWAS for its efforts to restore peace in Liberia, and urging the parties to cooperate in the implementation of the Yamoussoukro IV accord.[82] As Baccus Matthews, foreign minister of the interim government, later observed, "these two statements proved to be the most that Liberia, a founding Member of the United Nations . . . could elicit from the Security Council during the most critical hour of its history."[83]

The Security Council did not address the war in Liberia again until its discussion in November 1992 of the ECOWAS request for an embargo directed against the NPFL. During the discussion, the Council was not requested to and did not specifically address the legality of either the Standing Mediation Committee's initial decision to use force in 1990, or ECOMOG's ongoing use of force to reestablish a buffer zone around Monrovia by driving out NPFL fighters. Nonetheless, it is difficult to read the almost 100 pages of discussion, coupled with the Council's prior laudatory statements, without concluding that the Council at least implicitly approved of both decisions to use force.

Some delegates openly praised ECOWAS for providing "order and a bastion of security" by its "dispatch of a six-nation West African peace-keeping force in August 1990," and claimed to have "supported this effort from its inception"; others applauded more generally "the efforts of the countries of the region to restore peace to Liberia."[84] The only criticism came from the representative of Burkina Faso, who observed that his government had "not failed to express some reservations over certain measures and the manner in which they were implemented."[85] With that exception, all the delegates clearly approved, at least in general terms, the efforts by ECOWAS to bring peace to Liberia.

Most Council delegates appear to have intentionally avoided the need for an explicit authorization of ECOMOG's use of force by accepting at face value the ECOWAS characterization of ECOMOG as a "peacekeeping force." Even though the monitoring group did not have the consent of the NPFL when it entered Liberia in August 1990, delegate after delegate specifically referred to the deployment as the "dispatch of peace-keeping forces."

The denotation of ECOMOG as a peacekeeping force frees the delegates from having to consider awkward questions about retroactive validation of ECOMOG's use of force under chapter VIII of the Charter. Thus, while many of the delegates praise the ECOWAS intervention in Liberia as a model of regional action, sometimes with explicit reference to chapter VIII, they do not distinguish, at least overtly, between ECOMOG actions that might constitute peaceful regional measures under article 52 of chapter VIII (such as negotiating cease-fire agreements) and ECOMOG actions that might more appropriately be considered regional enforcement action under article 53 (such as the initial offensive to drive the NPFL from Monrovia). To the contrary, Security Council delegates generally describe the entire ECOWAS involvement in the conflict as a commendable regional effort to restore peace.

Similarly, the Council members fail to distinguish more recent ECOMOG actions clearly undertaken in self-defense (such as repelling NPFL attacks on ECOMOG positions in Monrovia) from more questionable ECOMOG preemptive actions (such as bombing raids on NPFL supply lines). Instead, the Council simply "condemns the continuing armed attacks against the peace-keeping forces of ECOWAS in Liberia by one of the parties to the conflict,"[86] and appears to accept, or at least fails to question, the Community's position that its military actions constitute either peacekeeping or self-defense.

Politically, the Council's approach is probably a wise one. The Council clearly welcomed the willingness of a regional organization to shoulder primary responsibility for at least one of the many costly and protracted internal conflicts now multiplying around the globe.[87] The simplest way politically to support ECOWAS was to accept its own characterization of its actions. But as a legal matter, the Council's characterization of those actions leaves much to be desired.

Notwithstanding the later question of self-defense, it seems clear that ECOMOG's initial offensive against the NPFL was a form of enforcement action. It is also clear that the Council never explicitly authorized enforcement action, although it ultimately approved, at least implicitly, the deployment of ECOMOG.

In the past, most commentators have insisted that the authorization requirement of article 53 means prior, express authorization.[88] In large part, this reading reflects a negative reaction to the U.S. position during the Cuban missile crisis. The United States argued then that the failure of the Security Council to condemn the naval blockade of Cuba amounted to implicit authorization of it. Most states rejected this view.

But the case for legitimizing regional action under chapter VIII seems much stronger when the Council unanimously approves of (rather than simply fails to condemn) the action taken, even if the approval is only implicit and after the fact. The danger of such an approach is that it will encourage regional organizations to act without authorization in the hope that the Council can later be induced, in light of the irreversible change that intervention has caused in the relative standing of the parties, to endorse or at least accept the intervention. This risk, however, must be balanced against the danger of discouraging regional interventions that genuinely merit, and eventually receive, Council approbation, but that would be rendered ineffective or unduly costly if forced to await prior authorization.

In this case, the statements of the Council, coupled with its decision to impose an arms embargo on all parties to the conflict except ECOMOG, seem sufficient to place the ECOWAS intervention within the bounds of chapter VIII. To hold otherwise would lead to the strange result of condemning ECOWAS for failing to obtain Council authorization for actions that the Council itself has chosen to construe as part of a peacekeeping effort, which thus characterized would not require Council authorization in the first place.

## Compatibility with the OAU and ECOWAS Charters

As Burkina Faso and other francophone states initially complained, it is not easy to reconcile the decision of the Standing Mediation Committee with the OAU Charter or the ECOWAS Charter and protocols. The OAU has always strictly interpreted the principle of nonintervention in its Charter. But the OAU, like the Security Council, has also implicitly ratified the ECOWAS intervention, and it continues to encourage the Community to pursue its efforts at restoring peace.[89] Still, reliance on such implicit ratification seems problematic under the OAU Charter, unless one accepts the argument that the UN has authorized the intervention under chapter VIII.

The compatibility of the ECOWAS intervention in Liberia with the Community's own constitutive documents is also problematic. The 1981 ECOWAS defense pact authorizes a collective response to internal strife, if it is "actively engineered or supported" from "outside."[90] In this case, Taylor's insurrection had the support of Libya, a state outside the subregion, and of Community members Burkina Faso and Côte d'Ivoire. Thus, even assuming the pact's provisions on internal conflict apply only in cases of extraregional support for internal strife, the situation met the primary criterion for a collective response. Other provisions of the pact, however, appear to contemplate the involvement of the government of the state experiencing the internal conflict in the decision-making process on a collective response; such involvement in this case would have appeared to legitimate the essentially defunct government of President Doe. For example, article 9 of the pact, which applies in cases of armed intervention by the Community in an internal conflict, provides that "the actions of the [ECOWAS] Force Commander shall be subject to competent political authority of the Member State or States concerned." Similarly, article 16 anticipates a written request for assistance from the head of state of the affected country. Thus, the pact's provisions regarding internal conflict seem designed primarily to provide assistance to an existing member government in combating external subversion,[91] which is not consistent with ECOMOG's claim to act as a neutral peacekeeping force. In addition, the pact as a whole seems to assume the creation of various institutions that have yet to come into being, such as a defense council with responsibility for supervising Community military action.

Perhaps for these reasons, the various communiqués issued by ECOWAS leaders throughout the conflict do not rely on the defense pact as authority for the formation of ECOMOG.[92] Somewhat surprisingly, however, Côte d'Ivoire, one of the countries most responsible for supporting Charles Taylor, announced during the Council's November 1992 discussion of the Liberian situation that "intervention by ECOWAS in Liberian affairs had its roots in the provisions of article 4B of the ECOWAS Mutual Assistance Protocol."[93] For the reasons noted above, it is difficult to conclude that the pact by itself validates ECOMOG's intervention under then existing ECOWAS rules.

But given the situation in Liberia at the time, the ECOMOG intervention was as close to conforming with the terms of the Pact as was possible. Although no functioning government existed in Liberia to participate in the decision-making process, as contemplated by the pact, President Doe, to the extent he retained any legal authority, did welcome the decision to intervene. Moreover, it would seem that the nonexistence of a defense council and other institutions contemplated by the pact should no more serve as a bar to Community military action than the failure of members of the UN to commit troops to it under article 43 of the UN Charter serves as a bar to enforcement action authorized by the Security Council.

In addition, under article 5 of the ECOWAS Charter, the Authority of Heads of State and Government of ECOWAS is the "principal governing institution of the Community," and has the power to take decisions and issue directives that "shall be binding on all institutions of the Community."[94] Arguably, under these provisions, the ratification by the ECOWAS heads of state of the Standing Mediation Committee's initial decision to intervene, coupled with article 4(b) of the defense pact, is sufficient to validate that decision for purposes of the Community.

Nonetheless, the purposes and constitutive documents of the organization limit the power of the Authority of Heads of State and Government. Thus, given that the application of the defense pact to the situation in Liberia is doubtful in the absence of effective consent by Liberia, it is questionable whether the ECOWAS heads of state possessed the legal authority to ratify the Standing Mediation Committee's decision to use force. Moreover, like the statements of the Security Council and the OAU, ratification by the ECOWAS heads of state occurred only implicitly and after the fact. Thus, it appears that ECOWAS stretched its mandate to deal with an extraordinary situation. But given the alternatives, it is hard to find fault with that choice.

## NORMATIVE ISSUES

Notwithstanding the international community's reluctance to approve overtly the use of force in Liberia, the ECOWAS solution to the problem of internal conflict suggests some lessons that may be applicable in other contexts.

First, ECOWAS has demonstrated that a subregional organization can muster the political will to tackle a seemingly intractable interethnic civil war. Many of the same warnings now raised with regard to intervention in Bosnia also surfaced prior to the ECOWAS intervention in Liberia. It was suggested that ECOWAS would have difficulty in separating the combatants, that the ethnic nature of the war would lead to an unending blood feud that could not be settled from the outside, and that peacekeeping troops would be vulnerable to continuing attacks. These warnings may yet prove accurate. But for several years ECOWAS leaders have found the risks of involvement manageable, and have demonstrated considerable imagination, flexibility, and resourcefulness in working toward a long-term political solution. The continuing fighting sparked by the NPFL's October 1992 offensive against Monrovia may yet undo what ECOWAS has sought to accomplish. But even though the final results are not yet in, the successes so far appear to justify the ECOWAS approach.

Moreover, the Liberian conflict suggests that at least in some situations, a regional or subregional organization may be more effective than the UN or big-power coalitions. In the past, arguments shaped by Cold War politics complicated the relationship between regional organizations and the UN. While that debate is now anachronistic, its successor may be a political debate over which organizations should take primary responsibility for resolving a given conflict. In many cases, particularly in Africa, where the preference has long been for regional solutions, regional organizations might be better suited than the UN to resolving a localized conflict, provided they can be induced to act: they are more likely to have a direct interest in solving the problems underlying the conflict; they may better understand the basis for the conflict and the relevant players; and they may be able to act more quickly, being preoccupied with other fewer other conflicts.

With fourteen new peacekeeping operations launched since 1989, UN personnel and finances are already stretched to the breaking point. As regional conflicts proliferate, pressure is likely to build on regional organizations to assist or even to supplant the UN in handling at least some of these crises.

Of course, the record of regional and subregional organizations to date, particularly in Africa, has not been encouraging. Few regional organizations, apart from the Organization of American States and the European Community, have much in the way of economic or military resources; fewer still have much in the way of political organization, unity, or will. Cumbersome decision-making procedures and inexperienced and understaffed bureaucracies and institutions further hamper most regional organizations.[95] Further, many regional organizations may shrink from collective military action for fear that it will prove an excuse for a regional superpower to extend its power and influence, or because one of the parties to the conflict considers the organization, or one of its key members, biased.

But the ECOWAS experience in Liberia suggests that if regional organizations can muster the necessary political will, spurred perhaps by massive cross-border refugee flows or threats to regional stability, then the other obstacles to regional action are surmountable. Like many other regional organizations, ECOWAS has no history of collective military action, and its institutions and decision-making procedures were not designed for such action. But ECOWAS, on a more or less ad hoc basis, was able to adapt itself to meet the needs of the moment.

In the process, the Community was also able to contain the risk that Nigeria might emerge as a regional hegemon. Some critics claim that ECOWAS did not contain Nigeria, and that the deployment of ECOMOG should be understood as a form of "Pax Nigeriana" rather than a "Pax West Africana."[96] Certainly, Nigeria played the lead role in forming and deploying ECOMOG, and it continues to supply most of the diplomatic, financial, and military support for ECOMOG. It is also true that Nigeria's president, Ibrahim Babangida, was a friend of Samuel Doe, and that Nigeria provided substantial political and economic assistance to Doe's regime, including military supplies in the early stages of his losing fight against the forces of Charles Taylor and Prince Johnson. In this context, some critics have seen the ECOMOG intervention primarily as a Nigerian effort to block Charles Taylor's drive to oust Doe from his executive mansion.

But in the end, Nigeria did not simply impose its will on Liberia. It did not intervene unilaterally, or at a point when Doe's regime might still have been salvageable. More importantly, Nigeria has frequently had to compromise on ECOMOG's goals and tactics in order to maintain a consensus within ECOWAS for continued involvement within Liberia. But for this need to compromise, ECOMOG might well have overrun Taylor's forces in August 1990. Indeed, many of the fits and starts of the ECOWAS approach to Liberia—the on again, off again economic sanctions and the repeated efforts to accommodate Taylor despite his string of broken promises—demonstrate that ECOMOG has indeed been a Community enterprise.

To date, ECOWAS has managed to move forward despite the difficulties imposed by the need to obtain consensus and despite the occasional willingness of some member states, Côte d'Ivoire and Burkina Faso in particular, "to pursue national policies toward the crisis which differed from those they endorsed within the organization."[97] As discussed below, the most pressing question now is whether ECOWAS can continue to adapt to meet the threats of a changing conflict.

Second, the political support accorded to ECOWAS throughout most of Africa suggests an increased willingness on the part of many African states to recognize that a blanket prohibition on outside intervention in a state's domestic affairs is no longer feasible or necessarily in the interest of most African states. In the past, many African states served as ideological and even military battlegrounds for superpower competition. Under such circumstances, the tendency in Africa, as in Latin America, was to condemn any form of outside intervention, for fear that exceptions would only invite further superpower involvement. With the end of the Cold War, many African states now fear neglect more than intervention. Consequently, at least some African leaders seem willing to view the issue of intervention in accordance with the circumstances of a specific case, rather than in terms of absolutes.

In particular, some African leaders seem willing to tolerate and even encourage intervention in cases of anarchy or massive human rights abuses. In part, that change may reflect the inclusion of many African countries in a larger global trend toward democratization and concern for human rights. A number of African states have substituted moderate democratic governments for oppressive, autocratic predecessors. These new governments are likely to feel less threatened by the treatment of human rights issues as matters of international concern.

Third, the willingness of the international community to acquiesce in but not overtly approve forcible intervention in Liberia suggests that, as in the past, states or groups of states willing to undertake interventions perceived as genuinely humanitarian will not incur condemnation or international sanction, especially when the decision to intervene stems from a multilateral decision-making process. In effect, such interventions are accorded a "second-tier" legality.[98]

This approach preserves the formal rules governing nonintervention, and lessens the likelihood that powerful states will rely on claimed humanitarian motives for interventions that are not in the interest of the affected state. But this approach may also unduly discourage desirable interventions, since typically such interventions are not formally "legal."

Ideally, the Security Council should alleviate the pressure for unauthorized humanitarian interventions by taking action in future crises more promptly than it did in Liberia. But as internal conflicts multiply, the UN may prove unable to respond to all (or even many) of them in a timely fashion. Moreover, the Council's ability to achieve consensus on decisions to intervene may not last forever. As a result, pressure for agreement on normative criteria for humanitarian intervention is likely to continue. One possible approach is to pursue the analysis presidents Museveni and Mugabe suggested: that is, to examine the interests that existing notions of sovereignty and territorial integrity protect, and to legitimate interventions in situations where those interests are not unduly infringed, such as when anarchy replaces any form of governmental authority.

Fourth, Liberia demonstrates the extent to which intervention in an internal conflict can draw the intervenors into the long-term political reconstruction, and the long-term political disputes, of the affected country. ECOWAS deployed troops to end the fighting in Liberia in August 1990. Elections originally scheduled for October 1991 were postponed to the spring of 1992, then to August 1992, then to November 1992, and then indefinitely. Throughout this period, ECOWAS has of necessity been intimately involved in attempts to broker a solution acceptable to all parties.

This involvement has required ECOWAS to develop detailed plans for encampment and disarmament of the warring factions; to sponsor political conferences; to hold innumerable meetings with the warring factions and various Liberian interest groups; to search for ways to pressure recalcitrant parties (in particular, the NPFL); to draw up election timetables and rules; and in general to involve itself in all aspects of Liberian political life. In short, once it entered Liberia, ECOWAS found that it could not get out, short of abandoning its peacekeeping mission, without first seeing to the reconstruction of a viable Liberian government.

ECOWAS has shown considerable flexibility, ingenuity, and patience in its efforts to stabilize Liberia. Moreover, throughout its involvement, ECOWAS has managed to maintain a working consensus among its member states, in part by entrusting much of the responsibility for a political solution to the states most reluctant to intervene in the first place.

But as the duration of ECOWAS involvement lengthens, so does the cost, both financial and political. To date, ECOWAS has found the alternative to continued involvement—the abandonment of Liberia to further conflict and possible anarchy—unacceptable. That calculus may change as renewed fighting jeopardizes the progress ECOWAS has achieved, and as domestic pressure builds within Nigeria and other ECOMOG members to end their involvement in Liberia. But it seems equally likely that having reached a consensus on involvement in Liberia, the ECOWAS states will decide to pursue that involvement to a satisfactory resolution, even if it means the further use of military force.

## CONCLUSION

To some extent, ECOMOG's initial success as peace enforcer has complicated and protracted the job of political broker and peace-keeper. When ECOMOG stopped the fighting in 1990 by sep-arating the warring parties, it also created the conditions for political stalemate. With the monitoring group present, Taylor could not exercise control over the entire country. But at the same time, he had little incentive to surrender what he did control. When ECOWAS did not move quickly to back its diplomatic pressure on Taylor with either economic or military coercion, the result was stasis.

The long delays in implementing the ECOWAS peace plan gave ULIMO the time it needed to organize itself as a political and military entity, and to mount a surprisingly successful military offensive. The formation of ULIMO gave Taylor the excuse he needed not to disarm, and ULIMO's offensive gave Taylor an excuse for attacking Monrovia. As a result, ECOWAS must now reconsider its mission and the viability of its peace plan, and find ways to adapt that plan to deal with the open hostility of the NPFL and the existence of a major new warring faction. Thus, if the future of Liberia is not to be decided in a military contest between the NPFL and ULIMO, ECOWAS will have to find ways to pressure both factions to accept a cease-fire, disarmament, and elections.

It is difficult to see how ECOWAS will accomplish that task. The character of the war now being fought, with its shifting fronts and uncertain battle lines extending through much of the country, makes effective military intervention far more difficult than it was when fighting was confined to Monrovia. Moreover, the size of the contending forces is considerably greater than it was at the time of the initial ECOWAS intervention. Perhaps most important, the largest of the warring factions again per-ceives ECOMOG as a military adversary rather than a neutral peacekeeper.

The increasing complexity of the conflict demonstrates the importance of timing in any outside intervention into an internal conflict. ECOWAS was sensitive to this issue when it first intervened, recognizing that premature involvement could appear to be an attempt to suppress a legitimate popular effort to overthrow a dictatorial government. ECOWAS also recognized that delay posed the danger of disintegration and loss of life. It appears, however, that ECOWAS did not fully appreciate the need for a prompt postintervention resolution, and that it relied too much on persuasion and too little on pressure as a means of holding the parties to their agreements.

It is too early, however, to conclude that ECOWAS has entirely missed its window of opportunity. ECOWAS has shown surprising resilience since 1990, and may yet find a way to revitalize its efforts to bring peace to Liberia. At the moment, the organization seems intent on exerting sufficient pressure on the NPFL to compel it to accept a Community-sponsored political settlement. But ECOWAS must also restrain ULIMO (and the AFL), and reestablish its credibility with all of the warring factions. If ECOWAS can manage to stop the fighting, whether through diplomacy or force, and continue with its plan for peace through disarmament and elections, it may yet achieve a major success.

The answer to this question will likely have implications beyond Liberia. If ECOWAS succeeds, its efforts may serve as a model for future regional action. If it fails, it will undoubtedly strengthen the hand of those who believe that such conflicts must be handled by a U.S.-led UN, or simply be allowed to burn themselves out, whatever the cost in human terms.

## NOTES

1. The historical background presented here derives in large part from Harold D. Nelson, ed., *Liberia: A Country Study* (Washington, D.C.: American University Foreign Area Studies, 1984); Hiram Ruiz, *Uprooted Liberians: Casualties of a Brutal War* (Washington, D.C.: U.S. Committee for Refugees, 1992); and Bill Berkeley, *Liberia: A Promise Betrayed* (New York: Lawyers Committee for Human Rights, 1986).
2. See Nelson, ed., *Liberia: A Country Study*, pp. 43–45.

3. Ibid., pp. 48–51.
4. See Berkeley, *Liberia: A Promise Betrayed*, p. 23.
5. Brenda M. Branaman, *Liberia: Issues for the United States*, Congressional Research Services Issue Brief 7–8 (Washington, D.C.: Congressional Research Service, 1991).
6. See Ruiz, *Uprooted Liberians*, p. 4.
7. Ibid., p. 5.
8. "Several Villages Said Seized," Paris Agence France Presse (AFP), FBIS-AFR-90-003 (January 4, 1990) pp. 13–14. Taylor himself is an Americo-Liberian. In the 1970s he helped organize opposition to the Tolbert government. When Doe overthrew Tolbert, Taylor became an official in the new government. In 1983, however, Taylor had a falling out with Doe and sought refuge in the United States. Doe sought to have Taylor extradited on charges of embezzlement. But Taylor escaped from a Boston jail as he awaited extradition, and after a long sojourn in Libya, he made his way to Côte d'Ivoire, where he organized his small invasion force. See Kenneth B. Noble, "In Liberia's Illusory Peace, Rebel Leader Rules Empire of His Own Design," *New York Times*, April 14, 1992, p. A3.
9. "Minister Reacts to Taylor's Claims," BBC World Service, in FBIS-AFR-90-002 (January 3, 1990), p. 19.
10. U.S. Department of State, *Country Reports on Human Rights Practices for 1990* (Washington, D.C., U.S. GPO, 1991), pp. 192–193.
11. See Ruiz, *Uprooted Liberians*, p. 5.
12. Ibid.; and U.S. Department of State, *Country Reports*, p. 192.
13. U.S. Department of State, *Country Reports*, p. 192.
14. "Business Closed, Air Guinea Suspends Flights," Paris AFP, FBIS-AFR-90-126 (June 29,1990), p. 28; and "Joint Effort Proposed For Doe's Resignation," Paris AFP, FBIS-AFR-90-124 (June 27, 1990), p.1.
15. The members of the Standing Mediation Committee are the Gambia, Ghana, Mali, Nigeria, and Togo.
16. "Information Minister on Doe Resignation Issue," BBC World Service, FBIS-AFR-90-142 (July 24, 1990), p. 26.
17. See Ruiz, *Uprooted Liberians*, p. 7.
18. See James Butty, "A Year of Terror," *West Africa*, January 7–13, 1991, p. 3151; and "NPFL Walks Out," Paris AFP, FBIS-AFR-90-163 (August 22, 1990), p. 26. Nonetheless, the United States has since applauded the ECOWAS countries for their efforts at restoring peace, and has lent both diplomatic and financial support to the peacekeeping effort of the Community's cease-fire monitoring group.
19. Tunji Lardner, Jr., "The Somalia Tragedy," *West Africa*, March 16–22, 1992, p. 449 (interview with UN Under Secretary James Jonah), quoted in John Inegbedion, *The ECOWAS Intervention in Liberia: Toward Regional Conflict Management in Post–Cold War Africa?* (Revised research paper for the Academic Committee on the United Nations System and the American Society of International Law Summer Workshop on International Organizations, Dartmouth College, Hanover, New Hampshire, July 1992.)
20. Ibid.
21. Neil Henry, "Doctors' Group Criticizes U.S. for Not Intervening in Liberia," *The Washington Post*, August 16, 1990, p. A17.

22. Julius Okolo, "The Development and Structure of ECOWAS," *West African Regional Cooperation and Development*, Julius Emeka Okolo and Stephen Wright, eds. (Boulder, Colo.: Westview Press, 1990), p.19. The members of ECOWAS are Benin, Burkina Faso, Cape Verde, Côte d'Ivoire, the Gambia, Ghana, Guinea, Guinea-Bissau, Liberia, Mali, Mauritania, Niger, Nigeria, Senegal, Sierra Leone, and Togo.

23. Stephen Wright and Julius Okolo, "Cooperation and Development in West Africa," *West African Regional Cooperation and Development*, pp. 3–5.

24. Ibid., p. 3.

25. See Protocol of Non-Aggression, reprinted in *West Africa*, May 25, 1981, p. 1153.

26. Protocol Relating to Mutual Assistance on Defence, A/SP3/5/81, reprinted in *Official Journal of the ECOWAS* (June 1981), p. 9. The defense pact entered into force on September 30, 1986.

27. It is unclear whether the term "outside" means outside the member state experiencing the internal conflict or outside the region.

28. See Okolo, "Development and Structure," p. 41.

29. Final Communiqué of the First Session of the Community Standing Mediation Committee, ECOWAS, Banjul, Republic of the Gambia, August 6–7, 1990.

30. Like Taylor, both Johnson and Doe viewed an ECOWAS intervention as a means of stopping the NPFL's drive to take complete control of Monrovia. Johnson went so far as to take foreign nationals hostage in the hope of provoking intervention. "ECOWAS Force Said Facing Difficulties," Paris AFP, FBIS-AFR-90-154 (August 9, 1990), p. 35.

31. "NPFL Rebels, Doe Troops Resume Fighting," Paris AFP, FBIS-AFR-90-151 (August 6, 1990), p. 25; and "ECOWAS Head Interviewed on Intervention," BBC World Service, FBIS-AFR-90-151 (August 6, 1990), p. 25.

32. "Conte Returns From Banjul ECOWAS Summit," Conakry Domestic Service, FBIS-AFR-90-153 (August 8, 1990), p. 45.

33. Peter da Costa, "The Cost of Peace," *West Africa*, September 3–9, 1990, p. 2391; and "ECOWAS 'Crisis of Confidence' on Peacekeeping," Dakar Pana, FBIS-AFR-90-167 (August 28, 1990), p. 1.

34. "Compaore Rejects ECOWAS Intervention," Ouagadougou Domestic Service, FBIS-AFR-90-157 (August 14, 1990), p. 24; and "Compaore Explains Support for Liberian Rebels," BBC World Service, FBIS-AFR-90-163 (August 22, 1990), p. 25.

35. See Final Communiqué of the National Conference of All Liberian Political Parties, Patriotic Fronts, Interest Groups and Concerned Citizens, Banjul, Republic of the Gambia, August 27–September 1, 1990, pp. 25–26.

36. Sawyer, who had been chairman of the commission that drafted Liberia's 1985 Constitution, was a well-respected Liberian politician and scholar, and a prominent opponent of President Doe.

37. Accra Domestic Service, FBIS-AFR-90-183 (September 20, 1990), p. 37.

38. "Aid Arrives—Slowly," *Africa News*, November 12, 1990.

39. Final Communiqué of the First Extra-ordinary Session of the Authority of Heads of State and Government of the Economic Community of West African States, Bamako, Mali, November 27–28, 1990.

40. Ibid.; and Joint Declaration on the Cessation of Hostilities and Peaceful Settlement of Conflict, Bamako, Mali, November 28, 1990. See also Ruby Ofori, "Ceasefire Signed," *West Africa*, December 3–9, 1990, p. 2954.

41. Joint Statement of the Warring Parties in Liberia, Banjul, Republic of the Gambia, December 21, 1990. The existing interim government, while maintaining that the August 1990 All Liberia Conference fully established its legitimacy, separately agreed to accept the results of a second All Liberia Conference.

42. See Final Communiqué of the Third Summit Meeting of the Community Standing Mediation Committee, ECOWAS, Lomé, Togo, February 12–13, 1991; Agreement on Cessation of Hostilities and Peaceful Settlement of Conflict, February 13, 1991; and ECOWAS, Modalities for Monitoring the Implementation of the Cease-fire Agreement by the ECOMOG, Lomé, Togo, February 12–13, 1991.

43. See Peter da Costa, "ECOMOG on Trial," *West Africa*, April 15–21, 1991, p. 560; and "Diversionary Tactics?" *West Africa*, April 29–May 5, 1991, p. 650.

44. ECOWAS, Final Communiqué of the Third Meeting of the Committee of Five on the Liberian Crisis Held in Yamoussoukro, October 29–30, 1991. ULIMO was not represented at these talks, because until its August 1992 offensive, ULIMO was not taken seriously as a warring faction.

45. "NPFL Obstructs ECOMOG," *West Africa*, June 1–7, 1992, p. 931.

46. "Troop Deaths in Liberia Spark Review by West Africans," Africa News, June 22, 1992.

47. Final Communiqué of the Fifteenth Session of the Authority of Heads of State and Government of the Economic Community of West African States, Dakar, Senegal, July 27–29, 1992.

48. "Trapped ECOMOG Soldiers Return to Monrovia," Xinhua General News Service, September 19, 1992.

49. "Some Africans Want U.N. Observer Role in Liberia," Reuters, October 7, 1992. Carter's involvement in Liberia began when representatives of the interim government, the NPFL, and ECOWAS requested his assistance in the organization and monitoring of elections.

50. Ibid.

51. The NPFL overran Caldwell base, where Prince Johnson and his INPFL were encamped, early in the fighting, leading Johnson to seek refuge with ECOMOG forces and effectively ending his role in the conflict.

52. Final Communiqué of the First Summit Meeting of the Committee of Nine on the Liberian Crisis, Abuja, Nigeria, November 7, 1992; and Final Communiqué of the First Joint Summit Meeting of the ECOWAS Standing Mediation Committee and the Committee of Five, Cotonou, Benin, October 20, 1992.

53. Final Communiqué of the First Summit Meeting of the Committee of Nine on the Liberian Crisis.

54. See Final Communiqué of the First Joint Summit Meeting of the ECOWAS Standing Mediation Committee and the Committee of Five.

55. Final Communiqué of the First Summit Meeting of the Committee of Nine on the Liberian Crisis.

56. In brief statements issued on January 22, 1991 (S/22133), and May 7, 1992 (S/23886), the Council had requested the warring parties to cooperate with ECOWAS in reaching a peaceful settlement to the conflict, but it had not otherwise discussed the war or the use of force by ECOMOG.

57. Final Communiqué of the First Joint Summit Meeting of the ECOWAS Standing Mediation Committee and the Committee of Five, paras. 6–9.

58. Final Communiqué of the First Session of the Community Standing Mediation Committee.

59. "Doe, Johnson Said 'Happy' for Intervention," BBC World Service, FBIS-AFR-90-151 (August 6, 1990), p. 23.

60. See, e.g., "The Gambia's Dawda Jawara on ECOMOG Role," Dakar PANA, FBIS-AFR-90-168 (August 29, 1990), p. 35.

61. Peter da Costa, "Hopeful Signs," *West Africa*, August 27–September 2, 1990, p. 2355.

62. Kaye Whiteman, "Towards Peace in Liberia," *West Africa*, November 26–December 2, 1990, p. 2895.

63. Similar arguments were made with some success in 1961, in the context of UN peacekeeping troops' extensive military operations in the Congo, and in 1965, with reference to U.S. and Latin American peacekeeping forces in the Dominican Republic. See, e.g., R. Simmonds, *Legal Problems Arising from the United Nations Military Operations in the Congo* (The Hague: Martinus Nijhoff, 1968), pp. 127–130; Michael Akehurst, "Enforcement Action by Regional Agencies, with Special Reference to the Organization of American States," The British Year Book of International Law, vol. 42 (1969), p. 212 and note 5 (quoting statement of the U.S. representative to the Security Council).

64. Taylor's postintervention consent to the presence of ECOMOG, and his agreement to encamp and disarm his forces under ECOMOG supervision, arguably gave the monitoring group legal rights as a peacekeeping body that Taylor could not unilaterally revoke. Compare Akehurst, "Enforcement Action," p. 212.

65. See Final Communiqué of the First Joint Summit Meeting of the ECOWAS Standing Mediation Committee and the Committee of Five.

66. "Liberia: U.S. Insists It Backs Peacekeeping Force," Inter Press Service, November 12, 1992.

67. Permanent Representative of Nigeria to the United Nations, letter to the secretary-general, August 9, 1990 (attaching letter from Dr. Rilwanu Lukman, honourable minister of external affairs of the Federal Republic of Nigeria).

68. A variety of authors have proposed tests by which to judge humanitarian interventions; the criteria Professors Richard Lillich and John Norton Moore have suggested are representative. Those criteria include: the immediacy and extent of the violation of human rights; "existence of an invitation by appropriate authorities"; the degree of coercion used; the "relative disinterestedness" of the intervenors; "minimal effect on authority structures"; "prompt disengagement consistent with the purpose of the action"; and "full reporting to the Security Council." See Richard Lillich, "Humanitarian Intervention: A Reply to Ian Brownlie and a Plea for Constructive

Alternatives," in John Norton Moore, ed., *Law and Civil War in the Modern World* (Baltimore: Johns Hopkins Press, 1974), pp. 229 and 248–249.

69. Individual leaders often cited the threat to ECOWAS nationals as a justification for refusing to consider the conflict a purely domestic one. While many states have at one time or another asserted a right to intervene in order to protect their own nationals, that right, to the extent that it exists in customary international law, would not by itself justify the continued presence of foreign troops after all foreign nationals have been released. Thus, while the danger to foreign nationals supports the claim that the Liberian civil war was a threat to international peace and security, it does not by itself justify the role of ECOMOG in Liberia.

70. "OAU's Salim Interviewed on Liberian Crisis," Dar es Salaam Domestic Service, FBIS-AFR-90-151 (August 6, 1990), p. 2. See also "Africa's Destiny," *West Africa*, October 22–28, 1990, p. 2690.

71. Ben Ephson, "Right to Intervene," *West Africa*, February 4–10, 1991, p. 141; and "Uganda's Museveni on ECOWAS, OAU Role," BBC World Service, FBIS-AFR-90-189 (September 28, 1990), p. 52.

72. "Doe, Johnson Said 'Happy' for Intervention," p. 23. Similar arguments have been made to justify intervention in Somalia. UN Secretary-General Boutros Boutros-Ghali, for example, in December 1992 rejected the criticism that intervention there violated Somalia's sovereignty, on the ground that Somalia had no government. See "The Concept of Sovereignty Is Flexible," Agence France Presse, December 10, 1992.

73. Ben Ephson, "Right to Intervene," p. 141.

74. It has been suggested, for example, that the temporary breakdown of authority in Grenada in 1983 constituted a justification for intervention by forces acting under the auspices of a subregional organization, although the true extent of that "breakdown" has been widely questioned. See John Norton Moore, "Grenada and the International Double Standard," *American Journal of International Law*, vol. 78 (1984), pp. 145, 154, and 163; compare Edward Gordon, Richard B. Bilder, Arthur W. Rovine, and Don Wallace, Jr., "International Law and the United States Action in Grenada: A Report," *International Lawyer*, vol. 18 (1984), p. 331, 369–71.

75. Ben Ephson, "Right to Intervene," p. 141.

76. In Liberia's case, there can be little doubt that massive cross-border refugee flows, the danger to foreign nationals, and the probability of a spillover of fighting to neighboring countries constituted the requisite threat to international peace and security.

77. Akehurst, "Enforcement Action," p. 175.

78. As in the case of Grenada, ECOWAS leaders repeatedly cited the threat posed to their own nationals as one justification for intervention. But again, the extent and duration of the intervention far exceeded what was necessary to rescue foreign citizens. Similarly, ECOWAS leaders noted that President Doe, who was arguably still the de jure head of state, welcomed ECOMOG's intervention. But by the time he did so, his authority to speak for Liberia was doubtful at best.

79. See Gordon et al., "International Law."
80. See General Assembly, Provisional Verbatim Record of the Twenty-Seventh Meeting, A/45/PV. 27, October 19, 1990, p.61; and Provisional Verbatim Record of the Two Thousand Nine Hundred and Seventy-fourth Meeting of the Security Council, S/PV. 2974, January 22, 1991, p. 3.
81. Note by the President of the Security Council, S/22133, January 22, 1991.
82. Note by the President of the Security Council, S/23886, May 7, 1992.
83. Provisional Verbatim Record of the Three Thousand One Hundred and Thirty-eighth Meeting of the Security Council, S/PV.3138, November 19, 1992, p. 13.
84. Ibid., pp. 74–75, 76 (remarks of Mr. Edward Perkins, United States); and p. 78 (statement of Mr. Herve Ladsous, France).
85. Ibid., p. 33.
86. Security Council Resolution 788, November 19, 1992.
87. As the U.S. representative observed, "if the united ECOWAS effort fails in Liberia, the regional organization is unlikely to venture into the difficult realm of peace-keeping and conflict resolution in the future, and pressure will build rapidly for direct United States or United Nations intervention." See S/PV.3138, p. 77.
88. See, e.g., Akehurst, "Enforcement Action," p. 214. But see John Norton Moore, "The Role of Regional Arrangements in the Maintenance of World Order," in *The Future of the International Legal Order*, vol. 3 (Princeton, N.J.: Princeton University Press, 1971), pp. 122 and 159 ("authorization may be subsequent").
89. See, e.g., Statement of the Fifth Session of the OAU Ad Hoc Committee of Heads of State and Government on Southern Africa, A/45/496, S/21743, September 12, 1990, p. 2; and S/PV.3138, p. 76 (statement of Mr. Edward Perkins, United States).
90. Article 4B of the Protocol Relating to Mutual Assistance on Defense, A/SP3/5/81, provides that "Member states shall also take appropriate measures . . . (b) in case of internal armed conflict within any Member State engineered and supported actively from outside likely to endanger the peace and security in the entire Community. In this case the Authority shall appreciate and decide on this situation in full collaboration with the Authority of the Member State or States concerned."
91. See John Inegbedion, *The ECOWAS Intervention in Liberia*, p. 9 ("the inclusion of internal armed conflicts as objects of collective action appears a device for the maintenance of the *status quo*—regime or presidential survival").
92. An additional problem that reliance on the pact poses is that it apparently was not properly registered with the UN until after the intervention took place, as required for invocation before any UN organ under article 102 of the UN Charter. A similar argument was made with respect to the OECS Charter in the Grenada intervention. But failure to comply with the registration requirements does not invalidate the treaty among the ECOWAS members, the point under discussion here. Compare Moore, *Grenada and the International Double Standard*, p. 164.
93. S/PV.3138, p. 27 (remarks of Mr. Amara Essy, Côte d'Ivoire).

94. Although an unstated rule of unanimity prevails in the ECOWAS decision-making process, the ECOWAS Charter does not require unanimity. See Samuel K. B. Asante, *The Political Economy of Regionalism in Africa* (New York: Praeger, 1986), pp. 69–73. Thus, the inability of Liberia to participate in decision-making should not constitute a bar to decisions under the unanimity rule.

    One could argue that decisions of the Authority are binding only on Community "institutions," and not on member states, absent ratification by the individual states. But it is unclear precisely which Community decisions require ratification, and to date none of the ECOWAS states has challenged the validity of the Authority's decisions for want of ratification.

95. See, e.g., Stanley Hoffmann, "Delusions of World Order," *New York Review of Books*, April 9, 1992, vol. 39, no. 7, p. 40.

96. For a fuller discussion of this issue, see Emeka Nwokedi, *Regional Integration and Regional Security: ECOMOG, Nigeria and the Liberian Crisis* (Bordeaux: Centre d'Etude d'Afrique Noire, 1992), pp. 9-17 (concluding that "ECOWAS, as a body, and not Nigeria exclusively was committed to the restoration of peace in Liberia").

97. Ibid., p. 15.

98. For a critical discussion of the theory of "acceptable breaches" of international law for humanitarian ends, see Jean-Pierre L. Fonteyne, "The Customary International Law Doctrine of Humanitarian Intervention: Its Current Validity under the U.N. Charter," *California Western International Law Journal*, vol. 4 (1974), p. 203.

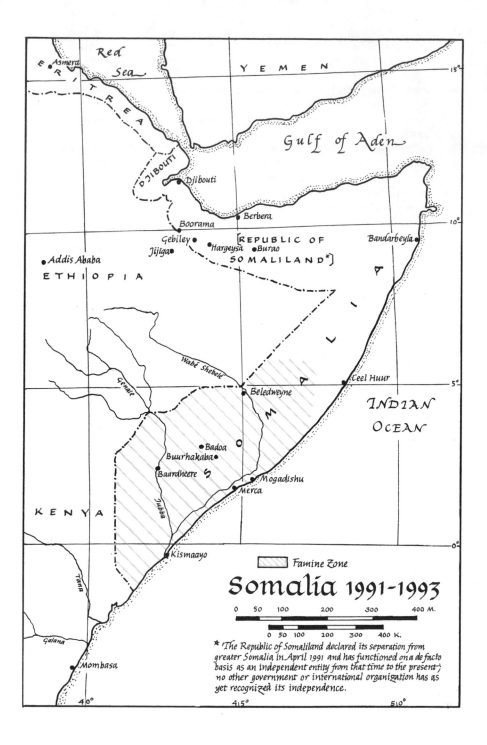

Red Sea

ERITREA
Asmera

YEMEN 15°

Gulf of Aden

DJIBOUTI
Djibouti

Boorama

Berbera 10°

Gebiley
Jijiga
Hargeysa
Burao

[REPUBLIC OF SOMALILAND*]

Bandarbeyla

Addis Ababa

ETHIOPIA

Wabé Shebele

Genale

S O M A L I A

Ceel Huur 5°

Beledweyne

INDIAN OCEAN

Badoa
Buurhakaba
Baardheere

Jubba

Mogadishu
Merca

KENYA

Tana

Kismaayo

Famine Zone

## Somalia 1991-1993

0   50   100      200      300      400 M.

0   50  100    200    300    400 K.

*The Republic of Somaliland declared its separation from
greater Somalia in April 1991 and has functioned on a de facto
basis as an independent entity from that time to the present;
no other government or international organization has as
yet recognized its independence.

Galana

Mombasa

40°      45°      50°

# Debacle in Somalia: Failure of the Collective Response

## JEFFREY CLARK

### THE PLUNGE INTO THE ABYSS

Following a United Nations Security Council vote authorizing force to rescue both starving Somalis and a highly imperiled relief operation, in early December 1992 President George Bush ordered a dramatic U.S. military intervention into the searing famine and advanced anarchy of Somalia. The drama of that genuinely unprecedented large-scale intervention, and the news media's fixation on looters and "warlords," threaten to obscure the fact that prior to late 1992, the international response to Somalia's long agony was itself a disaster of serious dimensions. In truth, inadequate and halfhearted multilateral measures had contributed not insignificantly to the very violence and starvation that the almost 35,000 U.S. and multilateral military troops were sent to address.

American (and world) public and political leaders, including President-elect Bill Clinton and the congressional leadership, greeted the intervention with widespread support. Early success in meeting at least the Pentagon's stated objectives and the rapid addition to the force of troops from France, Belgium, Saudi

Arabia, Canada, and other nations deepened that support. Operation Restore Hope did largely stop the marauding bandits and warlords from stealing relief supplies; the numbers of deaths in the infamous Baidoa camps dropped quickly from as high as 200 per day to ten. The operation thus appears to be, at least in the near term, a successful demonstration of American commitment to humanitarian principles—at acceptable risk and cost. More significantly, however, the intervention exposed the acute dangers inherent in the collective failure to restructure international humanitarian assistance policies and multilateral relief and political organizations to meet the realities of the post–Cold War world. President Clinton has acknowledged as much in comments addressing the need for policy realignment to chart U.S. involvement in Somali-like trouble spots around the globe.[1]

The ultimate success of the intervention will rely largely on whether or not the UN, the United States, and the other players decisively seize the opportunities created to both structure a national reconciliation process and forge a more coherent and forceful UN presence in the country. Prospects for that success remain modest. Neither objective had been even credibly attempted prior to the American-led military operation, and the UN today remains fundamentally ineffective in Somalia.

Operation Restore Hope should realistically be viewed as the first of several difficult steps necessary in renewing the political and economic viability of Somalia. If the ultimate achievement does not extend beyond the restoration of basic security for an external relief operation, the harsh manifestations of the country's fractured state will likely again extract a great and horrible price from the people of Somalia, as well as the international community.

Neither the UN relief agencies' initial operational response to the crisis nor the conflict mediation efforts of UN diplomats got under way with demonstrated professionalism. Until Secretary-General Boutros Boutros-Ghali publicly embarrassed the UN Security Council and Washington into action, the former responded only halfheartedly and ineffectually to clear indicators of Somalia's approaching tragedy, while the latter assumed a stance that was strangely passive and schizophrenic when contrasted with the sudden and forceful measures it took by year's end and the prominent role it has played in the Horn of Africa over the past two decades.

Various UN officials exaggerated security concerns to excuse their agencies' own scant presence and faulty performance, factors that in turn contributed to the very real level of violence prevalent by mid-1992. The unvarnished history of the UN's role in Somalia is a tragic one of opportunities missed and strategic and operational blunders not justified by situational realities. Western donor governments did little better, and African entities—in particular the Organization of African Unity (OAU)—contributed virtually nothing to efforts to avoid calamity. Only the nongovernmental relief organizations, all underprepared and ill-equipped for the roles forced upon them, survive scrutiny with honor intact.

The world, after all, is witness to the starvation of hundreds of thousands of the Somali people, including 75 percent of all children under age five in the most affected regions—amounting to the loss of a generation. An accurate accounting of how such a catastrophe unfolded is troubling and not convenient for those in part responsible. But harsh realities require stern and sober judgments, along with candid and urgent appraisals of systems in need of drastic and immediate overhaul. *Accountability can be postponed no longer.*

THE ROAD TO DEBACLE

How did Somalia come to its current unraveling? Even a cursory look at historical and indigenous factors reveals the fractured nature of a country long molded by political decentralization. More than a century ago, Sir Richard Burton described the Somali nomads as "a fierce and turbulent race of republicans"[2] who do not readily submit to anyone's authority. The societal structuring is a complex and rigid clan system (the Somalis are generally divided into six major clans[3] and innumerable subclans) that purportedly allows many children to recite the names of ancestors going back more than 20 generations.[4] Today the prevalence of modern weapons, Somalia's most significant legacy of superpower involvement during the Cold War, has undermined the very foundation for order in Somalia's society—the authority of clan elders.

The relevant historical starting point for comprehending Somalia's current denouement may be in 1896, when the army of Ethiopian Emperor Menelik II soundly defeated the Italians in battle as Italy attempted to expand from its Eritrean colony to take over Ethiopia itself. In subsequent negotiations Great Britain—Italy's de facto sponsor in the colonization of Africa—ceded control of the Ogaden to Menelik and the Ethiopian empire. The problem was—and is—that the Ogaden is a huge area populated by Somalis, and the decision triggered tension and bursts of warfare that have lasted through the present era.

The British later colonized the northern regions of Somalia as Somaliland, and the Italians took the southern two-thirds; the Europeans remained in at least nominal control until 1960, when the two colonies were merged into an independent and relatively democratic Somalia.

For nine years the fragile but functioning democracy survived; then, in 1969, the Somali army took control after the assassination of the president. Under General Mohamed Siad Barre, the new government embarked upon a concerted effort to erode the clan system and diminish the authority of the elders; to symbolize this goal, Siad Barre conducted funeral-like ceremonies marking the burying of the clans.[5]

Siad Barre's new government was oriented toward "scientific socialism"—or at least military alliance with the Soviet Union. The president's son-in-law set up a national security service under East German guidance, and the huge influx of external weaponry and military advisors—Soviet bloc at this time—that would eventually undermine the Somali nation began.

In 1974 history repeated itself as events unfolding in Ethiopia dramatically affected Somalia. Army officers frustrated with the stagnation and repression of Emperor Haile Selassie's latter years on the throne and his failure to respond to the famine gripping his country deposed the Ethiopian leader. The turmoil in Addis Ababa and an intensifying war in Eritrea weakened Ethiopia's grip over the Ogaden. Siad Barre, despite his suppression of the clan system, responded to the agitation of his fellow clansmen—and in fact widespread, intense nationalism—to renew claims on the region.

An Ogadeni guerrilla campaign to drive the Ethiopian army from the region led, in 1977, to full-scale war between Somalia and Ethiopia just as the Dergue government's embracing of Marxism was rupturing Addis Ababa's long-standing relationship with the United States. Simultaneously, the Soviets abandoned and betrayed Siad Barre, and rushed military advisors and equipment to the Ethiopians (who were strategically more valuable and newly available) under Mengistu Haile Mariam.

Soviet support enabled Mengistu to crush the Somali invasion of the Ogaden, humiliate Siad Barre, and send half a million Ogadeni refugees and guerrillas pouring across the border into Somalia. Many brought with them modern weapons—the next wave of guns in the rising tide.

The exit of the Soviets from Mogadishu set the stage for the first significant American involvement in Somalia—initially in the form of a modest quantity of defensive weapons to check any potential Ethiopian reprisal across the long border. U.S. military aid to Somalia would eventually total over $200 million; economic assistance to Siad Barre was an additional half billion dollars.

The Ogaden disaster also unleashed the first wave of serious discontent with the rule of Siad Barre. A coup attempt occurred in 1978; its organizers escaped to Addis Ababa, from where, with Mengistu's encouragement, they staged raids across the border. In London, in 1981, a group of exiles formed the Somali National Movement (SNM), its strength based in the northern Issak clans of the former British Somaliland.

Resentment against Siad Barre's increasingly brutal and discriminatory rule was then building among the Issak, who felt their region was not receiving its due in development or education funding from the Mogadishu government. Siad Barre's perceived support of the Ogadeni refugees' intrusion on their traditional grazing lands and into their livestock exporting business triggered hostility. The SNM began to raid government facilities, and Siad Barre's repression of the Issaks intensified.

By 1988, Siad Barre's fragile grip on the reins of power in Somalia had a parallel in Mengistu's desperate attempt to keep the upper hand in a series of civil wars that were going badly for him and threatening his bloodthirsty rule in Ethiopia. In that year, the two despots struck a deal to abandon support for insurgent groups using their respective territories for maneuvers against the other's regimes. Fearing forced isolation from the border areas or even expulsion, the SNM entered northern Somalia en masse, engaging and initially overwhelming Siad Barre's troops.

The retribution was savage. Hargeisa, the regional capital, was destroyed, thousands of Issak civilians were killed in cold blood and hundreds of thousands (along with the SNM) were sent scurrying into Ethiopia, where the United Nations High Commissioner for Refugees (UNHCR) established a series of deplorable refugee camps.[6] Siad Barre's air force strafed the fleeing Issak, killing many thousands. (It is discouraging to note that U.S. military aid to Siad Barre continued through June 1988, when congressional action finally ended it.)

As the Issak example and Siad Barre's demonstrated weakness encouraged others to take up arms, the retaliation proved to be the Somali president's undoing. The United Somali Congress (USC) came together as a force in the spring of 1989 as the struggle moved south. Siad Barre controlled only Mogadishu by the end of his tenure, during which he frantically attempted to divide clan against clan. The last three months of his rule, however, saw increasing military and political coordination among his many enemies as civilians joined hands with the USC for the final push. Siad Barre desperately launched a massive distribution of weapons and ammunition from his vast arsenals; his power all but evaporated when he turned his army loose on Hawiye sections of the city, destroying much of the infrastructure and provoking a violent and deadly uprising in the process.

The destruction of his capital was Siad Barre's last major installment of terror on the Somali people; he fled Mogadishu in January 1991. One million inhabitants also temporarily fled the destruction and violence for the countryside.

Siad Barre's flight was, however, not the end of the violence and chaos. To the contrary, the situation only deteriorated. In the south, the USC forces split in two. Troops under General Mohamed Farah Aideed set off in pursuit of Siad Barre, while others, under Ali Mahdi Mohamed, a wealthy Mogadishu businessman, remained in the capital and declared themselves leaders of a new government. In the north, the Issak subclans, responding to Ali Mahdi's self-appointment as president and his refusal to call a conference on national reconciliation, declared their region independent—as the Somaliland Republic.[7] The SNM saw another Siad Barre in the making in Ali Mahdi and wanted no part of it. (Siad Barre himself fought on after fleeing Mogadishu, taking advantage of the division between his foes. In April 1991, his forces advanced to within about 20 miles of the capital. But his efforts faltered, and he fled to Nigeria in the summer of 1992; as of the spring of 1993, his followers, under the command of General Morgan, his son-in-law and the former head of the national security apparatus, were still engaged in skirmishes.)

During 1991 the struggle between Aideed, chairman of the USC, and Ali Mahdi intensified. On November 17 a full-scale civil war erupted. That intense conflict persisted until March 3, 1992, when a cease-fire was brokered under the auspices of external players, primarily the UN. The fighting was so severe in Mogadishu that most of the remaining infrastructure of the city was totally destroyed: virtually every building in the central city was ripped apart by artillery shelling; bridges and water lines were blown up; underground utility lines were dug up for the copper wiring they contained.

An unparalleled number of guns and advanced weapons flooded into Somalia during this period, some from the soldiers of Mengistu's crumbling army and others captured from Siad Barre's forces and arsenals. These weapons facilitated the destruction of Mogadishu and other cities, and laid the foundation for the looting that would later hinder relief operations.

Complementing the 1988–1991 struggle to oust Siad Barre and the subsequent civil war between Aideed and Ali Mahdi, a lingering drought drove people from their land in a futile search for food and exposed them even more directly to the ongoing violence. Civil war and drought combined to trigger the acute famine that seared the land by the spring of 1992 (though drought alone clearly would not have provoked the onset of famine in Somalia).

Somalia has had no functioning government since January 1991. Only Ali Mahdi's own followers recognize his claims to be president of Somali—and the patrolling marines are diminishing even his control of the northern sections of Mogadishu, until early 1993 cordoned off from the rest of the city behind a Beirut-style green line. The various clan militia, once united in opposing Siad Barre but then preoccupied with dividing the country into zones of control, are today being effectively disempowered by the intervention forces. Either Siad Barre or the civil war destroyed most national institutions—there was not a functioning police force anywhere in Somalia in 1992, for example. The ability of surviving intellectuals, business and professional people, elders, and clerics to step into the resulting void will soon determine the prospects for national recovery.

## DEGENERATION: FAMINE, LOOTING, AND VIOLENCE

As early as January 1992, Andrew Natsios, director of the U.S. government's international humanitarian assistance efforts, described the Somali famine as "the greatest humanitarian emergency in the world."[8] The U.S. Centers for Disease Control and Prevention has verified mortality rates "among the highest ever documented by a population survey among famine-affected civilians."[9] The Somali tragedy is by some measures worse than the 1984–1985 Ethiopian famine—the universal benchmark for incomprehensible human suffering. The Ethiopian famine was somewhat limited to specific geographic pockets; in contrast, in July 1992 the International Committee of the Red Cross (ICRC) was estimating that 95 percent of the people in Somalia suffered from malnutrition, with 70 percent enduring severe malnutrition.[10]

The famine in Somalia engulfed vast regions of the country, including the capital, Mogadishu. The September 1992 ICRC estimates were that 1.5 million individuals faced imminent starvation; three times that many were totally dependent on external food assistance. At least 350,000 Somalis perished from severe malnutrition and its associated diseases in 1992,[11] while well over 900,000 fled to squalid relief camps in Ethiopia, Kenya, Djibouti, and Yemen. Another 150,000 Somalis are in Saudi Arabia. These figures are for a population numbering less than six million.

In Baidoa and other especially hard-hit locations, thousands of silent, gaunt figures slowly awaiting death—seemingly beyond caring and, in many cases, beyond saving—jarred the composure of startled international military peacekeepers arriving a few days before Christmas.

Relief officials were faced with the enormous hurdle of moving a minimally required 60,000 metric tons of emergency food rations per month[12] into a country with a destroyed infrastructure and no functioning government, and were also confronted by the most intensive looting ever to plague any relief operation.

By November 1992, some 80 percent of relief commodities were being confiscated. The anarchy and chaos were diminishing the prospects that the relief effort would be even minimally effective, and starvation was claiming in excess of a thousand victims a day. President Bush by then was receiving convincing reports that the entire relief operation would have to be suspended, as the risk to the life of relief workers was rising well above acceptable levels. Public outrage at the lurid scenes from Mogadishu and Baidoa freed (or, perhaps, forced) the president to catapult over questions of mandates and authorities to take decisive action. The "CNN factor" simply did not allow the UN and the international community to continue avoiding action as the situation deteriorated.

Relief items were being stolen for a number of reasons, all related to the fact that food was serving as the currency of the land: food equaled money and power. Merchants stole food, hoarding it to keep the price high; warlords stole it to feed armies. Hungry individuals possessing loaded automatic rifles took (and still take) food—and hungry individuals with guns were numerous.

The theft of food was also occurring in Somalia as part of a crude but ultimately comprehensible effort on the part of some clans and subclans to guarantee their members a larger share of the most urgently required commodity. That is, the chaos and the overall shortage of supplies available to relief groups resulted in a haphazard and uneven distribution of food among clans; part of the looting was a violent and dangerous redistribution effort.

## EXTERNAL PLAYERS: EXPECTATIONS ESTABLISHED

The perpetrators of Somalia's misery are Somali. The passive accomplices, however, are officials of the UN, of other multilateral organizations, and of the governments of major powers who contributed to that misery by neglect, denial, evasion of responsibility, and bungling relief operations and peacemaking initiatives launched without coherent strategy until, by late 1992, more decisive and expensive intervention was unavoidable. More than 350,000 Somalis have died from starvation, and vast numbers remain in peril, in part because as dictators and warlords assaulted them, the international humanitarian assistance system failed them. Relief that could have reached many was not delivered, not because of looting, but because Somalia fell through the cracks of that system, and decision-makers did not accord it the priority that "the greatest humanitarian emergency in the world" required if catastrophe was to be avoided. Somalia's famine developed over several years as UN and Security Council member government officials, distracted by a series of crises around the globe, ignored the clear signals of imminent disaster. Somalia, no longer strategically important after the end of the Cold War, could not compete for the political attention that is manifestly a prerequisite for the sustained and complex humanitarian assistance required. That the tragedy stemmed in large part from the effects of two decades of militarization by outside powers and their support for the authoritarian rule of Siad Barre was of little consequence as those powers distanced themselves from the messy situation and avoided further involvement.

Humanitarian assistance has as its purpose to ensure the most critical of human rights—the right of survival—to populations temporarily unable to fend for themselves. But the Somali people—subjected to dictatorship, civil war, drought, the collapse of civil authority, lawlessness—were largely left to fend for themselves until the suffering was too horrific to be ignored.

It is especially difficult to explain the level of failure by the international humanitarian assistance system, given the history of external intervention in countering the cycle of famine in the Horn of Africa. There is *all too much experience* in confronting the massive dislocation of hungry people in the region. Untold billions of dollars have gone to relief programs, since 1984 in particular, and those efforts have taught bitter lessons. Disaster assistance officials, diplomats, and politicians struggling to meet expectations for swift, generous and effective relief for the hungry and displaced have logged invaluable, often painful experience.

The lessons have been political, as well as operational. Recriminations against the slowness of the UN, the United States, and other donors (not to mention the Ethiopian government) to respond to early indicators of famine in Ethiopia in 1983–1984[13] led to a discernible determination to avoid repeating that costly error. President Ronald Reagan, in reference to Ethiopia, declared that "a hungry child knows no politics," expressing the will of the American public that the United States respond according to human need, not to the political orientation of governing regimes. Reagan's statement, however tardy in being applied during the 1984–1985 crisis, reverberated in 1987 when a drought-triggered food emergency again struck Ethiopia. Washington responded quickly and generously, spurring on the UN and other donors, and the emergency was contained; *no famine occurred*. Congressional and executive branch officials avoided the emotional, somewhat accusatory, confrontation that marked the 1984–1985 period.[14]

Thus it was that when famine began to stalk the people of Somalia in 1990, a number of major external players had established expectations for their involvements. Over a number of years, the UN had assumed increasing responsibility in the region for coordinating relief assistance for millions of people at risk, primarily from political turmoil. Such responsibility had by necessity included implementing the diplomatic and political strategies required for the relief to be delivered to and through zones of conflict. A series of "special representatives" of the secretary-general had acted as powerful and effective coordinators of external relief in Ethiopia and the Sudan.

The United States had demonstrated resourcefulness, generosity, and determination in getting more assistance to more individuals in the Horn than any other donor. And many regional observers believed the United States had a particular moral and political responsibility, given its long support of the Siad Barre dictatorship and the arguable contribution of American military and economic assistance to Somalia's descent into chaos. The U.S. government further established expectations through its high-profile, energetic, and highly successful role in negotiating an end to neighboring Ethiopia's civil wars and the Mengistu dictatorship during the spring of 1991.

All of the major donors had, of course, established collective expectations for involvement by their response via the UN Security Council in the Kurdish situation in northern Iraq following Operation Desert Storm, and by their concurrent attention to the internal chaos in the fractionalizing Yugoslav republics. Britain and Italy had obligations residual from the colonial era and, especially in the case of Italy, because of considerable business links and ties to Somali political factions.[15]

Regionally, assumptions for any OAU response to Somalia's deterioration were (and remain) more theoretical, given the OAU's history on "sovereignty" and noninterference questions and its crippling institutional weaknesses.

In fact, the OAU proved to be largely irrelevant as tragedy unfolded a few hundred miles from its Addis Ababa headquarters. More than two years into the turmoil, the OAU has yet to make a significant statement to the international community about humanitarian needs, national reconciliation processes, or peacekeeping in Somalia. The OAU secretary-general has not visited Somalia; the organization has dispatched no delegation of respected African elders to attempt a dialogue between conflicting factions; it has launched no concerted campaign to place or keep Somalia on the Security Council agenda.

Indeed, the OAU's most direct addressing of the Somali crisis may have been its rejection of a plan for intervening proposed in early 1992 by the transitional Eritrean government, on the basis of Eritrea's lack of membership in the OAU at the time. The Eritreans, unlike the OAU, had sent a delegation to Mogadishu during the Somali civil war. President Meles Zenawi and Ethiopian government officials, not those of the OAU, facilitated the January 1993 talks on Somali national reconciliation that the U.S. military intervention forced.

But the relative vigor of the current OAU leadership and its stated interest in improving internal conflict resolution mechanisms may have slightly boosted the assumptions for OAU involvement. Such expanded interest led to an OAU role in negotiating a contemporaneous cease-fire in the Rwanda conflict. Whatever might have been expected from either the Arab League or the Organization of the Islamic Conference in response to the Somali crisis, their roles were to remain minor, if not abstractions.

Regardless of institutional capacity or operational expertise, as Somalia's famine evolved, expectations built over the previous decade were largely abandoned. The humanitarian agencies were simply not able to deliver the food and medicine required for survival under the circumstances, and the political authorities at the UN, in Washington, and elsewhere declined to act to alter that situation until, for many, it was too late.

## DISASTER SQUARED: THE UN RESPONSE

What supports an assessment that much of the UN's contribution in Somalia was initially grossly incompetent, undisciplined, and unfocused? Damning assessments of the UN role in Somalia emanate from relief workers directly engaged in the Somali crisis, professionals in the humanitarian assistance community, journalists, and even the more candid UN officials involved.[16] The views of other well-placed and experienced observers and participants from a range of perspectives are no more positive. The pronouncements, supported by an investigation of factual evidence, stem from a series of UN blunders and the UN's basic failure to engage seriously in efforts to deal with the crisis when such engagement arguably would have diffused its intensity.

*Most egregiously, the UN was essentially absent from Somalia.* The UN withdrew from Mogadishu shortly before the January 1991 flight of Siad Barre, transferring staff to Nairobi, and stayed away until August 1991. A security incident in early September resulted in the reevacuation of the skeleton staff that had returned three weeks earlier. Criticism led to UNICEF's reestablishing offices in late 1991, but the UN agencies continued to suffer greatly from the absence of senior, qualified personnel and adequately staffed offices. The concerns over security that ostensibly prevented the UN from operating in Somalia during this period contrast with the stance of the ICRC, the International Medical Corps, Save the Children Fund/U.K., Médecins sans Frontières, and SOS (an Austrian nonprofit agency): these organizations *increased* staff because of the extraordinary needs . . . and the shortage of UN relief workers.

The absence of country expertise directly resulted in the debacle of Under Secretary James Jonah's January 1992 mission to Mogadishu. In response to criticisms for its neglect of Somalia (the ICRC created a stir by issuing highly unusual public criticisms of the UN's performance in Somalia),[17] the UN began formulating plans for a diplomatic initiative in December 1991. Jonah was dispatched to Mogadishu on January 3-5; he was to meet with General Aideed and with Ali Mahdi, to negotiate a cease-fire in the civil war and the safe passage of relief commodities. Two clans neutral in the Aideed/Ali Mahdi clash (the Hawadle and the Murasade) offered to escort Jonah to both Aideed and Ali Mahdi headquarters, and to serve as local peacekeepers. Jonah, apparently unaware of the existence of neutral elements in Mogadishu, made no arrangements to accept the offer. He then fell into a trap set by General Aideed.

Aideed's forces shelled the airport to prevent Jonah's UN plane from landing and had it diverted to an airstrip at Balidogley under the general's control; there, Jonah was met by Aideed. Manipulating Jonah's itinerary, Aideed took him on highly visible and extensive tours of territory under his control. When the Jonah party neared the planned point of crossing into Ali Mahdi's northern section of Mogadishu, an angry Ali Mahdi opened an artillery barrage. Jonah fled to Nairobi. The next morning, however, he flew to northern Mogadishu to (very) briefly visit Ali Mahdi, then publicly announced that Ali Mahdi had agreed to UN intervention in the crisis and that General Aideed stood as the obstacle.[18] Ali Mahdi immediately seconded Jonah's comments, seeing them as underscoring the legitimacy of his interim presidency. Aideed predictably became angry and more distrustful—and more violent.

The immediate results of the Jonah visit were that the airport was shut for ten days (blocking whatever arrivals of food were then possible) and the neutral position of the Murasade clan was undermined. Worst, the UN's particular advantage of being a neutral broker had been severely eroded. The war continued for another two months.[19]

The UN hierarchy had apparently absorbed no lessons on the finer points of negotiating in Mogadishu's internecine battles when its next high-profile delegation arrived, on February 5, 1992, this time headed by Special Coordinator Brian Wannop. No clan leaders or elders were invited to discussions with Aideed and Ali Mahdi about proposed peace talks in New York. That the UN apparently accorded the clans little standing made it easier for Ali Mahdi to launch attacks against the smaller clans, which he did the day after the UN issued invitations to the peace talks.

Yet another mission by James Jonah to Mogadishu in February finally led to a tentative agreement for representatives of Aideed and Ali Mahdi to convene under the auspices of the UN, the Islamic Conference, the OAU, and the Arab League; the meeting took place at UN headquarters on February 12 and 13. Despite a lack of preparation and the naive exclusion of relevant players,[20] the New York meetings produced the principles of a cease-fire. The Somali parties returned to Mogadishu, where the details, such as they were, were hammered out and agreed to by March 3. While violations have occurred, *the basic cease-fire between Aideed and Ali Mahdi has more or less held since early March 1992.*

One of the most ironic aspects of the UN's performance in Somalia is the failure to take advantage of the March 1992 cease-fire—a UN-brokered cease-fire. This failure rests at the very center of the flawed external involvement in the crisis and mirrors numerous other opportunities missed. The Security Council's dithering and its relief agencies' squandering of valuable time and opportunities paralleled the floundering of the UN's senior diplomats in the field during this period.

UNICEF and the other UN relief agencies were actually doing very little in the field. Repeated requests to UNICEF from the private relief agencies operating in Mogadishu and elsewhere for medicines and medical supplies went unheeded. Relief commodities that were delivered repeatedly went to arbitrary locations without UNICEF's consulting other agencies; the result was false expectations and unnecessary pressures as desperate people gathered to await further deliveries that never materialized. Save the Children/U.K., a relatively small private relief agency, delivered more food to Somalia in 1992 than did UNICEF.

Meanwhile, for some nine months, the United Nations Development Programme, the traditional coordinator of UN relief and development agencies, left untapped $68 million budgeted for Somalia *for lack of a signature* from the nonexistent Somali government. Efforts to obtain a waiver of the signature requirement commenced only after the press reported stinging criticism of the UN Somali relief operation from the director of Save the Children/U.K.[21]

From January through April 1992, the UNHCR and the World Food Programme were engaged in a dispute over the particulars of a contract to truck food from the port in Djibouti to camps for Somali refugees in the Hararge region of Ethiopia. In the meantime, more than 50 of those refugees were dying each day of malnutrition.

The UN's endless negotiations with General Aideed and Ali Mahdi during 1992 over the placement of UN peacekeepers to protect relief shipments came at the expense of an immediate opportunity—that of hiring and training some of the militia as police guards, an initiative that might have weakened the position of the two warlords and in the process seen more food moving.

As crisis turned to catastrophe in Somalia, the UN Department of Humanitarian Affairs (DHA) was largely unengaged in these fitful relief efforts. Prior to the late summer 1992 mobilization and the initial September 1992 visit of Under Secretary Jan

Eliasson, this theoretically central UN office had no discernible role whatsoever in mounting an effective response to the famine. It had been formed early in 1992 in response to the chronic blundering, uncoordinated performance of UN humanitarian agencies, to prevent just such responses as the one it passively watched unfold in Somalia.[22]

## HALF MEASURES AT THE SECURITY COUNCIL

The Security Council was not, of course, totally oblivious to the deteriorating situation in Somalia and busied itself during 1992 with a series of resolutions, after having taken no action during the year of anarchy following Siad Barre's flight. Its resolutions on Somalia before December are most notable, however, for their lack of resolve and for their inconsistency with actions regarding the Kurdish situation and the Balkan crisis. The great powers' reluctance to focus on Somalia was unmistakable. When the Council first addressed Somalia on January 23 at the instigation of Cape Verde—the Bush administration had blocked earlier attempts to put the crisis on the agenda[23]—the U.S. delegation insisted upon altering draft resolution language from "ensuring" a commitment to the cessation of hostilities and promoting a cease-fire to "seeking" such a commitment. The signal was clear: the United States sought a low-level UN investment in the crisis.

Resolution 773 called upon the secretary-general to increase humanitarian assistance and to work with the OAU and Arab League to seek a cease-fire. The resolution also established an international Somali arms embargo.

In March the Security Council adopted resolution 746, which called upon all parties in the civil war to abide by the cease-fire agreed to that month, but specified no measures to make that goal more likely. Resolution 751 (April) authorized a force of 50 UN observers to monitor the cease-fire and "in principle" a UN security force of 550 to be deployed. This deployment, minuscule as it would have been, remained one in principle; in early September the U.S. air force airlifted 500 UN troops into Mogadishu as part of the initial late summer mobilization on the crisis.

Resolution 767 (July) called upon all parties in Somalia to cooperate in the deployment of the security forces, and resolution 775 (late August) increased the authorized deployment to 3,500. (The secretary-general's special representative in Mogadishu, Mohamed Sahnoun, had requested 7,000 troops; in any case, the UN security force remained at 500—its level when the 24,000 American troops came ashore in December.)

Exactly what the Security Council imagined 500 peace-keepers with a vague but limited mandate would be able to accomplish in the midst of the violence then wracking Somalia remains unclear. The commander of the force, referring to U.S. troops in Mogadishu, later queried "Here we are with 6,000 troops in the city, and we have Chinese journalists being shot in the legs. We've got snipers here and there. So somebody give me the wisdom—how could I have done it with 500 troops?"[24]

The Security Council's evasion of decisive action ultimately led, in July, to an exasperated outburst from the secretary-general, who was moved to charge that members more concerned with "the rich man's war" in the Balkans than with the situation in Somalia were employing "a naked double standard."[25] Unfortunately for the Council, there was no plausible denial of his charges. The embarrassment stemming from the secretary-general's outburst led to UN and donor government galvanization on the Somali famine, including the August launching of food airlifts and September arrival of peacekeeping forces—some six months after initial consideration by the Security Council. Somalia's children were dying, and the world now knew it.

By this time, it was too late to avoid catastrophe. The peacekeepers were installed, additional senior UN personnel were dispatched, and the U.S. military began the huge airlift of relief commodities. The security situation, however, was such that far more dramatic steps were required three months later.

President Bush's late November decision to launch a major U.S. military intervention into Somalia brought about Security Council resolution 794, approved on December 3, which committed the UN to an armed humanitarian operation without historical or legal precedent. The lack of precision of that resolution and the continuing different interpretations of it by U.S. and UN officials reflect the sudden sense of panic that preceded the intervention—over 1,000 Somalis were starving each day. The resolution authorized "all necessary means to establish as soon as possible a secure environment for humanitarian relief operations in Somalia" and was based on an assertion that the "magnitude of human tragedy in Somalia constitutes a threat to international peace and security," thereby invoking chapter VII of the UN Charter.

Debate over the authorizing resolution is illustrative of the realization suddenly seizing the Council that the world public would not tolerate the carnage. The British ambassador remarked, "Every single member accepted the secretary-general's analysis that the top priority is to give aid to people who are starving. There is a remarkable convergence on the development of a multinational force."[26] African governments were quickly reassured that the operation was being undertaken by UN Charter authorization and was not a disguised form of big-power colonization on the continent, and none objected to the introduction of U.S. forces.

The Security Council action was both unprecedented and unspecific. The marines were still landing when differences surfaced between the secretary-general and President Bush over the time frame (originally 90 days) and the mandate of the forces (were they merely to achieve basic security, or to disarm the militias so that stability could be obtained?). Those differences continued into the Clinton administration.

Resolution 794 catapulted the Security Council into a radically different stance regarding collective interventions for humanitarian principles—perhaps not unintentionally as a precursor to an expanded intervention in Bosnia or Iraq.

The implementation of the precedent set in Somalia awaits events and Security Council determination of its meaning and application. What is clear is that the Council's avoidance of decisive action during 1992 contributed to the catastrophe that unfolded and has left unmasked its poor capacity to respond to humanitarian emergencies stemming from political disarray in the post–Cold War era.

## BOUTROS BOUTROS-GHALI

It was the UN secretary-general whose moral calls lanced the lethargy of the Security Council as it attempted to wish the Somali crisis away without decisive action or commitment. It was, however, the same Boutros Boutros-Ghali who presided over a pathetically incoherent UN performance in the field and who, more than a year after taking office, had yet to demonstrate any inclination to instill discipline or direction on the decidedly unchoreographed UN presence in Somalia.

Boutros-Ghali took office just as the frustration at inadequate UN response to previous humanitarian emergencies gave him the opportunity to seize control of the unwieldy system and place genuine authority and responsibility in the newly created DHA, headed by Under Secretary Eliasson. By the time the new secretary-general assumed office, the inadequacy of the UN diplomatic efforts of James Jonah and relief operations in the field in responding to the realities of Somalia were more than apparent. Yet, Boutros-Ghali failed to designate an overall coordinator for the UN in response to the crisis, to grant strong authority to Eliasson's unit (or, seemingly, even to insist that the DHA take on *any* role in Somalia), to support his first special representative in-country, or to replace him with a diplomat enjoying either much support or a strong mandate. The DHA, after the general mobilization on Somalia, eventually received a vague charge, but its role has been constantly thwarted by the operational agencies or by Under Secretary Jonah or both. (Jonah, a competitor of Boutros-Ghali for the secretary-general post, was promoted to under secretary *following* his dismal performance on the Somali front.)

The troubled stint of Mohamed Sahnoun as the secretary-general's special representative in Mogadishu is illustrative. Sahnoun, a respected Algerian diplomat, took the assignment after the UN had lost all credibility within Somalia. His tendency for candid remarks and the ongoing sabotage of his position by James Jonah and others made his position within the UN structure fragile from the beginning, and the refusal of the secretary-general to grant Sahnoun sufficient flexibility to act on the scene in negotiations with the militia leaders limited the latter's effectiveness. While it is by no means certain that Sahnoun's negotiations during the late summer and early autumn of 1992 would have resulted in any breakthrough in the crisis, he was able to win respect from many Somali elements through his energetic schedule of consultations with warlords, clan elders, intellectuals, women, and various professionals. The question of his ultimate effectiveness remains open as Sahnoun was forced to resign from his position in October 1992. His initial replacement, Ismat Kittani, an Iraqi diplomat, who lacked Sahnoun's candor, made an early impression by seeking an unqualified endorsement of the UN's role in Somalia—an endorsement withheld.

As the United States prepared to end its large military presence in Somalia in early 1993, the secretary-general had yet to indicate clearly the authority over UN efforts there that each of his coordinators—Kittani; Eliasson; Jonah; and Philip Johnston, the director of CARE/U.S., who had assumed the temporary title "UN coordinator of humanitarian assistance in Somalia"— would exercise, or exactly how he was going to coordinate all of his coordinators.

Furthermore, increasingly public U.S. resentment over disarray within the UN's mission in Somalia weakened the secretary-general's position on his expectations for an expanded and lengthened mandate for the American troops present in the country.

## CONFLICTING SIGNALS FROM WASHINGTON

The early success of the December military intervention and the increasingly (and increasingly welcomed) get-tough-with-the-UN stance of the State Department obscure the contradictory record of the United States in the Somali catastrophe. Official U.S. relief agencies[27] and their senior officers have a record of response to the crisis unmatched by UN or other donor government counterparts. Their operational achievements, however, were not supported with determination or political commitment at higher levels of government—prior to President Bush's personal involvement commencing in late July 1992.

While disaster assistance officials were committing significant U.S. government resources[28] to the ICRC and private relief
agencies, and pressuring the UN to move aggressively,[29] the State
Department's International Organization Bureau, the U.S. Mission to the UN, and the National Security Council were keeping
Somalia a low priority on the Security Council agenda and *avoiding commitments for multilateral action.*

State Department officials attribute the lack of attention
Washington gave to the famine in Somalia before July 1992 to a
lack of media attention and a system overloaded by concurrent
humanitarian crises in the Balkans, Iraq, and elsewhere (including turmoil in the former Soviet Union, which never reached the
point of humanitarian emergency). Sources indicate that the
department of state's Africa bureau tried but failed to put
Somalia on Secretary James Baker's agenda and to bring the crisis
to the attention of the White House.

The adoption of a Senate resolution in April 1992 that called
for "active U.S. initiatives" and encouraged UN and OAU mobilization in response to Somalia engendered little interest in the Bush
administration, as had earlier entreaties from within State's Africa
bureau. Indeed, press reports refer to administration rejection of
proposals to put Somalia on the Security Council agenda.[30]

Observers from Capitol Hill and within the administration
indicate that part of the rationale for not pressuring the UN to do
more was a loathing to set a precedent for U.S. financial obligations for UN peacekeeping. Thus, while AID funding was primary in enabling the ICRC to devote an unprecedented 50
percent of its worldwide emergency budget to Somalia, the lack
of resolve of the United States in the Security Council contributed
to the UN's balking at both humanitarian and peacekeeping
responsibilities.

The contradictory response of the United States continued
until mid-July, when media coverage and an emotional cable
from the American ambassador in Kenya following a visit to
Somali refugee camps brought stark reports of hunger and starvation to the attention of the president, who reportedly reacted
strongly and indicated he "wanted something done."[31]

Something *was* done, of course, and within a few days the departments of state and defense and the National Security Council recognized the situation as "the Somalia crisis." A U.S. military airlift of food commodities into Somalia and northern Kenya was ordered, and the United States was readying plans for UN resolutions on additional relief and national reconciliation conferences. On August 13, the White House announced that the United States would provide air transport for the 500 Pakistani troops who were to be the UN peacekeepers in Somalia—while the United States had earlier in the year forced the authorized level of UN peacekeepers for Somalia down to 50 from the proposed 500.

The August deployment of the U.S. military to move relief commodities to hungry Somalis was so rapid as to cause serious concerns among private relief agency workers in Somalia, who feared increased security threats, and a diplomatic incident with the Kenyan government (the airlift was based in Mombasa), which chose to portray the arrival of the U.S. armed forces as "an invasion." The timing of the announcement—on the eve of the Republican National Convention and on the heels of the increased press coverage, *but* more than five months after the March cease-fire and eight months after relief chief Natsios had described the famine as the world's greatest humanitarian emergency—evoked a high degree of cynicism among many observers.

Regardless of the various motivations that may have spurred the sudden activism, the high-profile U.S. attention to the Somalia famine changed the dynamics of the international response—as, of course, happened again on a grander scale in December—and quickly embarrassed the European and other donor governments and the UN into taking a more determined approach.

The initial U.S. position in the Security Council underscored a willingness to make naked calculations of political benefits and requirements in relationship to humanitarian emergencies. Until the secretary-general's tirade and news media focus forced a change in policy, the United States supported minimal UN response to Somalia—despite, not because of, the situational reality—*because no one was challenging such an approach.* At the time Washington announced the August airlift, conditions were no more or less safe within Somalia than they had been for six months; neither political factors nor logistics had altered; no significant new information had become available. The only difference was that the situation had deteriorated, largely because of inaction on the part of the international community: many more desperate people were hungry and dying of starvation.

The dichotomous U.S. reaction to the Somali famine illuminates the lack of accountability for the U.S. government's international humanitarian assistance programs—which is also the problem at the UN. Weak congressional oversight and limited meaningful input from the private humanitarian community leave humanitarian assistance policies and programs susceptible to political manipulation by the executive branch. No clearly established standards, criteria, or guidelines are being violated when huge sums are pumped through "humanitarian" channels for political reasons, such as to the former Soviet republics, at the expense of genuine catastrophes, like Somalia.

## PROFILES IN COURAGE

At least one chapter in the history of the response to the Somali crisis offers inspiration. When the final saga is written, the profiles in courage that will emerge are those of the staff members of the ICRC and four private relief agencies that stayed in Somalia during the darkest days of civil war and the subsequent mayhem. The four agencies (the International Medical Corps, Save the Children/U.K., Médecins sans Frontières, and SOS) and the ICRC basically assumed the role the UN relief agencies traditionally played, and in the process saved untold thousands of lives.

These agencies' professionalism in providing relief assistance under the most difficult and complex conditions stands in stark contrast to the bungled efforts of the UN. Further, their capacity to operate in such a setting exposes the hollowness and hypocrisy of the UN claims that Somalia was too dangerous for its personnel. (A handful of expatriate relief workers have been killed in Somalia, while several dozen peacekeepers, relief workers, and journalists have died in the Balkans as part of the multilateral intervention during the same period without eroding the conviction that such intervention is mandatory.)

The ICRC's role in Somalia in particular invites comparison to that of the UN relief agencies. The ICRC devoted 50 percent of its entire worldwide emergency budget for the Somali relief effort and orchestrated a massive feeding program, which is not a traditional Red Cross role. It set aside its policy of refusing armed escorts—a policy dating back more than a hundred years—adapting its posture radically, because doing so was required to be effective in Somalia. In fact, the ICRC did everything within its means to prevent the catastrophe from becoming even worse.

## INTERVENTION AFTERMATH: U.S.–UN TENSIONS MOUNT

Despite Operation Restore Hope's considerable success in protecting the delivery of relief commodities to the hungry Somalis, tensions between U.S. government and UN officials flared as the proper role and length of stay for the American military forces and the preparations for the UN management of the next phase of the response were contested. Such tensions were predictable, given the Security Council's vague mandate for the forces, the Bush administration's unrealistic predictions concerning the duration of the American military presence in Somalia, the continued lack of coherence in the UN response, and the uncertainty of resources and authorities to be provided to any successor UN peacekeeping force.

U.S. officials accused the secretary-general of deliberately stalling the transfer of responsibility to UN peacekeeping forces because of reluctance to assume the financial and political costs of the operation—though without much visible American mobilization to obtain support for a UN operation. UN officials countered with comments concerning American arrogance[32] and more relevant concerns that once the large American force departed, the country's warlords and militias would return in force and overwhelm UN peacekeepers.

The tough and shrewd U.S. special envoy, Robert Oakley, a retired foreign service officer and former ambassador to Somalia, quickly became established as the dominant international player in Mogadishu as looters were being disarmed and warlords and elders prodded to discuss a national reconciliation process. Oakley eclipsed Special Representative Kittani as a force, illustrating the UN's lack of credibility within Somalia, if not Kittani's own limitations. Oakley's candid expressions of frustration at the UN's slowness in organizing the peacekeeping force and a national police force—the United States undertook the latter task after the UN failed to proceed on such an obvious priority[33]— were meant to manipulate the UN into a more proactive stance.

State Department officials were at the same time indicating through the press that the United States had begun to withdraw troops from Somalia, in part to "nudge the UN off center,"[34] while others were less publicly pressing the secretary-general to appoint a diplomat with more stature than Kittani to direct operations in Mogadishu. Kittani was resisting the "nudge" as late as February 1993—some two months after the U.S. military intervention—where he told journalists (after a month's absence from the country) that the UN was not yet ready to assume primary responsibility in Somalia. "The UN has a number of questions they are discussing. What is the mandate? What are the costs?" he asked.[35] The U.S.–UN tensions on display surrounding Somalia are indicative of a larger struggle and the expanding U.S. annoyance with Secretary-General Boutros-Ghali. The Clinton administration sent an early signal that it intends to resist the secretary-general's plan to replace the departed Dick Thornburgh, the former UN under secretary for management, with a non-American—as part of the continuing U.S. push for UN reform.

One can only hope that the U.S. campaign to prod the UN in Somalia will result in a broader commitment to reforming the international humanitarian assistance system and making the UN's role in that system dramatically more credible and effective than it has been in this tragedy. Such a commitment would not only help establish greater UN credibility, but would also help

redeem the United States for its long neglect of the UN's humanitarian mechanisms.

## PROSPECTS FOR RECOVERY IN SOMALIA

A cautious and very conditional vision of a pacified Somalia
capable of again feeding its population is now possible. The
international military forces and the tough, no-nonsense diplomacy of Robert Oakley have marginalized the warlords to some
extent. The conferences on demilitarization and reconstruction
held in Addis Ababa in late January and again in March 1993[36]
reached agreements that, if honored, would see the surrender of
all heavy weapons and encampment of all militia forces—within
90 days of the March 27 final accord—as part of a national
reconciliation process.[37]

There is no guarantee that the agreements will hold or that
the lack of participation in the conference by the Itihad movement—a mysterious fundamentalist group seemingly more op-
portunistic than ideological—will not ultimately wreck the
accord.

But if the various Somali factions *are* prepared to undertake
national reconciliation, what of the international community?
The UN is a seriously discredited presence in Somalia, and the
United States is clearly impatient to surrender its present role.
Any disarmament or political agreement will rest as much
upon the appearance of alternatives to the thousands of militia
members conditioned to surviving by force as it will upon the
restoration of civilian administration of the country. From
where will the funds for a reconciliation and reconstruction
process be generated?

Few answers to such critical questions are readily apparent,
but a number of positive factors or indications of potentially
positive developments are evident. First is Somalia's tradition of
consensus building and its earlier experience with a democratic
society. If the international relief community can encourage civil
Somali management of the rehabilitation process, that tradition
can serve as the foundation for a more stable system. That is, the
identification of beneficiaries and the local management of com-

modity distribution by elders and village committees can help restore local administrative capacity. If the donor governments and multilateral organizations can move quickly to match any Somali reconciliation progress with the required reconstruction financing, then current (and future) relief and peacekeeping requirements can be reduced. If the relief emphasis can be geared toward restoring productive agricultural production and away from emergency food imports (that is, designing interventions from an economic perspective), then the basis of the Somali economy can be restored.

A logical and constructive transition from U.S. dominance to a UN-led operation is required. Despite the lack of demonstrated UN competence or credibility, it is clearly advantageous for reconstruction to be a multilateral process. The United States already carries a burden for its 20-year involvement in Somalia's internal affairs during the Siad Barre era and, in any case, does not need and cannot afford to be seen as either the guarantor of Somalia's pacification or involved in the "recolonization" of Africa. (Furthermore, the Clinton administration is hardly seeking complex foreign commitments.) However, everyone would stand to gain if the UN registered greater capacity to assist with reconciliation and reconstruction than it did in responding to the emergency situation. A candid recognition of prior shortcomings and the imposition of discipline and clear authority upon the UN's operational agencies would be a major step in building a new basis for a major UN contribution to that process. The appointment of a respected high-level envoy of the secretary-general to facilitate reconciliation and reconstruction *and* to galvanize international support for both would further add to UN credibility.

What is required is a phased and linked national process that addresses humanitarian, military, political, and economic components, and that has the support of an international coalition of donors prepared to facilitate reconstruction programs. Vigorous leadership of such a coalition is critical, and the ability of the UN to assert such leadership now may largely determine the restoration of its credibility. Preliminary discussions have taken place on a World Bank lead role in coordinating an economic rehabilitation package for Somalia, though the Bank has extremely limited experience working in such environments; the logical overall coordinator for the process remains, *in theory*, the UN.

It is not just the UN but the larger international community that has much to atone for in Somalia. The generosity, vigor, and sophistication of that community's response to the reconciliation and reconstruction needs of the country will be clear indicators of whether or not any lessons have been absorbed from the carnage and misery visited upon the Somali people.

## REFORMING HUMANITARIAN INTERVENTION: ACCOUNTABILITY

In the wake of the Somali debacle, the UN—and the Security Council in particular—is compelled to examine a number of broad policy issues and operational modalities if it is to avert the same failures and tragic consequences elsewhere. And the Clinton administration is faced with an immediate challenge to articulate new criteria for U.S. humanitarian intervention.

The UN will need to move swiftly and convincingly to regain credibility following its performance in Somalia. And the U.S. government, despite its public antipathy toward perceived UN reluctance to assume responsibility in Somalia and elsewhere, must move in its own interest and for the common good to help the UN gain that credibility. The United States will have to establish credible guidelines as to when and where it will intervene to feed starving children, restore law and order, or promote democracy. Former President Reagan, ironically, has already suggested a principle for the new era, proposing "nothing less than a human velvet glove backed by a steel fist of military force" to enforce humanitarian objectives by means of a permanent UN "army of conscience."[38] The Clinton administration will have to propose its own principles before crises impose others.

One fundamental question that has to be addressed is that of double standards. The international community's quick collective response to the situation in Kurdistan and its involvement in Iraq's internal affairs for humanitarian reasons stand in contrast to the initial response to Somalia. But eventually, a large multilateral military force *was* sent to protect relief operations in Somalia. How will the UN respond to the inevitable demands for intervention elsewhere? Will the UN, for example, protect the persecuted and hungry populations in southern Sudan? Are the marines to go to Liberia and Tajikistan? Are more than 350,000 deaths from starvation—and their stark documentation on camera—required before the international community responds?

Another question that has to be examined is that of cease-fires being in place before the introduction of UN peacekeeping forces. Such application gives any number of minor players potential veto power over the UN action required to assist non-participants in civil strife situations. The failure to move on the opportunity to introduce international peacekeepers into Somalia in March 1992 contributed to heightened levels of violence. Additionally, the imposition of this criterion forced the UN to act as if all of Somalia were engulfed in Mogadishu's extreme circumstances, contrary to the reality. Linking initiatives on the humanitarian program front to concurrence to agreements on the positioning of peacekeepers in Somalia was a major mistake, and the UN paid a heavy price as it squandered opportunities to exploit positives—the relative lack of both violence and food insecurity in key areas.

The Security Council must construct new guidelines concerning the acceptable safety risks for UN personnel intervening in internal conflict. Much of the UN's problem in Somalia stemmed from the lack of on-the-ground expertise following the evacuation of its staff, the stated justification for this measure being staff safety. This claim struck many as disingenuous, and Under Secretary Jonah's assertion that the lack of "insurance" for staff was a primary reason for not having a UN presence in-country underscores the necessity of more responsible guidelines in this area.[39]

It is obvious that without securing adequate financial resources, the UN can be expected to do little. The secretary-general states that "the financial foundations of the Organization daily grow weaker, debilitating its political will and practical capacity to undertake new and essential activities."[40] The long neglect of the UN by the United States and other powers has taken a heavy toll on the professionalism of its agencies. How is that professionalism to be rebuilt without funds? At the same time, however, the UN must look toward internal reform to recapture both credibility and savings if its budgetary woes are to be seriously addressed. The bungled response to Somalia has dramatically exposed the extent of its ineptitude[41] and it is clear that Somalia is but one example of the UN's failing to meet its obligations for reasons other than financial constraints. As institutional shortcomings increasingly come to light, the world public may not be as forgiving as it has been in the past.

A public airing of all that went wrong with the UN response to Somalia is both warranted and desirable if meaningful reform is to replace floundering approaches and double standards. The UN must tackle the lack of professional capability within its humanitarian agencies—and the hiring and placement practices that do little to enhance that professionalism. The individuals who failed so badly in Somalia must answer for those failures if confidence and credibility in the agencies are to be recaptured.

Concurrent with the conclusion of Operation Provide Hope, the U.S. government should mobilize the political will required to guarantee that a humanitarian assistance reform commission be impaneled at the UN. In Washington, a blue-ribbon commission should be convened to review bilateral programs. Both of those bodies should be charged with mapping out a new set of policies to guide programs now venturing into largely uncharted waters. President Clinton has an early opportunity for genuine leadership in reforming humanitarian policies by pushing to form these two panels.

Beyond bureaucratic consolidation and coordination, the humanitarian reform commission at the UN should be charged with identifying the needed strengthening of mandates and authorities required for collective involvement in internal conflicts, including the terms for asserting the right of survival over sovereignty. Notwithstanding the institutional bias of the UN toward governments—even when governments are morally reprehensible—public outcry from repeated exposure to innocent children starving forces a new interpretation of "sovereign."

236 ◆ *Jeffrey Clark*

The domestic body's priority would be to bring more consistency to U.S. humanitarian programs by opening a system too closed to public scrutiny, and to restore a nonpolitical basis for the provision of humanitarian assistance.

Ultimately, the most important question is that of accountability. To whom are the relief agencies of the UN accountable? Who determines when and how the U.S. government extends humanitarian assistance in the name of the American public? What is the collective responsibility to people in need who do not merit a special political status or the sustained attention of the media? What is the U.S. responsibility if reports of starving children do not reach the president?

Greater accountability needs to be established now at the international level and in our bilateral program, which has such disproportionate impact on the efforts of the UN and other players. Without such accountability, there is no reason to believe that the international community will absorb the horrible lessons apparent from the current Somali catastrophe. Instead, the same stories of neglect, evasion of responsibility, and lack of determination will lead to massive suffering in Mozambique, Tajikistan, Zaire, or other lands not likely to make a smooth transition in the post–Cold War era.

To fail to act now guarantees we will again pay a price too high to bear.


NOTES

1. See Thomas Friedman, "Clinton Inherits Conflicts That Don't Follow Rules," *New York Times*, December 13, 1992, in which the president-elect is quoted as saying, "On balance, let's make one thing clear: It is a wonderful thing that the Cold War is over. But let's also admit that the end of the bipolar world has made it possible to peel a layer off human aggression and made it possible in some parts of the world for people to be starved, brutalized and killed with much greater abandon.

   "I have two choices. We can either focus on these problems, come up with a decent policy and aggressively pursue it, or wait for it to explode."
2. See Edward Rice, *Captain Sir Richard Francis Burton* (New York: Charles Scribner's Sons, 1990).
3. The major Somali clans are the Darod, the Digil, the Dir, the Hawiye, the Issak, and the Rahanwein.

4. See Ioan Lewis, "In the Land of the Living Dead," *Sunday Times*, August 30, 1992, p. 8.

5. Ibid.

6. For a critique of an earlier UN failure to meet its obligations to suffering Somalis, see Jeffrey Clark, "Hell on Earth: A Trip to Dar Anagi," in United States Committee for Refugees, *World Refugee Survey, 1992* (Washington, D.C., 1992).

7. A government recognized by no other to date.

8. Statement of Andrew Natsios, assistant administrator for food and humanitarian assistance, U.S. Agency for International Development (AID), before the House Select Committee on Hunger, January 30, 1992. Roger Winter, executive director of the U.S. Committee for Refugees, had accurately warned of the tragedy to come in congressional testimony in May 1991.

9. See David Brown, "Data Indicates Somali Famine among Worst" *Washington Post*, January 9, 1993, p. A17.

10. "Emergency Plan of Action-Somalia," International Committee of the Red Cross, Geneva, Switzerland/Nairobi, Kenya, July 21, 1992.

11. 350,000 is my own professional analysis of the likely death toll based on data from: a) Center for Disease Control (see "Data Indicates Somali Famine Among Worst," by David Brown, *Washington Post*, p. A17, January 9, 1993); b) ICRC; c) Office of Foreign Disaster Assistance, AID and d) miscellaneous nongovernmental organizations and media reports. This is also the number used in *National Geographic* (August 1993). I would judge the UN figure of 500,000 to be too high, but no one has an accurate number.

12. The tonnage of food actually delivered into Somalia never approached the minimum monthly requirement prior to December 1992.

13. Observers detected and reported on the onset of the famine in Ethiopia from early 1983; many reports from credible observers went largely ignored, and measures that could have mitigated the emergency were not taken.

14. The problem with President Reagan's declaration has been its selective application, even in the Horn of Africa—a politicizing that distorts the humanitarian assistance efforts of the United States through the present. In Sudan in 1988–1989, when those most desperately in need of relief assistance and political protection were the victims of a ruthless and brutal persecution by a government traditionally allied with the United States, Washington failed to register the shrill public protests that characterized its dealings with the neighboring Mengistu regime in 1984 and 1985. When Somalia's children became hungry, the initial U.S. response was far less vigorous than the concurrent high-profile, dramatic response to far less compelling requirements in Russia and other former Soviet republics. Political calculations, alas, were not to prove irrelevant or even minor considerations as the government formulated its response to both situations.

15. See Wolfgang Achtner, "The Italian Connection: How Rome Helped Ruin Somalia" *Washington Post*, January 24, 1993, p. C3, for a discussion on

the disrupting and damaging impact of Italian economic and development assistance to Somalia throughout the 1980s and the linkage between that aid and political corruption in Italy.

16. "Somalia is the greatest failure of the United Nations in our time," said Aryeh Neier, executive director of Human Rights Watch (Keith Richburg, "In Africa, Lost Lives, Lost Dollars," *Washington Post*, September 21, 1992, p. A16). "We are a year and a half late," stated Mohamed Sahnoun, the secretary-general's special representative in Somalia ("The UN Up Against It," *Guardian*, September 2, 1992). "The UN, in terms of its life after the Cold War, is a shambles. If you look at Somalia, what you see is an ill-equipped, ill-informed and uncoordinated response," said Nicholas Hinton, director-general of Save the Children Fund/U.K. (Phil Davison, "Somalis Pay Price of UN Shambles," *Independent*, August 8, 1992, p. 1). "The UN agencies have no excuses. The dithering in the Security Council need not have stopped them from following the lead of the Red Cross and starting humanitarian work. . . . The money was there, but they chose not to use it. While sitting on their hands in neighboring Kenya, they did not even draw up contingency plans," accused Rakiya Omaar, former executive director of Africa Watch (Rakiya Omaar, "UN Relief Agencies are Incompetent," *Los Angeles Times*, August 26, 1992, p. B7); "It's so bad because we've let things simmer without paying proper attention. We've had inexperienced people who don't know what they are seeing, who don't know what the implications are and didn't blow the whistle! Because of the disorganization of the United Nations, less than a third of the food that is needed has been delivered," bemoaned Trevor Paige upon arriving in Somalia for the UN World Food Programme (Jane Perlez, "UN Let the Somali Famine Get Out of Hand," *New York Times*, August 16, 1992, p. 12).

17. "How come UNICEF/Somalia has thirteen people in Nairobi and no one in Somalia?" asked Pierre Gassmann, delegate-general for Africa, ICRC, in conversation with Jane Perlez, *New York Times*, December 11, 1991. "In a situation of war, we don't operate," Marco Barsotti, the UN Development Programme's acting resident representative for Somalia, responded, angering many who pointed to the concurrent UN presence in Yugoslavia and Sudan.

18. Jonah later unveiled a "comprehensive plan" for resolving Somalia's conflict after a two-hour visit that, by definition, allowed for extremely limited consultation with relevant players.

19. On this episode, see Africa Watch, *Somalia: A Fight to the Death?* (London, 1992).

20. It would have seemed logical to include neutral Somali groups and operational relief units of the UN in the talks; none were invited.

21. See Julie Flint, "UN's $68m Somali Aid Blunder," *Observer*, September 6, 1992.

22. See Leonard Doyle, "UN's Aid Supremo Post Goes to Swede," *Independant*, February 14, 1992, which begins: "A senior Swedish official is to become the new United Nations aid coordinator, taking charge of disaster relief operations worldwide, following the debacle of the slow UN response to the plight of the Kurds last year."

23. See Jane Perlez, "Somalia Self-Destructs, and the World Looks On," *New York Times*, December 29, 1991, p. 1.

24. See Keith Richburg, "Top UN Officer in Somalia Says Tactics Were Apt," *Washington Post*, January 23, 1993, p. A12.
25. See Trevor Rowe, "Aid to Somalia Stymied," *Washington Post*, July 29, 1992, p. A1.
26. See John Goshko and Trevor Rowe, "UN Nears Vote on Somali Plan; Little Opposition Seen to U.S. Proposal," *Washington Post*, December 2, 1992, p. A1.
27. Primarily AID's Humanitarian Assistance Bureau, incorporating the Office of U.S. Foreign Disaster Assistance and Food for Peace operations.
28. AID figures indicate that relief assistance provided to suffering Somalis (since 1991) totaled some $248 million by the end of January 1993— exclusive of the costs of Operation Restore Hope.
29. In testimony before the House Select Committee on Hunger on January 30, 1992, as he had earlier, Andrew Natsios, AID's humanitarian chief, called for greater UN presence and leadership in the Somali crisis.
30. See Perlez, "Somalia Self-Destructs."
31. See Don Oberdorfer, "U.S. Took Slow Approach to Somali Crisis," *Washington Post*, August 24, 1992, p. A13.
32. See Paul Lewis, "U.S. Offering Plan for Somali Relief," *New York Times*, September 18, 1992, p, A10, in which an unnamed UN official says in reference to Under Secretary Eliasson, "The Americans are coordinating the world, so they might as well coordinate the coordinator as well, I suppose." Such comments were increasingly sharp-edged as tensions mounted over the continuing role of the U.S. military in Somalia.
33. See Keith Richburg, "U.S. to Set Up Somali Police Unit," *Washington Post*, January 29, 1993, p. A21.
34. See John Lancaster, "Mogadishu's 'Green Line' Is Erased—in Theory," *Washington Post*, January 20, 1993, p. A23.
35. See Keith Richburg, "UN, U.S. Still Differ on Transfer in Somalia," *Washington Post*, February 4, 1993, p. A1.
36. A conference at which Ethiopian government officials, not UN negotiators, provided the critical interventions that resulted in an accord's being reached.
37. It is notable that the U.S. government avoided direct participation in the Addis Ababa conference so as not to establish expectations for an official American role in the political restructuring of Somalia, despite the major de facto role in just such a process concurrently under way.
38. See "Somalis Beckon Like Sirens," *New York Times*, January 24, 1993, p. E1.
39. See Keith Richburg, "In Africa, Lost Lives, Lost Dollars," *Washington Post*, September 21, 1992, p. A1, in which Jonah is quoted as saying: "The UN, as it is now, is not structured for emergency situations. How do you cover them [UN staff members] by insurance? It is very difficult to find a credible insurance company to cover them."
40. See Boutros Boutros-Ghali, *An Agenda for Peace* (New York: United Nations, 1992), para. 72.
41. See in particular "The UN Empire," a four-part series, *Washington Post*, September 20 (William Branagin, p. A1), September 21 (Keith Richburg, p. A1), September 22 (William Branagin, p. A1), and September 23 (William Branagin, p. A1), 1992.

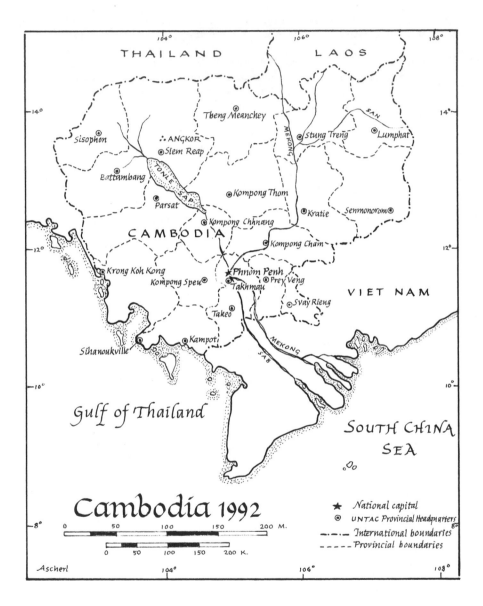

THAILAND  LAOS

Theng Meanchey

SAN

Sisophon  .·. ANGKOR  Stung Treng  Lumphat
Siem Reap

Battambang

TONLE SAP

Kompong Thom

Parsat  Kratie  Senmonorom

CAMBODIA  Kompong Chhnang

Kompong Cham

Krong Koh Kong  Phnôm Penh
Kompong Speu  Prey Veng
Takhmau  VIET NAM

Takeo  Svay Rieng

MEKONG

Sihanoukville  Kampot  SAB

Gulf of Thailand  SOUTH CHINA
SEA

## Cambodia 1992

★  National capital
◉  UNTAC Provincial Headquarters
—·—·—  International boundaries
— — — —  Provincial boundaries

0    50    100    150    200 M.

0    50    100    150    200 K.

Ascherl

# The United Nations in Cambodia: A Model for Resolution of Internal Conflicts?

## STEVEN R. RATNER*

On October 23, 1991, at the ornate Kleber Center in Paris, foreign ministers gathered with great ceremony to sign a set of accords on Cambodia. Their feat marked the culmination of years of negotiations aimed at bringing an end to the 20-year-old conflict in that country. The Paris meeting was also the beginning of another process—an unprecedented role for the United Nations in the implementation of the settlement of a conflict. The interval since that optimistic day has witnessed numerous obstacles to the fulfillment of the UN's mission; but the accords and their execution may yet pave the way for a more intrusive UN presence for countries ravaged by internal dissolution.

The linchpin of the Cambodia settlement was the agreement by the Cambodian and external parties to the establishment of a large and powerful UN operation to supervise the implementation of the accords. The agreements gave the United Nations Transitional Authority in Cambodia (UNTAC) vast authority: not only was UNTAC responsible for overseeing a demobilization of warring factions, the return of hundreds of thousands of refugees, and the monitoring of a ban on military assistance to the factions, but it had an extensive mandate over the civil admin-

---

* The author served as legal adviser to the U.S. delegation to the Paris Conference on Cambodia and to negotiations among the five permanent members of the Security Council on Cambodia. The views expressed are not necessarily those of the U.S. government.

istration of the country. UNTAC was to ensure the political neutrality of the governments in place in Cambodia, monitor human rights conditions, and organize and conduct—not merely oversee—free and fair elections.

This chapter reviews the approach the international community took to the resolution of the Cambodia conflict, with particular attention to the UN's authority in the governance of Cambodia, and examines the applicability of that model to other disputes. The civil conflicts examined elsewhere in this book that now plague the former Yugoslavia, Somalia, and Liberia, and the ongoing unrest in Haiti and parts of Iraq, may also be amenable to some type of long-term solution through an enhanced UN presence.

Any discussion of Cambodia in a book on collective involvement in internal conflicts must begin by acknowledging that the situation in Cambodia does not represent a typical post–Cold War internal conflict. Rather, it is a long-running interstate dispute, with direct involvement by Cambodia's neighbors and several major global powers. That regional conflict has, however, had devastating domestic repercussions. The external forces behind it—including historic Sino-Vietnamese and Sino-Soviet rivalries, as well as the Cold War—manifested themselves through a civil war among four factions, each of which had once governed the country since independence. Buttressed by foreign military aid, they struggled for decades for control of the country. As a result of the conflict, gross violations of human rights have occurred repeatedly; hundreds of thousands of Cambodian refugees have lived as displaced persons inside and outside the country; the economy is in shambles; a corrupt and untrainable government apparatus is in place; and hundreds of thousands, if not millions, of land mines will maim Cambodians for generations. The Cambodian people, then, have suffered the most damaging consequences of this "regional conflict."

In light of these conditions, as well as the geopolitical dimensions to the dispute, the international community's response has addressed more than just the external elements of the conflict: troop withdrawals, arms cutoffs, and guarantees of neutrality were only the beginning of a truly comprehensive resolution. A long-term settlement also needed to begin a process of true self-determination and resurrection of an entire country. Thus, regardless of the ultimate cause of Cambodia's woes, their effects and the methods to overcome them make Cambodia an appropriate subject to examine.

## BACKGROUND TO THE PARIS ACCORDS AND UNTAC

The UN mission in Cambodia represented the culmination of years of effort to end a conflict with long historical origins within and outside the country. For centuries Cambodia has been a witness to and victim of struggles for power in Southeast Asia.[1] Since the apogee of Khmer dominance during the era of Angkor (eleventh through thirteenth centuries), Cambodia has been losing territory, population, and influence to its two larger neighbors, Thailand and Vietnam. More recently, four of the 20th century's greatest powers have shaped Cambodia's destiny: France held Cambodia as a protectorate and colony from 1863 until 1953, and the Soviet Union, China, and the United States competed for influence throughout the Cold War period.

Since Cambodia gained independence from France, its history has been marked by domestic instability and involvement in confrontations outside its borders. Prince Norodom Sihanouk, the country's hereditary king, who first ruled from 1941 to 1970, attempted to build an independent Cambodia free of foreign domination, but the country was drawn into the Vietnam war when he permitted use of Cambodian territory by communist forces. Cambodia thus became a battleground for the global East-West confrontation and suffered from prolonged bombing (first covert and later overt) by the United States, whose ultimate enemy was not Cambodia itself but the Viet Cong's Soviet and Chinese backers.

In March 1970 General Lon Nol overthrew Sihanouk, ushering in the authoritarian rule of the Khmer Republic. After five years of fighting between Lon Nol's forces and the insurgents of the Communist Party of Kampuchea (the Khmer Rouge), in alliance with Sihanouk, the Khmer Rouge gained control of Cambodia by April of 1975. During its reign of three and a half years, the Khmer Rouge's government of Democratic Kampuchea attempted a complete reorganization of Khmer society, including a rejection of foreign influences and reliance upon a communal agrarian economy. The horrors of this period constitute among the worst cases this century of state-sponsored killing and other human rights abuses; in the end, more than one million Cambodians had been executed or died from starvation, exhaustion, or disease.

In December 1978, partly in response to cross-border attacks by the Khmer Rouge, Vietnam invaded Cambodia; by January 9, 1979, the Vietnamese had seized Phnom Penh. This aggression inaugurated the fourth regime to govern Cambodia since independence: the Vietnamese-supported People's Republic of Kampuchea (PRK). The Khmer Rouge occupied small areas principally near the Thai-Cambodian border; hundreds of thousands of Cambodians fled to Thailand and the West. Despite a call by the UN General Assembly for the withdrawal of all "foreign forces" from Cambodia, the regime, with Vietnam's help, retained control of most of Cambodia throughout the 1980s. Officials from the ousted Khmer Rouge regime continued to occupy Cambodia's UN seat.[2]

The Vietnamese invasion spurred the first multilateral attempt to resolve the conflict since the 1954 Geneva accords on Indochina. In 1981 the General Assembly convened the five-day International Conference on Kampuchea, attended by 79 states, including delegates-in-exile from Democratic Kampuchea (led by Ieng Sary, deputy to Khmer Rouge supremo Pol Pot), but boycotted by the PRK and its Soviet-bloc allies. The Conference addressed the Vietnamese invasion, not the Khmer Rouge's atrocities, and its final declaration scarcely mentioned human rights.[3] The General Assembly condemned the situation in annual resolutions beginning in 1979, but Cold War rivalries, Sino-Soviet tensions, and Sino-Vietnamese animosity rendered a settlement elusive.

In the late 1980s the peace process took on a decidedly regional emphasis. After two meetings between Sihanouk and PRK Prime Minister Hun Sen, the government of Indonesia—the de facto leader of the Association of Southeast Asian Nations

(ASEAN)[4]—convened the Jakarta Informal Meetings in July 1988 and February 1989. The Jakarta Meetings represented the first occasion on which the parties most directly involved in the conflict—the four Cambodian factions (the Vietnamese-backed PRK, the Khmer Rouge, and two noncommunist groups led by Sihanouk and former Prime Minister Son Sann), Cambodia's two Indochinese neighbors (Vietnam and Laos), and the ASEAN states—had discussed the elements of a settlement. Resulting communiqués outlined areas all agreed were the key components of a comprehensive solution to be endorsed at an international conference.

That conference met during the summer of 1989, following Vietnam's announcement that it would withdraw its troops from Cambodia by the end of September. France and Indonesia agreed to hold the Paris Conference on Cambodia, with all interested actors,[5] to reach a comprehensive settlement to the conflict, including its internal and international dimensions.[6] The need to address both facets had long been at the core of the position taken by the UN and ASEAN. An external settlement that resulted in the withdrawal of Vietnamese troops and cutoff of assistance, but left the Phnom Penh regime in place, was unacceptable; similarly, an election held by the PRK was rejected as inherently unfair and merely validating aggression. All states at the Conference, except the PRK (renamed the State of Cambodia, or SOC) and its allies, thus emphasized the importance of the internal components— namely, some reconciliation among the factions to permit the holding of a fair election in which Cambodians could choose their own future.

During the month-long 1989 session of the Paris Conference, the participants achieved some progress on the external issues, including military arrangements, neutrality guarantees, and refugee matters. Disagreements persisted, however, over numerous issues. Most telling was the Conference's failure to resolve the central question of power-sharing among the factions prior to elections. The three resistance factions insisted on a coalition government; the SOC demanded that it remain in power and that any interim authority be subservient to it and limited to organizing elections. The irreconcilable positions led to the adjournment of the Paris Conference on August 30, 1989.

With the collapse of the Paris Conference's first session, participants in the peace process, especially in Washington, Paris, and Canberra, began to contemplate new approaches to overcoming the impasse on power-sharing. Australian Foreign Minister Gareth Evans, with encouragement from U.S. Congressman Stephen Solarz, called in late 1989 for a UN administration of Cambodia.[7] In response, the five permanent members of the Security Council met in January 1990 to discuss the prospects for an "enhanced role" for the UN in Cambodia. Their deliberations throughout 1990 produced a series of communiqués defining the Five's position on the components of a solution: the need for a comprehensive settlement; free and fair elections conducted directly by the UN; UN verification of foreign troop withdrawal and peacekeeping to oversee a cease-fire, cantonment of forces, and an end to foreign military aid; creation of an entity, the Supreme National Council (SNC), to embody Cambodian sovereignty prior to elections; establishment of UNTAC; protection of human rights; and guarantees for Cambodia's independence, territorial integrity, and neutrality. They issued a peace plan, the Framework Document, in August 1990.[8]

During this process, the Five remained in contact with those Khmer forces they were supporting diplomatically, economically, or politically. In particular, China and the USSR, as the chief arms suppliers to the resistance and the SOC, respectively, discussed the Five's work with their Cambodian allies, both prodding them to accept elements of the emerging proposal and representing their concerns in the deliberations. The unique constellation of the permanent members' interests—four of them (all except Britain) had been involved in the conflict, and two (China and the USSR) had exercised considerable influence over the main antagonists—made them a prime forum for drawing up a peace plan. In addition, the Five were beginning to cooperate on other regional issues as the Cold War was winding down. This feature was most noticeable in the role of the Soviet Union, which endorsed a plan that could mean the demise of the regime it had supported in Phnom Penh for more than ten years. The weakening Soviet position also resulted in a stronger Chinese card, as the latter pushed hard for a settlement to protect the interests of the Khmer Rouge while attempting to avoid perceptions of blocking any peace efforts.

Other external factors were also at work. No solution to the Cambodian war would be possible until the ancient adversaries, Vietnam and China, were ready to cut a deal. That process began to transpire during 1990, as they saw the need for a political rapprochement because of their increasing isolation at the end of the Cold War. Their interests converged upon removing the chief obstacle to that goal by facilitating an end to the Cambodian conflict. The bargain struck at Chengdu in September 1990 accepted the Five's plan as allowing both China and Vietnam to protect their clients' interests—Vietnam's regime would remain in place, but the resistance would be bolstered through a political neutralization of the SOC. Other outside powers also exerted pressure on the parties to accept the Five's plan. Australia, the originator of the idea, peddled it heavily. The ASEAN states, once one-sidedly supportive of the resistance, accepted the need for compromise, as the conflict had too long hampered ASEAN's goal of a peaceful and prosperous region.

After the issuance of the Framework Document, diplomatic activity intensified, with the four factions accepting it in toto as the basis for a settlement and establishing the SNC, consisting of twelve members—six from the SOC, and two from each of the three resistance factions. The Security Council endorsed the Framework Document in resolution 668, which it adopted on September 20, 1990. The Five, aided by Indonesian and UN Secretariat officials, elaborated the plan into draft legal agreements, a process completed by late November 1990, and released their proposed texts.[9] The resistance immediately accepted these drafts, but the SOC found the UN's authority too broad and the plan for complete demobilization of its troops unacceptable.

After a six-month break in negotiations while the attention of most diplomatic actors shifted to the Persian Gulf crisis, a final round of talks began in the summer of 1991. In meetings in Beijing (at which Prince Sihanouk was elected president of the SNC), Pattaya (Thailand), New York, and Paris, the Five, Indonesia, and the SNC, assisted by UN officials, revised the 1990 texts to respond to the concerns of the SOC and other participants in the Paris Conference. These modifications permitted signature of the accords at the October 23 ministerial meeting.

## THE CAMBODIAN SOLUTION

The Paris accords adopt a two-pronged approach to the settlement of the Cambodia conflict: one set of commitments aimed at resolving the international elements of the dispute, and one directed toward the struggle among the warring factions. At the center of all these undertakings—as peacekeeper, civil administration overseer, human rights monitor and educator, and election organizer—is UNTAC.[10]

### UNTAC's Powers under the Paris Agreements

As the Five originally envisioned it, UNTAC's mission was to create the two key prerequisites for a free and fair election in Cambodia—a peaceful situation on the ground and a politically neutral environment. The first would entail the deployment of a massive UN military component, greater in size and assigned functions than most prior peacekeeping operations. The second, however, necessitated a wholly new role for the UN because of the factions' inability to agree on a formula for sharing power. The UN would act as an "authority" to sit above the two competing governments—the large administrative apparatus of the SOC, which controlled 90 percent of Cambodian territory, and smaller organs set up by the resistance in areas it occupies—and undertake any action needed to create political neutrality. UNTAC's mandate in this sphere was expansive.

Before turning to the details of that mandate, however, one must address how the UN is even permitted such extensive power over the governance of a member state. A UN trusteeship of a member state was not permissible under article 78 of the Charter.[11] If, as the Five sought, the UN were to oversee the administration of Cambodia, then under most views of the Charter, an entity authorized to represent Cambodia would need to delegate power to the UN or otherwise indicate Cambodia's consent. Such consent would eliminate any concerns regarding the ban in article 2(7) of the Charter upon UN intervention "in matters that are essentially within the domestic jurisdiction of any state." (Alternatively, the Security Council could approve an enforcement action under chapter VII to restore international peace and security in Southeast Asia, but the Council did not consider this option because of the practical impossibility of dispatching a large UN presence without any agreement by the factions and the Council's unwillingness to impose a settlement.) But herein lay the rub: in view of international isolation of the SOC (including the continued seating of the resistance at the UN), Cambodia lacked a single government that all states accepted as politically legitimate and legally able to perform this delegating function.

The Five thus invented the idea of the Supreme National Council, to include representatives from all four factions and to serve as the unique, legitimate authority in Cambodia—above the two governments—until the formation of a government following elections. The SNC's primary purpose, as envisioned in the Framework Document and the Comprehensive Settlement Agreement, was to delegate to UNTAC the authority needed to implement the settlement. In defining the SNC as "the unique legitimate body and source of authority in which, throughout the transitional period, the sovereignty, independence and unity of Cambodia are enshrined," [12] the Agreement contains the essential political approval by all parties to the conflict, within and outside Cambodia, for the SNC to delegate governmental powers to UNTAC. [13] The SNC then "delegates to the United Nations all powers necessary to ensure the implementation of this Agreement." [14] Thus, the Agreement provides the necessary consent for the UN to perform functions normally considered internal governmental matters.

The peace agreements also describe UNTAC's relationships to the SNC and the existing administrations and its tasks—specifically, the depth and breadth of its power. The depth of UNTAC's authority is governed as follows: UNTAC must comply with the SNC's advice on any aspect of the settlement (except electoral matters, where UNTAC's power is plenary) if the SNC speaks unanimously or Prince Sihanouk, its president, provides the advice on the Council's behalf; and if the advice is "consistent with the objectives of the present Agreement," *as determined by the chief of UNTAC,* the secretary-general's special representative. If the SNC does not provide advice to UNTAC or its views are, according to the special representative, incompatible with the goals of the Agreement, the special representative retains the prerogative to act as he wishes.[15]

This formula reflects the political realities of the Cambodian settlement. If the twelve Cambodians representing the four factions can agree upon a course of action, or Prince Sihanouk relies upon his stature to speak on behalf of the SNC, the special representative can reject its views only if he finds them inconsistent with the objectives of the accords. At the same time, the special representative has significant authority to act when the SNC is deadlocked and Prince Sihanouk does not wish to resolve the matter. Moreover, the special representative has absolute discretion to determine whether the SNC's advice is consistent with the settlement. The settlement strikes a balance between the need to respect Cambodian wishes and the urgency of implementing the settlement, but clearly gives the final word as a legal matter regarding execution of the plan to the UN.

The breadth of UNTAC's authority includes military operations, civil administration, organization and conduct of elections, and human rights monitoring.[16] UNTAC's military operations include verifying the withdrawal of Vietnamese troops; monitoring the cease-fire; supervising the regroupment, cantonment, and demobilization of forces; receiving and guarding the weapons and equipment from cantoned forces; monitoring the cessation of outside assistance; interacting with neighboring governments; destroying caches of weapons; assisting with prisoner-of-war exchanges; and contributing to mine-clearing.

With respect to civil administration, the Agreement breaks new ground for the UN. For the first time, the UN was empowered to undertake key aspects of the civil administration of a member state. Although previous plans had proposed UN participation in governance—such as sections of the 1947 Peace Treaty with Italy for a Security Council role in the Free Territory of Trieste, the Palestine partition plan's call for the creation of a *corpus separatum* for Jerusalem under a "special international regime," and establishment of the UN Council for Namibia— only a handful of proposals had ever materialized into actual territorial administration by an international organization. The League of Nations governed the Saar Basin from 1920 to 1935; and the UN Temporary Executive Authority administered the western half of New Guinea for six months in 1962–1963, during the territory's transition from Dutch to Indonesian rule.

Despite its immense mandate, UNTAC was not, like the Saar and western New Guinea precedents, meant to administer Cambodia. Rather, the peace plan calls for it to control, oversee, and work through the existing regimes according to a three-tiered scheme.[17]

First, "all administrative agencies, bodies and offices acting in the field of foreign affairs, national defense, finance, public security, and information"—the five areas most important to creating conditions for fair elections—would be placed "under the direct control of UNTAC";[18] the special representative may exercise whatever control he deems necessary to ensure their strict neutrality, including issuing binding directives.

Second, UNTAC maintains "supervision or control" over any other governmental components that "could directly influence the outcome of elections."[19] That is, it oversees entities— such as agencies responsible for education, agriculture, fisheries, and communications—in which partisan administration could impinge on electoral neutrality. Civilian police will operate under such supervision or control, and other judicial processes may be placed under UNTAC supervision in order to protect law and order, as well as human rights. The special representative can issue "guidance" to these agencies, but legally this guidance is as binding as the directives he can issue to the bodies under direct control.

Third, the least degree of UNTAC intervention is reserved for those agencies that, in the special representative's judgment, "could continue to operate in order to ensure normal day-to-day life in Cambodia."[20] These organs, charged with less politicized matters, such as cultural affairs, are not subject to supervision or control, but the special representative may conduct investigations to ascertain if they are subverting the settlement's objectives, and may take corrective steps as necessary.

Lest any doubt about the special representative's authority remain, the Agreement specifies that, with respect to all governmental entities, he may insert UN personnel with access to all operations and documents and require the removal of any Cambodian personnel.

UNTAC's electoral responsibilities were even broader. Throughout the peace process, elections have remained a sine qua non of the resolution of the Cambodia conflict. Because of the great mistrust among the factions, UNTAC had direct responsibility for organizing and conducting elections, another unprecedented aspect of its mandate. Moreover, under the accords, UNTAC was not beholden to the SNC—even if the Council speaks unanimously—with respect to elections. UNTAC would establish electoral laws and procedures, nullify laws that would not further the settlement, set a timetable, register voters and parties, organize and conduct the polling, respond to complaints, arrange for foreign observation, and certify the elections as free and fair.[21] Its mandate thus surpassed that of the UN in the four most recent instances of electoral control—Namibia, Nicaragua, Haiti, and Angola—although a similarly expansive UN role is planned in Western Sahara.[22]

Lastly, UNTAC had a central part in implementing the human rights provisions of the Paris accords, which were important to the settlement in view of the atrocities of the Khmer Rouge and the continued violation of human rights by the SOC. UNTAC was charged with monitoring human rights conditions in Cambodia, responding to violations, and conducting a comprehensive education program. The goals here are both immediate and long-term: to prevent a climate of fear from tarnishing the election, and to foster a long-term consciousness among Cambodians about universally accepted human rights.[23]

### The Reality: UNTAC on the Ground in Cambodia

The conclusion of the Paris accords marked the beginning of the UN's greatest test in so-called second-generation peacekeeping.[24] Secretariat officials immediately began planning the details of

UNTAC's structure and operation, and the secretary-general appointed Under Secretary-General Yasushi Akashi of Japan as his special representative. The secretary-general's plan of implementation organized UNTAC into seven components—human rights, elections, military matters, civil administration, police, repatriation, and rehabilitation.[25] The elections were set for no later than May 1993. After an unfortunately long interval of planning, the Security Council finally created UNTAC on February 28, 1992 (resolution 745), and Akashi took up his duties in Phnom Penh on March 15.

Since then, UNTAC has deployed more than 15,000 troops; UNTAC and the UN High Commissioner for Refugees have repatriated the 360,000 refugees and displaced persons living in Thailand; and human rights education and monitoring has been well developed. Plans for the 1993 elections moved forward: in August 1992 Special Representative Akashi promulgated an electoral law for Cambodia.[26] UNTAC registered political parties and voters; most significantly, more than 90 percent of the roughly 4.5 million eligible voters voted peacefully in May 1993.[27]

Nevertheless, the settlement's implementation unraveled in important respects, and UNTAC was not able to accomplish its mandate as originally hoped. First and most important, UNTAC was not able to execute fully the military aspects of the peace plan because the Khmer Rouge has refused to canton, disarm, and demobilize its forces and to grant UNTAC access to the areas it controls. As a result, cantonment and demobilization of the SOC stopped, and elections took place in a country that remains highly militarized. Cease-fire violations occurred sporadically, but with often terrifying results. The Khmer Rouge massacred groups of ethnic Vietnamese, temporarily detained groups of UNTAC forces who appeared in its zone without permission, and even killed some UNTAC personnel.

The Khmer Rouge offered two public reasons for refusing to cooperate on the military aspects of the settlement. First, it asserted that large numbers of Vietnamese forces remain in Cambodia, either as troops or disguised as civilian settlers. UNTAC was slow in verifying these charges (for which the Khmer Rouge provided little hard evidence), revealing only in February 1993 that it had found a handful of demobilized Vietnamese troops.

Second, the Khmer Rouge repeatedly criticized the weakness of the SNC vis-à-vis the SOC administration. It blamed UNTAC for failing to neutralize the SOC apparatus and called for the establishment of "consultative committees" of the SNC within each ministry, in addition to UNTAC oversight. The Khmer Rouge position, while a convenient excuse for noncooperation, was buttressed by the slow pace with which UNTAC has accomplished one of its two key purposes—the political neutralization of the existing administrations through the three levels of administrative control. In addition, some politically clumsy moves by UNTAC early in the implementation—such as its advocacy of an economic rehabilitation plan that the resistance groups saw as merely propping up the SOC before elections—further alienated the Khmer Rouge. Whether the Khmer Rouge would have complied even had UNTAC been more successful in these matters remains open to speculation.

Only in the several months immediately preceding the May elections did UNTAC begin to create the requisite neutral political environment. The SOC regime continued, like the Khmer Rouge, to rely upon forms of intimidation to accomplish its ends.[28] In January 1993, in response to attacks on resistance politicians by SOC forces, UNTAC gave itself the power to arrest Cambodians and oversee their trial in the admittedly nonindependent SOC judicial system. It also, on several occasions, used its authority to remove SOC officials, but did so through discreet requests, rather than any direct orders. As UNTAC attempted to neutralize the powerful SOC apparatus, it faced entrenched resistance at both the central and the local levels.

In addition to these violations of the accords, the relationship among the SNC, UNTAC, and the existing regimes changed from that contemplated during the negotiations. Whereas the Five assumed that the SNC would attempt little decision-making because of factional differences, the Council, at times, became a significant entity on the Cambodian political stage. Rather than simply assuming deadlock and leaving all important decisions to UNTAC, the SNC became a forum for the parties to argue their respective positions and attempt to reach a consensus to forward to the special representative. As noted, the Khmer Rouge, as the strongest resistance faction, was especially vocal about the need for a powerful SNC. It asserted that the SNC is the repository of all authority and that the Phnom Penh regime must surrender power to it. At one point early in the settlement, it even demanded the total dismantling of the SOC government.

The special representative himself responded to—as well as perhaps contributed to—this transformed role for the SNC. Rather than viewing disagreement among the SNC's members or their failure to attend SNC meetings as a green light for his own independent action, he sought to forge a consensus on the issue under consideration. Critics label this the weak approach of a career United Nations civil servant, while others might consider it simply the "Asian way" to make decisions. Either way, the special representative, aware of the difficulty, if not impossibility, of imposing a policy on an unwilling faction, was reluctant to assert the full scope of his powers by acting without SNC guidance. The risk to UNTAC's credibility of a string of orders from the special representative that the factions ignored, and the Security Council did not back up, compelled great caution by UNTAC. In the absence of SNC consensus, Akashi asked for Prince Sihanouk's decision, to place the political burden on him to make policy, before proceeding with implementation.[29] Only in the most egregious circumstances did the special representative test his full authority under the accords. For instance, he promulgated an electoral law on his own after the SNC proved hopelessly deadlocked (because of extremist positions by resistance groups and Prince Sihanouk's refusal to speak on the Council's behalf) and occasionally requested that SOC remove or reassign officials.

In many respects, then, the special representative was less of an administrator and more of a mediator, attempting to carry out UNTAC's mandate by persuading and working with the SNC and its factional representatives, rather than merely consulting them and making decisions when consensus was lacking. In taking action to effect political neutrality, the UN found itself performing a balancing act of seeking SOC cooperation in administration while challenging its more nefarious activities. The complexity of achieving UN administrative oversight in even a small country is thus becoming apparent.

As for attempts to overcome difficulties facing the operation, the Security Council first demanded compliance from the Khmer Rouge in a statement by its president and two resolutions.[30] In November 1992, after several months of negotiations led by representatives of France and Indonesia (as cochairmen of the Paris Conference) proved unsuccessful in persuading the Khmer Rouge to cooperate, the Security Council imposed a selective trade embargo on the Khmer Rouge–controlled areas and threatened other sanctions (resolution 792). The Council and the secretary-general repeatedly affirmed their view that elections must take place in May 1993, even without Khmer Rouge cooperation and in the absence of a demilitarized environment, in order to fulfill "the fundamental objectives," if not all the provisions, of the peace accords. In the end, the Khmer Rouge boycotted, but did not disrupt, the elections, in which the resistance won the most votes and the SOC came in second.

## Assessment

It is far too early to analyze fully the functioning of UNTAC. Nevertheless, it now seems clear that despite a legal framework that gave it immense powers over the governance of Cambodia, it came face-to-face with the same factional divisions and unwillingness to make peace that plagued the long negotiating process. The negotiators recognized the precariousness of the agreements forged in 1990 and 1991, but also believed that the presence of UNTAC on the ground would pressure the parties into complying with their obligations. Instead, the reluctance of the SOC to allow UNTAC to intrude upon its operations, the Khmer Rouge's mistrust of UNTAC and outright violations of the accords, UNTAC's logistical constraints and management shortcomings, and the hesitancy—or inability—of outside powers to back up UNTAC's mandate by effective pressure upon the Cambodian factions circumscribed UNTAC's powers and forced it to adjust its modus operandi. Rather than controlling the existing regimes, UNTAC was usually trying to win over those elements with its ideas, seeking SNC endorsement for nearly all significant initiatives. Only rarely did it respond to a deadlocked SNC by taking action, and the results were rejection by the faction with the most to lose. This process highlights the predicament of any UN mission—whether traditional peacekeeping or more intrusive forms, such as UNTAC—operating where the parties that have accepted its mandate one day reject their commitments the next.

But such an explanation for the setbacks to UNTAC's mission is incomplete. The UN and its member states merit criticism. Both were caught unprepared to provide the large civilian presence (including civilian police) the Paris accords envisaged. UNTAC's full deployment took too long, and its political neutralization functions advanced too slowly. As a result, UNTAC lost some credibility with both the SOC and the Khmer Rouge during the early, critical "honeymoon" months of the operation. Moreover, most UNTAC personnel, when finally recruited, knew little about Cambodian history, culture, or politics, let alone any words of the difficult Khmer language; and many were ill-equipped for the work of overseeing the governmental administration of any country. These and other systemic problems clearly suggest a need for careful analysis of institutional weaknesses if the UN is to try such ambitious peacekeeping operations again. The luxury of a peacekeeping operation requiring only military expertise is a relic of the past.

At the same time, one should not dismiss UNTAC's accomplishments. Those aspects of the mission in which the factions cooperated and for which planning did occur were great successes—especially the repatriation, the registration of parties and voters, and elections. Its military operations proceeded well until the Khmer Rouge refused to participate. A public awareness program has educated Cambodians about human rights, the elections (especially ballot secrecy), and mines. Moreover, UNTAC's ability to carry out the letter of its mandate should not lead to the conclusion that it was the wrong response to the conflict. Given the obdurate parties both inside and outside Cambodia, the employment of the UN to implement major aspects of the settlement still seems, in hindsight, the best possible policy response. Although expectations had to be adjusted regarding its ability to fulfill its entire mission (as with any peace settlement), the effect of UNTAC's presence in Cambodia should not be underestimated. It represented not only, in a conspicuous way, the interest of the world community in the future of a small Southeast Asian state, but an outside, generally neutral presence whose sole aim was to permit Cambodians to exercise their right to self-determination. The insertion of this actor into the maelstrom of Cambodian politics had a stabilizing influence, protecting the politically weak elements of Cambodian society, and it is difficult to imagine how fair elections could ever have taken place without UNTAC's ambitious mandate.

Regarding the Khmer Rouge's lack of cooperation, it is simply too easy to blame UNTAC's inability to force compliance from an uncooperative party on UNTAC alone. Rather, however incorrect this may now seem, the accords gave UNTAC a task to perform, assuming the parties' general observance of their most important obligations—either willingly or through outside political pressure. Any operation based upon consent and not upon UN enforcement action must tread lightly when that consent evaporates, although both logistical and managerial shortcomings and some political errors exacerbated the difficulties UNTAC faced. The accords' provisions that give a continuing role during implementation to the cochairmen of the Paris Conference foresaw the possibility of serious violations that UNTAC could not rectify. But peace enforcement properly belongs, in the first instance, to the Security Council and the member states, not UNTAC. And the reluctance of troop donor countries and other international players to enforce the Paris accords undoubtedly tied UNTAC's hands.

## BEYOND CAMBODIA: A NEW PARADIGM FOR RESPONDING TO INTERNALLY RAVAGED STATES?

The establishment of UNTAC may point the way to expanded roles for the UN in restoring order to other states riven by violence, anarchy, and economic collapse.

### The Problem: Failed States

The past decade has witnessed a gradual increase in the number of these so-called failed nation-states,[31] countries incapable of sustaining themselves as functioning members of the international community. Current cases include Cambodia, Somalia, and Bosnia, and perhaps Sudan, Liberia, and Haiti, as well. The future appears bleak for other states, such as several of the former Soviet republics (e.g., Tajikistan) and Afghanistan.

Most failed states were born during the proliferation of countries resulting from the decolonization of Africa and Asia after World War II. Indeed, the Charter made the "self-determination of peoples"[32] one of the UN's primary goals, and the UN relied upon a variety of mechanisms to provide assistance to the newly emerging states. However, the idea that states could fail—simply be unable to function as independent entities—was anathema to the raison d'être of decolonization and offensive to the notion of self-determination. A fundamental premise of decolonization was that peoples could best govern themselves through independent nation-states free from the shackles of foreigners. The Cold War prolonged the viability of some new states. Countries with underdeveloped economies and weak governmental structures received significant aid from their former colonial masters and the superpowers, regardless of any internal corruption. Many targets of such assistance did not survive solely because of it, and many (e.g., most of the ASEAN states) went on to become thriving independent states. But some new states became highly dependent on external aid.

Over time, the hurdles some young countries have faced have proven overwhelming, and the reduction in Cold War–related assistance beginning in the late 1980s has made their situations all the more difficult. Not all states—indeed, relatively few—that have suffered economic hardships have faced the prospect of collapse of governing institutions. Most have muddled through, albeit with a low standard of living or significant human rights abuses. But a small number have begun to prove incapable of self-government. The disintegration of the Soviet Union and Yugoslavia has added more candidates to the list of endangered nation-states. Inexperience in government, weak civic institutions, limited economic prospects, and ethnic and tribal strife inevitably will reduce some to helplessness.

## UN Conservatorship

For the bulk of poor states, traditional responses—such as development assistance to remedy economic woes and international pressure to rectify human rights abuses—may well be the most that can be expected from the international community. But the core group of failed states—those truly in extremis—needs a special remedy. A new conceptual and juridical framework can be developed for responding to the needs of these states.[33]

This effort would seek its basis in the idea of conservatorship. In domestic systems, where the polity confronts persons incapable of functioning on their own because of broken families, illness, or economic destitution, the law often provides a regime whereby the community itself manages the affairs of the victim. These notions entail placing the hapless individual under the responsibility of another (the trustee or guardian), with the latter charged to look out for the best interests of the former. In the commercial context, the bankruptcy codes accomplish a similar purpose—to provide a transitional period under which businesses are given a second chance at economic viability. UNTAC constitutes a move in this direction, although its establishment was also tied to extraneous geopolitical concerns.

Although the term "conservatorship" might be new (and raise fears of neocolonialism), the UN is already showing evidence of movement in this direction. In a highly significant report, Secretary-General Boutros-Ghali described the concept of "post-conflict peace-building," which he defines as "action to identify and support structures which will tend to strengthen and solidify peace in order to avoid a relapse into conflict."[34] He argues that to prevent future conflict, the international community should create a new political, economic, and social environment for states devastated by war, through strengthening of governmental institutions, protection of human rights, and demilitarization.

The secretary-general justified this aid for devastated states largely on the UN's obligation under the Charter to "maintain international peace and security."[35] Surely, as shown elsewhere in this book, the collapse of a state often is characterized by violence affecting other states, whether through refugee flows, illicit arms traffic, solidarity activities by related ethnic groups, or armed bands seeking a safe haven. The UN's actions in nation-building in Cambodia, Central America, and, in a certain sense, Namibia clearly fall under this rubric. But for failed states that do not represent a threat to international peace and security as that term is traditionally understood, the UN has been slower to promote multilateral involvement. Whether invoking Charter article 2(7)'s bar on UN interference in matters "essentially within the domestic jurisdiction" of a state or the mantra of "sovereignty," most states that have achieved independence since 1945 are quick to identify and resist such involvement in their internal affairs. They view a strict doctrine of sovereignty as protection against stronger states.

But even here, evidence of change has emerged. The secretary-general has observed that "the time of absolute and exclusive sovereignty . . . has passed; its theory was never matched by reality."[36] Historically, many economic assistance programs have required, through "conditionality," that the recipient state undertake policies of a wholly domestic nature. Article 2(7) has historically not prevented UN scrutiny or action to respond to human rights abuses. The UN, governments, and private agencies have delivered humanitarian assistance whether or not host governments have given formal assent to all such operations. International legal scholars have remarked on these trends, suggesting that sovereignty should now be viewed more as the trait of a people than as belonging to a state or government.[37] Even the

General Assembly, in resolution 46/182 (June 17, 1992), set forth the somewhat remarkable principle that UN humanitarian assistance "*should* [not *shall*] be provided with the consent of the affected *country* [not *state* or *government*] and *in principle* on the basis of an appeal by the affected country" (emphasis added). The intervention of the Economic Community of West African States in Liberia, while perhaps justified as responding to regional instability, was primarily targeted at anarchy within Liberia; and the military mission in Somalia received support even among African leaders long opposed to such ideas.

The long-term acceptance of limitations on absolute sovereignty, the views emerging among the world community regarding the propriety and legality of humanitarian assistance to countries in distress, and member states' increased willingness to entrust more authority to the UN, all point to new alternatives for responding to the phenomenon of failed states. Employment of a conservatorship model for saving states would build on these trends and flow from the UN's goal (even if not realized) with respect to trusteeships over non–self-governing territories, that is, promoting the advancement of their inhabitants toward self-government and encouraging respect for human rights.[38] Limiting the UN's conservatorship role to the Trust Territories (of which only Palau remains) is based upon the incorrect premise that only territories not yet independent require UN protection and fails to promote the Charter's values regarding human rights and stability in international relations. Failed states like Somalia are at least as "non–self-governing" as many colonial entities ever were.

## Models of Conservatorship

A range of models can be developed for such conservatorship programs. At one end, where the state still maintains a minimal governmental structure—where the state is failing, but not yet failed—the UN could provide governance assistance. It would offer personnel to work with governmental officials on administering the state, although the final decision-making authority would remain with the government. Conditions for providing such assistance might include both economic change and modification of the political structure if this restored the health of the state. To enable the state to get on its feet again, the aid should be directed at those sectors least equipped to respond to the country's needs, such as law enforcement, the military, or transportation.

The little-remembered, but massive, civilian assistance component of the 1960-1964 UN Congo operation (ONUC) followed this model, assisting the weak central government by effectively running those parts of the administration crippled by the civil war and the departure of Belgian personnel.[39] ONUC did not always seek consent from the Congo government for its operations, prompting Dag Hammarskjöld to observe shrewdly: "You try to save a drowning man without prior authorization and even if he resists you."[40] The UN's mission in El Salvador is also attempting this type of effort in the context of postconflict peace-building. Obviously, the UN faces a delicate task if the government itself is corrupt. The line between reforming it and undermining it may be thin.

The Cambodia model offers a second possibility for conservatorship, with a grant of power by representatives of warring factions. That delegation, with a reservation of some power to the local elites, has the advantage of its consistency with the Charter while offering an extensive UN role. This formula may represent the limit to which the world is currently willing to consider guardianship of member states. It may also form part of a solution to the tragedy in Bosnia—for example, if a committee authoritatively representing Croats, Muslims, and Serbs (including their militias) could agree to delegate certain functions to the UN, pending elections or some other long-term resolution.

A third, more radical model, would propose restoration of the trusteeship system under the Charter, though perhaps under another name. This would require a Charter amendment, the difficulties of which should not be underestimated. The Charter is based upon the important principle of "the sovereign equality" of UN members.[41] Today, however, if the forces in the country cannot agree upon the basic components of a political settlement—such as free and fair elections—then the Charter should provide a mechanism for effective international management.

The trusteeship plan would go further than the Cambodia model in that the local authorities would turn over power to the UN and follow its orders, rather than retaining any veto over UN action.

The administering power would in almost all cases be the UN itself, although this function could possibly go to a group of states, such as the European Community with respect to Bosnia. The UN will usually be the sole organization that the parties in the failed state and others in the international community view as possessing sufficient neutrality, and therefore legitimacy, to conduct a conservatorship. (Even the UN may be regarded as biased: for years, the SOC stated that the UN's annual resolutions on Cambodia disqualified it from a peacekeeping role; recently, the Khmer Rouge has seen the UN as tilted toward the SOC.) The UN and the affected state would negotiate a trusteeship agreement, containing the elements upon which the authorities of the state could agree.

### Limitations, Objections, and Modalities

In 1991 the suggestion that the UN oversee the administration of a member state would have seemed unimaginable. Today, however, the Cambodia operation has occurred, and diplomats and commentators mention the word "trusteeship" as a solution to Somalia's plight.[42] But the idea has many pitfalls, which merit careful examination. The normative and practical aspects to consider include consent, neocolonialism, duration, and cost.

*Consent.* The models above rely upon the consent of the failed state to a UN operation. The irreducible minimum of sovereign equality and nonintervention would suggest that conservatorships generally not be created without some form of consent. Beyond legal concerns, because most failed states face severe civil strife, it will prove nearly impossible as a practical matter to run any conservatorship until the belligerents agree upon a mandate for the UN.

But how does the UN achieve, or even determine, that consent? And what if consent is not forthcoming? Ideally, the UN should seek some formal agreement among the sources of effective power for its presence—the Paris accords on Cambodia are illustrative. For civil wars, this process will take time, but it should not be passed over quickly in favor of reliance upon less clear forms of consent. Conservatorship should be the product of, not a substitute for, UN peacemaking efforts. Formal consent clarifies the extent of the UN's mandate and commits the parties legally to the operation. Even such agreement, as shown in Cambodia, does not guarantee a smooth operation.

If the parties are unwilling to sign an accord outlining the terms of the conservatorship, less-formal consent may be possible. For instance, the parties may agree to accept a report of the secretary-general on the operation—the means by which the secretary-general has attempted to obtain the approval of the parties in Western Sahara to establish a UN electoral control mission. As a legal matter, either formal or informal consent would have to be reconciled with usual UN practices regarding peacekeeping operations: if the UN continues to recognize a regime, the latter will have to agree to the report; if anarchy has descended on the country and the recognized government is unable to do so, the consent of the belligerents to the report will have to suffice.

Beyond this stage, the normative and legal questions become exceedingly complex. In a case of pure anarchy, as prevails in Somalia, even acceptance of a plan of implementation by all factional leaders could prove impossible. Would the concurrence of the key leaders suffice? What normative valence should be attached to the consent of the people, as opposed to the armed parties? Should the consent be based upon inclusion of all elements in society, including those universally despised but well armed, as in the Cambodia context? Could consent be interpreted as the absence of resistance? And is it irrevocable? At a certain point, as consent becomes difficult to determine—or impossible to achieve—the concept of conservatorship intersects with international law notions of humanitarian intervention (which typically involves a use of force). Those who would call for imposing a UN guardianship on a member state absent clear, prior consent will have to consider arguments used to justify humanitarian intervention in both failed and other states.[43]

It seems reasonable, for example, that in a state of complete anarchy, the norms of proscribing intervention should be loosened. Where an invitation—normally a prerequisite of lawful intervention—is impossible because of a lack of any government, "consent" itself should be interpreted differently than in the case where a government exists. Here, acquiescence or absence of resistance may well constitute consent. If the UN proceeded on the basis of its view that resistance would not occur, a conservatorship might be created without the advance approval of the factions. This would move such an operation—normally viewed as "chapter VI $1/2$"—closer to chapter VII.

As an additional or alternative legal basis, the UN could rely upon chapter VII enforcement action, requiring the determination of a threat to international peace and security. The definition of such a threat, already enlarged for the Kurds, Yugoslavia, and Somalia, may have to be expanded further, perhaps to the point where the international community effectively considers the destruction of one of its members through anarchy as per se a threat to the peace. Such evolutions in the practical interpretation of the Charter are hardly novel. (In the extreme, one might even justify imposed conservatorships on the grounds that because an essential attribute of statehood, under international law, is an effective government, failed states are no longer legally states.)

Regardless of the doctrinal underpinnings, the practical difficulties of a forcible operation appear immense: imposition of a solution while the effective power sources still resist it seems an unpromising avenue for the UN. Again, the optimal solution in such a case remains diplomacy—that is, the UN's seeking domestic concurrence. Consent could be achieved in stages, with humanitarian relief of the utmost priority, followed by peacekeeping to freeze the conflict in place, and later by an administrative and electoral role.

This preference for diplomatic efforts to achieve consent should not suggest that the UN shirk its responsibility to intervene forcibly for a limited humanitarian purpose, such as delivery of food supplies. Such intervention is, for instance, eminently justifiable in the case of Somalia. Indeed, the presence of foreign troops may help to stabilize the situation in the country. But using those troops to force a UN occupation and administration upon a country remains normatively and practically troublesome. Rather, they should be viewed as helping to stabilize a volatile situation and laying the groundwork for some type of diplomatic activity to achieve domestic approval of a conservatorship.

*Neocolonialism.* The terms "conservatorship" and "trusteeship" will raise fears among developing countries regarding a renewed attempt by the rich and powerful states to control their destiny. The trusteeship system under the Charter, in fact, often worked against the interests of the inhabitants to benefit the "trustees." The placement of member states under such intrusive UN supervision could also be said to violate the "sovereign equality" of members enshrined in article 2(1), and to undermine basic notions of sovereignty. But neocolonial concerns, even if legitimate, should not carry the day. First, conservatorships will be based upon consent, not force. Second, the purpose of the conservatorship is to enable the state to resume responsibility for activities that are the traditional characteristics of sovereignty— namely, control over its internal governance and foreign affairs. Thus, conservatorship furthers sovereignty, so defined, in the long run. Third, if one accepts the concept of popular sovereignty, conservatorship will promote it, as well. The goal of UNTAC, for example, was to permit the Cambodian people to exercise their right of self-determination, the same end that the Charter posits for the trusteeship system.

Finally, the mechanism for creating and managing the conservatorship could also address these fears. The organ establishing the operation should represent developing states' views. As the General Assembly is too large for efficiently setting up a conservatorship, this suggests either enlarging the Security Council—with additional developing countries—or reviving or reorienting the Trusteeship Council. The former seems more likely, if not inevitable in the long run, as the developing countries continue to demand "democratization" of the Council in exchange for agreeing to allow Japan (and perhaps Germany) a permanent seat. And the operation should be managed by a group of countries that share regional, economic, cultural, and religious attributes with the pertinent state. For example, African officials should oversee African states; countries in the Islamic Conference and Europe would be among those supervising a Bosnian conservatorship. This practice would be consistent with the precedent the General Assembly set in creating the UN Council for Namibia in the 1960s.

*Duration.* Among the many uncertainties facing UNTAC's mission is Cambodia's ability to remain on the path of peace and development once UNTAC departs in late 1993. Although UN programs will continue in Cambodia after the installation of a new government, UNTAC itself was never meant to be a permanent UN investment in Cambodia. But disengagement may be very difficult as long as the postelectoral environment remains tense and national reconciliation occurs slowly. The international community will thus need to confront the possibility of an extended presence there and elsewhere.

Any permanent Band-Aid would be a mistake for the UN. Conservatorships should not endure and turn into long-term custody. If a given program fails to show serious progress after, for example, three years, then the various entities within the state and the international community should reassess the question of political viability, through the Security Council or the General Assembly. In certain situations, the appropriate solution could conceivably be a referendum by the citizens of the state on partition or union with a neighbor.

*Cost.* Mention of cost need only be brief here. Conservatorships will doubtless be very expensive for the UN. The Cambodia operation is expected to cost nearly $2 billion during its duration of less than two years. For a country greater in population, the resources will be larger, although much will depend on the mix of civilian and peacekeeping activities required. Thus, of course, member states will have to make sizable assessed and special contributions at a time when many are looking at their domestic priorities. Reform of the Secretariat and consolidation of functions associated with conservatorships that are now performed by a variety of UN components could realize cost savings. The challenge ahead is to demonstrate to the states that contribute most to the UN's budget that conservatorships will be cheaper in the long run than ad hoc arrangements of peacekeeping, refugee aid, and humanitarian assistance.

Conservatorships should not, however, be applied to the numerous states that are in difficult economic straits, but have functioning political and economic institutions; these are not failed states in the first place. Rather, these countries should be directed to the usual institutions disbursing foreign assistance. The UN might wish to develop criteria for determining when a state is near failure on the basis of sustained political, economic, and human rights distress. States should also be reluctant to surrender so much authority to the UN unless their situation is nearly hopeless.

CONCLUSION

The years since 1988 have seen a profound accretion in the UN's authority to respond to regional and internal conflicts. While most attention remains focused upon chapter VII sanctions and military action, the UN's accomplishments under chapter VI have been equally remarkable, especially through its peace-making and peace-building roles. From midwifing the birth of Namibia in the late 1980s, to electoral and human rights responsibilities in Central America, to the massive mandate in Cambodia, the international community has gradually entrusted the UN with greater responsibilities to build or restore states victimized by regional or internal strife. Thus far, its operations in nation-building, while laudable, have necessarily been ad hoc. Moreover, except possibly in Namibia, these operations have rarely solved all the problems they were mandated to tackle. Nevertheless, the new challenge of failed states is real, and the UN needs to develop a coherent method to respond to them.

Somalia, Bosnia, and Cambodia represent the most recent challenges to the UN in this area, but other states will surely follow. It is incumbent upon the UN and its member states to begin planning now for these contingencies. Close cooperation between the developed states—with the most to pay—and the developing states—with the most to fear—will be imperative for any type of conservatorship model to take hold. Sacrosanct principles under the Charter will require careful reexamination, and structural change within the Secretariat and the Security Council may be needed to make such an idea operational. A logical first step in the process would involve better coordination of existing peacekeeping, human rights, and election efforts. The ultimate goal of such an effort should be toward more routinization of UN activities to respond to failed states, following the UN's pattern for traditional peacekeeping and more recent election monitoring tasks.

This planning cannot and should not, however, produce a blueprint for all operations. The UN has functioned well through its common-law approach of building new operations upon the successes and failures of prior missions. Precedents and practices will need to develop over time, and lessons will need to emerge; each situation will be different from the previous one. The patient application of diplomacy, including effective mediation, will be critical to the creation and ultimate success of any conservatorships. But candor in what the UN is doing—resurrecting fallen countries—and some guidelines to steer it remain imperative as the UN faces a future of nation-saving responsibilities.

## NOTES

1. See Nayan Chanda, *Brother Enemy: The War after the War* (New York: Collier Books, 1986); David P. Chandler, *A History of Cambodia* (Boulder: Westview Press, 2d ed. 1992); Elizabeth Becker, *When the War Was Over: The Voices of Cambodia's Revolution and Its People* (New York: Simon and Schuster, 1986); Ben Kiernan, *How Pol Pot Came to Power* (London: Verso, 1985).
2. In 1982 the Khmer Rouge agreed with the two noncommunist resistance groups (led by Sihanouk and former Prime Minister Son Sann) to form the Coalition Government of Democratic Kampuchea (CGDK). The CGDK represented Cambodia's official government-in-exile, but the Khmer Rouge continued to dominate military operations and diplomatic activity.
3. Declaration on Kampuchea, in Report of the International Conference on Kampuchea, New York (13-17 July 1981), A/CONF.109/5, annex 1, p. 7.
4. ASEAN, formed in 1967, comprises Brunei, Indonesia, Malaysia, the Philippines, Singapore, and Thailand.

5. The Paris Conference included the four Cambodian factions, the ASEAN states, the five permanent members of the UN Security Council (the United States, the Soviet Union, Britain, France, and China), Vietnam, Laos, Japan, Australia, India, Canada (which had participated in earlier, unsuccessful peace supervision groups in Indochina), Zimbabwe (as the chairman of the Non-Aligned Movement), and the UN secretary-general (with his special representative).

6. The Conference's mandate was as follows: "to reach, through a consistent, balanced and co-ordinated approach, a comprehensive agreement providing for the internationally supervised withdrawal of foreign troops, restoring the independence of Cambodia, guaranteeing its sovereignty, territorial integrity and neutrality, promoting peace and national reconciliation in the country, ensuring self-determination for the Cambodian people through internationally supervised elections, arranging for the voluntary return of refugees and displaced persons to their country and paving the way towards the economic reconstruction of Cambodia." See Paris Conference on Cambodia, text adopted by the conference at its 4th plenary meeting, August 1, 1989, CPC/89/4.

7. See Steven Erlanger, "Diplomats Step Up Drive in Cambodia," *New York Times*, December 17, 1989, p. A15; and Stephen J. Solarz, "Cambodia and the International Community," *Foreign Affairs*, vol. 69 (Spring 1990), p. 99, esp. pp. 107–11.

8. Statement of the Five Permanent Members of the Security Council of the United Nations on Cambodia, A/45/472-S/21689 (1990).

9. See Permanent Representatives of France and Indonesia to the United Nations, letter to the secretary-general, January 8, 1991, annex II, A/46/61-S/22059 (1991).

10. The text of the Paris accords appears in *International Legal Materials* 1, vol. 31, (1992), p. 180.

11. "The trusteeship system shall not apply to territories which have become Members of the United Nations, relationship among which shall be based upon respect for the principle of sovereign equality."

12. Comprehensive Settlement Agreement, art. 3.

13. The precise legal status of the SNC is uncertain; the SNC lacks the attributes of a government and is not generally recognized as such. For a discussion of this point going beyond the scope of this paper, see Steven R. Ratner, "The Cambodia Settlement Agreements," *American Journal of International Law*, vol. 89 (1993), pp. 9–12.

14. Comprehensive Settlement Agreement, art. 6.

15. Ibid., annex 1, sec. A.

16. Ibid., annex 1, secs. B–E. UNTAC also has powers regarding refugee repatriation and economic reconstruction.

17. Ibid., annex 1, sec. B.

18. Ibid., annex 1, sec. B, para. 1.

19. Ibid., annex 1, sec. B, para. 2.

20. Ibid., annex 1, sec. B, para. 3.

21. Ibid., annex 1, sec. D.

22. See "Enhancing the Effectiveness of the Principle of Periodic and Genuine Elections", Report of the Secretary-General, November 18, 1992, A/47/668.
23. Comprehensive Agreement, annex 1, sec. E.
24. Georges Abi-Saab, "La Deuxième Génération des Opérations de Maintien de la Paix," *Le Trimestre du Monde*, November 1992, p. 87; and Victor-Yves Ghébali, "Le Développement de la Technique des Operations de Maintien de la Paix Onusiennes depuis la Fin de la Guerre Froide," *Le Trimestre du Monde*, November 1992, p. 67.
25. Report of the Secretary-General on Cambodia, February 19, 1992, S/23613 (1992).
26. "UNTAC Chief Signs Cambodian Election Laws," FBIS East Asia Daily Report, August 19, 1992, p. 20.
27. See the Secretary-General's Reports of May 1 (S/23870 and corrs. 1 and 2), June 12 (S/24090), July 14 (S/24286), September 21 (S/24578), November 15 (S/24800), January 25 (S/25124), and June 10 (S/25913).
28. See, for example, Mary Kay Magistad, "Cambodian Regime Harassing Opposition Leaders, Diplomats and Parties Say," *Washington Post*, November 27, 1992, p. A41; and Asia Watch, *Political Control, Human Rights, and the UN Mission in Cambodia* (unpublished study, 1992), pp. 13–27.
29. Prince Sihanouk has spoken on behalf of a deadlocked SNC regarding a ban on exportation of logs and a loan from the Asian Development Bank, both of which the Khmer Rouge members of the SNC opposed.
30. Note by the President of the Security Council, June 12, 1992, S/24091; resolution 766 (July 21, 1992); and resolution 783 (October 14, 1992).
31. Gerald B. Helman and Steven R. Ratner, "Saving Failed States," *Foreign Policy* 89 (Winter 1992/93), p. 3.
32. UN Charter, art. 1(2).
33. See Helman and Ratner, "Saving Failed States."
34. Boutros Boutros-Ghali, *An Agenda for Peace* (New York: United Nations, 1992), pp. 6 and 16–17. See also Boutros Boutros-Ghali, "Empowering the United Nations," *Foreign Affairs*, vol. 71 (Winter 1992/93), pp. 89–92.
35. UN Charter, art. 1(1).
36. Boutros-Ghali, *An Agenda for Peace*, p. 4.
37. See, for example, W. Michael Reisman, "Sovereignty and Human Rights in Contemporary International Law," *American Journal of International Law* 1, vol. 84 (1990), p. 866; Thomas M. Franck, "The Emerging Right to Democratic Governance," *American Journal of International Law*, vol. 86 (1992), p. 46; and Boutros-Ghali, "Empowering the United Nations," p. 99.
38. UN Charter, art. 76. See also art. 1(3) (purposes of the UN include promotion of human rights and cooperation in solving economic problems).
39. See generally Arthur H. House, *The U.N. in the Congo: The Political and Civilian Efforts* (Washington, D.C.: University Press of America, 1978).
40. Statement on UN Operations in the Congo Before the General Assembly, October 17, 1960, reprinted in Wilder Foote, ed., *Servant of Peace* (New York: Harper & Row, 1962), p. 323.

41. UN Charter, art. 2(1).

42. For the view of the Security Council's then-president, see Trevor Rowe, "U.N. Management Urged for Somalia," *Washington Post*, November 28, 1992, p. A1.

43. For a review of the positions on this issue, see Lori F. Damrosch and David J. Scheffer, eds., *Law and Force in the New International Order* (Boulder: Westview Press, 1991).

# CHAPTER SEVEN

## The Civilian Impact of Economic Sanctions

### LORI FISLER DAMROSCH

Starving children, fleeing families in leaky boats, surgery without anesthesia, barren fields: Do these images spring from crisis, or from the international community's response?

The outside world has reacted to the internal conflicts of the 1990s with a barrage of programs of economic sanctions, in the hope that nonforcible responses could curb ongoing violence and avert additional bloodshed. The United Nations has imposed arms embargoes against Iraq, all of the former Yugoslavia, Somalia, and Liberia.[1] In the cases of Iraq and the Yugoslav republics of Serbia and Montenegro, the UN followed up restrictions on military trade with comprehensive and mandatory economic embargoes, which have interrupted most trade, transportation and financial transactions with those areas. A hemispheric embargo on Haiti has cut off that nation from most sources of sustenance. Selective economic sanctions have been initiated to press recalcitrant factions in Liberia and Cambodia to comply with agreements for resolving long-running conflicts. Each of these programs began with the noblest of motivations: to reverse or deter breaches of the peace, to contain civil strife, to restore a legitimate government, or some combination of these objectives. In each case, forcible alternatives were forsworn, or at least postponed, to see whether firm economic pressure could render them unnecessary.

Yet as months stretch into years, the international community has become painfully aware that some programs of collective economic sanctions, begun with the best of intentions, may severely harm the very people they are intended to help. There is the perception, and possibly the reality, that the *sanctions*, rather than the crises to which they respond, have created humanitarian emergencies. Some religious groups, public health experts, and relief organizations, among others, oppose the continuation of crippling programs of economic isolation that have cut off civilian populations from their traditional means of livelihood and driven many to desperation. While it may be difficult to sort out the degrees of deprivation attributable to the sanctions themselves—as opposed to preexisting conditions, the underlying conflict, or the actions of ruling elites that exacerbate sanctions' impact on civilians—the moral questions cannot be ignored.

The facts that in the cases under consideration, the international community did endeavor to act with wisdom and prudence and to learn from past mistakes render these questions even more difficult. Indeed, the objectives of the sanctions programs were the most widely shared and deeply held values of the entire community,[2] rather than the partisan ideology of a mere bloc. The appropriate international body, acting within the scope of its legitimate authority and with widespread support, adopted the programs. As intended, virtually all states implemented them, and steps have been taken to track down and punish violators. Moreover, the sanctions programs have features meant to target perpetrators of violence and spare innocent civilians—hence the emphasis on cutting off supplies of weapons while creating certain express (but limited) exceptions for the inflow of food, medicines, and other humanitarian commodities.

The present wave of collective sanctions has made it necessary for the international community to confront for the first time the stark moral issues arising out of the civilian impact of sanctions. Were the sanctions programs misguided after all? Knowing what we now know, should we have made different decisions?

Should normal economic relations with the target countries be restored? What might we wish to do differently in future crises?

## A FRAMEWORK FOR ANALYSIS

Because our focus is *internal* conflicts, I will ask some questions aimed at identifying special problems that those kinds of conflicts may pose for the adoption of economic sanctions programs, in contradistinction to the types of transboundary conflicts that were presumably in the minds of the drafters of the UN Charter's provisions on sanctions. Furthermore, because our focus is *collective* involvement rather than unilateral U.S. sanctions programs, I will suggest a framework for evaluating sanctions adopted through the UN or regional organizations. No previous program of unilateral or coordinated multilateral sanctions has brought about the kind of total isolation of a target state that is theoretically possible with UN-mandated or concerted regional sanctions.[3]

### Beyond Policies to Principles

Unilateral sanctions need not be principled; collective sanctions ideally should be. National decision-makers have leeway to pursue self-interested policies or even to act without apparent rationale, as long as they stay within the limits of tolerance of their own polities. Thus if the United States so chooses, it can keep up favorable economic relations with its favorite dictators while stringently punishing the ones it doesn't like. But as we move from unilateral to collective sanctions, we should also attempt to move in the direction of evolving principled standards for the application of economic sanctions. Not the least of the reasons for doing so is that most of the human beings whom sanctions will affect have little or no voice in the decision to adopt them or in bringing about conditions for their termination.

Perhaps the call for principle will seem premature. After all, the international community was unable to acquire more than the most embryonic experience with collective sanctions during the era of the Cold War, when the only operative principle seemed to be that each superpower would oppose what the other one wanted. During that period, the only targets of compulsory UN sanctions were Rhodesia and South Africa,[4] and in the latter case, such sanctions remained limited to an arms embargo rather than the more sweeping measures that were theoretically available. Only in the 1990s have political conditions made it possible for the UN Security Council to begin to develop some relevant experience with a wider range of sanctions programs.

Selectivity in the adoption of sanctions may be inevitable for the foreseeable future, as key international actors set the agenda in accordance with their own perceptions of interests and resource constraints. It may well be that more experience with particular cases is an indispensable predicate for making wise judgments about standards to govern future ones. But over the longer term, as the international community matures, elaboration of normative criteria for the application of sanctions will be a critical step, leading to the eventual goal of treating like cases alike.

As discussed in the conclusion to this volume, the concept of treating like cases alike is an essential aspect of the evolution of international society toward a fuller embodiment of the rule of law. With respect to the application of economic sanctions, several questions are relevant to this concept, including the following: how to define categories of cases warranting a collective response (so as to overcome the current criticism that the international system acts on the basis of double standards by addressing only certain crises and ignoring others); whether the choice among available measures (for example, the choice between forcible and nonforcible measures) should itself be guided by identifiable standards; and on what scale to evaluate the measures decided upon.

For better or worse, most analysts have focused on "effectiveness"—in the sense of achievement of articulated objectives—as the touchstone for appraising economic sanctions.[5] While effectiveness is certainly an important dimension, it is not the only one. A growing body of literature draws attention to the value of economic sanctions, especially collective ones, in affirming the international community's commitment to certain fundamental norms, such as nonuse of force, peaceful settlement of disputes, and international human rights.[6] I endorse the trend in that literature to appreciate the norm-reinforcing reasons for going ahead with sanctions against violators of international norms, even when there might be little reason to expect the sanctions to achieve their declared objectives in the short term. Yet it is also necessary to refine our criteria for the appraisal of sanctions in order to get beyond the false dichotomy of "effective" ("instrumental") and "symbolic" ("expressive") sanctions:[7] some "ineffective" sanctions can serve important functions, such as norm reinforcement and deterrence; equally important, even "merely symbolic" sanctions can have effects in the real world. While some of those effects may sooner or later advance collective objectives, we must not ignore the potential for devastating effects on real people in the meantime.

A different sense of the term "effectiveness" connotes the degree of implementation of sanctions: How successfully are they put into effect and enforced? How complete is compliance? Are violations punished? Each of the sanctions programs considered in this chapter has raised important problems of effectiveness in this sense, as there have been well-known difficulties in ensuring that all parties who are supposed to abide by the sanctions in fact do so. Yet even if a sanctions program could be made perfectly effective in the sense of plugging all loopholes and enforcing 100 percent compliance, it might fail to achieve its intended objectives. This could be the case if, for example, the target has sufficient domestic resources to enable it to weather even a comprehensive and well-enforced embargo, or if the targeted regime can manipulate the internal economy to insulate itself from the brunt of externally generated pressure. Thus, even if all obstacles to enforcement could be overcome, important issues would remain. Indeed, to the extent that improvements in enforcement will increase the burden on the civilian population within the target state, the moral issues may become all the more acute.

With these considerations in mind, I propose two criteria for evaluation of collective sanctions programs addressed to internal conflicts:

- The *conflict containment criterion*: that a collective response to an internal conflict should be designed with a view to containing the theater and mitigating the level of violence

- The *differentiation criterion*: that the collective response should, to the extent possible, target the perpetrators of violence or other wrongdoing and minimize severe adverse consequences on civilians who are not in a position to bring about cessation of wrongful conduct

I will explore these criteria in the context of two types of collective responses that the international community has made to the internal conflicts under study: imposition of an arms embargo in the area of conflict; and imposition of a comprehensive economic embargo covering exports, imports, transportation, financial transfers, and other transactions.

The first of these techniques, the arms embargo, is now more or less in place for all of the conflicts studied in this volume, and on the basis of this growing body of experience we may be able to arrive at some conclusions as to whether—or under what conditions—these precedents may allow us to formulate a principled response to future crises. In brief, my assessment is that arms embargoes hold the promise of containing conflict, but that this expectation has been disappointed because perpetrators of violence have been allowed to consolidate and perhaps even improve their position of armed advantage. As for the second technique—the comprehensive economic embargo—we have rather less experience, probably not enough to justify attempting to describe a class of cases that would warrant similar treatment in the future. Thus it is important to clarify what has been done, and what more could be done, to respond to concerns about adverse impact on civilian populations.

## Refinement of the Criteria

I suggest the criteria of conflict containment and differentiation, in the first instance, as standards to be taken into account in deciding whether to adopt and how to fashion a program of collective economic sanctions in response to an internal conflict. At the initial stage, the criteria can assist in clarifying objectives and desiderata that the designers of any such program should bear in mind. These two criteria are obviously not the only relevant ones, but they will provide ample issues for consideration in what is of necessity a chapter-length, rather than book-length, treatment. I have deliberately refrained, for example, from expanding on the previous brief mention of the norm-reinforcing purposes of sanctions (even though I am wholly supportive of those purposes), as a substantial literature is already devoted to that topic.

I also intend these criteria to provide benchmarks for evaluating sanctions programs while they are in progress—as decisions arise about their continuation, modification, or termination—and for assessing them retrospectively. As standards for evaluation, these criteria are partly responsive to "effectiveness" questions: How well are we doing the job we set out to do? Would refinements in the program enable us to achieve our objectives more successfully, or with less cost to persons who are not in a position to bring about achievement of those objectives? Yet I have in mind that at least to some extent, these same criteria should take us beyond "mere effectiveness," to focus on questions with a deeper moral significance than the best way to achieve defined objectives. In what way should core principles and moral values shape our evaluation of sanctions programs wholly apart from (or at least in addition to) judgments about effectiveness?

*Conflict Containment Criterion.* The conflict containment criterion requires little elaboration. The value of containing conflict, rather than widening or aggravating it, underlies much of the system of international law and may well give us a principled basis for choosing nonforcible economic sanctions over forcible alternatives for collective response (or at least over those forcible options with significant escalatory potential). The conflict containment criterion can also serve as a basis for evaluating a sanctions program either while it is in progress or retrospectively, as one element of a judgment as to whether sanctions have been effective. The conflict containment criterion reminds us that wholly apart from whether sanctions have contributed to achieving a declared goal (such as restoring an elected government to power), we should be willing to put at least some positive credit in the balance sheet if sanctions have kept an internal conflict from spreading across national boundaries, or have kept a civil war from becoming even more ferocious than would otherwise have been the case. Likewise, if sanctions turn out—perversely—to extend or exacerbate conflict, then to that extent we must admit that they have failed. Such failures, if any, should not be perpetuated, and those charged with designing responses to the next set of similar crises should take them into account.

*Differentiation Criterion.* The differentiation criterion may require more explanation. It is an innovation as compared with criteria typically used to evaluate unilateral sanctions, under which analysts have generally concerned themselves with effects on the target state without worrying about how those effects might be distributed within that state.[8] It is analogous to a well-established principle in the international laws of warfare requiring discrimination between combatants and noncombatants and minimization of harm to the latter, but the analogy is only suggestive and not perfect. The criterion may be disaggregated into three claims: civilian impact criterion (absolute form); wrongdoer impact criterion (absolute form); and wrongdoer/civilian impact criterion (relative form).

*Civilian impact criterion—absolute form*: **A program of economic sanctions should not diminish the standard of living of a significant segment of society below the subsistence level.** This is not the same as a claim that the international community has an affirmative duty to ensure a subsistence standard of living, which is a much more ambitious proposition than needs to be defended here.[9] For present purposes, all that needs to be addressed is the moral responsibility of the international community to refrain from inflicting harm that crosses a defined threshold.

We may assume that any significant program of economic sanctions will drive down (or hold down) the standard of living of the civilian population of the target state to some degree. This inherent feature of sanctions does not of itself render them morally questionable. Only when sanctions would cause (or have caused) a significant segment of society to fall below the subsistence level would this formulation be violated.

Problems of multiple causation may complicate the application of this criterion. For example, the inability of a population to subsist may be due to the cumulative effects of its preexisting state of development, or natural disaster, aggravated by civil strife (the internal conflict), aggravated by the international community's response to the conflict. Only the last of these is subject to evaluation under this criterion. The conclusion will be that the international community should refrain from a sanctions program that aggravates an already bad situation, if the civilian population is already below the subsistence level before the decision on sanctions arises, or if the population will be able to subsist in the absence of sanctions but not after their implementation. (Alternatively, the implementation of such a sanctions program could entail a duty to ensure humanitarian assistance or other relief, such as temporary refuge, for the duration of the sanctions.)

*Wrongdoer impact criterion—absolute form*: **A program of economic sanctions should target those in whom a change in behavior is sought, and should either diminish their capacity to continue the wrongful behavior or penalize them so that they are induced to desist from the wrongful behavior.** This presupposes a separate moral framework for evaluating the wrongfulness of conduct to be sanctioned. With respect to the conflicts studied in this volume, certain conduct has been universally condemned, while other conduct is either controversial or considered morally neutral. "Ethnic cleansing," genocide, and war crimes are among the behaviors that have (or should have) no defenders; and although there may be acute practical problems in identifying wrongdoers and targeting a sanctions program at them, the idea of attempting to do so should be unobjectionable in principle. In Europe and the Americas, regional consensus has been reached on the wrongfulness of the irregular interruption of democratic governance,[10] so that selective targeting of sanctions against the perpetrators or beneficiaries of a coup d'état should similarly be a question of implementation rather than of principle.

In other conflicts, either no universal or regional consensus exists on the applicable norms, or consensus in applying norms in controversial factual situations is unlikely. For example, with the exception of the above-mentioned issue of overthrow of a democratic government, nothing in the existing norms of international law or morality purports to forbid civil war as such (as opposed to forbidding particular modes of warfare within civil war);[11] on the contrary, a right of rebellion against antidemocratic or colonial regimes is generally acknowledged. Moreover, the international legal system has heretofore insisted that outsiders *should refrain* from taking sides in civil wars;[12] thus it would be a significant departure from preexisting conceptions for the Security Council or another outside body to attempt to characterize one side in an internal conflict as in the right and the other side as in the wrong. At most, judgments of wrongfulness would have to be predicated upon wrongful *behavior*, such as commission of atrocities, and not on purported wrongfulness of a faction's objectives. It would be appropriate to reach a judgment of wrongdoing, however, in the case of a party that refuses to abide by a cease-fire agreement or other obligation: the Security Council has increasingly been making such judgments in the conflicts we have studied.[13]

*Wrongdoer/civilian impact criterion—relative form*: **To the maximum feasible extent, a program of economic sanctions should be designed and implemented so as to avoid enriching the perpetrators of wrongdoing at the expense of their victims.** The formulation that addresses *relative impact as* between wrongdoers and civilians shares with the previous formulation the assumption of an accepted basis for assigning blame to some actors and exculpating others: in the absence of such a basis, neither of these formulations would be applicable. But if normative criteria exist for making judgments of relative fault, then such judgments should be made in the design of a sanctions program, in subsequent decisions about its implementation and continuation, and in evaluating it ex post facto. The international community should neither approve nor approve *of* a sanctions program that would enrich war criminals and coup plotters at the expense of vulnerable segments of society, at least where the sanctioning body has the means to avoid or overcome such adverse relative effects.

The formulation in *relative* terms signifies that there may be cause for concern about the design or implementation of a sanctions program to the extent that the program itself causes a detrimental shift in wealth distribution within the target state, even if the program does not cause dire impoverishment of the civilian population. Thus a program might satisfy the absolute civilian impact criterion, but run afoul of the relative impact formulation. This is not to say that such a program could never withstand scrutiny, but only that every effort should be made to avoid such effects.

Conceivably, a program with adverse relative effects, or even adverse absolute effects, might have to be tolerated—reluctantly—in deference to the value of containing conflict, which in my view is and should remain hierarchically superior. In the final section of this chapter, I will ask whether and under what conditions this presumed hierarchy might be inverted: Should an otherwise disfavored forcible option be deemed legitimate when the nonforcible courses of action would either drive a civilian population below the subsistence level or enrich wrongdoers at their victims' expense?

## SANCTIONS AIMED AT CONTROLLING VIOLENCE: ARMS EMBARGOES AND INTERNAL CONFLICTS

The arms embargo as a technique of conflict containment has obvious intuitive appeal. If we want to stop people from killing each other, what could be a more natural response than to deny them the implements of destruction? If it seems self-evident, or at least highly likely, that unrestrained access to weapons and ammunition will fuel a conflict, then cutting off that access ought to dampen the conflict—or so we may hope. Moreover, if the possibility of external use of force in a policing capacity remains an option, then an arms embargo can impede the target's efforts to maintain stockpiles of weaponry that might eventually be turned against the intervening force.

In addition to its possible contributions toward the objective of conflict containment, an arms embargo also has psychological benefits for those of us outside the conflict. It makes us feel that at least *we* aren't contributing to the violence—indeed, we are trying to do something about it. If the embargo is effectively multilateralized, we can enjoy whatever comfort may come from knowing that the bad guys won't have external patrons (and, incidentally, that our own arms industry will not be losing sales to the competition). Finally, an arms embargo seems to satisfy our preference for targeting perpetrators of violence, rather than ordinary civilians, who would not normally need guns to obtain butter.

The international community has acted on these intuitions in several recent crises.[14] When Iraq invaded Kuwait, one of the first Security Council resolutions imposed a comprehensive arms embargo, which remains in effect and will continue for as long as Iraq is subject to the post–cease-fire regime of enforced demilitarization.[15] Thus a measure that began as a response to a transboundary invasion, and that has a continuing rationale for the maintenance of international peace and security, also may limit the capability of the Iraqi regime to wage war against its Kurdish and Shi'ite minorities or domestic political opponents. In the case of Yugoslavia, in September 1991, prior to international recognition of the independence of any Yugoslav republics, the Security Council mandated "a general and complete embargo on all deliveries of weapons and military equipment *to Yugoslavia*."[16] The Council has reaffirmed the applicability of the arms embargo to *all* of the former Yugoslavia, even though several of its republics have become new members of the UN,[17] notwithstanding the separate decision to impose a more sweeping program of economic sanctions on Serbia and Montenegro only.[18]

Somalia has been subject to a UN-mandated arms embargo since January 1992.[19] Liberia was placed under such an embargo upon the renewed outbreak of savage fighting in the fall of 1992, more than two years after a West African peacekeeping force had entered the country in an attempt to restore order.[20] While the Security Council did not exercise compulsory powers with respect to Haiti until June 1993, the Organization of American

States (OAS) voted within days of the coup to "urge all states to provide no military, police, or security assistance of any kind and to prevent the delivery of arms, munitions, or equipment to that country in any manner, public or private."[21]

In this pattern of arms embargoes we see the multilateralization of what in the past had been the unilateral policies of states, adopted either ad hoc or in pursuit of a general policy of refusing to sell arms to areas where active combat is in progress.[22] Midway between unilateralism and universalization of an arms embargo would be agreements among principal suppliers, sometimes undertaken as part of a comprehensive settlement of a conflict, to refrain from selling arms to any of the antagonists.[23] While such a multipartite agreement among major suppliers could theoretically approximate the effect of a formal embargo (especially if made subject to verification), nonparties to the agreement might undercut its effectiveness in achieving the objective of demilitarization. A mandatory embargo imposed pursuant to chapter VII of the UN Charter would presumably enhance effectiveness by extending the ban to all UN members, and could have the further advantages of publicizing the policies at stake and providing a firmer legal basis for criminalizing private conduct.[24]

While some resolutions adopting arms embargoes recite that the parties have already agreed to a cease-fire,[25] the typical situation entails an ongoing armed conflict, and the international sanction is seen as a means of mitigating that conflict. In other cases (of which the Haitian coup is an illustration), involving a sudden violent act or chronic armed repression, as opposed to outright combat, denial of access to arms may partake less of the character of conflict containment and more of the character of symbolically isolating the perpetrators.

Despite the apparent appeal of arms embargoes as a technique of conflict containment, experience suggests a much more complex picture, with more negative or even counterproductive effects than might have been expected. One lesson of the embargo on the former Yugoslavia is that a "general and complete" embargo may well have the undesired effect of consolidating preexisting imbalances, thereby increasing the likelihood that the side that started out with greater military power can achieve its aims by means of force. Indeed, such an undifferentiated embargo may even worsen existing imbalances, to the extent that the stronger side controls any indigenous arms industry—as turned out to be the case with Serbia.[26] A rough prediction would be that general application of arms embargoes in internal conflicts would typically favor incumbent governments (which are relatively likely to control the country's military forces and stockpiles, as well as its arms industry) and would disfavor insurgents, who are relatively unlikely to have internal sources of supply. In the worst case, of which Bosnia-Herzegovina provides a vivid and tragic example, the inability of a weaker side to acquire the means to defend itself could even embolden the stronger side to attack areas that had not been involved in the conflict, and thus defeat the conflict containment criterion.

The foregoing concerns about an undifferentiated arms embargo raise the question of the desirability and feasibility of attempting *differentiated* arms embargoes. If such a concept could be put in place, it could arguably come closer to satisfying the criteria that I have put forward as the framework for appraisal of sanctions—at least, it seems closer to the spirit of the differentiation criterion, even though it may never more than speculatively improve the prospects for conflict containment through deterrence or defense. Although I am a skeptic about the possibilities for differentiated arms embargoes, it may be worth thinking through what they might entail.

By analogy, in cases of transboundary breach of the peace,[27] the victim always retains the right to acquire arms with which to defend itself; indeed, any purported interference with this right would violate the express terms of the UN Charter unless the Security Council ensured the maintenance of international peace and security.[28] Iraq was placed under an embargo after it invaded Kuwait, but nothing prevented Kuwait from seeking to acquire arms in the exercise of its inherent right of self-defense.[29] If the decision on the Yugoslav arms embargo had been taken *after*, rather than before, international recognition of the independence of Yugoslavia's several republics, the embargo might have been targeted at Serbia as the party seeking to change the status quo through force, while leaving Croatia and Bosnia-Herzegovina free to acquire armaments necessary for their defense. As it was, the embargo went into effect at a time when the conflict was largely contained within the boundaries of an existing nation-state (Yugoslavia), and its scope was defined in terms of Yugoslavia's external boundaries, rather than the responsibility of any internal faction for initiating the conflict.

Before I proceed on a purported analogy to transboundary invasions, I should underscore that the embargo imposed on Iraq after its invasion of Kuwait is exceptional, at least in the practice of the UN to date. Although the framers of the UN Charter (like the framers of the League of Nations Covenant) surely contemplated that such a response to aggressive acts could both deter and reverse them, there has in fact been essentially no use of the arms embargo as a UN-mandated response to a transboundary attack, apart from the Iraq-Kuwait case.[30] Selective *unilateral* responses have occurred—for example, the congressionally mandated U.S. arms embargo on Turkey following the invasion of Cyprus[31]—but experience with the arms embargo as a collective sanction against transboundary breaches of the peace has been minimal. Indeed, on one of the few occasions in the Cold War period when the Security Council came close to imposing such an embargo, the target would have been not the initiator of the conflict, Iraq, but the initial victim, Iran, which some years later was perceived as the party obstructing efforts to bring about a settlement.[32] While one might discount this example as a relic of past political conditions, it illustrates how difficult it has been for the international community to arrive at judgments of fault even in cases of transboundary conflict, where the bases for normative condemnation are supposedly clearer than in internal conflicts.

Even if we did have an established practice of singling out initiators of transboundary conflict with the sanction of an arms embargo, the attempt to adapt such a differentiation concept to internal conflicts would be fraught with complexity. The appeal of an arms embargo as a response to *internal* conflicts lies precisely in the fact that the technique can be seen as a *nondiscriminatory* attempt to confine the conflict without taking sides in it. This attribute corresponds to traditional international law doctrine, which insisted on the illegitimacy of any efforts by outsiders to decide who should win a civil war.[33] Moreover, even when the facts of a particular case make it possible to assign blame to one faction rather than others for violation of an accepted norm, such as war crimes, it is far from clear that the remedy should be to increase the levels of weaponry for self-help: in addition to the ever-present risk of escalation of the cycle of violence, there are risks that the weapons will fall into the wrong hands or will be used for revenge attacks. Those opposed to lifting the arms embargo on Bosnia-Herzegovina have pointed out that even the UN Protection Force (UNPROFOR) and the deliverers of humanitarian relief are at risk, and that any increase in the absolute numbers of armaments available in the theater of conflict would aggravate those risks.

Whether an early distinction between wrongdoer and victims could have constrained the violence in Yugoslavia—or, on the contrary, might have exacerbated it—must remain a matter for speculation. In view of the difficulties of making such differentiations on the basis of fault in an internal conflict, the fundamental choice will probably remain between a nondiscriminatory arms embargo and none at all. But moral responsibility does not end once this choice is made: on the contrary, the international community may have a heightened responsibility to protect those whose ability to protect themselves is impaired by virtue of the international sanction. Thus, since the international community has effectively denied to Bosnia-Herzegovina the means to sustain the defense of its own national territory, the logical consequence may well be collective responsibility to secure that defense through sufficient collective force.

The Yugoslav arms embargo has been differentiated to the limited extent of allowing the import of arms for the benefit of UNPROFOR,[34] which is seeking to maintain peace in Croatia and to secure delivery of humanitarian assistance in Bosnia-Herzegovina, and whose mandate includes the disarming of forces in UN-protected areas.[35] This apparently uncontroversial exception in aid of an internationally authorized peacekeeping force has been extended to regional activities in the case of Liberia, where it is potentially more problematic.[36] The Liberian case is a curious mixture of an embargo that is nondifferentiated as between indigenous Liberian factions (one of which would probably have prevailed long ago in the absence of external intervention), but that is differentiated *in favor of* the nonindigenous peacekeeping force sent by the Economic Community of West African States (ECOWAS). How one assesses this differentiation depends on whether one views the ECOWAS intervention as a disinterested peacekeeping effort or as a projection of power on the part of Nigeria, which dominates ECOWAS. One may also question whether the embargo exemption for ECOWAS will contribute to containing the conflict or to keeping it alive. Notably, the Security Council resolution imposing the embargo lays great stress on the fact of violations of various obligations, including a cease-fire agreement, as well as on violations of international humanitarian law.[37]

Has the handful of arms embargoes in internal conflicts yet given us a sufficient basis to formulate any principled rule? General resort to arms embargoes for internal conflicts would seem presumptively attractive from the point of view of conflict containment. Yet in practical terms, substantial changes in the patterns of international political life—not to mention the economic interests of arms suppliers—would be required before anything like a general rule could become feasible. Even if it has become possible to abate (in part at least) the destructive habits of the Cold War, in which the superpowers continually kept up the supply of armaments to factions in internal conflicts, it is no simple matter to mandate the interruption of arms transfers in today's polycentric world. The sheer number of conflicts that would be candidates for application of such a rule illustrates the formidable difficulty of attempting to prescribe one. For each case in which an arms embargo has already been imposed, there are many multiples of equally deserving candidates: Somalia and Liberia would be reference points for Angola, Mozambique, Rwanda, Sudan, Zaire, and others; the former Yugoslavia for half a dozen or more "hot spots" in the former Soviet Union;[38] and so on.

Moreover, even if the political obstacles to formulation of a general rule could be overcome, caution would be necessary in particular cases because of the risk of entrenching precisely the sorts of imbalances that have turned out to be so harmful in the Yugoslav case. Since an approach of attempting to differentiate an arms embargo according to degrees of fault in the initiation of an internal conflict does not seem either workable or wise, the international community might have to take responsibility for effective protection of an endangered territory, such as Bosnia-Herzegovina, or of an endangered group, in the event that a well-intentioned embargo backfires. This factor may well serve as a disincentive to the adoption of arms embargoes in the first place.

## TRADE EMBARGOES AND THEIR LINKAGES TO HUMAN RIGHTS AND HUMANITARIAN CONSIDERATIONS

More drastic than an arms embargo are comprehensive sanctions reaching exports; imports; financial transactions; and in some cases even transportation, communication, and the movement of people. In sweeping terms, article 41 of the UN Charter grants the Security Council power to impose such sanctions.[39] In the exercise of its responsibilities for the maintenance of international peace and security, the Council may oblige all members of the UN to implement such measures.[40] It is up to the Council to decide whether to impose drastic measures in one fell swoop, or whether to tighten the screws progressively. In the discussion that follows, I will assume that major sanctions are to be adopted only in response to commensurably grave provocations, such as the violation of a norm to which the international community attaches high significance; I will not address the separate moral problems that would emerge if the Council or a regional body were to call for sanctions disproportionate to the underlying situation.

The practice to date in the application of collective economic sanctions has been highly selective, almost never coming close to the full sweep of the Council's powers. Prior to the present era, the sole target of wide-ranging UN sanctions was Rhodesia.[41] Only in the 1990s have political conditions made it possible for the Council to begin to consider comprehensive trade and financial sanctions. The principal UN experience in this regard has been with Iraq: the original purpose of the massive sanctions imposed in August and September 1990 was to induce Iraq to withdraw from Kuwait, but much more complex objectives have subsequently evolved, some of which pertain to Iraq's repression of its civilian population (including, but not limited to, the Kurds and Shi'ites). Beginning in May 1992, the former Yugoslav republics of Serbia and Montenegro were placed under an embargo that, although not as sweeping as the measures inflicted on Iraq, is quite severe. As for regional sanctions, while the OAS has had some experience with coordinating concerted pressure,[42] the current program of draconian sanctions against Haiti has achieved a much more effective isolation than was ever possible before.[43]

## Threshold Legal Questions

There has been little authoritative clarification of the international legal aspects of economic sanctions—whether unilateral or multilateral. Targets and other opponents of sanctions have frequently claimed that such programs constitute "economic coercion" that should be considered barred by one or another doctrine of international law, as Cuba has argued in its campaign for a General Assembly resolution denouncing U.S. measures against it.[44] The paucity of instances of collective sanctions prior to the 1990s has given little opportunity for consideration of the special legal issues concerning sanctions adopted under the authority of the UN or regional organizations, but that situation is changing. Indeed, in 1992 and 1993, two cases have come before the International Court of Justice in which sanctions mandated by the Security Council have been challenged as exceeding the Council's powers.[45] In theory, challenges to the legality of sanctions could come either from the target state[46] or from states that would prefer to continue normal relations despite a Security Council decision; affected individuals or companies may also have some forums available to them for raising legal issues, including in the courts of states participating in the sanctions.[47]

Litigation before the International Court of Justice,[48] including the *Nicaragua* case,[49] has raised questions concerning the legality of economic sanctions to influence the political situation within a state.[50] In *Nicaragua*, the United States had implemented measures—including ceasing economic aid, reducing Nicaragua's sugar import quota, and imposing a trade embargo—that Nicaragua challenged as violative of the principle of nonintervention. The Court rejected this claim, stating "that it is unable to regard such action on the economic plane as is here complained of as a breach of the customary-law principle of nonintervention."[51] Although the Court gave no reasons for this conclusion, possibly it was mindful that a contrary holding would in effect have obligated donor states or trading partners to continue preexisting aid or trade relations even with a state whose government had taken an unfriendly turn.

But the premise that each state may choose its trading partners, which could sustain the conclusion that each state may elect not to trade with another state, does not control cases of *collective mandatory* sanctions, where the Security Council decides that *all* states must interrupt their ordinary relations with the target. Then the question is no longer one of acknowledging that any state may sever a bilateral relationship without running afoul of the principle of nonintervention,[52] but of ascertaining the conditions under which it is legitimate for the Security Council to exercise power to compel not only the target but also third states that might have been perfectly content to continue their relationships with the target. It is commonly understood that the Council's authority to impose such sanctions derives from its responsibilities under the UN Charter for the maintenance of peace and security,[53] and thus the Council has been careful to recite in each resolution mandating such measures that the situation with which it is dealing does indeed constitute a threat to peace. As regards the internal conflicts addressed in this volume, the requisite finding was relatively easy to make with respect to Iraq and Yugoslavia, and in both cases the Council adopted sweeping economic measures.[54]

With respect to Haiti, the UN has followed the lead of the OAS as the responsible regional organization; only in June 1993 did the Security Council determine that the situation constitutes a threat to peace and then universalized the OAS embargo.[55] The failure of the Council to act in the Haitian situation is probably attributable in large part to political considerations and a preference for regional action, but some members of the Security Council (China in particular) resisted the view that the legal requisites for applying mandatory sanctions had been met (in other words, that the situation could properly be characterized as a "threat to the peace").

Although the Council has moved cautiously in its application of economic sanctions, it will inevitably be asked not only to build on precedents but to go beyond them. Other UN organs are also being urged to exercise available economic leverage in order to deal with human rights problems that are the underlying causes of many internal conflicts. We may take note of the insistence of the U.S. Congress that U.S. delegates to international financial institutions should exercise their voice and vote to deny loans and credits to regimes that engage in serious human rights violations.[56] This attempt to translate U.S. policies into a form of multilateral economic sanction has had little success so far, since other states that participate in these voting decisions do not necessarily share the view of the legitimacy of applying collective economic leverage toward internal political change,[57] or of the criteria that might be relevant in particular cases. Scholarly writers and nongovernmental organizations have advocated a greater degree of activism in the application of multilateral economic pressure than governments and international organizations have yet been willing to embrace.[58] Nonetheless, the normative appeal of these proposals is strong, and we may expect and hope that they will progressively gain acceptance. With time and further experience, the concerted application of economic pressure in support of human rights objectives should come to seem natural, rather than extraordinary.

## Moral and Humanitarian Concerns

A starting point for evaluating comprehensive economic sanctions can be the two suggested criteria of conflict containment and differentiation between wrongdoers and civilians. In general, such sanctions programs would be fully compatible with the conflict containment criterion: they neither contribute to violence nor are likely to cause escalation or extension of conflicts already in progress. The hope is that in time they will attenuate the capabilities of combatants and induce them to stop fighting.

The differentiation criterion is more problematic. Let us first consider it in the form of *absolute impact on civilians* and then go on to consider *targeting of wrongdoers* and *relative effects on wrongdoers and victims*.

*Absolute Impact: Humanitarian Exemptions.* In the tentative formulation in which I have proffered it, the absolute civilian impact criterion would be violated if an economic sanctions program were to cause a significant segment of a civilian population to fall below the subsistence level. This criterion is applicable only to those humanitarian emergencies *caused by sanctions*, even though other moral principles may also require humanitarian relief on a different or more general basis.

The international community has made at least some gestures in the direction of fashioning sanctions programs to shield the civilian population from serious negative effects. Uniformly, each of the sanctions programs under consideration has contained explicit exemptions for humanitarian needs, generally formulated along the lines of an exception to the import ban for "supplies strictly for medical purposes and, in humanitarian circumstances, foodstuffs," and an exception to financial controls for funds transfers in support of similarly defined purposes.[59] (The humanitarian qualification concerning foodstuffs is aimed at eliminating any loopholes that might otherwise enable the military to stockpile foodstuffs or the ruling elites to divert food imports for their own aggrandizement; as such, it is partially responsive to the relative impact criterion, which I discuss below.) National legislation and regulations implementing the collective sanctions embody humanitarian exceptions in similar terms.[60]

In general, parties seeking to avail themselves of the humanitarian exemptions are supposed to follow certain procedural requirements before effecting the transaction, typically consisting of notification to a committee charged with implementing the sanctions.[61] Flights for humanitarian purposes have been exempted from otherwise applicable prohibitions, provided that specified procedures are followed for obtaining approval.[62] The system has led to some annoyance on the part of humanitarian relief organizations and to criticisms that the new bureaucracy is bogged down in paperwork and preoccupied with trivial details (such as determining whether whiskey and caviar fall within the humanitarian exception).

Formal availability of a legal exception for humanitarian relief indicates consciousness of the moral and humanitarian dimensions of a sanctions program, but might well fall far short of fulfilling the actual needs of the civilian population. Thus the Security Council has taken some steps aimed at assuring delivery of humanitarian supplies,[63] wholly apart from the question of their formal exemption from the embargoes. The Security Council has demanded cooperation of all factions with humanitarian efforts, and has warned that in the absence of such cooperation, the Council "does not exclude other measures to deliver humanitarian assistance."[64] More forcefully, with respect to Bosnia-Herzegovina the Security Council called upon states and regional agencies to take "all measures necessary" to facilitate the delivery of humanitarian assistance (implicitly including the use of force),[65] and the Council subsequently authorized the use of force to ensure the delivery of humanitarian assistance to Somalia.[66]

Although removing impediments to delivery of humanitarian relief is surely important, it too is not the end of the inquiry. As the case of Haiti shows, over the long term the sanctions themselves may impair the subsistence prospects of vulnerable sectors of the population, and reliance on the generosity of external donors can only be a short-term and not a long-term solution. The OAS has exhorted member states "to increase humanitarian aid to the poorest sectors of the Haitian people," while underscoring that a comprehensive program for economic recovery should be implemented "in consultation with Haiti's constitutional authorities as soon as the country's democratic institutions have been reinstated."[67] If that objective comes to seem unattainable through economic sanctions, then the international community may have to reassess whether to change course, either by resorting to forcible measures or by abandoning the effort. (I will address some considerations bearing on that choice in the final part of this chapter.)

## Differential Targeting of Wrongdoers

The various sanctions programs have made some effort to differentiate between perpetrators and victims, but these distinctions have proven exceedingly elusive to make and apply.

A very broad-brush form of differentiation has to do with the geographic scope of application of the sanctions. Significantly, although the arms embargo was made applicable to all of Yugoslavia, the further economic sanctions the Security Council imposed in May 1992 (after the breakup of Yugoslavia) apply only to Serbia and Montenegro.[68] This geographic differentiation may have some abstract logic, but in practical terms it is less than meaningful. Not only are the borders between sanctioned and unsanctioned states highly porous,[69] but there are wrongdoers all over Croatia and Bosnia-Herzegovina (some, but not all, of whom are responsive to Serbian direction), and even within Serbia's borders the brunt of the sanctions falls on civilians, who are not engaged in the wrongful conduct.[70]

With respect to Iraq, the embargo formally applies to all of Iraq's territory, but the actual situation is one of de facto autonomy for Iraqi Kurdistan, policed by coalition troops operating out of Turkey. The Iraqi regime has itself implemented a severe internal blockade of the Kurdish region, as well as of the southern marsh areas in which many Shi'ites and other opponents of the regime are clustered. Relief efforts to deliver food, fuel, medicines, and other essential humanitarian commodities to the besieged populations have proceeded with the approval of the Security Council and with the protection of coalition forces and a small number of UN guards.[71]

The conditions the Security Council established for the lifting of the embargo on Iraqi oil exports may be considered a complex variant of differentiation.[72] The idea is to maintain controls to ensure compliance with a variety of obligations pursuant to Security Council resolutions (including demilitarization), while also making it possible to generate some revenue that would be denied to the regime but channeled for purposes of reparation, compensation, and humanitarian needs. Under a formula devised in the summer of 1991, dubbed "oil for food," Iraqi oil would have been sold and the proceeds earmarked in specified proportions. The formula would have enabled an allocation to civilian needs of at least as much as Iraq had been spending before the crisis, while redirecting a proportion commensurate with Iraq's previous military budget to the internationally approved purposes of compensating Kuwait (and others injured by the invasion) and funding the operations of the UN in carrying out demilitarization and other functions under the cease-fire resolution. The proposal, therefore, was directly responsive to the dual idea of denying military capability while providing for civilian needs. Iraq repeatedly rejected the proposal.

In the case of Haiti, the OAS and its member states have made gestures in the direction of singling out the coup perpetrators and officials illegitimately holding power for the application of selectively targeted sanctions. In particular, the OAS has called on states to deny visas to such persons and to freeze their individual bank accounts.[73] The United States has attempted to identify these individuals and penalize them accordingly. But no evidence indicates that the individual targets have felt particularly pinched by these minor efforts—certainly the effects do not compare with the general embargo's drastic effects on ordinary citizens.

*Relative Effects as Between Wrongdoers and Victims.* In the internal conflicts we have studied, and in others that have not yet reached the stage of collective involvement, a disturbing pattern of activity is evident on the part of incumbent regimes to control economic activity to their own benefit and to the detriment of vulnerable civilian populations.[74] Elites have proven to be exceedingly adept at bleeding the local economy during a period of internationally imposed sanctions, and at manipulating whatever transactions are allowed to occur notwithstanding the sanctions. The sweeping economic sanctions directed at Iraq have not noticeably weakened any of Saddam Hussein's perquisites, even as the standard of living in the country as a whole has diminished. In Haiti, the authorities who hold power illegally have developed sophisticated means of exploiting control over scarce goods and contraband, and of benefiting from financial transfers that individual Haitians are allowed to receive from their relatives outside the country. The examples could be multiplied. Indeed, one could argue that sanctions *inevitably* will redound to the benefit of an autocratic regime that is the ostensible target of the measures, precisely because such a regime will always be in a better position than the civilian population to wield control over external transactions and the internal economy. Thus the rich are likely to get richer and the poor poorer even under the most skillfully designed program of differentially targeted sanctions, and there is the further likelihood of the creation and enrichment of a criminal class that profiteers in bootleg or scarce items.

Earlier in this chapter, I suggested that sanctions programs should be carefully scrutinized to guard against the possibility of contributing to enrichment of the wrongdoers at the expense of their victims, whether or not civilian suffering reaches the level that would trigger concern under an absolute impact criterion. Evidence of detrimental wealth shifts certainly deserves full investigation and appropriate corrective measures, to the extent that the outside world is capable of overcoming the problem. I am not persuaded, however, that such evidence would necessarily provide a sufficient basis for abandoning sanctions or resorting to forcible options. To understand my position, it is necessary to consider the reasons why, in my view, economic sanctions are generally preferable to either forcible options or inaction, even when such wealth-distorting effects are unavoidable.

## ECONOMIC SANCTIONS AND FORCE
## AS POLICY ALTERNATIVES

It is now time to ask whether, or in what circumstances, collective force would present a preferable alternative to the undesirable or morally objectionable consequences of economic sanctions. The case of Haiti presents the issues most sharply. Could the Haitian people have been spared months, and now years, of devastation and desperation if the international community had been ready and willing to intervene with precisely targeted force? Some observers urged this course of action in the very first days of the Haitian crisis,[75] and probably even more think in hindsight that this would have been a preferable policy. Now that we have seen deployment of multilateral forces to several areas of internal crisis, as well as serious attention to proposals for creation of standing forces under international authority, we should consider the potential interrelationships among forcible and nonforcible options.

### Force as a Remedy of Last Resort

The UN Charter, and indeed the whole body of international law,[76] assumes that force should be a last resort. The Charter specifies that the Security Council "may decide what measures *not involving the use of armed force* are to be employed to give effect to its decisions";[77] only if such measures "would be inadequate or have proved to be inadequate" does the Charter contemplate military measures.[78] Implicitly, it is open to the Council to decide that nonforcible measures "would be inadequate" without actually trying them or giving them much time to work, but the presumptions should be in favor of holding force in reserve until nonforcible means have been exhausted.

There should be little reason to upset this traditional framework of assumptions. No matter how grievous the civilian impact of economic sanctions, war would almost always be more devastating, not only to the combatants, but to civilians and to the environment and infrastructure of affected countries. Nor do economic sanctions pose the same kinds of risks of escalation or sudden, irrevocable miscalculation: they are usually incremental and reversible, and their consequences are generally remediable.[79] Moreover, if the military option remains a *last* resort, then *prior* application of economic sanctions should weaken the military capabilities of the target and make it possible to achieve the objectives of sanctions at a lower level of violence.[80] Finally, maximum mobilization of peaceful pressure can serve important symbolic and moral values, and indeed it may be impossible to build or sustain domestic or international political support for more drastic action except by beginning with nonforcible measures.

Nonetheless, we have to ask whether we may be at a moment in the evolution of international society when authorized application of military force may in some circumstances be preferable to protracted, painful, and not necessarily effectual application of economic sanctions. In a well-regulated domestic society, we would expect to arrest and incarcerate a criminal, rather than to seal off his house and starve his whole family (especially if we knew that his wife and children would starve long before he would). If the political climate in the Security Council now makes it possible to move toward international police capabilities, then we should ask in what circumstances it might be preferable to interject a military presence either before any application of economic sanctions or before they have run their course.

While the determination of the legitimacy of the use of force in a particular case would need to take into account many considerations beyond the scope of this chapter, I suggest that the presumption against the use of force should not be overcome in the kinds of cases under examination here, unless we can be satisfied that the forcible option is so clearly preferable in terms of its ability to avert harm to civilians as to justify the inevitable risk to the conflict containment value. We might reach this judgment if the absolute impact of economic sanctions on civilians were so deleterious as to jeopardize prospects for subsistence, *and* if the forcible option could reasonably be predicted to avoid such adverse effects. We would also need to consider whether the ultimate objective is one that can in fact be secured by force—which is far from clear in the case of securing democratic governance for Haiti.

Collective forcible measures may also be justifiable when collective *nonforcible* sanctions, such as an arms embargo, have impaired the ability of a territory or population to defend itself against forcible attacks, including those tantamount to genocide. The interjection of a protective military force in such circumstances is more likely than an adjustment of the sanctions to advance the value of conflict containment that underlay the original choice for sanctions.

### The Attitudes and Capabilities of the People of the Target State

I have so far not explicitly addressed what may well be the most critical set of assumptions underlying the choice between sanctions and other policy options, ranging from inaction to military force: Do we assume that the people of the target state are innocent and passive bystanders—victims of their own rulers and perhaps of the sanctions as well—or do we believe that they have the capacity to exercise free choice? With respect to the decision to adopt sanctions (prior to or in preference to other policy alternatives), what weight should be accorded to the views of persons who can speak with authority and legitimacy on behalf of the civilian population? If sanctions are adopted, will they empower the people of the target state to overthrow illegitimate rulers, to end repressive or atrocious conduct, to bring their state into compliance with international law? Or will sanctions breed passivity or, even worse, be counterproductive by allowing the regime to portray itself as the embattled defender of nationhood and the outside world as the cynical killer of innocent children?

These issues have received much attention in connection with past sanctions programs, especially the collective sanctions imposed against Rhodesia and South Africa. Some observers have contended that sanctions ran contrary to the interests of the very people they were supposed to help, and that sanctions may have perversely assisted the white minority regimes in consolidating their own positions within the two countries.[81] The better view, I believe, is that sanctions have decisively contributed to the ability of the majority populations in those two target states to achieve political empowerment—an objective that once seemed unattainable, but that was sufficiently realized in Rhodesia upon the establishment of the state of Zimbabwe in 1979, and that has come to seem within reach in South Africa. Along with many others, I attach great significance to the fact that the authentic leadership of the majority populations called for the imposition, strengthening, and perpetuation of sanctions (and in the case of South Africa supported the sanctions until late 1993).

Where authentic leaders—ones with a bona fide claim to authority to speak for their people, even if they have never been allowed to run for election or are in exile—plead for economic sanctions as a strategy for bringing down an illegitimate regime, I believe that that plea should carry great weight. Such a plea gives credible evidence that the people of the target state are willing to endure substantial hardship for the sake of external support in vindicating their own political empowerment. The plea for sanctions speaks all the more eloquently when authentic leaders simultaneously forswear (or at least do not encourage) forcible strategies toward the same objective. I do not argue that the renunciation of force should be a condition precedent to international action on the request for sanctions; realistically, sanctions against a repressive regime may help the mobilization of indigenous factions for armed insurgency, and the combined effect of sanctions and warfare may be what ultimately brings about the desired objective.[82] But where authentic leaders of the target's people assert a preference for nonforcible over forcible options, that preference should be honored—at least in the absence of extraordinary circumstances in which an interest of the international community as a whole would justify overriding the local preference (for example, credible intelligence that the illegitimate regime is on the threshold of deploying weapons of mass destruction).

These considerations allow us to make sense out of the Haitian case by recognizing that Father Aristide—the duly elected president and still the legitimate head of state—has consistently advocated strong economic sanctions and has equally consistently refrained from asking to be reinstalled by means of force. No evidence suggests that President Aristide has lost the confidence of his people or that he is cynically exploiting their misery; if such evidence were to emerge, the presumption of deference to him as leader might be overcome, since it is, after all, the people's rights, rather than his personal rights, that are ultimately at stake. Since the ultimate objective of the sanctions is to vindicate the democratic choice of the Haitian people, it is entirely appropriate for the international community to defer to that people's democratically chosen leader in ranking the available options of economic sanctions, force, and inaction or abandonment of the collective effort. No other community interest (for example, the elimination of weapons of mass destruction) is present to justify taking an action more forceful than that which the authentic Haitian leadership itself advocates.

A different problem arises where there is no authentic leadership to speak for the people of the target state, or where there is doubt that indigenous views can be authoritatively determined. Apart from the unique circumstances of Iraqi Kurdistan,[83] the Iraqi populace has had no opportunity to express opinions in opposition to those of the regime. Moreover, the regime has been so manipulative in portraying the sanctions as the cause of the country's misery as to call into question whether the genuine will of the population could even be formulated, let alone ascertained. It is true that various outside experts have ascribed devastating effects to the sanctions, and thus at some point the violation of the absolute civilian impact threshold may become (or may have already become) a matter of objective reality wholly apart from subjective perception. In that event, it would be incumbent upon the international community to decide whether the sanctions should be alleviated, or whether renewal or intensification of forcible efforts would be appropriate.

As indicated elsewhere in this volume,[84] the pressures on Saddam Hussein have included not only economic sanctions, but also very tangible military activities to deliver humanitarian relief, to police the no-fly zones, to enforce the obligations of demilitarization, and to protect segments of Iraq's civilian population from hostile attacks. Thus the spectrum of measures already embodies forceful action of a measured sort; but even those who believe that the coalition forces should have occupied Baghdad in early 1991 are not at this point contending for renewal of all-out hostilities to overthrow Saddam Hussein. As for the argument that sanctions should be eased because of their harsh effects on the civilian population, my conclusion is that the overriding interest of the international community in current and prospective conflict containment must take precedence. Saddam Hussein's repeated rejections of the "oil-for-food" formula, combined with the overwhelming evidence of bad faith with respect to weapons of mass destruction and obligations under the cease-fire agreement, are compelling reasons to suspect that any loosening of the sanctions would be more likely to enhance the destructive capabilities of the regime than to ameliorate the civilian plight.

Finally, especially troublesome questions arise where the people of the target state, through electoral processes or otherwise, seem to have aligned themselves deliberately with the policies that the sanctions seek to change. In December 1992, the people of Serbia chose Slobodan Milosevic, whom most of the outside world viewed as being primarily responsible for the initiation of the Yugoslav conflict and for its degeneration into atrocities such as "ethnic cleansing," over Milan Panic, who promised a change of policies that could have led to a lifting of the sanctions. One may seek to explain away this result by referring to Milosevic's superior control over the mass media or other manipulations—indeed, some have argued that the sanctioning system inadvertently exacerbated the advantages of the government-controlled press, since the independent media enjoyed no exemptions from sanctions.[85] Nonetheless, it would require a considerable feat of interpretation to overcome the position that the people of the target state consciously chose Milosevic and his policies when they had the opportunity to choose otherwise. To that extent, they are no longer merely innocent bystanders in a conflict foisted on them by a cruel regime, but are at least partly complicit in that cruelty. Under the circumstances, sanctions have to be continued and probably strengthened, regardless of the absolute impact on civilians. Unfortunately, no version of differentiation is available to spare those who voted against the incumbents or who were not in a position to exercise any choice at all (children, for example).

## The Quest for Principle Reexamined

I have argued that the international community should strive for a system in which economic sanctions will ultimately be applied on a principled basis. The quest for principle means in part that the international community must be prepared to respond to cases that share defining characteristics, whether or not the interests of powerful states favor the application of sanctions and, indeed, even where those states may have short-term interests contrary to the long-range principle. The aspiration for principled application may not be realizable for years or generations to come, but we should keep it in view. We have fallen short not only by failing to respond to similar cases with a seriousness of purpose comparable to that shown in the cases under study, but also by failing to act consistently even in the cases where the community has decided to act. As one small example indicative of a much broader range of problems, the United States weakened its credibility with respect to the Haitian embargo when it allowed exemptions benefiting certain U.S.–owned businesses—a gesture that many have interpreted as signaling an equivocal commitment to the objective of the sanctions.[86] The U.S. assertion of a humanitarian motivation for the exemptions rang hollow, since there was no concerted humanitarian strategy, but rather a self-interest in flows of profits rather than of refugees.

The quest for principle does not mean that the same sanctions need to be invoked in each instance. As others have pointed out in works concerned with unilateral sanctions,[87] different targets will respond to different forms of leverage: an oil embargo may be right in one case, a blocking of financial assets in another, and so on. These are essentially instrumental judgments, bearing on the effectiveness of the tools for their intended objective. But certain issues of principle transcend all the cases. Favoring nonforcible over forcible means of response is, in my view, such a principle, as is attempting to ensure that nonforcible means serve the ultimate values of conflict containment and avoidance.

The quest for principle also allows us to see the moral issues implicit in programs of stringent sanctions. After weighing several alternative formulations of criteria aimed at the problem of targeting wrongdoers and sparing civilians, I conclude that a threshold of moral concern is crossed when civilians are subjected to harm so serious that a significant segment of the population is pushed below the subsistence level, but my choice of the term "absolute" to distinguish this criterion from formulations focusing on relative (distributional) effects does not mean that the criterion cannot be overridden. Rather, as the case of Saddam Hussein shows, continuation of sanctions may be the least bad alternative in moral terms, when compared either with renewal of active fighting or with a loosening of the strictures that currently prevent him from remilitarizing the country. Conflict containment is, in my view, a hierarchically superior value.

The absolute civilian impact criterion may or may not be susceptible to application in principled terms. It has normative appeal, since it underscores the fundamental worth of human life and reflects the moral intuition that policies resulting in widespread deprivation and death ought to be suspect. Yet in its own way, it might undercut the principled application of sanctions, since it would apparently require pursuit of different policies, depending on the relative wealth or poverty of the target state.[88] Ironically, strict application of the criterion could mean that the poorest states would be more likely than others to become objects of external military intervention. The consequences of such a tilt are problematic, but if my methodology is followed, forcible intervention would be allowable only in cases when it would cause less damage to the people of the target state than would the continuation of economic pressure. This approach to the ranking of forcible and nonforcible alternatives is, in my view, the one most responsive to the call of principle rather than expediency.

## NOTES

1. In addition to the cases of internal conflicts discussed in this volume, a UN-mandated arms embargo is in effect with respect to Libya, to induce it to desist from supporting terrorism. See Security Council resolution 748 (March 31, 1992). An arms embargo imposed in 1977 against South Africa also remains in effect. See note 14, below.

2. In the case of Haiti, the value of maintaining a democratically elected government had attained universal endorsement within the hemisphere that organized the sanctions program, although that value may not yet be universal elsewhere. See, for example, Charter of the Organization of American States (OAS), article 5(d) (affirmation by American states of the principle of "the effective exercise of representative democracy"); and the Santiago Declaration on Representative Democracy, OAS Doc. AG/RES. 1080 (XXI-0/91), June 5, 1991.

3. In extraordinary cases where a unilateral embargo could inflict extreme hardship on a target country, some aspects of the analysis in this chapter might be applicable mutatis mutandis. The tightening of the U.S. embargo against Cuba in the fall of 1992 illustrates the issues, but also raises questions that go beyond the scope of this chapter, including the legitimacy of U.S. efforts to require nationals of third countries to comply with the U.S. measures.

4. For discussion, see, for example, V. Gowland-Debbas, *Collective Responses to Illegal Acts in International Law: United Nations Action in the Question of Southern Rhodesia* (Dordrecht: Martinus Nijhoff, 1990).

In other cases—for example, North Korea's invasion of South Korea in 1950—UN organs encouraged but did not require states to cut off arms transfers or other transactions with a target. The General Assembly recommended an arms embargo of North Korea and the People's Republic of China in resolution 500(V) (May 18, 1951).

5. In this vein, see, for example, G. Hufbauer, J. Schott, and K. Elliott, *Economic Sanctions Reconsidered*, 2d ed. (Washington, D.C.: Institute of International Economics, 1990). For a broader view of the bases for evaluating both positive and negative tools of influence, see D. Baldwin, *Economic Statecraft* (Princeton, N.J.: Princeton University Press, 1985).

6. See for example, Baldwin, *Economic Statecraft*, pp. 352–355; and L. Martin, *Coercive Cooperation: Explaining Multilateral Economic Sanctions* (Princeton, N.J.: Princeton University Press,1992), pp. 3–12.

7. Baldwin gives a cogent exposition of the position that sanctions that some would characterize as merely "symbolic" or "expressive" may indeed be instrumental toward the achievement of important objectives—in short, that images matter. See *Economic Statecraft*, pp. 96–114.

8. See for example, Hufbauer, Schott, and Elliott, *Economic Sanctions*; variables in their analysis include costs imposed on the target country in absolute terms and as a percentage of gross national product, and commercial relations between sender and target as a proportion of target's GNP.

   Even Baldwin's chapter "The Legality and Morality of Economic Statecraft," welcome as it is in a work of political economy, only scratches the surface of the complex problem of moral obligations of external actors toward persons within another state. See *Economic Statecraft*, pp. 336–369. For an exploration of such obligations in general (not specifically in the context of economic sanctions), see L. Brilmayer, *Justifying International Acts* (Ithaca, N.Y.: Cornell University Press, 1990).

9. Concerning such claims, see the essays on international humanitarianism and distributive justice in C. Beitz, M. Cohen, T. Scanlon, and A.J. Simmons, eds., *International Ethics* (Princeton, N.J.: Princeton University Press, 1985).

10. For expression of this consensus within the Conference on Security and Cooperation in Europe (CSCE), see Document of the Moscow Meeting on the Human Dimension, October 1991, para. 17, in International Legal Materials, vol. 30 (1991), pp. 1670, 1677. To similar effect within the OAS, see the Santiago Declaration.

11. The rules of war applicable to conflicts of a noninternational character are codified in common article 3 to the Geneva Conventions of 1949. See generally T. Meron, *Human Rights and Humanitarian Norms as Customary Law* (Oxford: Oxford University Press, 1989), pp. 25–37.

12. See resolution of Institut de Droit International on the principle of nonintervention in civil wars, *Annuaire de l'Institut de Droit International*, vol. 56 (1975), pp. 544–549, cited in O. Schachter, *International Law in Theory and Practice* (Dordrecht: Martinus Nijhoff, 1991), pp. 158–160.

13. For example, resolutions 787 (November 16, 1992), on Yugoslavia; 788 (November 19, 1992), on Liberia; and 792 (November 30, 1992), on Cambodia.

14. UN actions with respect to both Rhodesia and South Africa provide histori-cal precedent. Concerning Rhodesia, see resolutions 217 (November 20, 1965), calling on states to desist from providing arms to the illegal regime; 232 (December 16, 1966), para. 2(d), imposing selective mandatory sanc-tions, including an arms embargo; and 253 (May 29, 1968), expanding sanctions. Concerning South Africa, see resolutions 181 (August 7, 1963); 282 (July 23, 1970), which is recommendatory; and 418 (November 4, 1977), imposing a mandatory arms embargo.

As mentioned in note 1, a UN-mandated arms embargo is also in effect with respect to Libya. See resolution 748 (March 31, 1992). Other UN-sponsored programs aim to curtail the flow of arms to areas of regional conflict, as in Cambodia and Central America, pursuant to multilateral settlement agreements.

15. Resolutions 661 (August 6, 1990), para. 3(c); and 687 (April 3, 1991), para. 24.

16. Resolution 713 (September 25, 1991), para. 6 (emphasis added), reaf-firmed, inter alia, in resolutions 724 (December 15, 1991), para. 5; and 727 (January 8, 1992), para. 6. Recognition of new statehood took place in general on or after January 15, 1992.

17. See resolution 762 (June 30, 1992), para. 8.

18. Resolution 757 (May 30, 1992).

19. Resolution 733 (January 23, 1992).

20. Resolution 788 (November 19, 1992), para. 8.

21. MRE/RES. 1/91 (October 3, 1991).

22. See S. Engelberg, "Germany Raising Hopes of Croatia," *New York Times*, December 12, 1991, p. A6: "German law forbids the sale of weapons to areas of conflict. Most of the European nations have enacted similar bans."

23. Compare, for example, the Cambodian and Central American peace settle-ments, which embody detailed undertakings concerning demilitarization. See S. Ratner, "The Cambodia Settlement Agreements," *American Journal of International Law*, vol. 87 (1993), pp. 1 and 16–17 (discussing the obligation of Cambodian parties to cease receiving, and outside states to cease supplying, any military assistance, and the obligation of Cambodian parties to disarm and demobilize). The legal foundation of the restrictions on arms transfers to Cambodia derives from the settlement agreements, and not from any form of compulsory authority. As of the end of 1992, the UN Security Council had not acted in its chapter VII enforcement capacity with respect to Cambodia or Central America.

24. These presumed advantages may be neglected in certain cases. Inexplicably, the UN-mandated arms embargo on Somalia had been in place at the international level for a year before the United States promulgated its own regulations giving public notice of national implementation of the ban.

25. In this vein, see, for example, Security Council resolution 713 (September 25, 1991), addressed to the situation in Yugoslavia. The preamble to the resolution notes that two cease-fire agreements had been signed, but that they had been violated. To similar effect concerning cease-fire violations in Liberia, see resolution 788 (November 19, 1992).

26. One commentator considered it extraordinary that the Yugoslav represen-tative to the UN welcomed the application of sanctions against the very

state that he represented. See M. Weller, "Current Developments: The International Response to the Dissolution of the Socialist Federal Republic of Yugoslavia," *American Journal of International Law,* vol 86 (1992), pp. 578 and 580. The irony is easily explained: the representative of "Yugoslavia" would have had Serbian interests and the Serbian advantage in mind.

27. Other analogies that might be considered as examples of targeting arms embargoes against violators of international norms are the two apartheid cases (Rhodesia and South Africa) and the case of international terrorism (Libya).

28. Article 51 states: "Nothing in the present Charter shall impair the inherent right of individual or collective self-defence if an armed attack occurs against a Member of the United Nations, until the Security Council has taken measures necessary to maintain international peace and security."

    In an application to the International Court of Justice filed March 20, 1993, Bosnia-Herzegovina has claimed that the Security Council resolution imposing an arms embargo upon the former Yugoslavia must be construed so as not to impair Bosnia-Herzegovina's right of self-defense. *Case Concerning Application of the Convention on the Prevention and Punishment of the Crime of Genocide (Bosnia and Herzegovina v. Yugoslavia [Serbia and Montenegro]),* Request for the Indication of Provisional Measures, ICJ Reports 1993, Order of April 8, 1993.

29. What should the response of the Security Council be if Iraq, which is now under a regime of enforced demilitarization, were to become a victim of aggression? Arguably the Council would have to authorize appropriate measures of collective security. (The forcible actions that the coalition states have taken against Iraq in enforcement of Security Council resolutions do not give rise to any rights of self-defense on Iraq's part.)

30. In the case of Korea, the UN recommended, but did not require, an embargo against the initiator of the attack (North Korea) and its principal sponsor (People's Republic of China). See note 4.

31. For references to this and other examples from unilateral U.S. practice, see B. Carter, *International Economic Sanctions: Improving the Haphazard U.S. Legal Regime* (Cambridge: Cambridge University Press, 1988), p. 19, n. 45. One could also cite sanctions adopted by states participating in a multinational bloc (such as when members of the North Atlantic Treaty Organization, in response to the Soviet invasion of Afghanistan, incrementally strengthened their controls on militarily significant transfers to the Soviet bloc). For discussion of multilateral cooperation in the imposition of such controls, see Martin, *Coercive Cooperation,* pp. 191–198.

32. The Iran-Iraq war began with Iraq's invasion of Iran in 1980. The Security Council was paralyzed at that time, not only because of Cold War conditions that rendered the Council generally ineffective, but also because of the pendency of the Iran hostage crisis, which made it unthinkable that the Council would rally to support Iran against Iraq.

    A July 1987 Security Council resolution called for a cease-fire, which Iran refused to accept. In late 1987 and 1988 the Council took some steps in the direction of an arms embargo against Iran, but it never finally adopted the resolution. See Carter, *International Economic Sanctions*, p. 181, n. 34.

33. See note 12.

34. Security Council resolutions 743 (February 21, 1992), para. 11; and 757 (May 30, 1992), para. 10.

35. Resolution 752 (May 15, 1992), para. 13; "Report of the Secretary-General Pursuant to Security Council Resolution 721 (1991)," S/23280, (December 11, 1991) para. 12; and resolution 779 (October 6, 1992). UNPROFOR and other UN operations are also exempted from the ban on military flights over Bosnia and Herzegovina. See resolution 781 (October 9, 1992), para. 1.

36. Resolution 788 (November 19, 1992), para. 9, states that the arms embargo "shall not apply to weapons and military equipment destined for the sole use of the peace-keeping forces of ECOWAS in Liberia."

37. Ibid. See, for example, paras. 3 and 6.

38. Indeed, the interests of the former Soviet Union in Russia's "near abroad" regions indicate the difficulties of attempting to extrapolate a general rule from the cases of the early 1990s.

39. The catalog of available measures includes "complete or partial interruption of economic relations and of rail, sea, air, postal, telegraphic, radio, and other means of communication, and the severance of diplomatic relations." This listing is nonexclusive and indicative of other generically similar measures: for example, cultural and sports boycotts are also comprehended.

40. UN Charter, arts. 39 and 48–50. The Council has the authority to determine whether all or some of the member states should carry out its decisions (art. 48[1]); any state "confronted with special economic problems arising from the carrying out of those measures shall have the right to consult the Security Council with regard to a solution of those problems" (art. 50).

41. In addition to the resolutions cited in note 14, see resolutions 277 (March 18, 1970) and 388 (April 6, 1976). As previously noted, the mandatory sanctions in South Africa's case were limited to the arms embargo.

42. Notably in the cases of Cuba and the Dominican Republic.

43. As of this writing, only limited sanctions have been imposed (at the request of ECOWAS) against the areas of Liberia controlled by Charles Taylor's forces, and their import is not yet clear.

    With respect to Cambodia, the Security Council's call for selective sanctions against any Cambodian party not in compliance with the peace settlement has been formulated in hortatory, rather than mandatory, terms. Denial of petroleum products and freezing of overseas assets are specifically mentioned as potential sanctions against any party obstructing the settlement; a moratorium on the export of logs, minerals, and gems is also contemplated. See resolution 792 (November 30, 1992).

44. The General Assembly adopted a resolution along these lines (resolution 47/19) on November 24, 1992, by a vote of 59–3, with 72 abstentions. For a compilation of documents bearing on Cuba's contentions, see M. Krinsky and D. Golove, eds., *United States Economic Measures against Cuba:*

*Proceedings in the United Nations and International Law Issues* (Northampton, Mass.: Aletheia Press, 1993).

45. These are cases brought by Bosnia-Herzegovina and Libya, discussed in notes 28 and 46.

46. In early 1992 Libya tried but failed to persuade the International Court of Justice to restrain members of the Security Council from moving forward with a sanctions program against it. See *Questions of Interpretation and Application of the 1971 Montreal Convention arising from the Aerial Incident at Lockerbie (Libya v. U.K. and U.S.)* (Request for Provisional Measures, Order of April 14, 1992), 1992 ICJ Reports 3, 114. The posture of the case allowed the Court to dispose of the matter by denying interim relief, without engaging in a full-scale exploration of all the issues.

   A case brought by Bosnia-Herzegovina against Yugoslavia (Serbia and Montenegro) in the International Court of Justice contends that the resolutions of the Security Council should not be construed to prevent Bosnia-Herzegovina from defending itself against armed attack and genocide. See note 28.

47. The Haitian refugee litigation involves challenges to the immigration policies of a sanctioning state, but not to the legality of the sanctions per se. Past litigation in U.S. courts has included unsuccessful challenges to, inter alia, the U.S. trade embargo of Nicaragua.

48. In the Tehran hostages case, the Court apparently viewed the U.S. economic countermeasures as legitimate responses to serious violations of international law on Iran's part. *Case Concerning U.S. Diplomatic and Consular Staff in Tehran* (U.S. v. Iran) (Judgment), 1980 ICJ Reports 3, para. 53.

49. *Military and Paramilitary Activities in and against Nicaragua*, 1986 ICJ Reports 14.

50. See generally L. Damrosch, "Politics Across Borders: Nonintervention and Nonforcible Influence Over Domestic Affairs," *American Journal of International Law*, vol. 83 (1989), pp. 1, 28–34, and 45–47.

51. 1986 ICJ Reports at 126.

52. Compare UN Charter, art. 2(7). The Charter's nonintervention norm is expressly subordinated to the Council's enforcement powers.

53. Art. 39.

54. Similar findings have been made with respect to the situation in Somalia and, belatedly, in Liberia, but in neither case were economic sanctions (apart from an arms embargo) part of the Council's response.

55. See General Assembly resolutions 46/7 (October 11, 1991), 46/138 (December 17, 1991), and 47/20 (November 24, 1992). More than a year into the crisis, the UN became more actively engaged in the diplomatic effort (as discussed in the chapter on Haiti in this volume). The Security Council ultimately did adopt sanctions in resolution 841 (June 16, 1993).

56. See generally Carter, *International Economic Sanctions*, pp. 158–173.

57. Indeed, the charters of multilateral financial institutions typically require the institutions to eschew political considerations in their decision-making.

58. See, for example, Thomas Franck, "The Emerging Right to Democratic Governance," *American Journal of International Law*, vol. 86 (1992),

pp. 46 and 91. Franck argues for the progressive denial of access to international fiscal, trade and development benefits for governments that are unwilling to submit to international validation of their democratic credentials.

59. For relevant provisions, see the following, among others: *Iraq*: Security Council resolutions 661 (August 6, 1990), paras. 3(c), 4; 666 (September 13, 1990); 686 (March 2, 1991), preamble; and 687 (April 3, 1991), sec. F, paras. 20 ff. *Yugoslavia (Serbia and Montenegro)*: Security Council resolutions 757 (May 30, 1992), paras. 4(c), 5, 7(a), and 17–18; and 760 (June 18, 1992). *Haiti*: OAS resolutions 1/91 (October 3, 1991), para. 6; 2/91 (October 8, 1991), para. 4; and 3/92 (May 17, 1992).

60. For relevant U.S. laws and regulations, see, for example, International Emergency Economic Powers Act, 50 U.S.C. sec. 1702(b)(2)(A)–(C) (exception for donation of humanitarian articles); Exec. Order 12,722, sec. 2(b) (1990) (Iraq); 31 CFR Part 580 (Haitian Transaction Regulations). For regulations of the European Economic Community implementing the UN embargoes against Iraq and Serbia/Montenegro, respectively, see, for example, Council Regulations 2340/90 (August 8, 1990) and 1432/92 (June 1, 1992).

61. The Security Council has committed various implementation tasks to the Sanctions Committee, composed of representatives of all members of the Council, and this committee has been charged with administration of the humanitarian exemptions. For example, resolution 757, para. 4(c), reads: " . . . but not including supplies intended strictly for medical purposes and foodstuffs *notified to the Committee* (emphasis added)." With respect to Yugoslavia, the committee considered more than 2,000 communications in a period of half a year; most concerned notification of the export of foods and medicines to Serbia and Montenegro, and requests for approval to supply other products to meet essential humanitarian need. See "Second Report of the Security Council Committee Established Pursuant to Resolution 724 (1991) Concerning Yugoslavia," S/25027 (December 30, 1992), pp. 6–7.

62. See, for example, resolution 757 (May 30, 1992), para. 7(a), which states that all states shall deny permission for flights to or from Serbia and Montenegro, "unless the particular flight has been approved, *for humanitarian* or other *purposes* . . . by the [Sanctions] Committee" (emphasis added); and resolution 781, paras. 1 and 3, which state that the ban on military flights over Bosnia-Herzegovina does not apply "to flights in support of UN operations, including humanitarian assistance," and contain provisions for a mechanism of approval and inspection through UNPROFOR.

63. This problem has been acute in the cases of Yugoslavia and Somalia, where military forces and irregular armed bands have impeded humanitarian relief, as well as in Iraq, where the regime is implicated in sabotage of vehicles delivering humanitarian assistance to Kurdistan. (The case of Somalia is relevant for its stress upon the need for actual delivery of humanitarian assistance, notwithstanding the fact that the only nonforcible sanction imposed by the Council has been an arms embargo.)

64. In the case of Yugoslavia, see resolution 761 (June 29, 1992). Concerning Somalia, see resolution 767 (July 24, 1992).
65. Resolution 770 (August 13, 1992).
66. Resolution 794 (December 3, 1992).
67. Resolution 3/92 (May 17, 1992), paras. 5(g) and (h).
68. Resolution 757 (May 30, 1992). But note that the preamble asserts that "all parties bear some responsibility for the situation."
69. The Sanctions Committee has aptly noted that the territory against which the sanctions are directed "lies at the hub of intense economic and cultural activity, international commerce, trade and industry in the south-eastern region of Europe." See "Second Report of the Security Council Committee," S/25027 (December 30, 1992), para. 23.

    The Security Council has addressed problems of unlawful diversion of embargoed commodities to Serbia and Montenegro, inter alia, by prohibiting transshipment of certain commodities and by authorizing measures to halt shipping to inspect cargoes. See resolution 787 (November 16, 1992).
70. Moreover, there is cause for substantial concern that certain of Serbia and Montenegro's neighbors—notably the former Yugoslav republic of Macedonia, which is landlocked, but also several states bordering on the former Yugoslavia—have suffered more from the sanctions than have Serbia and Montenegro. Article 50 of the UN Charter provides a theoretical mechanism for addressing third-country injury, but the Council has had no way to provide practical relief under that article.
71. See resolution 688 (April 5, 1991). For a discussion of the internal blockade, harassment of foreign relief workers, and other problems, see Human Rights Watch, *World Report 1993* (New York, 1993), pp. 305–314.
72. The most pertinent Council resolutions are 706 (August 15, 1991) and 712 (September 19, 1991). In resolution 778 (October 2, 1992), the Council authorized the seizure and sale of certain of Iraq's overseas assets to generate funds for several specific purposes, including "the provision of humanitarian relief in Iraq."
73. Resolution 3/92 (May 17, 1992), para. 5f; see also resolution 4/92 (December 13, 1992).
74. Such activity may take the form of an internal blockade implemented by a government or dominant group against a region controlled by an insurgency or minority population: this has been the case, for example, with respect to the Iraqi blockade of the Kurdish-controlled region and the Shi'ite marshlands.
75. See, for example, R. Pastor, "Haiti Is Not Alone," *New York Times*, October 4, 1991, p. A31.
76. Traditional (pre-Charter) international law and "just war" theories have likewise insisted on exhaustion of nonforcible remedies as a legal and moral prerequisite to the use of force.
77. Art. 41 (emphasis added).
78. Art. 42.
79. These generalizations may not apply in particular cases. The degree to which sanctions should be incrementally imposed is itself a policy choice, but even if the international community does opt at the outset for the

maximum available measures, it will probably take some time for the sanctions to achieve their full impact. Some kinds of damage, such as to the infrastructure or environment of the target, may be difficult to reverse or repair. And of course, to the extent that sanctions actually do cause the death of civilians, those consequences are irremediable.

80. I do not address here the problems of using military force to enforce economic sanctions, as has been done in the cases of Rhodesia, Iraq, and Yugoslavia. That topic deserves a whole essay in its own right.

81. See, for example, J. Galtung, "On the Effects of International Economic Sanctions: With Examples from the Case of Rhodesia," *World Politics*, vol. 19 (1967), p. 378. The argument is refuted by Baldwin in *Economic Statecraft*, pp. 190–204.

82. For a discussion of this point in reference to Rhodesia, see Baldwin, *Economic Statecraft*, pp. 196–203.

83. Iraqi Kurdistan has indigenous leaders who, remarkably, have been able to hold an election and exercise governance functions during the period that coalition forces have effectively excluded Iraqi authorities from the region. Kurdish leaders favor continuation both of the embargo and of the coalition's military protection.

84. See the chapter on Iraq and the concluding chapter.

85. To this effect, see Human Rights Watch, *World Report 1993*, p. 270.

86. For example, ibid., p. 125.

87. For example, see Carter, *International Economic Sanctions*.

88. A number of analysts have noted that sanctions are more likely to be *successful* against poor and weak states than against rich and powerful ones. See, for example, Hufbauer, Schott, and Elliott, *Economic Sanctions Reconsidered*, pp. 97–99; and Martin, *Coercive Cooperation*, pp. 34 and 44.

# CHAPTER EIGHT

# A Paradigm of Legitimate Intervention

## TOM FARER

Despite the increasing porosity of frontiers and the decreasing ability of governments acting alone to protect the interests of their citizens, the "sovereign" nation-state remains the principal ordering mechanism of the global political system.[1] It is likely to remain so as long as it surpasses other institutions in the ability to evoke loyalty. National frontiers being a central structural element of international order, uninvited physical intrusion continues to seem anomalous; in the idiom of the lawyers, it is presumptively illicit. Hence, minimum global order presupposes some measure of agreement on the conditions required to overcome that presumption—the conditions, that is, of "legitimate intervention."

Given the normative understandings, the organizations, and the precedents that have accumulated since the founding of the United Nations in 1945, those conditions must be institutional, procedural and substantive. The legitimacy of intervention will thus turn on the identity of the intervenor or the ultimate authorizer of the intervention, as well as the intervention's goals (that is, on its general justifications and their applicability to the facts of the particular case) and its compliance with procedural safeguards.

My purpose in this chapter is to suggest a paradigm of legitimate intervention. Intervention being an instance (albeit perhaps the most common one) of the use of force, its legitimacy paradigm must be consistent with the conditions of legitimacy for the more general phenomenon of armed coercion. Since those conditions will largely govern the character of legitimate intervention, they are a logical point of departure.

## THE LEGITIMATE USE OF FORCE

Law is a matter of degree, the degree of consensus and of clarity about what behavior is demanded, permitted, or proscribed. Rather than being what the political theorist, Carl Friedrich, once called "frozen history," law is fluid, a process of claim and counterclaim, act and acquiescence, that affects as it reflects the ebb and flow of consensus among consequential actors in the sphere of international relations. Snapshots, therefore, are apt to mislead, to imply a greater stability and clarity in presently influential norms than they actually possess. But there are important generative moments. The adoption of the United Nations Charter was one of them. It continues to frame discourse about the legitimacy of force. In order to appreciate where we are today, it helps to see both the distance we have traveled from the original understanding and the salient events of our trip.

### The Original Understanding[2]

In its essential character, the model of legitimacy set out in the UN Charter corresponds structurally to the model found in national legal systems; both tolerate self-help while subjecting it to close normative discipline and authoritative review. Space for self-help exists even in efficient modern states, where courts, prosecutors, and security forces, able to concentrate power far exceeding that of any delinquent, maintain order. Take the United States: individuals can, for example, use deadly force when they reasonably believe it is necessary to protect themselves and their families from a potentially fatal assault.[3] Since the Charter did no more than anticipate the creation of an international police force,[4] and since it made the force's use subject to veto by any one of the great powers,[5] and since sovereign entities had perforce always assumed the principal—and often the entire—burden of protecting their interests and rights, the drafters not surprisingly left states free to defend themselves until the Security Council took action "to maintain or restore international peace and security."[6]

The Charter also envisions the use of force by regional agencies or by individual states acting under the auspices of regional arrangements, but in either case, only to the extent they are serving as instruments of the Security Council to maintain or restore peace and security.[7] Thus the Charter explicitly recognizes a three-level structure of what we might fairly call law enforcement, on the assumption that neither individual states, regional institutions, nor the Security Council itself could properly undertake or authorize the use of force against a state carrying out its duties or exercising its rights under international law.

At the time of the Charter's adoption, the only subglobal institutions on the horizon that would assume peace-and-security missions were the Arab League[8] and the Organization of American States (OAS).[9] Rather than being a deliberate element in the drafters' original vision, a role for regional organizations emerged as an ad hoc response to requests from Latin American states moved by the belief that a regional organization would give them additional means for securing economic assistance from and containing the interventionist impulses of the United States.[10] So it cannot be said that the drafters intended to privilege intergovernmental organizations whose members satisfied some principle of geographic concentration as against groupings of states connected by ties of religion, ethnicity, or history.

Of course, if regional institutions could authorize or undertake military action for purposes other than collective self-defense *only with specific authorization from the Security Council*, the privilege, if any, would not amount to much. But if such institutions had a wider range of authority—if, for instance, they could legitimize the use of force to preempt a still evolving threat to the peace, to enforce human rights, or to impose humanitarian relief—then the privilege would bulk large. In that event, it would need more justification than a mere negative pregnant in the Charter language.

## The Cold War Gloss

At its inception, the Charter appeared both to impose unprecedented restraint on unilateral recourse to force and to centralize law enforcement in the Security Council. The only right of self-defense noted was one exercised "in the event of an armed attack";[11] previously states had invoked the right in a much wider range of settings.[12] As for regional arrangements, while authorizing the Security Council to use them for enforcement action, the Charter immediately added the following caveat: "But no enforcement action shall be undertaken under regional arrangements or by regional agencies without the authorization of the Security Council."[13]

Spurred on by pressures and incentives born of the Cold War and later supplemented by regional and decolonization conflicts, a substantial number of scholars and governments soon began challenging these close constraints.[14] To widen the space available for unilateral action, they employed a variety of strategies. One was to resolve all textual ambiguities in favor of self-help.[15] For instance, nothing in the Charter explicitly addresses the issue of intervention in civil armed conflict at the request of the recognized government.[16] Where insurgents demonstrate staying power and a significant measure of popular support, assistance to either side on a scale possibly sufficient to determine the outcome can be seen as an invasion of sovereignty, for what is more at the core of sovereignty than the processes, peaceful or violent, by which a national people decide who shall govern them? Nevertheless, throughout the Cold War era, the United States, France, the Soviet Union, and other states consistently acted as if recognized governments had an unfettered right to seek foreign assistance in crushing domestic rivals.

The Charter also fails to define the scope of a legitimate response to instances of illegal assistance to insurgents. Can assistance in such forms as arms, training, and advice be treated as an armed attack justifying collective self-defense including a direct assault on the assisting state? The answer of the White

House was yes.[17] On the strength of that answer, it organized, financed, armed and trained the Nicaraguan contras. But in finding that the United States had violated legal duties owed to Nicaragua, the World Court said no.[18]

The Charter's failure to spell out the scope of the interests that could be defended against an armed attack opened another opportunity to elasticize restraints on self-judging self-help. Does the right of self-defense extend beyond territorial integrity to citizens threatened with death, grave injury, or arbitrary detention in foreign lands, whether as the result of internal conflict or for any other reason? By persistently invoking such a right without encountering substantial opposition to the abstract claim (as distinguished from its particular application), the United States and a number of the other countries able to project force internationally have effectively occupied the interpretive space the founding fathers left.[19]

For those determined to find ambiguities, they lurked as much in what was said as in what was not. Article 2(4) prohibits force or the threat thereof against the political independence or territorial integrity of a state or for any other end inconsistent with the purposes and principles of the Charter. In justifying Israel's 1956 thrust into Egypt's Sinai Peninsula, the Australian scholar Julius Stone denied that a temporary incursion designed to protect threatened legal rights could be deemed inconsistent with the Charter's language. Surely, he declaimed, the vindication of law is consistent with the Charter's principles.[20]

A small covey of scholars, most of them from the United States, rather than interpreting their way through the Charter's restraints circumnavigated them. It was in contemplation of collective enforcement by the Security Council, they argued, that states had yielded their inherent right to apply force proportionally as a last resort in defense of important legal rights. Thus when the collapse of the wartime coalition paralyzed that organ, states recovered a broad right to self-help.[21] In legal terms, either the failure of a condition or a fundamental change of circumstances had occurred.

Imaginative exegesis and the capacity of a superpower to manufacture precedent also loosened the restraints on regional arrangements. That regional organizations could coordinate collective defense against an armed attack seemed indisputable. But could they also authorize members to use force to liquidate a still remote threat to a region's security? In other words, could they, despite the language of article 53 of the Charter, act like mini–Security Councils without benefit of Security Council authorization?

Moscow's decision at the beginning of the 1960s to emplace nuclear-armed ballistic missiles in Cuba drew an affirmative response to this question from Washington and the great majority of its Latin American allies.[22] Determined to force removal of the missiles, but unable plausibly to claim that Fidel Castro and Nikita Khrushchev were about to attack the United States or any other state, Washington secured OAS authorization for a partial blockade of the island. In defending the "quarantine" and the 1965 occupation of the Dominican Republic, which the OAS authorized after American troops invaded that country, U.S. officials argued that authorization could be after the fact and could be induced from the silence of the Security Council.[23] They also argued that where the OAS merely authorized, rather than ordered, military measures (under the OAS Charter and the associated Rio Treaty of Mutual Defense, the organization's political organs actually lack authority to order the use of force), those measures did not constitute "enforcement action" and therefore did not fall within the terms of article 53.[24]

In the later years of the Cold War, normative dissonance intensified. To Soviet claims of right to intervene on behalf of international proletarian interests, Washington responded with the Reagan Doctrine, heralding military assistance to opponents of Marxist regimes.[25] Meanwhile, outside the framework of bipolarity, Third World states helped to loosen restraints on intervention. They proclaimed a right to assist national liberation movements.[26] In addition, they secured an expansive reading of Security Council jurisdiction under chapter VII. When, in the mid-1960s, a white minority government announced the independence of Rhodesia, the Council ordered economic sanctions against the de facto racist regime without attempting seriously to identify a threat to the peace.[27] The Council's subsequent decision to sanction South Africa[28] strengthened the initial precedent for treating chronic and gross human rights violations as a sufficient basis for initiating enforcement measures, at least when the violations assume the form of systematic racial discrimination.

## LEGITIMATE INTERVENTION AFTER THE COLD WAR

The Gulf War seems to have functioned as the inaugural event of a new political age.[29] By itself, the violent expulsion of Iraqi forces from Kuwait seemed no more than the realization of the Charter's original promise of collective resistance to classical forms of aggression. But when the Security Council empowered the makers of Desert Storm to carve out a protected zone for Kurdish people in northern Iraq,[30] it appeared to confirm that wide expansion of its jurisdiction and the corresponding contraction of "domestic jurisdiction" that the Rhodesian and South African precedents intimated. The imposition of a ban on Iraqi air force operations in southern Iraq[31] and then the U.S.–led military operation in Somalia[32] reinforced this impression of a watershed irrevocably crossed.

Although consistent in spirit with these several "humanitarian interventions," UN action in the Balkans[33] is unlike them in that it could be justified under the original understanding of the Charter. Croatia and Bosnia were widely recognized states before Council action.[34] The Serbian government's intimate connection to the notionally independent ethnic Serbians operating within those states is aggression even under the controversially austere criteria the World Court announced in the Nicaragua litigation.[35]

The Balkan case is, nevertheless, another sign of change in the assumptions and expectations that structure international politics, a change closely linked to the rising strength of human rights claims. Third World states, fearing the capacity of self-determination to turn in their hand, yet determined to slash away with it at the residue of the West's overseas empire, secured both Western and Communist-bloc support for a historically contingent interpretation of the right to national self-determination.[36] It applied only to territories occupied by European states in the colonial era and separated from them by salt water, race, or culture. And it could be exercised only once, and then by a majority of the people living within the boundaries the colonial powers established in their peculiar national interests. The right thus became almost coterminous in practice with the list of "non–self-governing territories" assembled at the UN shortly after its inception. As more and more territories emerged from the chrysalis of colonial status, the shrinking list correspondingly shrank the right to self-determination. Or so the Third World argued.

The United States and the former metropoles, suspicious of disorder, enjoying a paternal relationship with the great bulk of postcolonial regimes, and perpetually alert to the Soviet Union's hovering presence as an alternate patron, had ample incentive to share Third World hostility to secessionist claims. The pattern of international community response was set as early as the Congo crisis at the beginning of the 1960s, when a UN peacekeeping force acting at the behest of the rudimentary central government (strongly backed by Washington) defeated a secessionist bid by the former colony's richest province, Katanga.[37]

For a quarter century thereafter, the constellation of forces backing the postcolonial status quo rejected any and every justification for secession. Even in cases where secessionist bids were inspired by grave and systematic discrimination and awful violations of human rights, the community of states was adamant. When Nigeria's numerous Ibo people, concentrated in their traditional heartland by pogroms in other parts of the country and denied a fair share in the federal government, declared their independence and mobilized an initially effective resistance to federal forces, only four small countries[38] ultimately accepted their bid for recognition as an independent state, and no country at all openly lent them assistance. Meanwhile, both superpowers and Britain, the former suzerain, lavished arms and trainers on the federal authorities, thus assuring their victory.[39]

The international community proved equally inhospitable when East Pakistan, with India's backing, sought independence from the central authorities in Pakistan's Western sector.[40] In the face of gross discrimination in access to high government and military positions and in the allocation of public investment, the ethnically distinct people of the East had first pursued a high degree of regional autonomy. The central government responded with a genocidal campaign against the East's educated classes.

When, at that point, India intervened, in part for the stated purpose of assisting the people of the East in protecting their basic human rights,[41] only a Soviet veto protected it from a Security Council resolution designed to force its withdrawal. An equivalent resolution then passed in the General Assembly virtually without opposition other than that of the Soviet Union and its Warsaw Pact dependencies.[42] Against this background of unblinking hostility to secessionist claims, the widespread recognition of Slovenia, Croatia, and Bosnia-Herzegovina without the consent of the Yugoslavian government, and without a demonstration that they could make their claims good against the Serb-dominated federal regime, represents a sea change in the normative order.[43]

As I indicated at the outset, any paradigm must specify the conditions under which states, subglobal organizations, and the UN should be legally entitled to use (and in the case of the last two, to authorize use of) force or the threat thereof as means for intervening in internal conflicts.

*Unilateral Intervention.* The riptide of sentiment favoring action to combat unnatural disasters has not yet breached the wall of opposition to unilateral measures. Opposition stems in part from pessimism about the possibility of an altruistic international politics. Governments, it is widely assumed, will rarely shoulder the costs of intervention when the principal envisioned benefit is an easy conscience. Hence, if granted a license to intervene for allegedly humanitarian ends, they will abuse it as much through their acts as through their omissions. Disasters that cannot be converted into the coin of national interest will be deplored but otherwise ignored, while those that can (including those that can be invented) will be exploited to advance selfish ends.

Pessimism stems from a certain experience. Aggression has been known to sport a humanitarian cloak. Adolf Hitler, for example, prepared the ground for Czechoslovakia's extinction by alleging that his intended victim was abusing its German minority.[44] Sins of omission are more numerous. Even in the presumably more enlightened post-Holocaust era, where unspeakable abuses—mass murder, systematic torture—have not engaged the parochial interests of consequential states, such states have often been supine, as the victims of the Khmer Rouge[45] or Guatemala's counterinsurgency,[46] among others, would confirm if only they were able to speak.

No doubt the rise of transnational group empathy, spurred by the mobility of peoples and the globalization of the mass media, will sustain growth in the constituency for humanitarian intervention. Selfish national interests may join idealism as propellants of a public policy more sensitive to slaughter occurring beyond national frontiers. Refugees from murderous domestic conflicts display an unparalleled awareness of and ability to reach distant safe havens.[47] In their growing numbers they bear heavily on the social fabric, as well as the resources, of host countries.[48] Large and prosperous states, the haven of preference for most refugees, have yet another incentive for intervention—namely, to deter mimesis. The success of a barbaric response to political and social tensions in one country encourages a similar response in others. Intransigence in negotiation leads to conflict. The ripple of social conflict through the international system imperils international trade and investment, pillars of prosperity in the postmodern world. So the incentives for what in the past would have been seen as essentially humanitarian intervention are likely to expand.

It is nevertheless doubtful that they can eclipse the enduring incentives for supporting the formal prohibition of unilateral initiatives. One such incentive is the ease with which many regimes can imagine themselves as objects of intervention and the corresponding dearth of prospective intervenors. The latter are the most powerful and, in general, the most influential states. By virtue of their power, they enjoy a great comparative advantage in ability to take initiatives and thereby generate precedent. But where the great mass of weak states have a strong common interest in resistance, they can obstruct the alluvial growth of precedent into positive law. If they cannot do it in all cases, certainly they can when the leading states are not united. And that is certainly true with respect to humanitarian intervention. One can judicially notice that such intervention is not high among the priorities of the Chinese, the Japanese, or such regional powers as Iran and Brazil. In fact, if Bosnia is any indication, leading states approach opportunities for humanitarian intervention with extreme caution even where butchery has unpleasant side effects for them or their allies.

If any powerful country exhibits substantial enthusiasm for unilateral human rights enforcement, it is the United States. The strength of the interventionist constituency was sufficient to persuade President Clinton while he was still a candidate to criticize President Bush's passivity.[49] Nevertheless, since assuming office, Clinton has made it clear that the United States will not intervene unilaterally.[50] The combination of reluctance, indifference, and hostility will for the foreseeable future bar development of a normative license for unilateral action. If one state cannot act, it follows that many cannot either (unless, perhaps, they are acting within the framework of a regional arrangement), since each would come to the enterprise without the requisite license. One hundred times zero still equals zero.

The risk of carefully calculated abuse is not the only reason for refusal to license intervention. Yet another is the danger to minimum world order of competitive interventions carried out by states acting in good faith. In a given case, governments may perceive differently the gravity of human rights violations, or the allocation of responsibility, or the measures reasonably necessary to halt a massacre. Hence, what one deems an intervention in the service of humanity may appear to another like old-fashioned aggression. So a broad concern for the health of the international system joins parochial national interests in blocking unilateral initiative.

Yet it is not hard to imagine cases that will cry out for exceptional treatment. Murderous conflicts and monstrous pogroms are not always announced by long previews. They can burst suddenly through the brittle veneer of an apparently civil, even if strained, society. Few of the Argentineans calling on the armed forces to restore order during the chaotic days of 1976 anticipated the campaign of extermination that would quickly unfold.[51] The Indonesian holocaust of 1965, which consumed hundreds of thousands, perhaps over a million people in a matter of months, erupted without any warning at all.[52] West Pakistan did not announce the final solution to its Eastern problem.[53]

Aspiring mass murderers will not always march to the stately tempo of intergovernmental organizations. Where the slaughter has begun, should action by one or more states able and willing to halt it be prohibited? Must not imagined dangers defer sometimes to realized horrors?

The architects of legal systems may respond to the hard case for a general rule in one of two ways: They may carve out an explicit exception, but limit access to it by sharply defining the strict conditions under which it is available and imposing on the party invoking it the burden of proving that the conditions were satisfied. Alternatively, they may deny exceptions, but tolerate an unstated code of mitigation. The case of euthanasia epitomizes the second approach. Fearing abuse, legislators ban mercy killing. Samaritans proceed at their peril, but occasionally they succeed in persuading jurors that the conditions (incurable illness, great pain, appeal from the nominal victim, and so forth) justify a finding of not guilty.

Either approach is subject to abuse. Both require strict criteria and systematic and impartial review. Academic defenders of unilateral humanitarian intervention generally propose the following substantive criteria of legitimacy:

- There are no plausible alternative means for averting a massive violation of fundamental human rights.

- The violation will cause irreparable injury.

- The intervenor uses the minimum force necessary to prevent or halt the violations and withdraws as soon as the threat is terminated.

- The intervention is calculated to cause less damage to the target society than would inaction.[54]

To buttress these criteria, legitimacy or mitigation should be conceded only where the intervening state immediately reports the intervention to the Security Council and the political organs of any subglobal arrangement with jurisdiction over the parties. And if humanitarian intervention is deemed legal where the enumerated conditions exist, the intervenor should be required to announce its acceptance of World Court jurisdiction over any challenge to its action, whether brought by the target government or by any other state.

*UN Intervention.* Chapter VII of the Charter appears to envision enforcement of Security Council decisions by units of national armed forces placed under the direct command of the UN's own military staff committee pursuant to previously negotiated agreements. The onset of the Cold War froze implementation of the textual design, which remains dormant despite the grand thaw. Unable to deploy troops of its own, the Council has authorized national armed forces operating under national chains of command to carry out its decisions. By means of national proxies, it has expelled Iraq from Kuwait and protected Kurds in northern Iraq and food in Somalia.

Whether it has a right to command member states to perform or assist in the performance of military missions is unclear. Article 43 seems to condition the obligation to provide the Council with "armed forces, assistance, and facilities, including rights of passage, necessary for the purpose of maintaining international peace and security" on the existence of a special agreement between a country and the Council. However, the same article certainly can be read to oblige states to enter into such agreements. And presumably those agreements can be negotiated at the time the Council chooses to initiate enforcement measures.

When almost all of the states able to participate consequentially in military actions were either permanent members of the Council or dependents thereof, this question of the Council's power to command assistance would have seemed academic. The continuing spread of high-technology weaponry, technical knowledge, and industrial capacity, coincident with the collapse of the hierarchies incident to bipolarity, makes it less so now. For the moment it remains a dormant uncertainty. Concern over the Council's sudden impulse to exercise its powers under chapter VII focuses elsewhere.

One hears behind the curtains of contemporary statecraft a choral murmur of unease about the gathering precedents for Security Council licensing of interventions to halt civil conflicts, enforce humanitarian relief, and terminate outrageous violations of human rights. Before authorizing a safe haven for the Kurds, the Council had conceptualized the use of troops into the dyad of "peacekeeping" and "enforcement." Peacekeepers were an instrument of peaceful settlement under chapter VI of the Charter, to be introduced into a conflictual setting only with the consent of all parties to the conflict, usually to cement a cease-fire.[55] Lightly armed, they were authorized to use what little firepower they had strictly in self-defense. Peacekeepers functioned as UN fact finders, as a trip-wire to signal a renewal of factional conflict, and arguably as a deterrent to renewed fighting insofar as incidental injury to UN units might antagonize the governments that had provided them.

Now the dyad is multiplying. Neither the pilots protecting the Kurds of northern Iraq nor the troops protecting aid deliveries in Somalia can be encompassed within the established idea of peacekeeping forces. They are not where they are with the consent of local authorities; they are not lightly armed. And they enjoy a mandate to blast anyone or anything that threatens their mission. In the case of the forces in Somalia, that mission is to disarm local forces sufficiently so as to permit establishment of an effective national government.[56] Indeed, as it has evolved, the UN operation in Somalia has passed far beyond old-fashioned peacekeeping, beyond peace enforcement, to something approaching a de facto trusteeship.

In the Somali case, no aspirant to power controls much of the country effectively or has achieved international recognition. Since those two conditions are rare, and the level of human misery dramatic (albeit not singular), if the case stood alone, it could seem more an anomaly than a precedent for UN-authorized intervention to secure a people threatened or experiencing massive loss of life. But placed alongside the defense of the Kurds and the ban on Iraqi overflight of territory in the south where Baghdad is attempting to root out Shi'ite insurgents, and the selective blockade of Serbia (in pre-Charter customary law, a blockade was an act of war),[57] Somalia does have precedential force.

Earlier this century the irascible political boss of a city in New Jersey was accused of ordering his police force to violate the law, the Constitution in particular. "That's impossible!" he reportedly roared. "I am the law." Is the Security Council the only judge of the legality of its actions? Does it enjoy a plenary discretion to interpret the breadth of its jurisdiction under the Charter? It may, of course, solicit the opinion of the International Court of Justice,[58] but it is under no apparent obligation to do so.

To what should the Council be analogized? If the appropriate analogy is an arbitral tribunal, then individual states may conclude that the Council has exceeded its jurisdiction and decide not to comply. I believe, however, that the appropriate analogy is to the British Parliament; in this case, the Council enjoys a kind of legislative supremacy as long as it commands the support of, if not the great majority of states, then the great majority of states that count in international relations.

Why the Council's creative interpretation of its constitutional obligation to maintain international peace and security should occasion alarm among people other than the members of brutal parasitic governments in relatively weak states is unclear. Surely it cannot be construed as the renaissance of a Western global imperium. China, a decidedly non-Western state moving on a rising trajectory of national power, can paralyze the Council at will. Nor does it threaten a five-power condominium, since the permanent members cannot simply command the four additional votes required to pass a resolution. And then there is the matter of UN finances: Given the parlous state of the United States, Britain, and France and the financial constraints under which they labor, it is unlikely in the extreme that the Council will pursue policies that cut across the grain of German and Japanese preferences.

As the ongoing slaughter in the Balkans attests, the threat to a humane international order consists not of Council hyperaction, but rather of no action at all. The breadth of values, interests, and perspectives represented at the UN tends to limit even the Council to expeditious and decisive intervention only in exceptional cases, and then for ends considerably more limited than promoters of liberal values might prefer. We can therefore anticipate the recurrence of cases where, despite the extremity of a population's condition, either the requisite majority cannot be marshaled or a permanent member will veto any intervention, or at least any intervention of the sort required to deal with both causes and symptoms of political pathology.

The Council's refusal to authorize intervention will not always settle the question. Some states—whether because of ethnic and historical ties to the victims or for more material reasons, such as an avalanche of refugees—may experience an almost uncontrollable impulse to intervene. The danger to order springing from unilateral action makes the case for channeling such impulses through subglobal institutions.

*Regional and Other Subglobal Institutions.* As I implied above, for purposes of constructing a paradigm of legitimate intervention, intermediate institutions generate essentially three questions: One is how they should relate to the UN. A second, intimately tied to the first, is the extent of their authority. The third is whether it would be wise to distinguish among them in terms of the scope of their legitimating power and their autonomy.

The question of their relationship to the UN should not and, as a matter of the logic of international law, cannot be reduced to a simple dichotomy between independence and subordination. For certain purposes there are grounds for imputing to them an extensive freedom of action, while for others they should probably enjoy very little, if any, independence. I proceed from the assumption that states enjoy the freedom to surrender sovereignty entirely through voluntary integration into another sovereign unit. I further assume that having thus ceded sovereignty, neither the ceding authority nor the population it previously ruled has as such any right under international law to reclaim the bundle of rights and privileges that are sovereignty's operational essence.[59] At that point its right to self-determination would be no greater than that enjoyed by any other self-conscious people with similar grievances.

If, in order to advance their collective purposes, a people can cede sovereignty altogether, they should be able to cede any part of it, including the right to determine when foreign troops may enter their territory. What is less clear, however, is whether, despite ceding to others a right to intervene under stated circumstances, the state retains, by virtue of its continuing existence as a sovereign entity, an absolute right to revoke the ceded authority.

Suppose, for example, that a group of democratic Caribbean island states, together with Costa Rica, decided that the best way to safeguard democracy was to enter into a pact with those members of the North Atlantic Treaty Organization (NATO) that have particular interests in the Caribbean basin—namely, the United States, Canada, the United Kingdom, France, and the Netherlands.[60] The pact would provide that in the event of an unconstitutional seizure of power in one pact member, the others will continue to recognize the displaced elected officials as the only legitimate authority and, at their request, will take appropriate measures to reestablish constitutional government. If the officials are unable to communicate an appeal for assistance, the other pact members will consult and may by a vote of two-thirds or more of the member states choose to intervene militarily to restore democracy.

Should an intervention triggered by the two-thirds vote require Security Council authorization? Since such an action is carried out with the previously expressed consent of the target state, it is not an "enforcement action" within the meaning of chapter VIII. Hence, I would argue that specific authorization is not required. The institution created by the pact is not functioning like a mini–Security Council, trumping state sovereignty in matters involving threats to peace and security.

If, however, Costa Rica were to propose intervention in Nicaragua to assure the triumph of insurgents struggling against an allegedly undemocratic government that had, again allegedly, been attempting by means short of force to subvert the Costa Rican regime, it would be calling for the kind of measures the

Security Council can adopt under chapter VII. Hence, if the intent of the original members of the UN is deemed controlling for purposes of Charter interpretation, prior Security Council authorization would be required. But, as noted above, under the interpretation urged by the United States during the Cold War, authorization could be after the fact and implicit, assuming that the pact was deemed a regional arrangement or agency. If it is not so perceived, then arguably it would be merely a collection of states entitled to use force only in collective self-defense or when specifically authorized by the Security Council.

The most serious objection to collective intervention pursuant to prior agreement by the target state is the danger that agreement may have been coerced. Prior agreement to unilateral intervention was, of course, a commonplace feature of the age of imperialism.[61] Where the power of parties to a pact is very unbalanced, nominal reciprocity is valueless as evidence that the arrangement was voluntary. Hence, I would require, as a condition of the legitimacy of intervention under such pacts, that at their inception they be submitted to the Security Council for review. Moreover, while prior authorization should not be necessary, any intervention should be reported to the Council and justified at the time it occurs.

I turn now to the question of whether there are prudential grounds for attributing more extensive powers to associations of states that are in some way geographically concentrated as distinguished from associations of states with some other sort of connection—religion, for example, or ideology. At one point this seemed to me a fairly important question. After all, such organizations already exist—the Organization of the Islamic Conference is one example—and while technology may keep reducing the importance of space, differences based on ideology and sentiment are likely to endure.

But on further reflection I am persuaded that, for two reasons, the question is likely to prove academic. One is that, at least up to now, no one has appeared to care very much about the issue of what does and what does not constitute a regional security arrangement. Disinterest might well stem from the fact that until the past decade, only the OAS openly asserted the right to authorize the use of force by its members *for purposes other than self-defense against an armed attack*. In the discourse of statecraft and scholarship, the Americas have always appeared as a self-evidently distinct region. Moreover, it was the prospective members of the OAS who insisted on including in the UN Charter a special dispensation for regional arrangements.[62] Chapter VIII was not the drafters' response to a purely hypothetical scenario. It was intended to apply to the organization the leading states of the hemisphere said they planned to form.

In the 1960s, therefore, when the OAS, urged on by Washington, was trying to slip normative fig leaves over the U.S. quarantine of Cuba during the missile crisis[63] and the U.S. invasion of the Dominican Republic,[64] opponents of these adventures would not have expected a claim that the OAS lacked authority because it was not a chapter VIII arrangement to persuade any relatively neutral audience. In any event, the claim was not made. And yet the OAS did not include all of the hemisphere's sovereign states. Canada was not then a member. Neither was Guyana, nor Britain and France as suzerains of Caribbean island territories.

Partial inclusiveness has not seemed to disable an association of states with geographic connections from being deemed a regional arrangement. After all, the Arab League still fails to encompass three of the most important actors in the Middle East—Iran, Israel, and Turkey—just as the Organization of African Unity has excluded the continent's richest and most powerful country. Presumably, at some point underinclusiveness would cripple the claim of some neighborly grouping to be a chapter VIII arrangement. But I know of only one indicator of where that point might be—the General Assembly's response to the U.S. occupation of Grenada in 1983[65]—and it speaks with Delphic ambiguity. Among the justifications the Reagan Administration cited for the occupation was an appeal from the members of the Organization of Eastern Caribbean States (OECS) for assistance in wrenching dictatorial power from the cabal within the Grenadan administration of Maurice Bishop that had overthrown and then killed him and a number of his supporters.[66] Since the invitation seems to have been genuine in the sense that it was received before the occupation and was not coerced (although it may have been encouraged), the General Assembly's condemnation of the U.S. occupation could be read as an implicit finding that a few members of one regional organization cannot form a subregional organization endowed with authority to intervene in member states for the broad purpose of maintaining peace and security in the area.

Other readings are, however, possible. The language of the OECS Charter lends itself less readily than that of the OAS to the conclusion that the members have accepted intervention by majority vote.[67]

Moreover, in this instance the actual intervention was performed by a proxy. In addition, the OECS majority could not plausibly claim that the events in Grenada constituted an immediate threat to the subregion's peace and security. Finally, it was not clear that all remedies short of occupation had been exhausted. The mere threat to intervene unless the cabal agreed to internationally monitored elections or the release of political prisoners might have achieved whatever ends the organization could legitimately have sought under any conceivable interpretation of its Charter.

Despite these complicating contextual elements, Grenada standing alone could provide some precedential support for the claim that subregional organizations cannot legitimate intervention in member states (at least when not explicitly authorized by treaty). But Grenada does not stand alone. Africa has provided another and considerably less ambiguous case of a humanitarian, peace-enforcing intervention by a subregional organization. On August 23, 1990, after the United States and the Security Council had ignored appeals from Liberians and others, armed forces from five members of the Economic Community of West African States (ECOWAS) landed in Liberia's devastated capital, Monrovia. Their goal: to end a horribly brutal three-sided civil war and, in the process, to save hundreds of their own citizens trapped in the dying city without food, water, medicine, or shelter.[68]

This was no essay in mere peacekeeping. Charles Taylor, leader of the strongest faction, had promised to resist what he termed a violation of Liberian sovereignty. True to his word, he launched an attack on the ECOWAS units as soon as they arrived.

A desire to increase regional cooperation in the economic sphere had been the principal motive driving sixteen West African states to establish ECOWAS. The decision to intervene was taken by means of ad hoc procedures that did not include all of the members. In part for that reason, it engendered internal wrangling, primarily across the linguistic fault line between the anglophone and francophone members. Yet the intervention evoked not a peep of censure from either the wider African community of states or the UN. What little reaction that occurred seemed quietly approving.[69]

Liberia, like Somalia, is one of those hitherto rare instances where a universally recognized state lacks a recognized government. The vacuum of authority that, together with the humanitarian crisis, drew ECOWAS into Liberia is a contextual feature that may sharply limit the value of this case as a precedent for tolerance of intervention by regional or subregional organizations to end some unnatural disaster in a state with a functioning, albeit abominable, government. While the case therefore speaks ambiguously about the broader legitimating authority of institutions other than the Security Council, international community reaction—or the lack thereof in this instance—is consistent with the community's generally relaxed view of what sorts of arrangements can claim powers beyond those of coordinating self-defense against an armed attack.

To date, there is no reason to believe that *overinclusiveness* (from the standpoint of a geographer) will arouse more concern than has underinclusiveness. When the United States, Canada, and the nations of Western Europe formed NATO, they chose not to designate it as a regional arrangement. Their choice stemmed not from doubt that it qualified, but from a judgment that such designation might connect it more closely to the Security Council and thereby expose its decisions to a Soviet veto.[70] With 3,000 miles of ocean separating North America from Europe, why did the NATO member states see nothing dubious about describing their creation as a regional arrangement? In part, perhaps, because in the course of the 20th century, the United States had become deeply enmeshed in the European political system. Yet the United States is deeply enmeshed in the political system of the

Middle East. If it were to join Egypt, Saudi Arabia, Kuwait, Jordan, Morocco, and Tunisia in a "Middle East Treaty Organization," would their claim to have formed a chapter VIII arrangement be widely accepted?

It is hard to answer that question with any confidence. No UN organ has laid down criteria for identifying chapter VIII arrangements. As noted above, the issue of what sort of associations qualify for the designation has not been salient in the politics of the UN. Why has it failed to attract controversy? The most, perhaps the only, plausible reason is a widely shared conviction that nothing of consequence turns on the designation.

But how is that possible, in light of U.S. claims in the 1950s and 1960s about the authority of the OAS to legitimate the use of force for purposes other than self-defense? It is possible in the first place because the Soviet Union implicitly rejected those claims. Moscow insisted on the subordination of regional arrangements to Security Council jurisdiction. For instance, when in 1960 the OAS proposed economic sanctions against the Dominican Republic as punishment for the involvement of its dictator, Rafael Trujillo, in an assassination attempt against the president of Venezuela, the USSR claimed that under article 53 of the Charter, the OAS was obligated to obtain the Security Council approval.[71] While Moscow and its clients were vociferously hostile to U.S. claims about the autonomous power of regional arrangements, the other UN bloc likely to challenge U.S. positions, the Non-Aligned Movement, seemed indifferent. Indifference may have been a function of timing, for by the late 1960s, when the Non-Aligned Movement began to control the UN's agenda, the United States had lost effective control of the OAS. Never again did the OAS purport to authorize military intervention. In the case of Panama, the Latin members of the OAS blocked any sort of resolution that would in effect have stripped the color of international legitimacy from the Noriega-controlled government and thus opened the way to intervention in response to appeals from Noriega's political opponents.[72] The Non-Aligned Movement's indifference to the issue may also have had two other roots. One is the existence of regional arrangements dominated, respectively, by its Arab and African members. The other is the effective veto the Latin states, including members of the Non-Aligned Movement, have enjoyed in the OAS since the 1960s.

The increasing inability of governments to advance national interests through purely national measures and the coincident growth in the extraterritorial effects of national policies will generate additional intergovernmental arrangements, as well as deepening and enlarging some existing ones. Most participants in each of the arrangements that emerge or enlarge will share some sort of geographic connection, since despite the shrinking effect new technologies of communication and transportation have had on distance, neighbors still tend to experience a greater depth and velocity of interactions and tend to share more characteristics with each other than with distant countries. There is now talk, for instance, of an association of states clustered around the Black Sea. But for many reasons—including mutual distrust, a felt need to balance the power of another association of states, and cultural or ideological ties—neighbors may require or desire that one or more states with whom they have no direct geographic connection be included in their association.

Since the institutionalization of interstate relationships tends to increase the flow of information and transactions, and thereby to facilitate the formation of transnational interest groups embedded in national bureaucracies, both public and private, international community policy should generally favor the proliferation of subglobal organizations. A norm privileging geographically compact associations of states seems inconsistent with that policy. Could it nevertheless be justified with respect to the privilege that is the focus of this chapter—legitimating the use of force for purposes other than self-defense? Could one argue that the virtue of the geographic connection is its inherent limit, that regional enforcement action is less likely to inflame the globe?

But is it in fact much less likely to engage the concerns of extraregional states? Enforcement action may take the form of blockades. To be effective, they must be enforced against all states, not just members of the regional organization. Moreover, a state targeted for coercive measures, in addition to being a member of the regional organization, may be connected through treaty to an extraregional collective defense arrangement. So authorization of coercion by a regional organization would not necessarily limit the potential scope of ensuing violence even if there were well-understood, easily applicable, and generally accepted criteria for deciding what is and what is not a regional arrangement.

## CONCLUSION

Subglobal intergovernmental organizations with geographically diverse membership are a firmly established feature of the contemporary international system. Efforts to establish a hierarchy of privilege with respect to the capacity to authorize coercion are certain to generate a vast amount of heat and very little consensus. Geography is a perception, not a fact. And it does not, in any event, correspond systematically to national and international community interests. Reasonable restraints on the use of force must be sought elsewhere.

One approach would be to recognize a Security Council monopoly on authorizing force for purposes other than self-defense against armed attack. But, as noted earlier, individual states will occasionally feel an overwhelming compulsion to intervene for the defense of rights or values in circumstances where the Security Council is paralyzed by the veto of a permanent member or by the opposition of temporary occupants of Council seats who may be concerned about the precedent or determined to extract rent for their acquiescence. Submitting the self-help impulse to the discipline of multimember organizations should reduce the danger of intervention's igniting a regional conflagration, for collective authorization will credential the intervention as authentically humanitarian rather than a seizure of assets or the imposition of a client regime.

Architects of order need to incorporate into their designs the diversity of national values and material interests; the corresponding limits of universal consensus on substantive law; and the rudimentary character of global institutions for making, applying, and enforcing norms. For the reasons sketched above, subglobal institutions with the authority to legitimate the threat or use of force can help to contain violence and maintain law. But the consequent decentralization of coercive authority from the Security Council is not without risk. As suggested earlier, states may belong to more than one organization claiming authority to protect the security of member states or to enforce peace, human rights, or other shared values. Overlapping membership can occur unintentionally, since institutions established for some other reason—economic cooperation, for instance—can suddenly be driven by events, as ECOWAS was, to transform themselves into peace or human rights enforcing agencies. Thus one can envision cases where two subglobal institutions make competing claims of entitlement to undertake or authorize interventions. In addition, while they are engaged in disciplining a member state, subglobal arrangements may incidentally tread on the interests of a powerful nonmember even where they do not violate its legal rights. Furthermore, a dominant bloc may seize such arrangements and turn them to the end of exploiting a minority of members or maintaining an inherently unstable status quo.

To mitigate these and other risks, subglobal organizations should not have more than a limited and conditional autonomy. The Security Council needs to reclaim part of the authority that dribbled away from it in the course of the Cold War. Insistence on prior case-by-case consent by the Security Council to all peace and humanitarian enforcement activities is not desirable, for it is precisely when the Security Council is paralyzed by states without an intense interest in the result of a humanitarian crisis, but still unwilling to lend the Council's authority at a reasonable price, that the subglobal organization needs autonomy to provide individual states with an alternative to self-help. Review should not, however, be entirely after the fact, when it may well be otiose.

Requiring organizations to notify the Council immediately in the event they authorize the use of force for any purpose, including collective self-defense, strikes the appropriate balance. The secretary-general would receive notice for immediate dissemination to all Council members. The Council could also call on the secretary-general to inform members in the event a regional organization fails to make the required report, and should state that any use or threatened use of force about which the Council is not notified is presumptively illegal. Since the right to authorize intervention against a government in place derives from prior consent to participate in the regional organization, in theory the right terminates when consent terminates. What if the constitutional agreement establishing the organization says nothing about withdrawal? Sovereignty is the defining structural feature of the present international order. A central strand in the cluster of rights that the word "sovereignty" describes is the right to monopolize the use of force within the national territory. Hence, any concession to intergovernmental organizations of a right to intervene cuts against the logic of sovereignty and therefore seems anomalous. A grant in perpetuity would come close to ceding sovereignty itself. So unless the contrary evidence left little ground for dispute, it would be reasonable to assume that such a grant was not made. What should also be assumed, however, is that the parties to the agreement committed themselves to give reasonable notice prior to withdrawal.

Regional organizations are not yet and may never become ubiquitous. And they, too, can be paralyzed. The structure of legitimation I have proposed does not go far beyond the outlines of the contemporary consensus. It is consistent with the character of what remains a thinly institutionalized, if not altogether anarchic, political system. It will channel, but it cannot utterly subdue, the impulse to unilateral action. From time to time, states still will have to choose between compliance with formal prohibitions and response to urgent moral appeals. The Bosnian affair tells us that obdurate opponents of unilateral action—and, for that matter, opponents of intervention by regional organizations—have very little to fear.

## NOTES

1. See, for example, Robert Jackson and Karl Rosberg, "Why Africa's Weak States Persist: The Empirical and the Juridical in Statehood," *World Politics*, vol. 35, no. 1 (1982), p. 1. See also Stephen D. Krasner, "Economic Interdependence and Independent Statehood," unpublished paper (Stanford University, July 1991).

342 ◆ Tom Farer

2. See Tom J. Farer, "Law and War," in C. E. Black and R. A. Falk, eds., *The Future of the International Legal Order*, vol. 3 (Princeton: Princeton University Press, 1971), pp. 27–36.

3. See, for example, Model Penal Code, sec. 3.04, which allows the use of force when it is "immediately necessary for the purpose of protecting [oneself] against the use of unlawful force." Compare state laws: "Any person using force intended or likely to cause death or great bodily injury within his or her residence shall be presumed to have held a reasonable fear of imminent peril of death or great bodily injury to self, family, or a member of the household when that force is used against another person, not a member of the family or household, who unlawfully and forcibly enters or has unlawfully and forcefully entered the residence and the person using force had reason to believe that an unlawful and forcible entry had occurred" (Tenn. Code Ann. sec. 39-2-235 [Supp. 1988]). "No person in this state shall be placed in legal jeopardy of any kind whatsoever for protecting himself or his family by reasonable means necessary" (*Hoemig v. Indiana*, 522 N.E.2d 392, 396 [1988]). "If the defendant believed that he was in imminent danger of death or serious bodily harm and that deadly force was immediately necessary to repel such danger he was not required to retreat or consider whether he could safely retreat. He was entitled to stand his ground and use such force as he believed immediately necessary to protect his person" (CJI 7:9:02).

4. "All members of the United Nations, in order to contribute to the maintenance of international peace and security, undertake to make available to the Security Council, on its call and in accordance with a special agreement or agreements, armed forces . . . [the] agreement or agreements to be negotiated as soon as possible on the initiative of the Security Council" (UN Charter, article 43, paras. 1 and 3).

5. "Decisions of the Security Council on all other [i.e., nonprocedural] matters shall be made by an affirmative vote of nine members including the concurring votes of the permanent members" (UN Charter, article 27, para. 3).

6. Ibid, art. 51.

7. Ibid., arts. 52–54. Article 53 (1) states that "no enforcement action shall be taken under regional arrangements or by regional agencies without the authorization of the Security Council."

8. On the Arab League, see Istvan Pogany, *The Arab League and Peace Keeping in Lebanon* (London: Avebury Gower, 1987); Fawig Y. Hasou, *The Struggle for the Arab World* (Boston: KPI, 1985); Muhammed Khalil, *The Arab World and the Arab League* (Beirut: Khayats, 1962); Boutros Boutros-Ghali, *The Arab League 1945–55* (New York: Carnegie Endowment for International Peace, 1954); and Albert H. Hourani, *A History of the Arab Peoples* (Cambridge: Harvard University Press, 1991).

9. On the OAS, see Aida L. Levin, "The Organization of American States and the United Nations," in Berhanykun Andemicael, ed., *Regionalism and the U.N.* (Dobbs Ferry, N.Y.: Oceana Press, 1979), pp. 147–336.

10. See Tom J. Farer, ed., *The Future of the Inter-American System* (New York: Praeger, 1979), pp. xvi-xvii.

11. UN Charter, art. 51.
12. See Derek Bowett, *Self-Defense in International Law* (Manchester: Manchester University Press, 1958).
13. UN Charter, art. 53 (1).
14. See, for example, Myres McDougal and Florentino Feliciano, *Law and Minimum World Order* (New Haven: Yale University Press, 1961); and Julius Stone, *Aggression and World Order* (Berkeley: University of California Press, 1958).
15. See Farer, "Law and War," pp. 27–36.
16. See Tom J. Farer, "The Regulation of Foreign Intervention in Civil Armed Conflict," *Recueil des Cours*, vol. 2 (Leyden: A.W. Sijthoff, 1974) pp. 297–404.
17. For an exemplary piece reflecting official views of the governing norms, see John Norton Moore, "The Secret War in Central America and the Future of World Order," *American Journal of International Law*, vol. 80 (1986), p. 43. An earlier articulation of official U.S. views on the issue is the State Department memorandum "The Legality of U.S. Participation in the Defense of Vietnam," submitted to the Senate Committee on Foreign Relations on March 8, 1966, reprinted in Richard A. Falk, ed., *The Vietnam War and International Law* (Princeton: Princeton University Press, 1968), p. 583.
18. Case Concerning Military and Paramilitary Activities In and Against Nicaragua (*Nicaragua v. United States of America*), 1986 I.C.J. Rep. 14 (Judgment). See paragraphs 183–211, 229–242, and 246–252.
19. Tom Farer and Christopher Joyner, "The United States and the Use of Force," *Transnational Law and Social Problems*, vol. 1 (1991), p. 15.
20. Stone, *Aggression and World Order*, esp. pp. 43–44.
21. See, for example, W. Michael Reisman, "Coercion and Self-Determination: Construing Charter Article 2(4)," *American Journal of International Law*, vol. 78 (1984), p. 642.
22. See Abram Chayes, *The Cuban Missile Crisis* (New York: Oxford University Press, 1974); James G. Blight and David Welch, *On the Brink: Americans and the Soviets Re-Examine the Cuban Missile Crisis* (New York: Hill and Wang, 1989); and Raymond Garthoff, *Reflections on the Cuban Missile Crisis*, rev. ed. (Washington, D.C.: Brookings Institution, 1989).
23. See Leonard Meeker, "The Dominican Situation in the Perspective of International Law," *Department of State Bulletin*, vol. 53 (July 12, 1965); and Abram Chayes, "Law and the Quarantine of Cuba," *Foreign Affairs* vol. 41 (April 1963), p. 550.
24. Meeker, "The Dominican Situation," pp. 60 and 62.
25. On the Brezhnev Doctrine and Reagan Doctrine see W. Michael Reisman, "Old Wine in New Bottles: The Reagan and Brezhnev Doctrines in Contemporary International Law and Practice," *Yale Journal of International Law*, vol. 13 (1988), p. 171.
26. See, for example, W. Hays Parks, "Air War and the Law of War," *Air Force Law Review 1*, vol. 32 (1990), p. 136.
27. Resolution 253 (1968). This section extends the previous oil embargo of resolution 221 (1966), and calls for extensive additional economic sanctions against Rhodesia.

28. See resolution 418 (1977), calling for a mandatory arms embargo against South Africa.
29. See Micah L. Sifry and Christopher Cerf, *The Gulf War Reader* (New York: Random House, 1991). See also James Turner Johnson and George Weigel, *Gulf War and the Just War* (Washington, D.C.: Ethics and Public Policy Center, 1991).
30. Resolution 688 (April 5, 1991).
31. Resolution 687 (April 3, 1991). (See chapter two, above, and pp. 357–361 below.)
32. Resolution 733 (January 23, 1992); resolution 746 (March 17, 1992); resolution 751 (April 24, 1992), and resolution 794 (December 3, 1992).
33. Particularly the decision to impose an arms embargo—resolution 713 (September 25, 1991)—and to impose economic sanctions on the Serbia-Montenegro rump of former Yugoslavia—resolution 757 (May 30, 1992).
34. On January 15, 1992, the European Community (EC) unanimously agreed to recognize Slovenia and Croatia (*Washington Post*, January 16, 1992, p. A21). On April 6, 1992, the EC foreign ministers decided to recognize Bosnia (*New York Times*, April 7, 1992, p. 1).
35. See *Nicaragua v. United States of America*, 1986 ICJ 14.
36. See Hurst Hannum, *Autonomy, Sovereignty and Self-Determination* (Philadelphia: University of Pennsylvania Press, 1990); and Michla Pomerance, *Self-Determination in Law and Practice* (The Hague: Martinus Nijhoff, 1982).
37. See Ernest Lefever, *Crisis in the Congo* (Washington, D.C.: Brookings Institution, 1965); and King Gordon, *The U.N. in the Congo* (New York: Carnegie Endowment for International Peace, 1962).
38. Ivory Coast, Gabon, Tanzania, and Zambia. See "Why We Recognized Biafra," *Observer*, April 26, 1968.
39. On the Nigerian war, see Walter Schwartz, "Foreign Powers and the Nigerian War," *Africa Report*, vol. 15, no. 2 (February 1970), p. 12.
40. See Thomas Franck and Nigel Rodley, "After Bangladesh: The Law of Humanitarian Intervention by Military Force," *American Journal of International Law*, vol. 67 (1973), p. 275.
41. S/PV.1608, December 6, 1971, p. 141.
42. For the General Assembly debate, see A/PV.2002, December 7, 1971.
43. See note 34, above.
44. See Franck and Rodley, "After Bangladesh," p. 284.
45. James S. Fenton, ed., *Cambodia Witness: The Autobiography of Someth May* (London: Faber, 1986).
46. On terrorism in Guatemala, see Stephen Kinzer and Stephen Schlesinger, *Bitter Fruit: The Untold Story of the American Coup in Guatemala* (Garden City, N.Y.: Doubleday, 1982); Piero Gleijeses, *Shattered Hope: The Guatemalan Revolution and the United States* (Princeton: Princeton University Press, 1991); and Richard Immerman, *The CIA in Guatemala: The Foreign Policy of Intervention* (Austin, Tex.: University of Texas Press, 1982).
47. See, for example, Douglas Farah, "Prospects for Prompt Resolution of Haitian Crisis Begin to Dim," *Washington Post*, January 24, 1993, p. A24.
48. See "Desperate Voyagers," *Economist*, January 16–22, 1993, p. 22.

49. See David Lauter, "Clinton Charges Bush Appeased Iraq before War," *Los Angeles Times*, July 1, 1992, p. 1.
50. See Blaine Harden, "Sizing Up Serbia's Leaders," *Washington Post*, January 17, 1993, p. A44.
51. On the period of state terror in Argentina, see Inter-American Commission on Human Rights, *Report on the Situation of Human Rights in Argentina* (Washington, D.C.: OAS, 1980). See also Jacobo Timmerman, *Prisoner without a Name, Cell without a Number* (New York: Alfred A. Knopf, 1981); and John Simpson, *The Disappeared: Voices from a Secret War* (London: Robson Books, 1985).
52. See Franck and Rodley, "After Bangladesh," p. 295.
53. See Richard Sisson, *War and Secession: Pakistan, India, and the Creation of Bangladesh* (Berkeley: University of California Press, 1990).
54. See, for example, Michael Bazyler, "Reexamining the Doctrine of Humanitarian Intervention in Light of the Atrocities in Kampuchea and Ethiopia," *Stanford Journal of International Law*, vol. 23 (1987), pp. 547 and 598–611; and Jean-Pierre Fonteyne, "The Customary International Law Doctrine of Humanitarian Intervention: Its Current Validity under the U.N. Charter," *California Western International Law Journal*, vol. 4 (1974), pp. 203 and 258–268
55. See Indar J. Rikhye and Kjell Skjelsbaek, eds., *The United Nations and Peacekeeping* (New York: St. Martin's Press, 1991); Henry Wiseman, ed., *Peacekeeping* (New York: Pergamon Press, 1983); and Anthony Verrier, *International Peacekeeping* (New York: Penguin Books, 1981).
56. See "U.S. May Be Trapped in Somalia," *Washington Post*, February 26, 1993, p. A6.
57. See Julius Stone, *Legal Controls of International Conflict* (New York: Rinehart & Co., 1954), pp. 292 and 492; and Rosalyn Higgins, *The Development of International Law Through the Political Organs of the United Nations* (London: Oxford University Press, 1963), p. 202.
58. UN Charter, article 96 (1), states, "The General Assembly or the Security Council may request the International Court of Justice to give an advisory opinion on any legal question."
59. Consider, for example, the refusal of the UN's political organs to countenance Eritrean claims of a right to secede from Ethiopia in light of Emperor Haile Selassie's failure to fulfill his promise to the UN that if it incorporated the former Italian colony into the Ethiopian empire, Eritrea would be allowed to maintain democratic institutions and a high degree of local autonomy. See Tom J. Farer, *Warclouds on the Horn of Africa*, 2nd rev. ed. (Washington, D.C.: Carnegie Endowment for International Peace, 1979).
60. Compare Tom J. Farer, "The United States as Guarantor of Democracy in the Caribbean Basin: Is There a Legal Way?" *Jerusalem Journal of International Relations*, vol. 11 (1989), p. 40.
61. See, for example, the Platt Amendment, which conditioned the withdrawal of U.S. forces from Cuba after the Spanish-American War on a continuing right to intervene on the basis of a unilateral determination by the United States that the local authorities were unable to maintain order. See Louis A. Perez, *Intervention, Revolution, and Politics in Cuba, 1913-1921* (Pittsburgh: University of Pittsburgh Press, 1978).

62. See Tom J. Farer, ed., *The Future of the Inter-American System*, pp. xvi–xvii.

63. See Chayes, *The Cuban Missile Crisis*; Blight and Welch, *On the Brink*; and Garthoff, *Reflections*.

64. See Shir Kumar, *US Intervention in Latin America: The Dominican Crisis and the OAS* (New York: Advent Books, 1987); Theodore Draper, "The Dominican Crisis," *Commentary*, vol. 40 (December 1965), p. 33; Mark Bohan, "The Dominican Case: Unilateral Intervention," *American Journal of International Law*, vol. 60 (1966), p. 809; and Ved Nanda, "The United States Action in the 1965 Dominican Crisis: Impact on World Order," *Denver Law Journal*, vol. 43 (1966), p. 441.

65. General Assembly resolution 38/7 (November 2, 1983), declaring the "armed intervention" in Grenada a "flagrant violation of international law." The vote was 108–9, with 27 abstentions. Countries voting for the resolution included Australia, Denmark, France, Greece, Iceland, Italy, the Netherlands, Norway, Portugal, and Spain. While Canada, Great Britain, Japan, and West Germany abstained, their governments had earlier made public statements opposing the U.S. intervention. See Berlin, "U.S. Allies Join in Lopsided Vote Condemning Invasion of Grenada," *Washington Post*, November 3, 1983, p. A1.

66. Statement by the Honorable Kenneth W. Dam, Deputy Secretary of State, before the Committee on Foreign Affairs, U.S. House of Representatives, November 2, 1983, reprinted in major part in *American Journal of International Law*, vol. 78 (1984), p. 203.

67. See Christopher Joyner, "The United States Action in Grenada: Reflections on the Lawfulness of Invasion," *American Journal of International Law*, vol. 78 (1984), p. 131, see esp. pp. 135–142. But compare John Norton Moore, "Grenada and the International Double Standard," in the same volume, p. 145; see esp. pp. 153–166.

68. See the chapter by David Wippman in this volume.

69. U.S. reaction, for instance, was favorable. See *The Christian Science Monitor*, August 9, 1990, quoting an unnamed State Department official. The *Monitor* also cited approving remarks from a "UN official."

70. See Secretary of State Dean Acheson's testimony before the Senate Foreign Relations Committee, April 27, 1949 (Hearings, part I, pp. 22, 30). See also Sir Eric Beckett (U.K. Legal Advisor at time), *The North Atlantic Treaty* (Oxford: Oxford University Press, 1950).

71. See S/4476, S/4477, S/4481.

72. When Panama's de facto dictator used violence and fraud to maintain control of the government despite what international monitors confirmed to be his electoral defeat, the crisis decision-making organ of the OAS, the Organ of Consultation (of foreign ministers), did the following: It declared "that the solidarity of the American States and the high aims which are sought through it *require* the political organization of those States on the basis of the effective exercise of representative democracy" (emphasis added). However, it coincidentally affirmed that "no state or group of States has the right to intervene, directly or indirectly, *for any reason whatsoever*, in the internal or external affairs of any other state" (emphasis

added). It sought to walk the line between the first two propositions by appointing three of its members to promote "conciliation formulas for arriving at a national accord that can bring about, through democratic mechanisms, a transfer of power in the shortest possible time, and with full respect for the sovereign will of the Panamanian people." See resolution 1, approved at the second plenary session of the Twenty-first Meeting of Consultation of Ministers of Foreign Affairs (May 17, 1989).

After conciliation formulas failed to achieve the transfer of power, the United States invaded. The response of the Permanent Council of the OAS was "to deplore profoundly the military intervention in Panama [and] to exhort the removal of the foreign troops utilized for the military intervention." See resolution 534 (December 22, 1989).

# CHAPTER NINE

## Concluding Reflections

### LORI FISLER DAMROSCH

The case studies and thematic essays have suggested a number of cross-cutting issues, of which only a few can be addressed in this concluding chapter. They are the concept of deterrence as applied to collective efforts to restrain internal conflicts; the tension between preserving impartiality and passing judgment, which may suggest the desirability of allocating different roles to different collective organs; the problem of enhancing the authority and legitimacy of collective restraint of internal conflicts; and the problem of treating like cases alike. In formulating my views on these issues, I have benefited greatly from the contributions of all who participated in the present study, but the reflections in this chapter are my own.

## DETERRENCE AND INTERNAL CONFLICTS

The uneasy peace of the Cold War period was preserved at least in part because of deterrence—knowledge on both sides of a potential conflict that hostile acts would trigger a costly, even devastating response. The legal structure of the UN Charter bolstered deterrence by delegitimizing first use of transboundary force and legitimizing self-defense. There were, of course, significant failures of deterrence, as when Saddam Hussein ventured to attack one neighbor, Iran, in 1980 and another neighbor, Kuwait, in 1990. But the ability of the international community to muster a decisive response to the 1990 invasion will surely help deter future Saddam Husseins from attempting other such attacks.

Deterrence has always been a controversial concept, both in international relations and in domestic law enforcement. It is bound up with some of the most troubling and divisive issues of our times—nuclear strategy and capital punishment, among others. During the Cold War, the term acquired specialized connotations pertaining to relations between the superpowers that would seem remote from the present topic. But in the broader sense of discouraging the outbreak of conflict or the violation of community norms, deterrence may indeed be a relevant concept. What can the international community do to *deter* civil wars, war crimes, genocide, "ethnic cleansing," and other abhorrent conduct?

International politics and domestic law enforcement may have some common lessons for our subject, as both systems have grappled with the problem of deterring unacceptable behavior through the threat of a response (retaliation, punishment, and so on) that would impose sufficiently high costs on perpetrators to give them a motivation to refrain from the behavior in the first place. Deterrence in this broad sense always operates alongside other strategies, including efforts to eliminate the underlying causes of unacceptable behavior. Naturally, it would be preferable if we could overcome the sources of conflict and thereby obviate the need for deterrence through threats: social justice and economic development are desirable for the sake of internal as well as international peace. But just as every modern society recognizes that the threat of punishment is an essential part of the mix of crime prevention strategies, international society also must continue to rely on the threat of imposing unwelcome costs on those who may decide to violate community norms.

Deterring the outbreak of internal conflicts, and deterring atrocities and other norm violations within such conflicts, will pose difficult challenges. The structural features of the Cold War that prevented the outbreak of major conflict between the super-powers did not deter internal conflicts (or at least not all such conflicts): on the contrary, especially outside Europe, many such conflicts flourished with encouragement and contribution from the superpowers. There is reason to hope that some of those destructive tendencies belong to the past. To the extent that the major powers retain some influence over former clients, we may also hope that such influence can be exerted along the lines of preventive diplomacy, to lessen the chance that internal stresses will erupt into violence. But in parallel to these aspirations, it may be advisable to consider whether development of patterns of collective response to internal conflicts can serve some deterrent functions.

Our cases suggest a range of examples in which concepts of deterrence have or have not worked in the context of internal conflicts:

*Yugoslavia—1991:* The European Community registered concern about the impending use of force by the Serbian-dominated Yugoslav National Army against Croatia after the latter's declaration of independence, but threatened no specific consequences against Serbia. This weak signal failed to deter the eruption of conflict.

*Yugoslavia—1992–1993:* President Bush signaled more force-fully to Serbian leaders that any use of force in Kosovo (formally part of Serbia) would evoke a forcible response against Serbia, and the Clinton administration has reaffirmed Bush's warning. Similarly, the United States has warned the Serbs against expanding the conflict to Macedonia (formally a separate republic whose recognition was delayed for extraneous political reasons); the Security Council has backed up this signal with a commitment to a preventive deployment along the Serbian-Macedonian frontier.[1] So far, combat has not spread to those areas.

*Iraq—1991:* Ambiguous signals in the wake of the Persian Gulf conflict of January–February 1991 were followed first by a Kurdish and Shi'ite uprising, then by Saddam Hussein's ruthless crackdown, then by the international response embodied in Security Council resolution 688 and Operation Provide Comfort.

*Iraq—1992–1993:* The multinational coalition clarified its intentions vis-à-vis the zones north of the 36th parallel (Kurdistan) and south of the 32nd parallel (Shi'ite marshlands). The coalition has sent the signal that hostile actions on Saddam Hussein's part will evoke a military response. Saddam Hussein's probing of the coalition's resolve has elicited the threatened forcible response, with the apparent effect of bringing about an abatement of the objectionable conduct (temporarily, at least).[2]

*Haiti:* The Santiago Commitment of June 1991 established a normative trigger ("sudden or irregular interruption of the democratic political institutional process or of the legitimate exercise of power by the democratically elected government"), but the articulation of the response (merely to convene a meeting of foreign ministers to consider what measures should be taken) was too weak to constitute a deterrent. The perception that the international community did not act effectively against the poorest state in the hemisphere, and that it would be even less likely to act strongly against a more powerful state, has weakened deterrence of future coups.[3]

*Liberia and Somalia:* The signals sent, apparently, were that the major extraregional powers no longer had sufficient interest to warrant a prediction that they would react in any way at all to outbreaks of violence. Thus local forces were emboldened to seek to attain their objectives forcibly.

*Cambodia:* The UN Security Council has condemned the Khmer Rouge for its failure to abide by the settlement agreement, has recommended selective sanctions, and has indicated that it would "consider appropriate measures to be implemented should the [Khmer Rouge] obstruct the implementation of the peace plan."[4] Yet the Khmer Rouge and the incumbent government have been increasingly brazen in their violations of the agreement, including outright attacks resulting in the deaths of

UN personnel, extensive voter intimidation, and refusals to abide by the electoral process and outcome. The collective response has essentially been limited to reiterating that the elections would take place as planned, with or without all parties' cooperation; the patterns of noncompliance have continued.

What lessons may be learned from these examples, as well as from theories of deterrence in other contexts? If unacceptable behavior is to be deterred, the international community must clarify its expectations in at least two significant ways. First, it must identify the thresholds that will elicit an international response if crossed. This would include an affirmation of the importance attached to norms already in existence (for example, humanitarian law, and obligations under cease-fire agreements or Security Council resolutions); it could also include specific triggering points correlated to enforcement of norms and obligations (for example, geographic designation of military exclusion zones where necessary to police a cease-fire or to protect populations that have been victims of atrocities).

Second, the international community must clarify what responses will be forthcoming in the event that the thresholds so identified are crossed. The kinds of theories of deterrence that were prominent during the Cold War may or may not be relevant to internal conflicts; but if the concept has any applicability even by analogy to domestic law enforcement, the probability of deterring the unacceptable behavior is directly correlated to the likelihood that adverse consequences will be imposed, as well as to the costliness of the consequences in proportion to what the target hopes to gain from the violation. In short, the international community should be able to signal to the potential violator: Don't even risk it; it won't be worth your while!

For the reasons discussed in the chapter on economic sanctions, the international community should strive to impose adverse consequences on the actual violators of community norms and should attempt to avoid harm to civilian populations, especially to civilian populations that have already been victims of the conduct that the international community seeks to deter. To the extent that nuclear deterrence in the Cold War period relied on holding civilian populations hostage, it is obviously not an appropriate analogy for the international response to internal conflicts.

Punishment imposed on specific individuals may serve as a deterrent to future violations. The establishment of a war crimes tribunal for the former Yugoslavia (and possibly for Iraq) ought to remind individuals of the Nuremberg precedent that they can be held individually responsible for grave breaches of the laws of war and other important international norms.[5] That precedent has so far been insufficient to deter flagrant violations of Nuremberg-type norms in post–World War II conflicts, in part because of the perception of the remote likelihood that such a tribunal would be convened again. If a war crimes tribunal for Yugoslavia functions effectively, a deterrent effect on the commission of future war crimes may be plausible; but if the effort should falter or fail, potential violators may even be emboldened.

One should not underestimate the difficulties of deterring the outbreak of internal conflict and the violation of international norms in the course of such conflict. The fact that internal conflicts are by definition concentrated within a state's territorial boundaries complicates the task of identifying the thresholds that the international community insists must not be crossed. Even when unambiguous norms are breached (such as the prohibition on genocide or the laws of war), the feasibility of imposing serious costs on the violators may be questionable. Nonetheless, attention to developing and implementing international mechanisms analogous to domestic law enforcement should help deter violations of community norms in internal as well as international conflicts.

## PRESERVING IMPARTIALITY VS. PASSING JUDGMENT

To what extent should the UN (or other collective bodies) be passing judgment on actions or actors in situations of internal conflict? Traditional international law endeavored—ineffectually—to require outsiders to remain neutral during internal struggles. The international legal norm of nonintervention, though it is obviously undergoing change, still embodies some values worthy of preservation. As discussed in the introduction, the norm seeks to contain internal conflicts within state boundaries rather than allowing them to spread into other states (the conflict containment value), and it affirms that the people within a state should determine for themselves how they are to be governed, free from external domination (the autonomy, or self-determination, value).

As the focus shifts from unilateral intervention to collective involvement, the values of conflict containment and autonomy implicit in the nonintervention norm should not and need not be abandoned. In addition, international institutions have reasons of their own for favoring the preservation of impartiality in internal conflicts. Among these reasons are the desirability of allowing the institution to play the role of "honest broker" and to hold itself available for good offices or mediation functions.

Yet international institutions are more and more often being asked to pass judgment on one or another faction in an internal conflict, and have done so often enough that we may discern some trends. Among the variants are the following:

- Condemnation of behavior by one or more sides to a conflict in violation of universally accepted international norms— for example, war crimes, severe internal repression, "ethnic cleansing" (Iraq, Yugoslavia)

- Condemnation of violations of an agreement for a cease-fire or political settlement (Liberia, Cambodia)

Some of the relevant Security Council resolutions have singled out the offending party by name; in other cases it has been obvious which faction is being condemned even if its identity is not explicitly stated. Moreover, the threshold has been crossed for the imposition of sanctions on a particular faction, or territory under its control (for example, areas of Liberia controlled by Charles Taylor or of Cambodia controlled by the Khmer Rouge), when that faction appears to be the one obstructing the peaceful settlement of the conflict.

An obvious tension exists between preservation of impartiality or neutrality on the one hand, and fulfillment of functions of norm enforcement on the other. To the extent that the same organ is asked to play both roles, it may end up failing at both. This is a strong argument for having available a variety of potential mechanisms, so that functions can shift from one to another after it becomes clear that strictly neutral facilitation must give way to stronger forms of condemnation, pressure, and enforcement.

It may be premature to try to articulate fixed patterns for the allocation of responsibilities among a variety of institutions. Within a complex institution such as the UN, functional differentiation already exists, so that, for example, the secretary-general can offer good offices at an early stage of a conflict, with the locus of activity later shifting to the political or judicial organs as appropriate. Where organizations with overlapping mandates or membership exist within a given region (as is the case in Europe), efforts can begin within the framework of one body (such as the Conference on Security and Cooperation in Europe), which would be expected to perform neutral functions of peaceful settlement; a different body, equipped with enforcement powers, could step in if necessary at a later stage. And, of course, shifting can take place from regional efforts at mediation in the first instance to UN-based condemnation or compulsion after regional initiatives are exhausted.

Important as it is to have available some institutions that can play a strictly facilitative, nonjudgmental role, the strengthening of the norm enforcement function is ultimately critical for the maturation of international society. As we have seen, the Security Council is increasingly willing and able to discharge this function and should be commended for doing so. The International Court of Justice could also participate in both norm clarification and the passing of judgment; Bosnia has asked it to do so in the Yugoslav conflict, concerning allegations of genocide.[6] Moreover, the Security Council is able to exercise compulsory powers to array the entire international community against a violator of international norms, whether that violator is the government of a state (for example, Saddam Hussein's Iraq) or a faction in an internal conflict (such as Charles Taylor's followers in Liberia). Countries that identify themselves as "neutral" should understand that participation in UN-mandated sanctions, as in UN-authorized peacekeeping or collective security, is consistent with the proper reconceptualization of neutrality in the contemporary world. Indeed, even non-UN members such as Switzerland and Taiwan have cooperated with the UN to enforce international law against violators.[7] With more experience in mobilizing the entire weight of the international community to isolate those who transgress our shared norms, we will make significant progress toward the maturation of the international legal system.

## ENHANCING AUTHORITY AND LEGITIMACY: TEXTS AND PRECEDENTS

In some of the cases we have studied, the appearance of formal legality has been maintained by resort to legal fictions: for instance, that "consent" has been obtained to a peacekeeping deployment when the putative consent has come from sources whose authority is questionable, or when in fact all structures capable of conferring effective consent have broken down (Somalia). Some consider that the current treatment of the concept of "threats to the peace" has become fictional. One commentator has argued that

> continuing to stretch the concept of threat to the peace ultimately undermines the legitimacy and authority of the entire UN Charter. Once a threat to the peace can mean anything from famine to the invasion of a sovereign state, the concept is so broad as to be useless. We need a new concept.[8]

A response to this criticism is that the fallacy of insisting on proof of particular transboundary consequences was exposed as long ago as the cases of Rhodesia and South Africa in the 1960s and 1970s, when the Security Council implicitly acted on the premise that serious human rights violations are themselves a threat to peace.

In certain cases, questions can arise about collective actions that may be highly desirable from a policy point of view but that stretch the limits of existing legal authority. While practice seems to be evolving in normatively sound directions, the legal documents have not necessarily kept pace.

A possible example is the military enforcement of the no-fly zones over the protected areas for the Kurds and Shi'ites in Iraq. The allied decisions to designate the zones and to protect them with military force are eminently justifiable from the point of view of norms and policies, in light of Saddam Hussein's history of genocidal repression and the unleashing of a new round of intolerable brutality in the aftermath of the Gulf War. No doubt, the Security Council does have authority to adopt measures of military protection of endangered populations, both under chapter VII of the UN Charter and under the Genocide Convention.[9] Thus the policy is sound; the Council has ultimate authority to authorize that policy; and plausible arguments for the legality of the policy can be based on the resolutions that the Council has in fact adopted.[10] Nonetheless, it is arguable that military enforcements of the flight bans in Iraq have taken place more on a de facto than a de jure basis, since no resolution of the Council formally approves such action. A fragile consensus exists to the extent of acquiescence in the U.S.–U.K.–French initiatives, but the situation is less satisfactory from a legal point of view than if the Council were to authorize enforcement forthrightly through a resolution specifically addressed to the point (as it eventually did for Bosnia, but has not yet done for Iraq).[11]

We have also seen cases where a policy, having been initially implemented by one or more interested states acting on their own initiative, only later attained formal imprimatur. An example is the operation of the Economic Community of West African States in Liberia, which functioned for two years before the Security Council explicitly acknowledged its military component (although one could arguably have inferred "authorization" within the meaning of article 53 of the UN Charter[12] from acquiescence, or from a cautiously worded statement previously issued on the Council's behalf).[13]

To many American lawyers, concerns about legitimacy in the above situations are easily accommodated under jurisprudential techniques familiar from American constitutional law and the evolution of the common law. The term "threat to the peace" in the UN Charter can be interpreted expansively to meet new concerns, just as the meaning of terms such as "interstate commerce" and "due process" has evolved in ways that the framers of the U.S. Constitution could never have anticipated. The Security Council's authorization to member states to enforce its mandates against Iraq could be given the same kind of flexible construction as congressional delegations of authority to the president.[14] Implicit authority could be inferred from ambiguous texts, as well as from past practices under which authority was claimed and exercised without encountering significant resistance.[15] I am one of many lawyers who endorse the general thrust of these American legal methodologies in the international context, but others find such techniques objectionable in principle or unlikely to be acceptable to those coming from different legal cultures. Thus the question arises: would it be possible or desirable to codify emerging norms of intervention in a new international treaty?

For a variety of reasons, I favor allowing trends to continue to develop and precedents to accumulate, without any explicit move in the near term to change existing legal texts. Gradual growth in the Security Council's powers is fully consistent with methodologies of treaty interpretation, widely accepted in international law, that take account of the purposes of an instrument and practice under it;[16] interpretation can accordingly be dynamic and teleological rather than static and literal. Of course, it would theoretically be possible to clarify the meaning of Charter norms through General Assembly declarations, which if adopted by consensus with the requisite law-declaring intent can constitute an authoritative interpretation of the UN Charter.[17] This has been done in the past with some of the most important Charter norms, including the prohibitions on aggression[18] and (most importantly for our subject) intervention in internal affairs.[19] The General Assembly has taken certain limited steps in the direction of articulating contemporary trends concerning international assistance in situations of humanitarian need (although it deliberately avoided the term "intervention").[20] In the present transitional period, however, I believe that any attempt to address the general problem of intervention in internal conflicts by purporting to codify a consensus that is necessarily still in the process of formation not only would be premature, but could even be counterproductive. Rigid verbal formulations could retard necessary evolution and work against flexibility; insistence that states go on record for or against the proposals might polarize their positions rather than promote consensus.

In my view, a better alternative to the unlikely prospects for general codification of evolving norms is the current approach of arriving at case-specific consensus within the Security Council and then building on each new precedent as newer cases arrive. Structural reforms to increase the representativeness of the Security Council and to improve consultation and transparency of its deliberations could enhance procedural regularity and thereby strengthen the perception of legitimacy. So far, the limiting factor in the Security Council has been the extent to which China has been willing to agree, abstain, or acquiesce instead of exercising its veto. The current relatively veto-free period could end at any time for extraneous reasons (such as Chinese or Russian domestic politics), and the international system would once again have to improvise, as it did around the vetoes of the Cold War period.[21] In that event, other mechanisms outside the Security Council might be devised to embody procedural safeguards such as deliberation and approval by a cross-section of the international community.

Some voices have called for new treaties that, if feasible, could advance the effort to crystallize normative consensus, at least among parties to the treaties. In his chapter in this collection, Tom J. Farer has proposed a treaty to guarantee that like-minded states would act in support of participating democratic governments that come under anticonstitutional attack. Stanley Hoffmann of Harvard University has suggested as follows:

> [Among possible measures, the] boldest would be a treaty, open to (but unlikely to be signed by) all states, that would define rigorously the circumstances in which collective intervention for humanitarian purposes could be undertaken, for a limited period, by a group of states whose action would be authorized by a strong majority of the treaty's signers. The nations would act through a secretariat set up under the treaty, and would report all plans for action to the UN Security Council, which could at any time order the end of sanctions taken under the treaty.[22]

While such measures are conceivable on a regional or subglobal as well as a general basis, I doubt that any significant progress could be made along these lines at the present time. Efforts to formulate the substantive criteria for justifiable intervention would run into all the difficulties previously suggested, with the further complication that few governments and few national parliaments would want to place new interventionary authority in the hands of future voting majorities of signatories. In any event, the very regimes whose repressive character would make them the most appropriate targets for justifiable intervention would be the least likely to agree to such a system.

To be sure, progressive development of international law through the formulation of treaties articulating new norms has an important place. If such treaties attain sufficiently widespread acceptance, or if general practice crystallizes around the norms embodied in the treaties, international law can advance accordingly. Treaties expressing fundamental norms are among the most important sources of contemporary international law, as such landmarks of the post–World War II period as the Genocide Convention and other human rights treaties, the 1958 and 1982 conventions on law of the sea, and the Nuclear Nonproliferation Treaty of 1968 demonstrate. If a new treaty to articulate norms of justifiable intervention should become politically feasible, it could in principle take its place alongside such landmarks. But for the current transitional period, gradual accretion of precedents seems more plausible and advisable.

## THE CALL FOR PRINCIPLE: TREATING LIKE CASES ALIKE

As each of the crises considered in this volume has progressed, the collective response to one has served as a benchmark for evaluating the response or lack of response to others. When it seemed that the international community was ignoring Somalia even though the dimensions of the humanitarian tragedy were greater there than elsewhere, UN Secretary-General Boutros Boutros-Ghali insisted that the crisis in Somalia be given at least as much attention as Yugoslavia was then receiving. Later, when U.S. Marines landed in Somalia but had stayed out of the action in Yugoslavia, the tables were turned. Comparisons and contrasts have been continually made between Iraq and Yugoslavia. For example, a ban on military flights was formally declared over Bosnia in October 1992,[23] but no military action to enforce the ban was taken at that time; in contrast, the protected zones above the 36th and below the 32nd parallels in Iraq were not explicitly established by the Security Council, yet were enforced with military power. To many speakers in the UN, journalists, and other commentators, the existence of such differences constitutes a compelling argument for changing policies, or even casts doubt on the legitimacy of the system as a whole.

As a lawyer concerned with the operation of principles within institutions, I share the concern about differential treatment. The objective of treating like cases alike is fundamental to the evolution of a system based on law rather than power. Legal scholars have underscored that in order for a system to be viewed as legitimate and for its rules to exert a normative "pull" toward compliance, those rules must be seen as fitting within a coherent structure of principle, with consistent application in similar cases.[24]

It may be a long time before the international community will be able to act on the principle of treating like cases alike—even as to well-established norms with determinate content and acknowledged pedigree,[25] let alone norms that are still in flux (as is surely the case with those concerning intervention in internal conflicts). But with a view toward achieving the realization of that objective sooner rather than later, it may be helpful to identify some of the factors that hamper a principled collective response to internal conflicts and consider how they may be overcome.

The political reality is that effective action comes about when one or more strong states have interests that motivate them to take initiatives; otherwise, inertia generally prevails. Institutions provide arenas for coordinating state initiatives and mobilizing pressure for action, but they have heretofore lacked autonomous capabilities. Proposals for creating a standing UN military or police force[26] (or comparable forces at regional or subglobal levels) could enable effective responses to internal conflicts where the objective circumstances call for serious treatment, but where no major power has sufficient interest to initiate action.

The influence of the media, especially television, is one explanation for differing responses to crises that otherwise have similar features. Televised images of fleeing Kurds and starving Somalis galvanized the international community for action, yet media access to Sudan and other crisis areas has been denied. Over time, the artificial barriers to media access will surely fall. Only recently the Soviet Union and Eastern Europe were essentially "closed societies," but the Iron Curtain could not stop the flow of information or the revolution in communication technologies that hastened change within those societies. In the long run, the penetration of the media into what were once inaccessible areas will bring the outside world critical information about those areas, and vice versa. Inevitably, this process will contribute to equalizing the uneven treatment that different areas of crisis have received in international arenas in the past.

Fears about creating potentially unwise precedents have motivated some actors to prefer no action to ill-advised action. Fears about creating potentially insatiable demands are another factor that may have fostered an atmosphere of excessive caution. Fears, whether justifiable or not, that all (or many) states might become vulnerable to unwarranted intrusions have inhibited the creation of innovative but drastic "rescue" measures (for example, conservatorship for states whose authority structures have ceased to function).

Perhaps most important of all is that interventions are costly, not only financially, but also in risk to human life. Thus, the international community has chosen to act selectively—where the likelihood of achieving the desired result is substantial, where the expected benefits outweigh the expected costs, and where one or more states have been motivated to exercise leadership. In view of obvious limitations on resources and political will, it may seem ambitious enough to seek to address a few problems in an admittedly ad hoc and imperfect way.

This effort to explore some of the reasons for inconsistent treatment of cases with similar features has two rather different motivations. First, if I am right in my claim that eventual evolution toward consistent application of principles is not only desirable but essential, then it is important to expose the impediments to that evolution and suggest ways to overcome them. Equally important is my conviction that to offer the concept of principle as a rationale for inaction would be a misuse of the concept. That the system is incapable of responding effectively to all (or even to very many) crises is not a valid excuse for failing to act when some action is possible. Small achievements will lead to greater ones, and to more of them, and eventually to patterns that will reflect underlying principles. Thus, paradoxically, the strategy of choosing to respond selectively in the near term may produce the body of experience that will be necessary for realizing the longer-term objective of treating like cases alike.

Some analysts have argued for a progression from permissive (tolerated) intervention to a right and ultimately a duty to intervene in internal conflicts. Formulations of the scope of such a duty are obviously highly controversial, but at their core is the idea that prevention of preventable evils is morally required. This idea, or ideal, may never be wholly realizable, but it reminds us that states—and an international legal system constructed of states—are human creations whose legitimacy depends on continuing responsiveness to basic human values.

## CONCLUSION

In undertaking the present study, we have sought to contribute to understanding both the possibilities and the limitations of collective involvement in internal conflicts. We began with the preexisting structure of assumptions embodied in legal rules of long standing, and identified the objectives of conflict containment and autonomy that need to be kept in mind as the rules themselves undergo change. We then examined a series of cases that have produced a marked evolution in international norms in a remarkably short period of time. As recently as 1990 or early 1991, before the Persian Gulf war catalyzed international cooperation toward the enforcement of shared values, it was unthinkable that the community of nations could act collectively for any purpose, let alone to restrain conflicts occurring within nation-states; and traditional notions of state sovereignty and domestic jurisdiction held sway to inhibit contemplation of active intervention in such conflicts.

In a few short years the terms of debate have shifted dramatically. Instead of the view that interventions in internal conflicts must be presumptively illegitimate, the prevailing trend today is to take seriously the claim that the international community ought to intercede to prevent bloodshed with whatever means are available. Legal arguments now focus not on condemning or justifying intervention in principle, but rather on how best to solve practical problems of mobilizing collective efforts to mitigate internal violence.

The essays in this volume have shown how legal texts and doctrines formulated in a different era have influenced the international responses to current crises, for better or for worse. Lawyers have had to exercise considerable imagination to adapt inherited words and concepts to new challenges, and the pending challenges are formidable indeed.

A perennial criticism of international law is that the system has too often failed to restrain states from violations of norms when their own interests are at stake. More recently, the complaint has been turned inside out—that legal rules of nonintervention are a spurious form of restraint, which gives states and organizations an excuse to stand by and do nothing while conflict rages within a given state's borders. Fortunately, the dramatic changes of the last few years give cause for optimism that both criticisms can be overcome. The cases in the present study show an impressive transformation toward mobilizing collective energies to restrain violators of international norms and perpetrators of internal violence. By seeking to understand factors both motivating and inhibiting this transformation, we hope to contribute to the effective restraint of internal conflicts.

## NOTES

1. David Binder, "Bush Warns Serbs Not to Widen War," *New York Times*, December 28, 1992, p. A6. The article quotes a Bush administration

document as having warned Serbian officials: "In the event of conflict in Kosovo caused by Serbian action, the United States will be prepared to employ military force against the Serbs in Kosovo and in Serbia proper." The Security Council authorized the preventive deployment in Macedonia in resolution 795 (December 11, 1992).

2. See, for example, Thomas L. Friedman, "U.S. Leads Further Attacks on Iraqi Antiaircraft Sites," *New York Times*, January 19, 1993, p. A1; Elaine Sciolino, "New Iraqi Site Raided as White House Vows Firmness," *New York Times*, January 23, 1993, p. A3; and Thomas L. Friedman, "U.S. Asserts Iraq Changed Behavior," *New York Times*, February 3, 1993, p. A5.

3. Two attempted coups in Venezuela and an autogolpe in Peru (dissolution of the legislature by the president) occurred subsequent to the Haitian coup.

4. Resolution 792 (November 30, 1992).

5. In resolution 808 (February 22, 1993), the Security Council decided to establish an international tribunal for the prosecution of persons responsible for serious violations of international humanitarian law committed in the former Yugoslavia since 1991. In the context of both Iraq and the former Yugoslavia, the Council had affirmed that persons who commit or order the commission of grave breaches of international humanitarian law are individually responsible in respect of such breaches. See resolutions 674 (October 29, 1990), on Iraq; and 764 (July 13, 1992), on Yugoslavia.

6. Case Concerning Application of the Convention on the Prevention and Punishment of the Crime of Genocide (Bosnia and Herzegovina v. Yugoslavia [Serbia and Montenegro]), Request for the Indication of Provisional Measures, ICJ Reports 1993, Order of April 8, 1993.

7. The Swiss Federal Council voted to participate in the UN's economic sanctions against Iraq. See Schindler, "Turning Point for Swiss Neutrality?" *Swiss Review of World Affairs*, vol. 40 (December 1990), p. 10 (calling the action "a milestone in the development of Swiss neutrality policy"). Taiwan detained a Yugoslav-owned cargo ship in accordance with the UN embargo against Yugoslavia. See "Balkan Update," *New York Times*, June 8, 1993, p. A3.

8. A. Slaughter Burley, in L.W. Reed and C. Kaysen, eds., *Emerging Norms of Justified Intervention* (Cambridge, Mass.: American Academy of Arts and Sciences, 1993), p. 111.

9. According to article 8 of the Convention on the Prevention and Punishment of the Crime of Genocide (December 9, 1948): "Any Contracting Party may call upon the competent organs of the United Nations to take such action under the Charter of the United Nations as they consider appropriate for the prevention and suppression of acts of genocide [or related acts]."

10. Notably resolution 678 (November 29, 1991), authorizing all necessary means to eject Iraq from Kuwait "and to restore international peace and security in the area"; resolution 687 (April 3, 1991), establishing the terms of the cease-fire; and resolution 688 (April 5, 1991), condemning repression of Iraq's civilian population.

11. See resolutions 781 (October 9, 1992), establishing the flight ban; and 816 (March 31, 1993), in which the Council authorizes member states to take "all necessary measures in the airspace of the Republic of Bosnia and

Herzegovina . . . to ensure compliance with the ban on flights . . . proportionate to the specific circumstances and the nature of the flights."

12. Article 53 reads, in part: "But no enforcement action shall be taken under regional arrangements or by regional agencies without the authorization of the Security Council." (For further discussion, see the chapter on Liberia.)

13. Note by the president of the Security Council, UN Doc. S/22133 (January 22, 1991).

14. Abram Chayes of Harvard Law School has drawn such an analogy along lines that would entail limitations as well as authorizations. He adapts Justice Robert Jackson's model—under which presidential powers are not fixed but fluctuate depending upon the position Congress has taken with respect to the matter—to the authority of states to act in relation to the Security Council's position. State power would be at a maximum when exercised in accordance with the explicit or implicit approval of the Security Council, and at a minimum when exercised contrary to the Council's commands; in between, there would be a "zone of twilight" where the distribution of power is uncertain. See Chayes, "The Use of Force in the Persian Gulf," in L. F. Damrosch and D. J. Scheffer, eds., *Law and Force in the New International Order* (Boulder: Westview Press, 1991), pp. 3 and 8–9.

15. Among U.S. constitutional cases concerning these issues, see *Youngstown Sheet & Tube Co. v. Sawyer*, 343 U.S. 549 (1952), including Justice Jackson's influential concurring opinion referred to in the preceding note.

16. See, for example, Vienna Convention on the Law of Treaties, UN Doc. A/CONF.39/27 (1969), arts. 31–32.

17. On the use of General Assembly resolutions to interpret the Charter, see O. Schachter, *International Law in Theory and Practice*, pp. 85–86 (Dordrecht: Martinus Nijhoff, 1991).

18. "Definition of Aggression," General Assembly Resolution 3314 (December 14, 1974).

19. The General Assembly's treatment of intervention is surveyed in the introduction.

20. "Strengthening the Coordination of Humanitarian Emergency Assistance of the United Nations," General Assembly Resolution 46/182 (December 19, 1991).

21. After three years in which no permanent member of the Security Council had cast a negative vote, Russia vetoed a resolution concerning Cyprus on May 11, 1993. See F. Prial, "Russia Dusts Off a Long-Unused Security Council Tactic: The Veto," *New York Times*, May 12, 1993, p. A10. As of this writing, it is not clear whether this action will turn out to be an isolated incident or a harbinger of a new wave of vetoes.

22. Stanley Hoffmann, "Delusions of World Order," *New York Review of Books*, April 9, 1992, pp. 37, 41.

23. The relevant resolutions concerning establishment and enforcement of the Bosnian no-fly zone are cited in note 11 above.

24. See T. Franck, *The Power of Legitimacy Among Nations* (Oxford: Oxford University Press, 1990), pp. 150–182.

25. Franck elaborates the concepts of determinacy and pedigree in chapters 4–7 of his *Power of Legitimacy*, pp. 41–110.
26. Secretary-General Boutros-Ghali has called for the creation of peace-enforcement units in his "Agenda for Peace," UN Doc. A/47/277, S/24111 (June 17, 1992), para. 44, as well as for other improvements in the UN's capacity to respond to both international and internal crises.

# EPILOGUE

As this volume goes to press, we cannot yet say that any one of the six cases has come to a definitive resolution. Nonetheless, significant developments during 1993 have brought several of the cases to a point where closure has seemed almost within reach; and in several others the international involvement has moved to a qualitatively different plane. This epilogue traces the most important of those developments.

## FORMER YUGOSLAVIA

The bloodletting in the former Yugoslavia continued without abatement during 1993, especially in the Republic of Bosnia and Herzegovina. Even as international appreciation of the magnitude of atrocities increased, the international community stopped short of decisive intervention to impose a solution. The Clinton administration groped for a policy that might be acceptable to the U.S. public and Congress, and to the UN member states whose troops were already in the field. In June 1993, however, only five other Security Council members joined with the United States in voting for a draft resolution that would have selectively lifted the arms embargo in favor of Bosnia-Herzegovina.[1] The nine other Council members expressed a variety of objections, especially the concern that the proposal would be more likely to widen and intensify the conflict than to contribute to its resolution.[2] More intrusive measures, such as air strikes on Serbia or the introduction of U.S. troops into the theater of conflict, were also not forthcoming.

This is not to say that the international community was inactive on the Yugoslav question in 1993. On the contrary, many efforts were underway to bring pressure on the various factions to reach a settlement.

As 1993 began, peacemaking through the International Conference on the Former Yugoslavia (cosponsored by the UN and the European Community) focused on the Vance-Owen Peace Plan for a political settlement in Bosnia-Herzegovina, which was brought forward in January. The plan provided for a single state of Bosnia and Herzegovina with a decentralized structure consisting of ten provinces.[3] By the end of March the Bosnian Croats and Bosnian government had agreed to the plan: only the Bosnian Serbs held out against it, as it denied them their war aims. In an effort to press the Bosnian Serbs to agree, the Security Council in mid-April authorized a new package of economic sanctions, which not only tightened the May 1992 trade embargo against the Federal Republic of Yugoslavia (Serbia and Montenegro) but also made the Bosnian Serbs a target of sanctions.[4] Despite the stepped-up sanctions, the Bosnian Serb parliament rejected the Vance-Owen Plan in mid-May.

The international mediators (Thorvald Stoltenberg replaced Cyrus Vance in May) thereafter developed a different plan, which would partition Bosnia-Herzegovina into three ethnically based "Constituent Republics" that would coexist in a "Union of Republics of Bosnia and Herzegovina" for a finite period (two years under the September 1993 version of the plan), after which referenda to dissolve the "Union" could be held. As of October 1, 1993, the Bosnian Serbs and Bosnian Croats had accepted this plan, which would allow them to remain in control of much, but not all, of the territory seized during the conflict. The Muslim-dominated parliament of Bosnia-Herzegovina rejected the plan in late September, decrying it as a sellout to aggression and genocide.[5] It remained unclear whether the mediators could prevail on the three groups to accept a final package of concessions, or whether this plan too would fall by the wayside.

The international community continued to view Serbia, and the Serbs of Bosnia and Croatia, as principally responsible for perpetuating the conflict and obstructing a settlement. Thus, the Security Council not only maintained its compulsory and comprehensive embargo on the Federal Republic of Yugoslavia and extended the sanctions to Serbian areas of Bosnia[6] but also took certain steps to plug loopholes and strengthen enforcement. The Council authorized specific enforcement measures, including interdiction and inspection on the Danube and in the Adriatic, and also reaffirmed that states could act individually or collectively to enforce the embargo.[7] Naval forces under the command of NATO and the West European Union (WEU) undertook military enforcement of the sanctions, but the embargo remained porous nonetheless.

Ambivalence over military involvement persisted, and concerns over a worsening quagmire deepened. By September, more than fifty UN peacekeepers and numerous other international personnel had lost their lives. The future of the UN Protection Force (UNPROFOR) in Croatia also remained very much in doubt, as Croatia threatened to withhold consent to renewal of the mandate and the Security Council struggled to decide on terms for an extension.[8] UNPROFOR in Bosnia-Herzegovina has carried out its humanitarian assistance functions under increasingly dangerous conditions, which have led the Security Council to adopt several decisions aimed at restraining deterioration of the situation. Decisions in spring 1993 included extension of the previous flight ban to cover all flights over Bosnia-Herzegovina (except those authorized by UNPROFOR),[9] the declaration of certain Muslim centers as "safe areas,"[10] and the specification of conditions under which a military response to Serbian provocations would be authorized.[11] The preventive deployment of UN peacekeeping troops in Macedonia (including a small U.S. contingent dispatched in June 1993)[12] may have helped discourage the spread of conflict to that new republic, which gained admission to the UN in the spring of 1993.[13]

The series of more than forty-five Security Council resolutions on the conflict in former Yugoslavia provides explicit legitimacy for a limited range of unilateral military activities, as well as for concerted multilateral force alongside UNPROFOR's peacekeeping objectives. These currently include: "all measures necessary" to ensure the delivery of humanitarian assistance;[14] forcible measures of enforcement of the economic sanctions, including forcible interdiction of vessels bound to or from the Federal Republic of Yugoslavia;[15] measures to enforce the no-fly zone over Bosnia-Herzegovina, through operations toward that end in Bosnian airspace;[16] and the use of air power to support UNPROFOR in protecting the safe areas in Bosnia-Herzegovina.[17] Proponents of stronger military action have contended that the normative thrust of these and other resolutions should provide legitimacy for more drastic forcible measures, with or without further action from the Security Council.

Indeed, the Republic of Bosnia and Herzegovina has argued to the International Court of Justice (ICJ) and to UN audiences that the UN Charter and the Genocide Convention require states to come to Bosnia-Herzegovina's defense against armed attack and genocide, and that any Security Council resolutions purporting to require or imply the opposite (such as the arms embargo on all of the former Yugoslavia) should be considered *ultra vires* and void.[18] The ICJ's two preliminary rulings in April and September of 1993 have called on the Federal Republic of Yugoslavia to take all measures within its power to prevent genocide, but the ICJ has not ruled on the broader challenge to the Security Council's exercise of its powers under the UN Charter (and may lack jurisdiction to do so).

A development of considerable moral significance, but of uncertain practical consequences, was the UN's decision to convene a tribunal to prosecute and punish war crimes committed in the former Yugoslavia. The Security Council resolved in early 1993 to establish the tribunal under its compulsory powers (acting under Chapter VII of the Charter);[19] selection of judges and staff proceeded over the summer. Many factors will complicate the ability of the tribunal to carry out its charge, including the difficulties of moving forward while the conflict still rages, problems in obtaining custody of the principal offenders and sufficient reliable evidence to convict, and the delicate interrelationship with prospects for a negotiated settlement of the conflict.[20] Nonetheless, as the first such body since the Nuremberg and Tokyo trials, the tribunal could, in principle, mark a new step in the evolution of the application of law to wartime violence.

Some commentators have become increasingly vocal in their criticisms of the Clinton administration for failing to exert leadership toward stronger interventionary measures. By the time of President Clinton's address to the UN General Assembly on September 27, 1993, the contours of a cautious U.S. policy had taken shape. President Clinton has indicated that under certain strict conditions he would support sending up to 25,000 U.S. troops to assist in implementation of a settlement of the Yugoslav conflict. The conditions include: that any settlement be fair, freely arrived at, and enforceable; that U.S. troops serve under NATO rather than UN command; that their political and military objectives be clearly defined, with a strategy for review and termination of the U.S. involvement; and that the U.S. Congress support the deployment. Key members of Congress have remained skeptical as to the wisdom of any introduction of U.S. forces into the Yugoslav conflict; and the fact that U.S. troops were fighting and dying in Somalia a year after their dispatch there has only heightened congressional qualms about a much riskier commitment to the former Yugoslavia. Clearly, until the Yugoslav factions themselves agree to a peace settlement that they are prepared to live with, the U.S. involvement is unlikely to cross the line from "restrained" to "restraining."

## IRAQ

In comparison to the rest of the cases under examination in this book, the situation in Iraq remained relatively unchanged over 1993. The basic structural features were established with 1991's Operation Provide Comfort and the summer 1992 decision of the United States, U.K., and France to declare a no-fly zone below the

32nd parallel (Operation Southern Watch), comparable to the zone already being protected above the 36th parallel.[21] Periodic renewals were obtained into 1993 of the terms for the UN presence in Iraq (and also of the Turkish parliament's approval of access to the Incirlik base for coalition operations.)[22] The UN, however, had virtually no access in 1993 to the inhabitants of the southern marshlands, who remained under ongoing attack from Saddam Hussein's forces. Humanitarian activities by the UN elsewhere in Iraq continued with a small staff (the number of UN guards protecting the relief operations having been sharply reduced from 500 in 1991 to under 200 in 1993).[23] The demands on those operations grew ever greater, however, because of the worsening impact of the UN-mandated economic sanctions.

Discussions toward a compromise on possible resumption of Iraqi oil sales remained unresolved.[24] The United States and other Security Council members insisted that Iraq must, at a minimum, comply with the relevant terms of the cease-fire resolution (Resolution 687), which had reaffirmed and strengthened the embargo, and subsequent resolutions, including detailed obligations of disarmament under international supervision. A series of disputes over Iraq's violation of those obligations arose over the course of 1993, but one by one the disputes were addressed as Iraq showed greater willingness (under threat of new compulsion) to accept certain UN disarmament demands with specific and intrusive measures to verify compliance.[25] The position that compliance with all the Council's resolutions would be a prerequisite to lifting the sanctions made an implicit linkage between Resolution 687's sanctions and Resolution 688's demands concerning the treatment of Iraq's civilian populations. Other U.S. objectives—that sanctions might hasten Saddam Hussein's downfall or contribute to significant political change within Iraq—seemed no closer to attainment and possibly even more distant.

Military clashes between coalition forces and Iraq took place on some twenty occasions in the first eight months of 1993,[26] including a cluster of incidents in the weeks spanning the transition between the Bush and Clinton administrations. Saddam Hussein seemed to want to test the coalition's resolve, as he had in the past; but both the outgoing and the incoming U.S. adminis-trations maintained the previous policies of responding forcibly to Iraqi actions threatening the coalition aircraft protecting the two no-fly zones. The Clinton administration likewise repeated prior warnings that force could be used in the event of failures of compliance with Iraq's disarmament obligations. A different kind of military operation took place in June 1993, when President Clinton ordered an attack on military targets in Baghdad (which resulted in some civilian casualties), in response to evidence that the Iraqi regime had sponsored an assassination attempt against former President Bush on his April 1993 visit to Kuwait.[27]

Kurdish leaders drew attention to the acute need for continu-ing military protection, especially in light of fears that Saddam Hussein was preparing in spring 1993 for an incursion into Iraqi Kurdistan.[28] The Clinton administration renewed the previous sharp warnings (in which the UN delegates of the United States, U.K., France, and Russia had joined earlier in the year) promising a "firm and united response" to any such attack.[29] Within the Kurdish region, meanwhile, the Kurds nurtured a fragile auton-omy. The Iraqi Kurds had to tread carefully with respect to Turkey, in order to sustain coalition access to the Incirlik air base for policing the no-fly zone; this delicate position not only re-quired avoiding support for separatist activities of Turkish Kurds, but even put the Iraqi Kurds in the awkward posture of having to tolerate (if not cooperate with) Turkish activities in northern Iraq aimed at suppressing such separatism.[30]

Although northern Iraq remained under Kurdish control throughout 1993, formal partition of Iraq was in no way encour-aged (even though the international community had already accepted the disintegration of Yugoslavia and moved closer to accepting partition of Bosnia-Herzegovina in the same period). Indeed, partition of Iraq was actively discouraged, in part be-cause of concerns about growing Iranian influence in the region.


HAITI

The fate of the international endeavors to bring about the restora-tion of President Aristide remains murky. Despite the signing of the Governors Island agreement on July 3, 1993,[31] under which Aristide was supposed to return to Haiti by October 30, the de facto government has continued to flout world public opinion by condoning and sponsoring violent attacks on Aristide's supporters and even outright political murder.[32]

Many observers concur that Haiti's military rulers never took the OAS or UN diplomatic efforts seriously until June 1993, when Security Council Resolution 841 imposed a mandatory embargo on oil and petroleum products, arms and police equipment, as well as a freeze of the assets of the Haitian government and de facto authorities.[33] The UN embargo of Haiti is noteworthy as a new step in the Security Council's willingness to deal with an internal political crisis as a threat to international peace and security. Resolution 841 imposing the embargo takes the pattern of other crises as a departure point, by stressing factors that could be consistent with transboundary conceptions of "threats to peace" (as in the following preambular passages):

> Concerned that the persistence of this situation contributes to a climate of fear of persecution and economic dislocation which could increase the number of Haitians seeking refuge in neighbouring Member States and convinced that a reversal of this situation is needed to prevent its negative repercussions on the region. . . .
> Determining that, in these unique and exceptional circumstances, the continuation of this situation threatens international peace and security in the region. . . .

In this respect Resolution 841 is similar to the Council's characterizations in Resolution 688 on Iraq and in its early resolutions on the former Yugoslavia, which emphasized potential effects on neighboring countries. Resolution 841 also builds on prior practice by attaching significance to a request for sanctions from the recognized representative of the target's own government.[34] But the Haitian sanctions resolution goes farther than any other to date in applying universal, mandatory, and severe economic sanctions to influence a domestic political crisis over democratic governance. Its cautious wording (stressing more than once the "unique and exceptional" circumstances) cannot hide its precedential significance.

Following Resolution 841's formula, the Council suspended the sanctions in late August (Resolution 861), after the UN secretary-general reported that the de facto authorities had begun implementing in good faith the agreement for reinstating President Aristide's government.[35] According to the suspension resolution, definitive termination would come about only upon a conclusion "that the relevant provisions of the Governors Island Agreement have been fully implemented." The suspended measures could be reimposed at any time, if the secretary-general decided that the parties "have not complied in good faith with the Agreement."[36]

The illusion of compliance with that good faith standard vanished in early October, when a violent demonstration orchestrated by the de facto authorities blocked the debarkation of a crucial contingent of U.S. troops that was to have formed part of a UN deployment to Haiti. On September 23 the Security Council had approved the dispatch of a 1,300-member military and police mission, which was expected to carry out various tasks of training, monitoring, and assistance in reconstruction, in order to ensure a peaceful transition and to begin the rebuilding of a shattered nation.[37] The U.S. offer to contribute as many as half the military engineers and other personnel to the international mission was an important symbolic gesture, but one that relied on an evidently misplaced assumption of sufficient cooperation from the de facto government in Haiti.[38] When the transport ship carrying the first of the U.S. contingent met defiance rather than cooperation, it withdrew from Haitian waters, and the effort to deploy the UN mission was interrupted.

On October 13, 1993, the Security Council unanimously voted to reimpose the suspended sanctions.[39] The prospects for carrying out the plan for restoring President Aristide's government will depend on the UN's determination to support it: that in turn will depend on the strength of the U.S. commitment to the plan.

## LIBERIA

On July 25, 1993, the principal contenders in Liberia's civil war signed yet another agreement promising to bring peace to their exhausted country. But unlike the nearly twenty previous accords, the July 1993 agreement might actually mark the onset of a sea change in Liberian politics. The terms of the accord are deceptively simple. It mandates an immediate cease-fire (as did all the preceding agreements), and also requires the contending parties to form a new government, headed by a five-member Council of State, to run the country until elections can be held in February 1994. ECOMOG (the Military Observer Group of the Economic Community of West African States [ECOWAS]), augmented by forces from African countries outside the region, is authorized to disarm and encamp the combatants, under the supervision of a UN observer mission.

A combination of factors made the agreement possible. The military and economic pressure brought to bear on Taylor and the National Patriotic Front for Liberia seems to have forced them to accept a settlement.[40] The costs of continued fighting, economic disintegration, and international pressure constrained the other warring factions to pursue settlement also. In addition, the UN, assisted by the Organization of African Unity (OAU), played a substantial role in brokering the new agreement, and promised to monitor its implementation.

As of this writing, the cease-fire has largely held. More surprising, the parties have actually agreed on the composition of the Council of State, and named its members, although its inauguration has been delayed pending commencement of the disarmament process.

It is too early to predict whether the new agreement will bring about a lasting peace. Taylor has reneged on numerous prior agreements; Nigeria's internal political situation may produce a softening of the Nigerian commitment to peacekeeping in Liberia; and the UN has been slow to send its monitors. The Security Council did unanimously approve the dispatch of an advance team of thirty military observers in Resolution 856 of August 10, 1993, which also instructs the secretary-general to prepare for the eventual establishment of a UN observer mission in Liberia. Encampment and disarmament, inevitably the most difficult part of the peace plan, have yet to begin. Fighting can erupt at any time for many reasons; indeed, reports of renewed fighting in September 1993 (spilling over for the first time into the Ivory Coast) cast doubt on the prognosis for the settlement.[41]

If the plan does succeed, however, it will mark a major achievement for ECOWAS. Even though UN participation at a late stage was crucial to removing the final obstacles to settlement, it was the persistence of ECOWAS, against enormous odds, that made peace through elections a possibility. The reliance on UN involvement in the July 1993 settlement should not detract from the accomplishments of ECOWAS up to that time; instead, it should be understood as a reflection of the different but complementary roles that regional and international organizations can play in resolving localized conflicts.

## SOMALIA

The hopes that a major international intervention could bring a swift end to Somalia's miseries gave way to serious disappointments in 1993. The premise that the Somali people would welcome outside assistance in reestablishing order in their troubled country turned out to be far too simplistic. The U.S.–led Unified Task Force (UNITAF), which began its operation in December 1992, and the U.N.'s second-stage observer mission (UNOSOM II) which took over from UNITAF in spring 1993, both had to confront a range of problems far more intractable than the relatively straightforward tasks of securing airfields and routes for food delivery.

Security Council Resolution 794 of December 3, 1992, had articulated the primary objective of the initiative: "to establish a secure environment for humanitarian relief operations in Somalia as soon as possible."[42] But intermixed with that objective were other important desiderata, interconnected with overcoming the humanitarian crisis but also transcending it. Above and beyond the immediate and massive humanitarian needs, it would be essential to restore stability and order in order to ensure the nation's long-term survival. The chaotic, violent Somalian environment of 1993 offered no ready path toward that goal. The mandate to use "all necessary means"[43] to establish a secure environment for relief operations could be interpreted to authorize compulsory disarmament of recalcitrant factions, but UN member states had differing views on the wisdom of such a course of action. Resolution 794 had likewise called on all parties "to promote . . . reconciliation and political settlement in Somalia," but had laid down no blueprint for that program.

The U.S.–led UNITAF, which had deployed approximately 37,000 troops in southern and central Somalia,[44] did have substantial success in getting food to hundreds of thousands of Somalis who had been close to starvation, and it thereby saved innumerable lives. Within the first few months of 1993, preparations for the transfer of responsibility from UNITAF to the UN went forward as planned, on the expectation that the UN force would entail a military component of 20,000 troops and an additional 8,000 logistical personnel and 2,800 civilian staff.[45] In late March the Security Council authorized the mandate for a UN force (UNOSOM II) for an initial period through October 31, 1993.[46] Secretary-General Boutros-Ghali designated Jonathan Howe, a retired U.S. admiral, as his new special representative in Somalia; Lieutenant-General Cevik Bir of Turkey became force commander of UNOSOM II.[47]

Meanwhile, fifteen Somali political movements took part in meetings in January and March 1993 in Addis Ababa, Ethiopia, which were aimed at bringing about national reconciliation and reconstruction. Those meetings produced both a fragile political accord and an agreement by all parties to cooperate with UN-OSOM in disarmament.[48] When the Security Council subsequently authorized UNOSOM II's mandate in Resolution 814 of March 26, 1993, it specifically demanded that all Somali parties comply fully with the Addis Ababa agreements, including the undertakings on disarmament.[49] The same resolution also called for UN assistance to the people of Somalia in "the re-establishment of national and regional institutions and civil administration in the entire country" and in "the restoration and maintenance of peace, stability and law and order."[50]

Over the ensuing months, tensions mounted as General Mohammed Farah Aideed and his Somali National Alliance (SNA) came to view UNOSOM and its disarmament activities as an impediment to achievement of their own objectives. A fatal confrontation on June 5, 1993, produced a new round of controversy over the objectives and tactics of the international involvement. On that day, twenty-four Pakistani soldiers serving under UNOSOM command were ambushed and killed and an additional fifty-six were wounded, some while distributing food to Somali citizens and others while returning from inspection of a weapons storage site. The Security Council strongly condemned the unprovoked attack as part of "a calculated and premeditated series of cease-fire violations to prevent by intimidation UNOSOM II from carrying out its mandate."[51] In a significant but controversial directive, the Security Council called on the secretary-general "to take all necessary measures against all those responsible for the armed attacks . . . including to secure the investigation of their actions and their arrest and detention for prosecution, trial and punishment."[52]

A UN investigation subsequently found "clear and convincing evidence" that General Aideed had authorized the attack, that his faction had executed it, and that the attack violated multiple aspects of Somali criminal law and of international law.[53] The same investigation also charged the SNA with actions "consciously designed . . . to cause the wounding or killing of non-combatants," in violation of the central principle of international humanitarian law. In the meantime, the instruction to UNOSOM II to pursue efforts to arrest and detain the perpetrators of the attack intensified the confrontation between the UN and General Aideed, and also led to serious disagreements among UN member states over the course of action that UNOSOM should be following. In particular, Italy—a contributor of a substantial UNOSOM contingent, and a former colonial power in Somalia—urged a change in course to favor political dialogue over pursuit of Aideed, and threatened to withdraw its contingent if the confrontational posture continued.

Another devastating clash occurred on October 3, 1993, resulting in the deaths of eighteen U.S. peacekeeping troops and at least seventy other U.S. casualties, as well as the gruesome televised images of an American captive under interrogation and the body of a dead American soldier being dragged through the streets of Mogadishu. Tragically, the same incident produced an even higher toll among Somali civilians—possibly as many as 300 dead and 700 wounded. As some congressional leaders called for prompt withdrawal of U.S. troops and public opinion turned decidedly against the U.S. involvement, the Clinton administration struggled to redefine and explain the U.S. and UN objectives. President Clinton announced that he would increase the U.S. deployment in the near term but would also set a firm date of March 31, 1994, for a complete U.S. withdrawal. At the same time, other troop-contributing countries were also reconsidering their commitments; the French and Belgians proposed to withdraw their contingents by the end of 1993, while the secretary-general appealed to African states to contribute substantial new forces.

The events of 1993 underscored the inherently contradictory task for an external intervention into a situation of chaos. UNITAF and UNOSOM II had to work toward establishing conditions of minimum order, without at the same time antagonizing powerful forces who could command the loyalty of substantial segments of Somali society. The common portrayal in the Western media of the clan leaders as "warlords" obscured the origins of their power bases in the Somali clan structure. The effort to disarm them, well-intentioned as it may have seemed in the atmosphere of thuggery and looting that prevailed when the first UNITAF troops landed, soon took on quite different overtones, which Somali clan leaders (especially General Aideed) would naturally have interpreted as a direct challenge to their own authority. Yet without the cooperation of those same leaders, the objectives of the international intervention could not realistically be achieved.

U.S. and UN decisionmakers have not yet found a satisfactory resolution to this intractable dilemma. Between the June 1993 attack on the Pakistani peacekeepers and the response to the October 1993 attack, a double metamorphosis has been in progress: first, a shift away from Resolution 837's mandate to punish the attackers of peacekeeping forces, toward a policy of political isolation of those elements; and second, toward the acceptance of futility of isolation and the inevitability of working with those same elements in order to achieve a durable political solution.

Some have suggested that Somalia might be a candidate for direct or indirect UN governance, either on the model of past trusteeships or under a variant of the recent Cambodian experience. In late 1993 these possibilities seem remote. In Cambodia, the four contending factions had been willing to cede authority to the UN to carry out many governmental functions for a transitional period. Somalia, by contrast, had very recently emerged from a fifteen-year period (1945–1960) as a UN trust territory, and its people had no wish to resume that status. Nor, apparently, would they contemplate delegating powers to the very organization that had failed them in the humanitarian crisis of 1991-1992 and had fought with Aideed in 1993. With the United States preparing to withdraw from the operation it had initiated, the next phase of international involvement will need to continue addressing immediate humanitarian concerns, while at the same time providing time and space for the Somalis to work out their own political future.

## CAMBODIA

Cambodia's first free and fair elections occurred May 23–28, 1993. Despite considerable violence in the preceding two months, which compelled elimination of some polling stations in tense areas, the elections took place remarkably smoothly, without significant violence, disruptions, or irregularities. Over 4.2 million voters—nearly 90 percent of those registered—voted, through approximately 1,400 UN-operated fixed polling stations and 200 mobile teams reaching all Cambodia's provinces.

FUNCINPEC, the royalist opposition party under the leadership of Prince Sihanouk's son Norodom Ranariddh, won 45 percent of the vote and the incumbent State of Cambodia (SOC) party won 38 percent, with the remaining 17 percent divided among other resistance parties. The special representative of the UN secretary-general declared the voting free and fair on June 10,[54] and Security Council Resolution 840 endorsed the results on June 15, 1993.[55]

The peaceful election represented a high-water mark for the UN Transitional Authority in Cambodia (UNTAC). Even the severest critics of the Paris accords and UNTAC acknowledged the important contribution the UN had made to giving Cambodians a new beginning. The obstacles to creating a neutral political environment and the operation's inability to disarm the Khmer Rouge became less significant to diplomats and commentators in light of the final results.

In the aftermath of the elections, FUNCINPEC and the SOC agreed on an interim power-sharing arrangement pending promulgation of a new constitution, and also agreed to form a united national army. During the post-electoral period UNTAC worked on training that army and on other nation-building technical assistance matters, with a view toward completing the transition and withdrawing by November 1993. UNTAC also assisted the constituent assembly in the drafting of the constitution, focusing on ensuring consistency with the constitutional and human rights principles of the Paris accords. The constitution was formally adopted in late September, and Sihanouk returned to assume the throne of a constitutional monarchy on September 24, 1993.[56] In remarks after the ceremony, the king acknowledged that "there remains only one problem, the problem of the Khmer Rouge" — and indeed the possibility that the Khmer Rouge could continue guerrilla attacks remains very real.[57]

UNTAC's stock as a precedent for future operations would appear to have risen in the months after the elections, as the conclusion that the result would hold seemed more likely. Among the lessons from UNTAC's mission are: the centrality of cooperation from the parties (in this case, despite carrying out considerable harassment in the months leading up to the election, the Khmer Rouge decided at the end not to disrupt the polling); ample preparation (for which the extraordinarily detailed planning by UNTAC electoral staff deserves much credit); and the commitment of the international community to the mission (as indicated by the Security Council's repeated insistence that the elections would take place on time and by the substantial investment of several billion dollars and more than 20,000 persons in the UNTAC force). The results also confirmed the UN's ability to conduct an election, at least in a small country—an endeavor it may have to repeat in other shattered polities.

## CONCLUSION

Perhaps the most pertinent questions to ask about the six conflicts examined here are whether they are any closer to resolution than they were when this study began, and if so, what measure of credit properly belongs to the international efforts. Overall, the progress toward resolution has been substantial. It is striking to note how much has changed even in the few months between late spring 1993 when the bulk of the manuscripts went to press, and early fall when this epilogue was written. Just a few months ago, all six of the cases were still very much unresolved, but over the course of mid-1993 we could take satisfaction in the completion of the transition to an elected Cambodian government, the conclusion of a settlement agreement for Liberia, and an agreement for the return to Haiti of President Aristide and his government.

Of course, after those three steps forward, there came at least one step back, when the Haitian settlement fell apart in October 1993 and sanctions had to be renewed. In the other cases, forward movement was difficult. The Iraqi situation has remained structurally stable, but the continuation of economic sanctions has taken a heavy toll on the civilian population there as well. In former Yugoslavia, two settlement plans have foundered; the on-the-ground situation remains dire. In Somalia, although starvation is no longer claiming massive numbers of lives as it did in 1991–1992, the combat deaths of scores of peacekeepers and hundreds of civilians cast a shadow over that accomplishment; moreover, starvation may yet return if civil order cannot be restored with or without the peacekeepers.

Where progress is detectable, can it be credited to the efforts of international organizations? We would like to make that claim. The Cambodian, Haitian, and Liberian settlement agreements (and steps toward their implementation to date) are the direct achievements of cooperation between the UN and a relevant regional organization. In Somalia, the United States probably would not have ventured its massive humanitarian effort without the assurance that it could turn the operation over promptly to the UN, and the UN's approval at the outset strengthened domestic and international support for the U.S. initiative. In Iraq and Yugoslavia, though the successes and failures are harder to weigh and responsibility is harder to assign, the international efforts do reflect a united determination to discourage the spread of internal conflict beyond the borders of the affected territories and to apply peaceful leverage to bring about solutions.

As more of these cases reach their denouement, it will become possible to look back and reflect more deeply on the contributions of collective involvement to the resolution of internal conflicts. Until then, the provisional conclusion is that the international efforts, though far from perfect, have been justified.

L. F. D.
*October 1993*

## NOTES

1. See Provisional Verbatim Record of the 3247th Meeting, UN Doc. S/PV.3247 (June 29, 1993), at p. 148. The six states voting in favor were Cape Verde, Djibouti, Morocco, Pakistan, United States, and Venezuela.
2. Rather than formally voting against the proposal, these nine states abstained. They were Brazil, China, France, Hungary, Japan, New Zealand, Russian Federation, Spain, and the United Kingdom. *Ibid*. Since a Security Council decision needs at least nine affirmative votes to pass (UN Charter, art. 27), the draft resolution was not adopted.
3. See Report of the Secretary-General on the Activities of the International Conference on the Former Yugoslavia: Peace Talks on Bosnia and Herzegovina, UN Doc. S/25479 (Mar. 26, 1993).
4. Security Council resolution 820 (April 17, 1993).
5. John F. Burns, "Bosnia Legislators Reject Peace Plan in a Lopsided Vote," *New York Times*, Sept. 30, 1993, p. A1.
6. Resolution 820, *supra*.
7. *Ibid*., reaffirming resolution 787 (November 16, 1992).
8. Paul Lewis, "Russia Delaying U.N.'s Vote on Troops in Ex-Yugoslavia," *New York Times*, October 2, 1993, p. A3. The mandate has already been renewed several times, for example in Security Council resolution 815 (March 30, 1993).
9. The Council had originally imposed a ban on military flights over Bosnia-Herzegovina in resolutions 781 (October 9, 1992) and 786 (November 10, 1992). In resolution 816 (March 31, 1993), the Council extended the ban to cover "flights by all fixed-wing and rotary-wing aircrafts in the airspace of

the Republic of Bosnia and Herzegovina," except for flights authorized by UNPROFOR for humanitarian and other approved purposes.

10. See, for example, resolutions 819 (April 16, 1993), 824 (May 6, 1993), and 836 (June 4, 1993).

11. See, for example, Security Council resolution 816 (March 31, 1993); see also notes 14–17 below.

12. The deployment was authorized in resolution 795 (December 11, 1992); troops arrived in stages during 1993.

13. A compromise intended to allay Greek objections allowed Macedonia's UN admission under the name "Former Yugoslav Republic of Macedonia." Separately, the UN had determined that the Federal Republic of Yugoslavia (Serbia and Montenegro) could not automatically succeed to the UN seat of the former Socialist Federal Republic of Yugoslavia. See General Assembly resolution 47/1 (September 24, 1992); Security Council resolution 821 (April 28, 1993).

14. Security Council resolution 770 (August 13, 1992).

15. Security Council resolution 820 (April 17, 1993), para. 29 (reaffirming resolution 787 of November 16, 1992).

16. Security Council resolution 816 (March 31, 1993).

17. Security Council resolution 836 (June 4, 1993), para. 10.

18. The International Court of Justice has entered two preliminary orders on Bosnia's claim, relying in both instances only on the Genocide Convention and declining to take up broader questions under the UN Charter.

19. Security Council resolutions 808 (February 22, 1993) and 827 (May 25, 1993).

20. For commentary see Theodor Meron, "The Case for War Crimes Trials in Yugoslavia," *Foreign Affairs* 72, no. 3 (summer 1993), pp. 122–135.

21. Confusion persists as to who established these zones, and under what authority. After several misstatements, the *New York Times* published the following correction: "An article on July 26 about an American warplane that fired on a missile battery in southern Iraq misidentified the authority that barred Iraqi flights over the area. The ban was imposed by the United States, Britain and France, not the United Nations." *New York Times*, Aug. 11, 1993, p. A2. See discussion in "Concluding Reflections" at p. 357 above.

22. Paul Lewis, "U.N. Warns of End to Kurdish Relief," *New York Times*, May 23, 1993, p. A8 (concerning continuation of UN relief operations in Iraq); Alan Cowell, "Attacks Focus the Spotlight on Kurds' Tangled Affairs," *New York Times*, June 25, 1993 (concerning Turkish parliament's extension of the Iraq operation).

23. "U.N. Warns of End to Kurdish Relief," *supra.*

24. Paul Lewis, "U.N. Is Holding Talks on Lifting Its 3-Year Ban on Iraqi Oil Sales," *New York Times*, Sept. 6, 1993, p. A2.

25. Iraq's acceptance of the UN's delimitation of a new Iraq-Kuwait border was another sticking point in the dispute over the lifting of sanctions.

26. Eric Schmitt, "U.S. Bombs Iraqis for Firing at Jets," *New York Times*, Aug. 20, 1993, p. A8.

27. David Von Drehle and R. Jeffrey Smith, "U.S. Strikes Iraq for Plot to Kill Bush," *Washington Post*, June 27, 1993, p. A1.

28. Chris Hedges, "Iraq Said to Prepare Attack on Kurds' Enclave in North," *New York Times*, May 24, 1993, p. A6.
29. Douglas Jehl, "Christopher Warns Iraqi Chief Not to Attack Kurds in North," *New York Times*, May 25, 1993, p. A8. The warning applied not only to the northern no-fly zone, but also to territories south of the zone under Kurdish control.
30. Alan Cowell, "Attacks Focus the Spotlight on Kurds' Tangled Affairs," *New York Times*, June 25, 1993, p. A10.
31. The agreement is reprinted in "The Situation of Democracy and Human Rights in Haiti: Report of the Secretary-General," UN Doc. A/47/975, S/26063 (July 12, 1993).
32. Howard W. French, "Haiti Justice Minister Slain in Defiance of U.S. Warning to Military to Keep Peace," *New York Times*, Oct. 15, 1993, p. A1; and "Haiti in Turmoil as It Awaits Aristide," *New York Times*, Sept. 22, 1993 (UN officials comment on more than 100 killings in Port-au-Prince in two months after Governors Island agreement, including a prominent backer of Aristide who was shot to death on September 11).
33. Editorial, "Haiti: The Secret of Success," *New York Times*, July 7, 1993, p. A14: "For more than 20 months, as Washington sent mixed diplomatic signals, the Haitian military defiantly rejected all serious diplomacy. But less than two weeks after the Clinton Administration sought and won stiff U.N. economic sanctions, the generals were at the bargaining table ready to deal."
34. The arms embargoes against Yugoslavia and Somalia began this pattern. See "The Civilian Impact of Economic Sanctions," p. 285 above.
35. The secretary-general made the relevant report on August 13, 1993 (UN Doc. S/26297), and the Council voted unanimously to suspend the sanctions in Resolution 861 (August 27, 1993).
36. *Ibid.*, paras. 2, 3.
37. "U.N. Council Votes to Send Peacekeeping Force to Haiti," *New York Times*, Sept. 24, 1993, p. A3.
38. "U.S. Dispatching 600 on Haiti Assignment," *New York Times*, September 29, 1993, p. A5.
39. Paul Lewis, "U.N. Again Imposes Sanctions on Haiti After 40. Pact Fails," *New York Times*, October 14, 1993, p. A1. Oil imports during the period of suspension may have given Haiti as much as a 3–6 month supply, thereby cushioning the de facto government from the effect of the reimposition of sanctions. *Ibid.*
40. "War Factions in Liberia Peace Accord," *New York Times*, July 18, 1993, p. A6.
41. "Liberian War Is Said to Spill Into Ivory Coast," *New York Times*, Sept. 5, 1993, p. A21.
42. Security Council resolution 794 (December 3, 1992), paras. 7, 10
43. *Ibid.*, para. 10.
44. UN Department of Public Information, "The United Nations and the Situation in Somalia," p. 8 (April 30, 1993).
45. *Ibid.*, pp. 9–10.
46. Resolution 814 (March 26, 1993).

47. "The United Nations and the Situation in Somalia," pp. 9–10.
48. See Agreement on Implementing the Cease-Fire and on Modalities of Disarmament, UN Doc. S/25168, Annex III (January 26, 1993), and Further Report of the Secretary-General, UN Doc. S/25354 (March 3, 1993).
49. Resolution 814 (March 26, 1993), para. 8.
50. Resolution 814 (March 26, 1993), para. 4(c), (d).
51. Resolution 837 (June 6, 1993), para. 1.
52. *Ibid.*, para. 5.
53. Report Pursuant to Paragraph 5 of Security Council Resolution 837 (1993) on the Investigation Into the 5 June 1993 Attack on United Nations Forces in Somalia, UN Doc. S/26351 (August 24, 1993). The independent expert engaged to carry out the investigation was Professor Tom Farer.
54. Report of the Secretary-General, UN Doc. S/25913 (June 10, 1993).
55. Security Council resolution 840 (June 15, 1993).
56. "Sihanouk Again Becomes King and Picks Government," *New York Times*, Sept. 25, 1993, p. A3.
57. *Ibid.* King Sihanouk has since invited the Khmer Rouge to begin a dialogue with the new government.

# INDEX

# About the Authors

**Domingo E. Acevedo** has been principal legal adviser of the Organization of American States and is currently a special adviser to the Inter-American Commission on Human Rights and an adjunct professor of law at American University.

**Jeffrey Clark,** a consultant on development and humanitarian assistance issues, has long been affiliated with the United States Committee for Refugees and is now with the Refugee Policy Group in Washington. He previously directed an African food security program at the Carter Presidential Center and served as a senior professional staff member for the House Select Committee on Hunger.

**Lori Fisler Damrosch** is a professor of law at Columbia University in New York City and consultant on international law to the Council on Foreign Relations.

**Tom J. Farer,** former president of the Inter-American Commission on Human Rights of the OAS, is currently professor and director of the joint degree program in law and international relations at American University. This chapter was written when he was visiting Eberhard-Deutsch professor at Tulane University Law School.

**Max M. Kampelman** is former ambassador and chairman of the U.S. delegation to the Review Conference on Security and Co-operation in Europe (CSCE) in Madrid 1980–1983, CSCE Conference on the Human Dimension (Copenhagen 1990 and Moscow 1991), and CSCE Conference on National Minorities (Geneva 1991). He was head of the U.S. delegation to negotiations on nuclear and space arms (1985–1989) and counselor of the U.S. Department of State (1987–1989).

**Steven R. Ratner** is an assistant professor of law at the University of Texas. He was an International Affairs Fellow of the Council on Foreign Relations on leave from the U.S. Department of State, Office of the Legal Adviser, at the time that his chapter was written, and previously served as legal adviser to the U.S. delegation to the Paris Conference on Cambodia.

**James B. Steinberg** is a senior analyst in the International Policy Department at RAND. He previously served as a senior fellow at the International Institute for Strategic Studies, and as a special assistant in the U.S. Department of Justice.

**Jane E. Stromseth** is an associate professor of law at Georgetown University. She formerly served in the Office of the Legal Adviser of the U.S. Department of State.

**David Wippman** is an associate professor of law at Cornell University. From November 1990 to May 1992 he served as counsel to the interim government of Liberia.